the essential
baking
cookbook

the essential baking cookbook

bay books

Published by Bay Books, an imprint of Murdoch Books Pty Limited.

Murdoch Books Australia
Pier 8/9, 23 Hickson Road
Millers Point NSW 2000
Phone: + 61 (0) 2 8220 2000
Fax: + 61 (0) 2 8220 2558
www.murdochbooks.com.au

Series Editor: Wendy Stephen Managing Editor: Rachel Carter Editorial Director: Diana Hill
Designer: Wing Ping Tong Designer (cover): Annette Fitzgerald
Design Concept: Marylouise Brammer
Photographer (special features): Craig Cranko, Chris Jones Photographer (cover): Ian Hofstetter
Stylist (special features): Mary Harris Stylist (cover): Katy Holder
Food Editor: David Herbert
Food Director: Jane Lawson
Home Economists: Michelle Earl, David Herbert, Valli Little, Kerrie Mullens,
Kim Passenger, Christine Sheppard, Angela Tregonning
Additional text: Michelle Earl
Picture Librarian: Anne Ferrier

Chief Executive: Juliet Rogers
Publisher: Kay Scarlett

ISBN 978 0 68102 593 6

PRINTED IN CHINA
This edition printed in 2010.

OUR STAR RATING: When we test recipes, we rate them for ease of preparation.
The following cookery ratings are used in this book:
☆ A single star indicates a recipe that is simple and generally quick to make—perfect for beginners.
☆☆ Two stars indicate the need for just a little more care, or perhaps a little more time.
☆☆☆ Three stars indicate special dishes that need more investment in time,
care and patience—but the results are worth it. Even beginners can make these
dishes as long as the recipe is followed carefully.

You may find cooking times vary depending on the oven you are using. For fan-forced ovens, as a general rule,
set the oven temperature to 20°C lower than indicated in the recipe.
We have used 20 ml tablespoon measures. If you are using a 15 ml tablespoon, for most recipes the difference will not be
noticeable. However, for recipes using baking powder, gelatine, bicarbonate of soda, small amounts of flour and cornflour, add
an extra teaspoon for each tablespoon specified. We have used 60 g (Grade 3) eggs in all recipes.

IMPORTANT: Those who might be at risk from the effects of salmonella food poisoning
(the elderly, pregnant women, young children and those suffering from immune deficiency diseases)
should consult their GP with any concerns about eating raw eggs.

BAKING

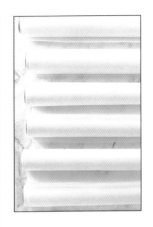

There are two things you need to know about baking. One — it's a miracle that a pile of flour, some shortening and a good blast of heat can form the base for such a varied and scrumptious array of food. Two — the sum of these raw materials is temperamental, moody and difficult, and will drive you mad if your first attempts at baking are not as successful as you'd hoped. If this does happen to you, try not to feel discouraged. As well as making sure our recipe methods are clear and informative, we've given a lot of thought to the problems you might encounter along the way, and have put together a series of "what went wrong?" pages to help you with your next baking adventure. It really is worth taking the time to learn the art of baking, and once you've mastered it, you'll be so proud of yourself, you'll wonder why you didn't get started years ago.

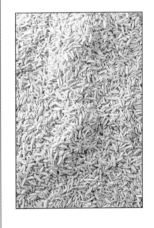

CONTENTS

SPECIAL FEATURES

WHAT WENT WRONG?

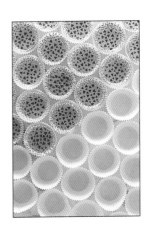

HISTORY IN THE BAKING

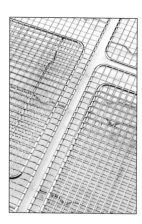

When looking at the history of baking we have to start with bread, which is certainly the basis for other types of baking such as cakes and biscuits. As people became more skilled at baking and leavening techniques, and a greater variety of ingredients became available, these baked goods began to assert their individuality and gradually earned names of their own. So now when we try to define 'baking' in its most general sense, we mean anything that has a flour base and is cooked in an oven. But let's go back to the beginning.

BREAD

Bread has been an important staple since Stone Age farmers created the first flat bread. A rough porridge was mixed together and spread thinly over hot stones to form a soft pancake-like bread. It truly is an amazing feat that the connection was made between wheat, water and sunshine to give us this most enduring of foods. The next step forward was achieved 5000 years ago in the Bronze Age, when it was discovered that inverting a pot over hot stones forms a primitive but effective oven.

But the honour of mastering the art of yeast fermentation goes to the ancient Egyptians, who observed that if dough was left out in the open for a few hours it would often bubble and smell a little sour. If this sour dough was baked, the resulting bread had a lighter texture and a pleasant yeasty flavour. The down side to this discovery was that it relied on airborne yeast particles, which made it completely unreliable. To overcome this, the Egyptians would simply save a piece of fermented dough from a previous successful batch, and mix it into the new dough. Brilliant!

Bread has always played rather a telling role in Europe's social history — the bread in your hands would always reveal your rank. Made from refined flour, white bread was regarded as infinitely superior and therefore only suitable for the upper classes. These days, of course, the reverse is true. Dense, wholegrain breads are now thought to be a healthy, more nourishing option and are priced accordingly. It is indeed ironic that people will pay a comparatively large sum of money for something that was once considered the bread of paupers.

But while we now have every imaginable variation to choose from, the basic bread recipe remains largely unchanged. And the discovery of yeast fermentation hasn't stopped us from continuing to bake flatbreads and hearthbreads either. The flat breads that are prominent in Indian and Arabian cooking prove this point well enough. It's very comforting to know that bread in its simplest form is hard to improve upon.

CAKES

During the medieval period the distinction between bread and cake was a hazy one, yet both words passed confidently from Anglo-Saxon into English. Size may have been one telling factor, as 'cake' was translated into Latin as 'pastillus', which means a little cake or pie.

By the 17th century, the haze had lifted and Europe was familiar with most of the key ingredients for modern cake-making, in particular, chocolate, sugar, vanilla and treacle. The developments were not restricted to ingredients either — cake hoops and tins also began to emerge at this time.

But it was the technology of the 19th century that brought about the greatest breakthrough. The chemical raising agent, bicarbonate of soda, made a grand entrance in the early 1800s, and was closely followed by baking powder

(a mixture of bicarbonate of soda and a mild acid). This powder replaced yeast (creating further distinctions between the two forms of baking) but still maintained excellent leavening power. A ready supply of white flour, granulated sugar and cheap shortening made the whole cake-baking experience much simpler (and therefore more popular). Another important development at this time was ovens with reliable temperature control. Imagine that!

Cast your eye over any classic movie set in the early to mid 20th century, and you'll quickly see that good cake-baking skills were something any housewife was proud to possess. Serving a generous slice of home-made cake not only suggested warmth and hospitality, it also displayed an air of abundance and comfort in the household. Of course, attitudes have changed significantly since then — not only do we have less time to spend in the kitchen, but we have become more health-conscious and this, sadly, restricts our intake of these delicious home-made goodies. Unlike bread, cakes tend to be viewed as more of a lovely treat than a staple.

BISCUITS

The word 'biscuit' is derived from the Latin 'panis biscotus' (which means 'bread twice cooked') because up until the 18th century, the dough was first baked in a hot oven, then transferred to a cooler oven to dry out (much like modern-day biscotti). Since then, however, cooks the world over have taken the basic recipe and run with it, giving us a staggering array of shapes, flavours and textures to choose from, and making a modern definition of the term rather more difficult.

Luckily there are two subcategories most people are familiar with. The 'cracker' is a thin, unsweetened, dry biscuit whose name probably comes from the cracking noise it makes when broken. The earliest biscuits would have been like these, in that they were unsweetened, hard rounds. Taking a sweeter turn, the word 'cookie' comes from the Dutch 'koekje', meaning little cake, and these tend to be richer, softer and quite chewy in texture. The most famous variety would have to be chocolate chip cookies. Created by Mrs Ruth Wakefield in the 1930s, these became known as Toll House cookies after the inn she ran with her husband. Feeling a little experimental one day, she cut a bar of chocolate into bits and added them to her cookie dough. Surprise, surprise, the chocolate held its shape and didn't melt into the dough, and history was made.

PASTRY

The Romans made a pastry of flour, oil and water, which was used to cover meat and poultry during baking, thus sealing in the juices. The pastry was not meant to be eaten, which is just as well as it was very dry and tough. In medieval Northern Europe, pastry was used for a similar purpose, but there is also evidence during this time of a finer, richer pastry made from fine white flour, butter and sugar that was certainly meant to be eaten.

Specific recipes for pastry began to appear from about the mid 16th century. In those days, pies generally contained savoury fillings — fruit fillings were very much the exception. It was not long, however, before sweet tarts became popular. These generally contained flower petals, which were chopped up and mixed with sweet biscuits, rosewater, cream, eggs and spices to make rich yellow cream centres.

TEATIME

Teatime gives us the chance to enjoy all of the baked goodies we have just been discussing. Delicate little sandwiches, pastries, scones, tea cakes and hot buttered toast, washed down with a perfectly brewed cup of tea. For this delightful custom, we must thank Anna, wife of the seventh Duke of Bedford. In the 19th century, lunch was a very light meal, and dinner was not served until eight o'clock. Not happy with this arrangement, The Duchess of Bedford asked that tea and cakes be served mid afternoon because, to quote herself, she had 'a sinking feeling'. She invited friends to join her and in no time at all this became a fashionable thing to do!

GLOSSARY

Terms used in recipes for baking sometimes seem mysterious but once understood, help you cook with confidence. Knowing the function of common ingredients also helps you on your way.

Bake blind means to partially or totally cook a pastry case before filling it. This prevents the pastry going soggy. Pastry should be partially cooked when it is going to be filled with an uncooked mixture (such as egg in a quiche), or fully cooked for fresh fruit flans. The uncooked pastry is lined with baking paper or foil and, to prevent it rising, it is filled with dried beans, uncooked rice or special-purpose beads.

Baking powder is a leavener used to aerate cakes, bread and buns. It is a mixture of bicarbonate of soda (baking soda), cream of tartar (an acid) and usually cornflour (to absorb moisture). As a substitute you can use a mixture of three parts cream of tartar and one part baking soda.

Batter is an uncooked mixture of flour, liquid and sometimes a leavener such as baking powder. It can be a thick, spooning consistency as with cake batter, or thin, pouring consistency such as the batter made for pancakes, crepes and pikelets.

Beat means to briskly combine ingredients, usually with electric beaters but sometimes with a wooden spoon, to introduce air into a mixture to make it smooth and light. Beating also helps to create a finer texture for cakes, biscuits and other baked products.

Bicarbonate of soda, or baking soda, is both a component of baking powder and a leavener in its own right, one that gets its leavening power with the aid of acid in yoghurt, sour cream, crème fraîche, molasses or buttermilk. It is best to work quickly with the mixture after it has been activated and to get the batter into the oven as soon as possible.

Biscuit base or crumb crust This is crushed bought biscuits combined with melted butter and sometimes spices. The mixture is pressed onto the base and/or sides of a cake or tart tin. It can be baked or unbaked and is mostly used as a base for cheesecakes and slices.

Bread dough is a mixture of flour, liquid, leaven (yeast) and sometimes other flavouring and enriching ingredients. The dough should be pliable enough to knead with your hands on a floured surface until it is smooth, non-sticky and elastic. Kneading by hand usually takes about 10 minutes. The dough is fully kneaded when it springs back after a finger is indented into the dough. The dough will be smooth, elastic and non-sticky and will often have small air bubbles on the surface.

Butter is produced when the fat content of milk (the sweet cream) is separated from the liquid (the buttermilk). The fat globules are churned until they combine and become solid, forming butter. Butter is the most commonly used fat for cake-making as it creams well and has an acceptable flavour. Salted butter has two per cent salt added. Originally salt was added as a preservative, but today it is included for taste. We specify unsalted butter (also known as sweet butter) for use in baking biscuits, slices, cakes and sweet pastries.

Buttermilk is traditionally the liquid that is left after cream is churned into butter. Today, it is made by adding a culture to skim milk and leaving the mixture for up to 24 hours to sour and thicken. It has a tangy flavour. Because of its acidic content it is used to act as a raising agent, especially in quick breads and scones.

Chocolate is made from components extracted from cocoa beans which grow in pods on the cacao tree. After the beans have been roasted, the shells are removed, leaving the nibs which are ground to produce chocolate liquor (bitter chocolate), which forms the base for all chocolate products. This liquor is either pressed to extract cocoa butter to make cocoa powder, or blended with varying amounts of cocoa butter and flavouring to produce different chocolates. Couverture chocolate is considered the best. It has a good flavour and glossy finish suitable for cake decoration.

Cinnamon is the dried aromatic bark from the laurel family of trees native to Asia. The paper-thin inner bark is rolled and dried to form quills or sticks. The sticks are used as a flavour infusion in syrups and poached fruits. Ground cinnamon adds flavour to cakes, puddings, biscuits and yeast breads.

Cinnamon sugar is used to decorate cakes, before or after baking, and to flavour buttered toast. Caster sugar and ground cinnamon are combined in a proportion of four sugar to one (or more, to taste) cinnamon.

Cloves are the strongly scented flower buds of the clove tree which are sun-dried until hard. They contain essential oils and are used whole or ground in baking. The flavour marries especially well with apple.

Cocoa is ground into a powder from the dry solids left when the cocoa butter (the fat) is removed. It is used extensively in baking. Cocoa is usually sifted in with the dry ingredients so it is distributed evenly. Sweetened cocoa powder is sold as drinking chocolate. Dutch cocoa, available from delicatessens, is considered to be the best flavoured cocoa for baking. It is rich, dark in colour and unsweetened.

Cookie is an American term for biscuit. It was originally a small dry flat cake that was twice baked so that it would be crisp and also so it would keep longer. Today, the terms 'cookie' and 'biscuit' cover a wide range of baked goods from crispy to chewy. The basic ingredients usually include flour, butter, eggs and sugar. Other flavours such as chocolate, nuts and dried fruit can be added.

Copha, or white vegetable shortening, is made from purified coconut oil that is processed into a white solid. Copha is generally used in making uncooked confections and slices or bar cookies.

Corn syrup is a liquid form of sugar refined from corn. A variety of corn syrups are produced, from light, which is less sweet, to dark, which is a caramel colour and has flavour added. Corn syrup adds flavour to baked products and is available at speciality shops and delicatessens.

Cornflour or cornstarch is a fine white powder made from maize or corn (gluten-free) or from wheat. It is used in small quantities in baking, such as in sponges and shortbread, to produce a lighter texture. It is also used to thicken sauces and fillings because it forms a gel when heated. Cornflour is usually mixed to a paste with a small amount of cold liquid before being added to the remaining liquid.

Cream is the fat globules that rise to the top of milk. The old method of collecting cream was to leave the unrefrigerated milk to stand until the cream separated to the required amount. Today the separation process is done by using centrifugal force. The fat content determines the type of cream. Cream is used extensively in baking, either as part of the mixture or whipped to decorate. For successful whipping, cream must have a fat content of at least 30 per cent and if the fat content is higher than this, a lighter foam results when the cream is whipped.

Cream of tartar This is a component of baking powder. It acts as a raising agent when combined with bicarbonate of soda. Sometimes it is used to help stabilize the beating of egg whites, as in meringue.

Cream together means to beat one or more ingredients, usually butter and sugar, until light and fluffy. Electric beaters or a whisk can be used. The creaming process dissolves the sugar, resulting in a light texture in the baked product.

Crème fraîche is a naturally soured cream with a nutty, slightly sour taste. You can make your own crème fraîche by mixing a little sour cream or yoghurt into cream and leaving the mixture in the refrigerator for up to 24 hours to sour. It makes an interesting flavour to accompany sweet desserts, especially tarts. It is available at delicatessens.

Dust means to cover lightly, usually referring to icing sugar or cocoa powder that is sifted over the top of a cake or pie for presentation.

Eggs In baking, eggs enrich and also add flavour, moisture, nutritive value and yellow colour. They have three main functional properties in cooking—coagulation, emulsification and foaming ability. To maintain freshness, eggs should be refrigerated. Bring them back to room temperature before using them in baking.

Egg whites increase in volume when whisked, due to the entrapment of air. There are four stages in the whisking of whites. The first is the large bubble stage where the foam is frothy and unstable. The soft peak stage is where the whites form a glossy mass and just hold shape (folded into creams and cake mixtures). The next

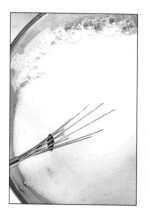

Egg whites *continued*
stage is medium peaks where the foam is very white and glossy—the peaks are soft and the tip falls a little (used for soufflés, mousses and ice creams). The final stage is stiff peaks where the bubbles are very fine and the peaks hold their shape (as in meringue). To successfully whisk by hand or beat with electric beaters, make sure all utensils are spotlessly clean and free of grease and that the bowl is deep enough to hold the volume of whisked whites. Egg whites also act as leaveners, adding volume and texture to soufflés, flourless cakes and sponge cakes. The whisked whites are folded into the mixture just before baking. When cooked, the air is trapped and the mixture expands and coagulates.

Essences are concentrated flavourings that enhance the taste of food. Vanilla essence is used extensively in the baking of cakes and biscuits. Almond essence is also used to boost chopped or ground almond flavour in cakes. An extract is a stronger, purer concentration.

Evaporated milk is canned milk with most of its water removed. After opening, it should be refrigerated and used within a couple of days. Diluted, it can be used as milk. Undiluted, it can replace cream. It is used to enrich sauces and moisten food. With the addition of lemon juice, chilled evaporated milk will whip to form a stable foam. Sometimes it is used to make ice cream.

Fat or shortening contributes flavour, colour and shortness (tenderness) to shortcrust pastries, cakes and biscuits, and flakiness to layered pastries such as flaky and puff. Lard, butter,

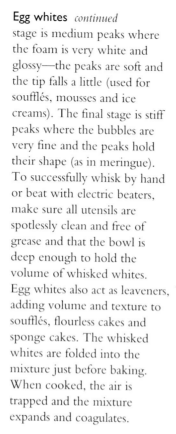

margarine and half butter, half lard, are all suitable fats for baking. Shredded suet is used in traditional baked pie crusts including steak and kidney pie. Oils are sometimes used in one-bowl or quick-mix cake mixtures such as carrot cake, resulting in a heavier texture. A little oil or butter is added to bread dough to add flavour and tenderness. Fat can be creamed with sugar, rubbed into the dry ingredients, melted and mixed into the dry ingredients, or kneaded into bread doughs.

Flour provides the basic structure of bread, cakes, batters and pastry. The process of manufacturing the whole grain where the grain is converted into a variety of flours is called milling. Wheat flour is the most versatile of all the flours. Roller milling produces all white flour and most wholemeal flours. Some wholemeal flours are produced by stone milling. Other non-wheat cereals are milled and used in cooking, for example cornflour, cornmeal, potato flour, rice flour and rye flour. These are not termed high-quality flours because, unlike wheat flour, they lack the protein gluten (the strength, elasticity and structure) necessary for baking. However, they are useful for people who are intolerant to wheat products. Bread dough made with non- or low-gluten flours do not have the elasticity of dough made with wheat-based flour so the bread will be dense.
Plain white flour, also called all-purpose flour, has a medium protein content of about ten per cent. Most baked goods use this flour. Self-raising flour has the same protein qualities as plain flour but has baking powder added to it. Self-raising flour can be made by adding 2 teaspoons of baking powder

to 1 cup (125 g/4 oz) of plain flour and then sifting thoroughly several times. Wholemeal flours are coarsely milled or finely ground and can be used instead of plain white flour. If you do use wholemeal, the baked product will have a denser crumb and less volume.
Bread flour is produced from hard wheat that has a higher protein (gluten) content, about twelve per cent, than all-purpose bleached or white flour. It is smoother in texture and is used to ensure that the dough is elastic and strong so that the bread has structure, strength and elasticity. It is available in supermarkets and health food stores. Sometimes it is called strong flour. It can be used for general baking.

Frangipane is creamed butter and sugar with eggs, ground almonds and a liqueur. It is used to fill a pastry or tart case.

Galettes are small open fruit tarts. They have a thin pastry base topped with raw sliced or halved fruit that is sprinkled with sugar, then dotted with butter and baked. Galettes are usually made with puff pastry, either home-made or bought, cut into individual rounds or squares, topped with the fruit and sugar and baked. They can also be made with filo or shortcrust pastry. Dried fruit and nuts can be used as a topping if preferred.

Gelatine is extracted from collagen, the connective tissue present in the bones and cartilage of animals. Gelatine is a setting agent available in powdered form and as leaves. 3 teaspoons of gelatine powder is equivalent to 6 leaves, which will set 2 cups (500 ml/16 fl oz) of liquid to a light jelly. To dissolve gelatine leaves, soften them in a bowl of cold water for 5 minutes, then remove and squeeze well. Next, dissolve them in warm to hot liquid. To dissolve gelatine powder, sprinkle the powder over a small bowl of water. Sit the bowl in a larger bowl of hot water and leave to dissolve. Agar-agar is a substitute suitable for vegetarian people. Follow the instructions on the packet.

Ginger Native to Southeast Asia, ginger is the rhizome or root of the ginger plant. It is available fresh or dried (ground). Fresh ginger should be bought while plump and firm with a pale outer skin. The outer skin is peeled away and the flesh is finely grated just before use. The powder is used in baking to flavour cakes, biscuits, puddings and gingerbread. Crystallized fresh ginger is used in cakes, desserts and as decoration. The flavour is pungent, sweet and spicy.

Glacé fruit is fruit that is preserved in sugar. The fruit, usually citrus or pineapple slices, or cherries, is cooked in a strong syrup solution until the fruit is impregnated by the sugar. Cherries are often coloured with various food dyes.

Glaze is a liquid such as milk, sugar syrup, melted butter, softened and sieved jam, beaten whole egg, egg yolk and water, or egg white that is brushed onto food, often before baking but sometimes after, to give colour and shine.

Gluten, a protein found in wheat flour, is the muscular substance of great elasticity that strengthens the cellular structure of the bread dough. Without the elasticity qualities of gluten, bread is flat and heavy. Gluten flour or powder

is often added to a bread dough to provide more protein and therefore improved volume, structure and texture. Non-wheat flours, notably rye, oat, barley and corn, lack gluten. If volume is wanted, these flours require added gluten in the form of gluten flour or the addition of some wheat flour. Breads made without the addition of gluten are heavy and dense as in German rye bread, corn breads and oatcakes. Gluten flour or powder is available at health food shops and some supermarkets.

Golden syrup is a by-product of sugar refining. It is a thick sticky syrup with a deep golden colour and distinctive flavour. It is used in the baking of gingerbread, tarts and some breads to give flavour and moisture. It can be substituted for treacle in baked goods.

Icing sugar Pure icing sugar is powdered white sugar used in the making of icings including buttercreams, glacé and royal, and fondants, to decorate cakes. Pure icing sugar should always be sifted before use to remove lumps and to obtain a smooth finish.

Icing sugar mixture is icing sugar to which a small amount of starch is added to prevent lumping during storage. It is used in the making of icings such as buttercreams and glacé, but is not suitable for royal icing. It is also known as confectioners' sugar.

Jams are traditionally made from whole ripe fruit that has been cooked to a pulp with sugar until it jells or sets. Jam heated and strained through a sieve then brushed over a cake or sweet bread makes a very attractive finish to baked goods.

Small amounts of jam or marmalade blended into a cake mixture add extra flavour and moisture.

Knead This means to work a bread dough with your hands on a flat floured surface. The dough is rhythmically pushed, stretched and folded in order to develop the gluten in the flour. It takes about 10 minutes for the gluten to be fully developed.

Knock back After the first rising, bread dough is 'knocked back' or punched down. This allows all the bubbles of carbon dioxide to be expelled, thus preventing the gluten walls from overstretching and collapsing. The dough is then ready to be shaped and left to rise a second time.

Lard is purified fat from pork. It is sold in solid form in packets and can be refrigerated for weeks. It is traditionally used in pastry-making. Lard is a good shortening (tenderizing) agent but lacks flavour and colour, so a blend of butter and lard will produce the most tender pastry with more flavour.

Leavened is a term describing baked products such as breads and cakes that contain a raising agent, usually yeast or baking powder, to increase the volume of the goods.

Malt extract is produced from grain, a process that converts grain starch to a sugar called maltose. The resulting powder or syrup is used widely in baking, brewing and distilling. It retains moisture, thus giving malted breads their distinctive flavour and moist texture. It also aids in the rising of the bread dough. It is a nutritious addition to breads, puddings and cakes. The powdered form is used in drinks.

13

Maple syrup is a light brown syrup processed from the sap of the maple tree. It is famous for its distinctive flavour and is often used as a topping for pancakes and waffles. It is also used in the baking of cakes and biscuits and to flavour icings and ice creams. Maple syrup is available at most supermarkets.

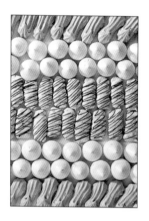

Marzipan is a mixture of almond paste (meal), egg white and icing sugar. It is mainly used by rolling out thinly to cover fruit cakes before they are finished with a layer of royal icing. Marzipan can be shaped, then tinted with food dyes to resemble fruits, and used to decorate cakes.

Meringue is stabilized egg-white foam and dissolved sugar crystals, brought about by whisking. The quantity of sugar required per egg white in order to form a stable meringue varies from 50 to 75 grams. There are three types of meringue. Swiss meringue produces an externally crisp and dry texture usually with a dry centre. It is suitable for piping, pie toppings and pavlovas. The standard proportion is 50 to 60 grams of sugar per egg white.

Soft and creamy in texture, Italian meringue is more stable than the Swiss and is used as a cake frosting, for Baked Alaska, and sometimes in ice creams and whipped cream (crème chantilly). The basic proportion is 50 to 60 grams of sugar to egg white—a sugar syrup is first made, then slowly poured onto the beaten white.

Meringue cuite (cooked) is a very firm dry meringue mostly used by pastry cooks in the making of meringue baskets and meringue decorations that can be stored for a time. 75 grams of icing sugar to one egg white is used for this.

Meringues need to be baked at a very low temperature, preferably in an electric oven, as they need to dry out and maintain their white colour.

Mixed peel is a mixture of chopped citrus fruit peel preserved in sugar and glucose syrup. It is mainly used in fruit cakes, mince pies and dried fruit puddings.

Mixed spice is a blend of ground spices, usually allspice, cinnamon, nutmeg, cloves and ginger. It adds a lightly spicy flavour to cooked fruit such as apples, and to cakes, fruit cakes, puddings and biscuits.

Nutmeg is the dried kernel or seed of the fruit of an evergreen tree native to Southeast Asia. The seed has a lacy husk called mace. Mace is used in flakes (blades) or powdered form and added to savoury dishes such as pickles and instead of nutmeg in sweet dishes. The nutmeg kernel is grated whole or used in powder form to flavour cakes and desserts. Freshly grated nutmeg has a much better flavour. Grate on the fine holes of a grater, or use a special nutmeg grater.

Nuts are formed after a tree or plant has flowered. They are the hardened and dried fruit encased in tough shells that have to be cracked to open (such as macadamias and chestnuts). However, the term 'nut' is also used to describe any seed or fruit with an edible kernel in a hard or brittle shell (almonds, walnuts and coconuts). Nuts are used extensively in baking. They are an important source of food and oil in all cuisines. Because of their high fat content it is advisable to refrigerate nuts in an airtight container to prevent them turning rancid.

Oils are similar to fats but differ in their physical state. Oils are liquid at room temperature and fats are solid. Animal fats (i.e. saturated fats) that are used in baking include butter, cream, ghee, lard and suet. Vegetable oils (i.e. polyunsaturated and monounsaturated fats), include fruit oils (olive oil), nut oils (walnut, hazelnut), seed oils (sesame, sunflower), pulse oils (soybean) and cereal oils (corn). All are used in one form or the other for the baking of cakes, biscuits, desserts, puddings and breads. Oils enhance the flavour and moistness as well as the keeping qualities in baked products.

Organic ingredients have generally been produced without the use of pesticides, insecticides, herbicides, fungicides or artificial fertilizers. Increasingly, ingredients that are commonly used in baking, such as flour, butter and eggs, are being produced organically and made more generally available. There is still more information to be gathered as to whether organic products do have a superior flavour and are actually of benefit to health. These products can be substituted in recipes and this decision is entirely personal.

Powdered milk is milk from which most of the moisture has been removed. The resulting milk powder can be stored in airtight tins or foil bags for up to a year. It is reconstituted to milk by adding water, or can be used in its powder form to enrich baked products, especially bread doughs. Powdered milks are made from both full-fat and non-fat (skim) milk.

Proving (also called the second rise) describes the process of the bread dough being knocked back, then shaped and left to rise on its baking tray until doubled in bulk, before baking. Test by gently pressing a finger into the dough and if the imprint remains, the dough is proved and ready for baking.

Ribbon stage Eggs and sugar are beaten, either with an electric beater or hand whisk, until the sugar has dissolved and the egg becomes pale and firm with very small bubbles. The beater or whisk will leave a raised mark on top of the mixture when the ribbon stage is reached. The term is used when sponge cakes are being made. The result of the beating is a very light aerated cake. Usually only small amounts of flour and maybe ground nuts are gently folded into the mixture before baking.

Salt is used as a seasoning, preservative and flavour enhancer. Salt improves the balance of flavours in sweet baking goods and most recipes will include some. The flavour of bread is greatly improved with the addition of salt. Iodised salt, often used as table salt, has a trace element of iodine added. Maldon salt, or sea salt, is produced in Essex in the UK and is made by extracting sea salt by natural means. Rock salt is mined from under the ground.

Suet is the fat that surrounds the kidneys of beef cattle. Before use, suet needs to be skinned and cleaned, then grated or shredded. It is often used in dried fruit puddings. Fresh suet can be bought from a butcher. Dried, shredded suet can be found at supermarkets. Butter can be used instead.

Sugar is the common name for sucrose, the simplest form of carbohydrate. The sugars are found in virtually all plants, including many fruits and vegetables. There are several types of sugar. The most widely used is white sugar (granulated, caster, cubed and icing sugar). It is usually manufactured from sugar cane or sugar beet and is used extensively in baking and general table use. In baking, sugar is important as it adds flavour, taste and moisture, and has a tenderizing effect.

Coloured sugars, also manufactured from sugar cane, include brown sugar, often known as soft brown sugar, a golden brown refined sugar, which is used in baked goods. These sugars add colour and flavour and help create a moist texture, especially in cakes. Brown sugar is also available as dark brown sugar. The colour in these sugars comes from the molasses content.

Raw sugar, coarse straw-coloured crystals, is also produced from sugar cane. It can be substituted for white sugar to add texture, but is difficult to dissolve. Demerara sugar, a coarse amber-coloured crystal, similar to raw sugar, is also used in baking, especially in crumble topping.

Treacle is a blend of concentrated refinery syrups and extract molasses. It is used in baking to give a distinctive colour and flavour. It also adds moistness and keeping qualities to a baked product. Golden syrup can be substituted in baking.

Vanilla is extracted from the pods of a climbing orchid plant native to South America. The pods or beans are dried and cured. For use in cooking, the pod is split open and infused with the food to allow for maximum flavour. The pod can be washed, dried and re-used. Vanilla is also available as pure essence or extract, which has a more concentrated flavour and is widely used in cakes, biscuits and desserts.

Vanilla sugar is made by placing a whole vanilla pod or bean in a jar of caster sugar and leaving it to stand so the flavour can be absorbed into the sugar. This is a good method of storing a vanilla pod as it flavours the sugar and prevents the pod from drying out. For a flavour boost in baking, use the vanilla sugar instead of caster sugar.

Yeast is a biological (naturally occurring) raising agent. Fresh yeast (compressed), available from some bakeries, needs to be blended with water to form a smooth cream, then added to any remaining liquid and left to foam before being added to the dry ingredients. Dried yeast, available in long-life sachets from supermarkets, can be added to liquid or mixed straight into the dry ingredients. For fermentation of the yeast to take place, it needs the right conditions of food (sugar), warmth (26– 29°C) and moisture (liquid).

Zest or rind is the outside rind of any citrus fruit. The rind contains all the essential oils and therefore the flavour. Be careful when removing it that you do not include the bitter white layer beneath. If the fruit has a wax coating, wash it off in hot water before removing the rind. Grated or shredded rind is used to flavour cakes, biscuits, syrups and doughs. The rind can also be thinly peeled from the fruit, leaving the white pith behind, then thinly shredded with a small sharp knife.

BASIC UTENSILS

When you decide to investigate the secrets of baking at home, you will need to invest in some basic utensils. If you buy good-quality ones you will find they last longer.

LATTICE CUTTERS
For topping pies and tarts, these simplify cutting a lattice pattern into rolled out pastry. They are usually made from plastic so they will not mark work surfaces.

WOODEN SPOONS
These are useful for beating, mixing and stirring because they do not conduct heat or scratch non-stick surfaces. Choose spoons with hard, close-grained wood for durability.

GRATERS
Graters with perforations of different sizes are designed for specific functions, from grating cheese to citrus zest. Nutmeg graters are small and concave, often with a compartment for the whole spice.

METAL SPOONS
Large metal spoons are best for folding in dry ingredients, or combining one mixture with another without losing too much air.

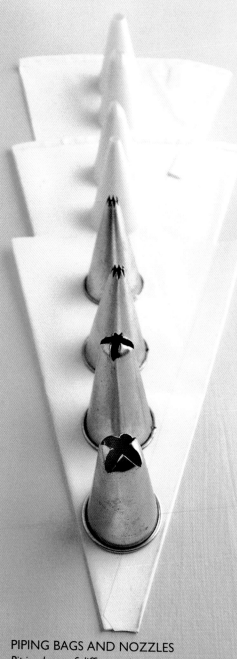

PIPING BAGS AND NOZZLES
Piping bags of different sizes accommodate small metal or plastic nozzles with various shaped openings. The bags should be washed thoroughly after use and dried inside-out to prevent odours developing.

DOUGH SCRAPERS
These are used to divide, separate and scrape dough on a work surface. They are used mainly for pastry and bread doughs.

ROLLING PINS
These should be large enough to roll out a full sheet of pastry, ensuring a smooth surface. Good-quality rolling pins are made from hard wood with a close grain and very smooth finish. Wood is preferable to ceramic and marble as its surface collects and holds a fine layer of flour.

COOLING RACKS
These footed metal grids enable air to circulate around food during cooling.

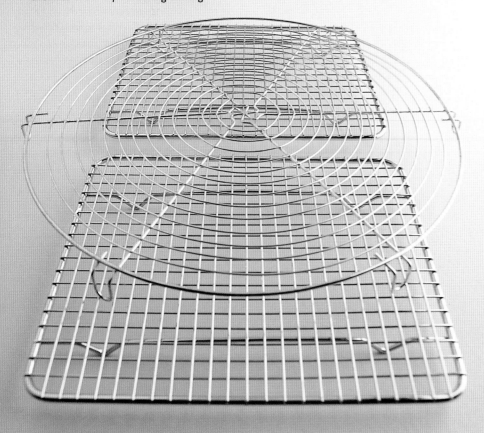

FLOUR SIEVES AND DREDGERS
These are ideal for incorporating air into flour or dusting flour onto work surfaces. They can also be used when decorating or dusting with icing sugar or cocoa.

BAKING BEADS
Small reusable ceramic or metal beads used when blind baking pastry. Uncooked rice or dried beans can be substituted.

CUTTERS
These come in a variety of shapes and sizes, ranging from plain and fluted rounds to hearts and gingerbread people. Metal cutters have a better edge than plastic but need to be stored carefully as they can rust and squash easily.

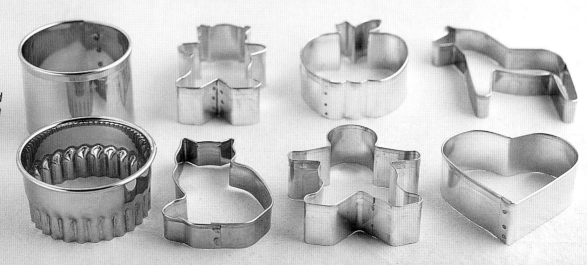

WHISKS

Whisks beat air into ingredients and remove any lumps. Balloon whisks consist of loops of stainless steel joined by a handle. They range from large ones for whisking egg whites to smaller ones for batters and sauces.

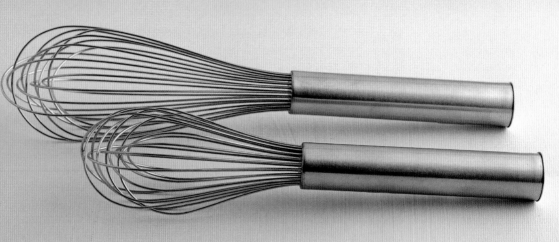

CITRUS ZESTERS

Zesters have a row of holes with sharp edges running across the top. When they are drawn down firmly across a citrus fruit, they peel off the zest or rind in long thin shreds.

APPLE CORERS

These have a cylindrical blade that fits neatly around an apple core and removes it whole without damaging the shape of the fruit.

MEASURING CUPS AND SPOONS

All spoon and cup measures in this book are level, not heaped. Dry ingredients should be levelled off with a knife.

PASTRY BRUSHES

Made with nylon or natural bristles, these can be flat or round and are used for glazing. Care should be taken when using nylon bristles with very hot liquids as the bristles may melt. Brushes should be washed and dried thoroughly before storage and separate brushes should be used for oil and butter.

PASTRY WHEELS

These are metal or plastic wheels used for cutting fluted edges on pastry.

PALETTE KNIVES

These are available in various sizes and degrees of flexibility. The blade is thin and flat with a rounded end and is useful for transferring flat items such as biscuits and for spreading decorative icings.

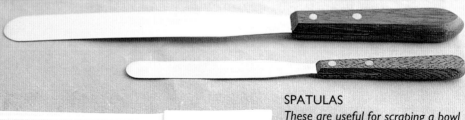

SPATULAS

These are useful for scraping a bowl completely clean and getting residue out of blender and food processor bowls. Rubber spatulas are more flexible than plastic ones but do tend to absorb colour and flavour so keep separate ones for sweet and savoury use.

PARING KNIVES

With a short blade, these are a handy all-purpose knife. They are perfect for cutting fruit as well as trimming pastry and making small incisions.

SERRATED KNIVES

These are best for slicing through bread and cakes neatly and evenly.

MIXERS

These can be hand-held or table models. They make creaming mixtures, mixing batters and whisking whites much easier than by hand.

SIFTERS

This hand sifter is used to aerate lumpy flour. It is also useful for sifting small amounts of flour to a light consistency.

METAL SKEWERS

Long and thin with a sharp, pointed edge, these are useful for testing to see whether a cake is cooked through.

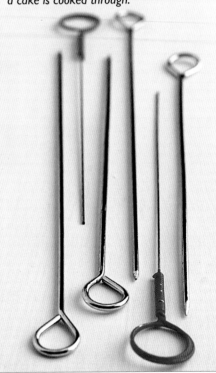

SCALES

Essential for weighing ingredients, kitchen scales vary from balance scales to digital display and most of them provide both metric and imperial weights.

MIXING BOWLS

Stainless steel bowls are durable and are good conductors of heat and cold. Heatproof bowls are essential for slow heating over a water bath. Glass and ceramic bowls need to be sufficiently heavy to sit firmly in place while ingredients are combined.

OVEN THERMOMETERS

These are designed to stand or hang in the oven. When doing any baking it is essential to check the accuracy of the oven temperature.

CITRUS JUICERS

These are available in glass, ceramic, plastic and wood, as well as electric.

BREAD TINS

ROUND TINS

deep tins

shallow or
sandwich tins

Genoise tin

fluted tart tins with
removable base

CAKE AND SLAB TINS

BAKING TRAYS, SLICE TINS AND LOAF TINS

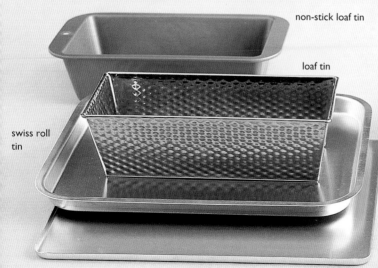

non-stick loaf tin

loaf tin

swiss roll
tin

baking or biscuit tray

bar tin

slice or
brownie
tins

loaf tin

SPECIALITY CAKE TINS

deep fluted ring tin

nut-roll tin

angel food tin

round springform tins

Charlotte tin

tube tin

savarin tin

kugelhopf tin

MUFFIN AND SMALL CAKE TINS

mini muffin tin

shallow patty tins

Texas muffin tin

regular muffin tin

friand tins

madeleine tins

TEATIME

A warming fireside, a squashily comfortable armchair, perhaps a little sprinkle of rain outside. The kettle whistles noisily in the kitchen and everyone's spirits brighten — it's time for tea. The tradition of teatime conjures up a cosy, safe and reassuring feeling and is an excellent opportunity to indulge in some of your favourite comfort foods. Light-as-air scones with home-made strawberry jam and clotted cream, muffins, friands, wonderfully old-fashioned cream buns and madeleines . . . mmmm lovely. Pour yourselves a nice cup of tea, crook your little finger daintily as you drink, and enjoy the moment.

SCONE SECRETS

Scones are so easy, it is quicker to make them than go out and buy them.

For perfect scones, handle them quickly and lightly and cook in a hot oven.

LIGHT AND EASY

All scones are made according to the same principles: add the wet ingredients to the dry and mix the dough as briefly and lightly as possible. Because the moisture content of flour varies, you may not need all the liquid stated in your recipe. The amount of liquid the flour absorbs can also change according to the room temperature and even the altitude.

Although our recipe uses self-raising flour, some people prefer to use plain flour and add more raising agents such as baking powder. Salt is added to enhance the flavour of all scones, even sweet ones, and the taste is not noticeable.

MAKING PERFECT SCONES

Follow these simple directions to achieve a good batch of high, light and golden scones. Remember that unlike bread, which requires vigorous kneading, scone dough just needs quick light handling. To make ten to twelve scones, you will need 2½ cups (310 g/10 oz) self-raising flour, 1 teaspoon baking powder, a pinch of salt, 40 g (1¼ oz) chilled unsalted butter, cut into small cubes, and 1 cup (250 ml/8 fl oz) milk. Assemble all the ingredients as well as a large bowl, a

flat-bladed metal spatula or knife for mixing, a round scone or biscuit cutter, a pastry brush and a baking tray. You will also need a clean tea towel to wrap the scones. Before you begin mixing, preheat the oven to hot 220°C (425°F/Gas 7) and lightly grease the baking tray or line it with baking paper. Sift the flour, baking powder and salt into a bowl. Sifting aerates the dry ingredients and helps achieve lighter scones. Many bakers sift the flour twice. Rub in the butter briefly and lightly with your fingertips until the mixture is crumbly and resembles fine breadcrumbs. Mixing in 1 tablespoon of sugar at this stage will lessen any floury taste. Make a well in the centre. Pour in almost all the milk and mix with a flat-bladed knife, using a cutting action, until the dough comes together in clumps. Rotate the bowl as you work.

Use the remaining milk if the mixture seems dry. Handle the mixture with great care and a very light hand. If you are heavy-handed and mix too much, or knead, your scones will be very tough. The dough should feel slightly wet and sticky. With floured hands, gently gather the dough together, lift onto a lightly floured surface and pat into a smooth ball. Do not knead. Pat or lightly roll the dough out to 2 cm (¾ inch) thick. Using a floured 6 cm (2½ inch) cutter, cut into rounds. Don't pat out too thinly or the scones will not be a good height. Gather the scraps together and, without handling too much, press out as before and cut out more rounds. Place close together on the baking tray and lightly brush the tops with milk. Bake in the top half of the oven for 12– 15 minutes, or until risen and golden. It is important to cook

scones at a high temperature, otherwise the raising agents will not work. If you aren't sure they are cooked, break one open. If still doughy in the centre, cook for a few more minutes. For soft scones, wrap them in a dry tea towel while hot. For scones with a crisp top, transfer to a wire rack to cool slightly before wrapping. Serve warm, or at room temperature, with butter or jam and whipped or clotted cream. As scones contain little fat, they dry out quickly so are best eaten soon after baking. They freeze successfully.

FRUIT SCONES

To make fruit scones, add ½ cup (75 g/ 2½ oz) currants or chopped pitted dates (95 g/3 oz) to the mixture after you've rubbed in the butter. Mix well to distribute the fruit, then proceed with the recipe.

ABOVE: Sultana scones

SCONES

Scones are the most popular of the 'quick breads' as they can be mixed and baked in a short time, unlike yeasted breads. *Devonshire Tea*, known all over the world, consists of freshly baked scones with jam and cream served with a pot of tea. The name originally came from the beautiful thick rich cream of Devon, called clotted cream, but whipped cream is an adequate substitute. Sweet additions to a scone dough can include sugar, spices and dried fruits such as chopped pitted dates, raisins and mixed peel. Savoury flavours can include a variety of herbs, ham, pumpkin or cheese.

ABOVE: Sultana scones

SULTANA SCONES

Preparation time: 10 minutes
Total cooking time: 15 minutes
Makes 12

2 cups (250 g/8 oz) self-raising flour
1 teaspoon baking powder
30 g (1 oz) unsalted butter, chilled and cubed
$^1/_2$ cup (80 g/2$^3/_4$ oz) sultanas
1 cup (250 ml/8 fl oz) milk, plus extra, to glaze

1 Preheat the oven to hot 220°C (425°F/Gas 7). Lightly grease a baking tray or line with baking paper. Sift the flour, baking powder and a pinch of salt into a bowl. Rub in the butter using your fingertips, then stir in the sultanas. Make a well.
2 Add almost all the milk and mix with a flat-bladed knife, using a cutting action, until the dough comes together in clumps. Use the remaining milk if necessary. With floured hands, gently gather the dough together, lift out onto a lightly floured surface and pat into a smooth ball. Do not knead or the scones will be tough.
3 Pat the dough out to 2 cm (³⁄₄ inch) thick. Using a floured 5 cm (2 inch) cutter, cut into rounds. Gather the trimmings together, press out

as before and cut more rounds. Place close together on the tray and brush with milk. Bake for 15 minutes, or until risen and golden brown on top. Serve warm or at room temperature.

CHEESE SCONES

Preparation time: 15 minutes
Total cooking time: 15 minutes
Makes 12

2 cups (250 g/8 oz) self-raising flour
1 teaspoon baking powder
$^1/_2$ teaspoon dry mustard
30 g (1 oz) unsalted butter, chilled and cubed
$^1/_4$ cup (25 g/³⁄₄ oz) grated Parmesan
$^3/_4$ cup (90 g/3 oz) finely grated Cheddar
1 cup (250 ml/8 fl oz) milk

1 Preheat the oven to hot 220°C (425°F/Gas 7). Lightly grease a baking tray or line with baking paper. Sift the flour, baking powder, mustard and a pinch of salt into a bowl and rub in the butter with your fingertips. Stir in the Parmesan and $^1/_2$ cup (60 g/2 oz) Cheddar, making sure they

don't clump together. Make a well in the centre. Add almost all the milk, and mix with a flat-bladed knife, using a cutting action, until the dough comes together in clumps. Use the remaining milk if necessary. With floured hands, gently gather the dough together, lift out onto a lightly floured surface and pat into a smooth ball. Do not knead or the scones will be tough.

2 Pat the dough out to 2 cm (³/₄ inch) thick. Using a floured 5 cm (2 inch) cutter, cut into rounds. Gather the trimmings and, without over-handling, press out as before and cut more rounds. Place close together on the tray and sprinkle with the remaining cheese. Bake for 12– 15 minutes, or until risen and golden brown. Serve warm or at room temperature.

PUMPKIN SCONES

Preparation time: 15 minutes + cooling pumpkin
Total cooking time: 30 minutes
Makes 12

250 g (8 oz) butternut pumpkin, cut into cubes
2 cups (250 g/8 oz) self-raising flour
1 teaspoon baking powder
pinch of ground nutmeg
30 g (1 oz) unsalted butter, chilled and cubed
2 tablespoons soft brown sugar
¹/₂ cup (125 ml/4 fl oz) milk, plus extra, to glaze

1 Steam the pumpkin for 12 minutes, or until soft, then drain well and mash until smooth. Cool to room temperature. Preheat the oven to hot 220°C (425°F/Gas 7). Lightly grease a baking tray or line with baking paper.

2 Sift the flour, baking powder and a pinch of salt into a bowl and add the nutmeg and butter. Rub the butter into the flour with your fingertips, then stir in the sugar and make a well in the centre.

3 Mix the milk into the pumpkin, add to the well in the flour and mix with a flat-bladed knife, using a cutting action, until the dough comes together in clumps. With floured hands, gather the dough together (it will be very soft) and lift out onto a lightly floured surface. Do not knead or the scones will be tough.

4 Pat the dough out to 2 cm (³/₄ inch) thick. Using a floured 5 cm (2 inch) cutter, cut into rounds. Gather the trimmings and, without handling too much, press out and cut out more rounds. Place close together on the tray and brush with milk. Bake for 12– 15 minutes, or until well risen and lightly golden. Serve warm.

BELOW: Pumpkin scones

MUFFINS

Wonderfully simple, muffins can be plain, sweet or savoury. Master the basic muffin, then experiment with different flavour combinations and enjoy them for breakfast, snacks, lunch or dinner.

PERFECT MUFFINS

Follow these simple instructions to make twelve delicious muffins. You will need 2½ cups (310 g/10 oz) self-raising flour, ½ cup (125 g/4 oz) caster sugar, 1½ cups (375 ml/12 fl oz) milk, 2 lightly beaten eggs, 1 teaspoon vanilla essence and 150 g (5 oz) unsalted butter that has been melted and cooled. We used the regular (100 ml/ 3½ fl oz) size American-style non-stick

tins but tins are also available in mini and Texan sizes. Even though most muffin tins have non-stick surfaces, it is worth greasing the holes, especially when making sweet muffins, as the sugar can make them very sticky. Assemble your ingredients and utensils and preheat the oven to moderately hot 200°C (400°F/ Gas 6). Sift the flour into a bowl to aerate the flour and ensure a light muffin. Add

the sugar to the bowl and stir through the flour. Make a well in the centre. In a jug, mix together the milk, eggs and vanilla essence. Pour the liquid into the well in the flour and add the cooled butter. Melted butter doesn't always combine well with other liquids so it is often added separately. Fold the mixture gently with a metal spoon until just combined. Be careful not to overbeat or the muffins

will become tough and rubbery. The mixture should still be lumpy at this stage. Divide the mixture evenly among the holes using two metal spoons—fill each hole to about three-quarters full. Always try to use the hole size indicated in the recipe because if you use a different size the cooking time changes. The larger the hole, the longer the baking time.

COOKING

Bake the muffins for 20–25 minutes, or until they are risen, golden and come away slightly from the sides of the holes. Test them by pressing lightly with your fingertips—they are cooked when they feel firm, and spring back. Another test is to insert a skewer into the centre—if it comes out clean they are ready. Most muffins should be left in the tin for a couple of minutes once out of the oven, but don't leave them too long or trapped steam will make the bases soggy. Using a flat-bladed knife, loosen the muffins and transfer to a wire rack. They can be eaten warm or cool and can be decorated or iced.

SIMPLE VARIATIONS

The basic recipe can be adapted to add many flavours. You can use the same tin but the muffin holes will be quite full.

CHOC CHIP

Add 1½ cups (260 g/8 oz) choc bits to the flour and replace the caster sugar with ½ cup (95 g/3 oz) soft brown sugar.

BLUEBERRY

Add 300 g (10 oz) blueberries to the flour. If fresh blueberries are unavailable, frozen ones can be used. Add while still frozen to avoid streaking the batter.

BANANA

Add an extra ¼ cup (60 g/2 oz) caster sugar and ½ teaspoon mixed spice to the flour and 1 cup (240 g/7½ oz) mashed ripe bananas to the butter. Use only 1 cup (250 ml/8 fl oz) milk. Proceed with the recipe.

PECAN

Replace the caster sugar with ¾ cup (140 g/4½ oz) soft brown sugar. Add ¾ cup (90 g/3 oz) chopped pecans with the flour. Mix to distribute, then proceed with the recipe.

STORAGE

Cold muffins can be frozen for 3 months in a freezer bag. When required, thaw them, wrap in foil, then reheat in a moderate 180°C (350°F/Gas 4) oven for about 8 minutes, or until heated through.

CHOCOLATE MUFFINS

Preparation time: 15 minutes
Total cooking time: 25 minutes
Makes 12

2¹/₂ cups (310 g/10 oz) self-raising flour
¹/₃ cup (40 g/1¹/₂ oz) cocoa powder
¹/₂ teaspoon bicarbonate of soda
²/₃ cup (180 g/6 oz) caster sugar
1¹/₂ cups (375 ml/12 fl oz) buttermilk
2 eggs
150 g (5 oz) unsalted butter, melted and cooled

1 Preheat the oven to moderately hot 200°C (400°F/Gas 6). Lightly grease twelve regular muffin holes. Sift the flour, cocoa powder and bicarbonate of soda into a bowl and add the sugar. Make a well in the centre.
2 In a jug, whisk the buttermilk and eggs together and pour into the well. Add the butter and fold gently with a metal spoon until just combined. Do not overmix—the mixture should still be lumpy.
3 Fill each hole about three-quarters full. Bake for 20–25 minutes, or until the muffins are risen and come away slightly from the side of the tin. Allow to cool for a couple of minutes, then loosen with a flat-bladed knife and transfer to a wire rack. Serve warm or at room temperature.

APPLE CINNAMON MUFFINS

Preparation time: 15 minutes
Total cooking time: 25 minutes
Makes 12

400 g (13 oz) can pie apple
2¹/₂ cups (310 g/10 oz) self-raising flour
2 teaspoons ground cinnamon
²/₃ cup (125 g/4 oz) soft brown sugar
1¹/₃ cups (350 ml/11 fl oz) milk
2 eggs
1 teaspoon vanilla essence
150 g (5 oz) unsalted butter, melted and cooled
¹/₂ cup (60 g/2 oz) walnuts, finely chopped

1 Preheat the oven to moderately hot 200°C (400°F/Gas 6). Lightly grease twelve regular muffin holes. Place the pie apple in a bowl and break up with a knife.
2 Sift the flour and cinnamon into a bowl and add the sugar. Make a well in the centre. Whisk together the milk, eggs and vanilla in a jug and pour into the well. Add the melted butter.
3 Fold the mixture gently with a metal spoon until just combined. Add the pie apple and gently stir through. Do not overmix—the batter should be lumpy. Overmixing will make the muffins tough.

FLAVOURING MUFFINS
Using buttermilk instead of milk in muffins results in a softer texture and a good crust. It also adds to the flavour. To achieve the same effect, you can sour your own milk by adding a few drops of lemon juice or vinegar, just until it curdles the milk, or you can use milk that has gone sour. Muffins can be iced with a simple icing if you like. Make it by combining 1 cup (125 g/4 oz) sifted icing sugar with 10 g (¹/₄ oz) butter and about 1 tablespoon hot water to form a smooth paste. Flavour it with vanilla or grated citrus rind. For a chocolate-flavoured icing, add 1 tablespoon cocoa powder to the sifted icing sugar. Use a small metal spatula to ice the muffins.

RIGHT: Chocolate muffins

4 Fill each muffin hole with the mixture (the holes will be quite full, but don't worry because these muffins don't rise as much as some) and sprinkle with walnuts. Bake for 20–25 minutes, or until the muffins are risen, golden and come away slightly from the tin. Allow to cool for a couple of minutes, then gently loosen each muffin with a flat-bladed knife and transfer to a wire rack. Serve warm or at room temperature.
NOTE: Completely cool the melted butter before adding it. It doesn't always combine well with other liquids so it is often added separately.

ORANGE POPPY SEED MUFFINS

Preparation time: 15 minutes
Total cooking time: 30 minutes
Makes 12

2¹/₂ cups (310 g/10 oz) self-raising flour
¹/₄ cup (40 g/1¹/₄ oz) poppy seeds
¹/₃ cup (90 g/3 oz) caster sugar
125 g (4 oz) unsalted butter
1 cup (315 g/10 oz) orange marmalade
1 cup (250 ml/8 fl oz) milk
2 eggs
1 tablespoon finely grated orange rind

1 Preheat the oven to moderately hot 200°C (400°F/Gas 6). Lightly grease twelve regular muffin holes. Sift the flour into a bowl. Stir in the poppy seeds and sugar, and make a well in the centre. Put the butter and ²/₃ cup (210 g/ 7 oz) of the marmalade in a small saucepan and stir over low heat until the butter has melted and the mixture is combined. Cool slightly.
2 Whisk together the milk, eggs and rind in a jug and pour into the well. Add the butter and marmalade. Fold gently with a metal spoon until just combined. Do not overmix—the batter should still be lumpy. Overmixing will make them tough.
3 Fill each hole about three-quarters full and bake for 20–25 minutes, or until the muffins are risen, golden and come away slightly from the tin.
4 Heat the remaining marmalade and push it through a fine sieve. Brush generously over the top of the warm muffins. Leave them to cool in the tin for a couple of minutes, then gently loosen each muffin with a flat-bladed knife and transfer to a wire rack. Serve warm or at room temperature.
NOTE: A variation of this muffin can be made using lime marmalade and finely grated lemon rind. Muffins are most delicious if eaten on the day they are made and served warm. If you want to store muffins for a couple of days, let them cool completely, then store them in an airtight container. Muffins are also suitable for freezing (see page 29).

EGGS
Eggs quickly lose their quality so it is important to store them correctly. Check the use-by date when you buy them and look to make sure none of the eggs are broken. Store eggs in their cartons to protect them. They are commercially packed with the pointed end down to prevent damage to the air cell and to keep the yolk centred. Eggs should be refrigerated as this slows down moisture loss. For every day that an egg is left out of the refrigerator, as much as four days in quality can be lost.

LEFT: Orange poppy seed muffins

FRIANDS

Friands (pronounced *free-onds*) are small oval-shaped cakes baked in special-purpose oval tins called friand tins or barquette moulds. Sometimes the same mixture is baked in a rectangular tin and is then named *Financier*, meaning 'gold ingot', which the shape resembles. Both are very popular in cafés and come in a variety of flavours. The tins can be purchased from kitchenware shops. Traditional friands are made with almond meal.

ALMOND FRIANDS

Preparation time: 10 minutes
Total cooking time: 20 minutes
Makes 10

160 g (5½ oz) unsalted butter
1 cup (90 g/3 oz) flaked almonds
⅓ cup (40 g/1¼ oz) plain flour
1⅓ cups (165 g/5½ oz) icing sugar
5 egg whites
icing sugar, extra, to dust

1 Preheat the oven to hot 210°C (415°F/Gas 6–7). Lightly grease ten ½ cup (125 ml/4 fl oz) friand tins (barquette moulds).
2 Melt the butter in a small saucepan over medium heat, then cook for 3–4 minutes, or until the butter turns deep golden. Strain to remove any residue (the colour will deepen on standing). Remove from the heat and set aside to cool until just lukewarm.
3 Place the flaked almonds in a food processor and process until finely ground. Transfer to a bowl and sift the flour and icing sugar into the same bowl.
4 Place the egg whites in a separate bowl and lightly whisk with a fork until just combined. Add the butter to the flour mixture along with the egg whites. Mix gently with a metal spoon until all the ingredients are well combined.
5 Spoon some mixture into each friand tin to fill to three-quarters. Place the tins on a baking tray and bake in the centre of the oven for 10 minutes, then reduce the heat to moderate 180°C (350°F/Gas 4) and bake for another 5 minutes, or until a skewer comes out clean when inserted in the centre of a friand. Remove and leave to cool in the tins for 5 minutes before turning out onto a wire rack to cool completely. Dust with icing sugar before serving.
NOTES: These friands will keep well for up to three days in an airtight container.

To make berry friands, make the mixture as above and place a fresh or frozen raspberry or blueberry in the top of each friand before placing in the oven.

To make lemon friands, add 2 teaspoons grated lemon rind to the flour and sugar mixture and proceed as above.

HAZELNUT AND CHOCOLATE FRIANDS

Preparation time: 20 minutes
Total cooking time: 40 minutes
Makes 12

200 g (6½ oz) whole hazelnuts
185 g (6 oz) unsalted butter
6 egg whites
1¼ cups (155 g/5 oz) plain flour
¼ cup (30 g/1 oz) cocoa powder
2 cups (250 g/8 oz) icing sugar
icing sugar, extra, to dust

1 Preheat the oven to moderately hot 200°C (400°F/Gas 6). Lightly grease twelve ½ cup (125 ml/4 fl oz) friand tins (barquette moulds).
2 Spread the hazelnuts out on a baking tray and bake for 8–10 minutes, or until fragrant (take care not to burn). Wrap in a clean tea towel and rub vigorously to loosen the skins. Discard the skins. Cool, then process in a food processor until finely ground.
3 Melt the butter in a small saucepan over medium heat, then cook for 3–4 minutes, or until the butter turns deep golden. Strain to remove any residue (the colour will deepen on standing). Remove from the heat and set aside to cool to lukewarm.
4 Place the egg whites in a clean, dry bowl and lightly whisk until frothy but not firm. Sift the flour, cocoa powder and icing sugar into a large bowl and stir in the ground hazelnuts. Make a well in the flour, add the egg whites and butter and mix to combine.
5 Spoon some mixture into each friand tin to fill to three-quarters. Place the tins on a baking tray and bake in the centre of the oven for 20–25 minutes, or until a skewer comes out clean when inserted in the centre of a friand. Remove and leave to cool in the tins for 5 minutes before turning out onto a wire rack to cool completely. Dust with icing sugar before serving.
NOTE: These friands will keep for up to four days in an airtight container.

OPPOSITE PAGE:
Hazelnut and chocolate friands (at left on plate); Almond friands

WHAT WENT WRONG?

MUFFINS

PERFECT The texture of the muffin is even with a nicely risen centre and good golden colouring. If a skewer is inserted in the centre it will come out clean. The muffin has started to come away from the side of the holes. Muffins need to be cooked in a preheated moderately hot 200°C (400°F/Gas 6) oven so the batter will set and peak correctly as it has above.

TOO PEAKED The crust is too coloured and the muffin too peaked. This is caused by mixing too much or baking in an oven that is too hot. The result is muffins with a tough, rubbery texture and uneven shapes. Make sure all the dry ingredients are evenly distributed by sifting and mixing them, including the raising agent, before adding them to the wet ingredients. A perfect muffin mixture should be lumpy so do not combine the ingredients too much.

POORLY RISEN The muffin texture is too heavy and dense. This can be caused by insufficient raising agent or a missing ingredient. To avoid leaving out any vital ingredient, check that you have all the ingredients assembled and correctly weighed out before you start.

OVERFLOWING MIXTURE Make sure you use the size of muffin tin suggested in the recipe. Do not fill the muffin holes more than two-thirds full. This leaves room for the batter to rise as it will often rise by half its volume.

UNDERCOOKED The finished muffin is moist in the centre with insufficient peaking. The muffin is not properly coloured and didn't shrink away from the tin. The oven was probably not sufficiently preheated or not hot enough, or the cooking may have been too short.

MORE ABOUT MUFFINS

If you like the idea of having freshly baked muffins for breakfast but don't want to start the day making a mess in the kitchen, you can make a muffin mixture, then spoon it into the muffin tin and refrigerate it overnight, ready for baking the following day. Uncooked mixture for the plainer muffins such as chocolate or blueberry, or those without fillings, can be frozen in paper-lined muffin tins for up to a month. When you want to cook them, remove them from the freezer and bake in a preheated moderately hot 200°C (400°F/Gas 6) oven for 25–30 minutes, or until golden and slightly shrunk away from the sides.

FRIANDS

PERFECT The friand is nicely domed and has a moist, even texture and a good golden colour. The batter has shrunk from the side of the tin.

UNDERCOOKED The friand is a pale colour and has a wet, buttery and dense texture. The oven was not hot enough. Make sure you cook friands in an oven that has been preheated to hot 210°C (415°F/Gas 6–7).

OVERCOOKED The friand has a badly cracked top and the top and base are over-coloured. The friand is dark and crusty around the edges. Either the oven was too hot, or the cooking time was too long.

SCONES

PERFECT The scone is evenly risen, has a soft crust and soft inside texture and is light golden. The dough should not be overworked, but just lightly mixed with a flat-bladed knife until combined.

POORLY RISEN If the scone texture feels heavy and dense, the dough may have been either too dry or too wet, or the dough may have been mixed or worked too much.

UNDERCOOKED The scone is pale, sticky in the centre and has a dense texture. The cooking time was too short or the oven temperature too low. The oven must be at hot 220°C (425°F/Gas 7).

OVERCOOKED The scone has a dark crust and a dry texture. Either the cooking time was too long or the oven temperature was too hot, so check the oven temperature before baking scones.

MORE ABOUT BAKING

For all baking, make sure the ingredients are fresh and not past their use-by date. For example, baking powder should be replaced every six months as it loses its effectiveness as a raising agent if stored for too long. Proper storage of baking ingredients is also important. Flours should be stored in a cool, dry, dark cupboard. They can be kept for up to 3 months. Flours that contain a lot of oil, such as soy flour, should be kept refrigerated in hot weather to prevent them turning rancid.

Because oven temperatures vary a great deal, it is a good idea to invest in an oven thermometer (see page 19) so that you can check the oven temperature.

The time required to heat an oven to the correct temperature varies considerably from oven to oven but it takes at least 10 minutes. So, when baking, plan ahead and leave plenty of time for the oven to heat and be sure to wait until it has reached the specified temperature before placing the item in the oven.

Filling

30 g (1 oz) unsalted butter

1 tablespoon caster sugar

1/2 cup (100 g/3 1/2 oz) coarsely ground
  blanched almonds

1/2 cup (95 g/3 oz) mixed dried fruit

1/2 cup (100 g/3 1/2 oz) glacé cherries,
  cut in halves

Icing

1 cup (125 g/4 oz) icing sugar

1– 2 tablespoons milk

2 drops almond essence

1 Lightly grease a baking tray or line with
baking paper. Dissolve the yeast in 2 tablespoons
warm water in a bowl and leave in a warm place
for 10 minutes, or until bubbles appear on the
surface and the mixture is frothy. Heat the milk,
butter, sugar and 1/2 teaspoon salt in a saucepan
until just warmed.

2 Sift 2 cups (250 g/8 oz) of the flour into a large
bowl. Add the yeast and milk mixtures and beaten
egg and mix to a smooth batter. Add enough of
the remaining flour to make a soft dough. Turn
out onto a lightly floured surface and knead for
10 minutes, or until the dough is smooth and
elastic. Place the dough in a large, lightly oiled
bowl and brush the dough with oil. Cover with
plastic wrap or a damp tea towel and leave in a
warm place for 1 hour, or until well risen.

3 Meanwhile, to make the filling, cream the
butter and sugar, then mix in the almonds,
mixed fruit and cherries.

4 Punch the dough down and knead for
1 minute. Roll the dough to a 25 x 45 cm
(10 x 18 inch) rectangle. Spread the filling over
the dough, leaving a 2 cm (3/4 inch) border. Roll
up and form into a ring with the seam underneath.
Mix the egg yolk with 1 tablespoon water and
use a little to seal the ends together. Place on the
tray. Snip with scissors from the outside edge at
4 cm (1 1/2 inch) intervals. Turn the cut pieces on
the side and flatten slightly. Cover with plastic
wrap and leave in a warm place for 45 minutes,
or until well risen.

5 Preheat the oven to moderate 180°C (350°F/
Gas 4). Brush the tea ring with some of the egg
yolk and water and bake for 20– 25 minutes, or
until firm and golden. Cover with foil if the tea
cake is browning too much. Remove and cool.

6 For the icing, combine the ingredients until
smooth. Drizzle over the tea ring.

NOTE: This will keep for three days in an airtight
container. It will freeze, un-iced, for a month.

SWEDISH TEA RING

Preparation time: 1 hour
  + 1 hour 45 minutes rising
Total cooking time: 30 minutes
Makes 1

★ ★ ★

7 g (1/4 oz) sachet dried yeast

2/3 cup (170 ml/5 1/2 fl oz) milk

60 g (2 oz) unsalted butter,
  softened

2 tablespoons caster sugar

3 cups (375 g/12 oz) plain flour

1 egg, lightly beaten

1 egg yolk, extra

ABOVE: Swedish tea ring

DATE AND WALNUT ROLLS

Preparation time: 25 minutes
Total cooking time: 1 hour 10 minutes
Makes 2

3/4 cup (90 g/3 oz) self-raising flour

3/4 cup (90 g/3 oz) plain flour

1/2 teaspoon bicarbonate of soda

1 teaspoon mixed spice

1 cup (125 g/4 oz) chopped walnuts

100 g (3 1/2 oz) unsalted butter, chopped

3/4 cup (140 g/4 1/2 oz) soft brown sugar

1 1/2 cups (280 g/9 oz) chopped pitted dates

1 egg, lightly beaten

1 Preheat the oven to moderate 180°C (350°F/ Gas 4). Lightly grease two 17 x 8 cm (7 x 3 inch) nut-roll tins and their lids. Sift the flours, soda and spice into a large bowl, then stir in the walnuts. Make a well in the centre.
2 Combine the butter, sugar, dates and 1/2 cup (125 ml/4 oz) water in a saucepan. Stir constantly over low heat until the butter has melted and the sugar has dissolved. Remove from the heat and set aside to cool slightly. Add the butter mixture and egg to the flour and stir well.
3 Spoon the mixture evenly into the prepared tins. Bake, with the tins upright on a baking tray, for 1 hour, or until a skewer comes out clean when inserted into the centre of the loaves. Leave in the tins, with the lids on, for 10 minutes before turning out onto a wire rack to cool. Serve in slices. Delicious buttered.

BANANA BREAD

Preparation time: 20 minutes
Total cooking time: 45 minutes
Makes 1

2 cups (250 g/8 oz) plain flour

2 teaspoons baking powder

1 teaspoon mixed spice

150 g (5 oz) unsalted butter, softened

1 cup (185 g/6 oz) soft brown sugar

2 eggs, lightly beaten

1 cup (240 g/7 1/2 oz) mashed ripe bananas
   (about 2 medium-sized bananas)

1 Preheat the oven to moderate 180°C (350°F/ Gas 4). Grease and line the base of a 23 x 13 x 6 cm (9 x 5 1/2 x 2 1/2 inch) loaf tin.
2 Sift together the flour, baking powder, mixed spice and 1/4 teaspoon salt into a bowl.
3 Cream the butter and sugar in a large bowl with electric beaters until soft. Add the eggs gradually, beating well after each addition, and beat until smooth. Mix in the banana. Gradually add the sifted dry ingredients and mix until smooth. Pour into the loaf tin and bake on the middle shelf for 35–45 minutes, or until the top is nicely coloured and a skewer inserted into the centre comes out clean. Cool in the tin for 10 minutes before turning out onto a wire rack. The bread is delicious warm and keeps for a few days wrapped in plastic wrap. The flavour improves on keeping. Can be toasted.

BELOW: Date and walnut rolls

CREAM BUNS

Preparation time: 40 minutes
+ 1 hour 25 minutes rising
Total cooking time: 20 minutes
Makes 12

7 g (¹/₄ oz) sachet dried yeast
2 tablespoons sugar
1¹/₃ cups (350 ml/11 fl oz) milk, warmed
3¹/₂ cups (435 g/14 oz) plain flour
60 g (2 oz) unsalted butter, melted
¹/₂ cup (160 g/5¹/₂ oz) strawberry jam
1¹/₄ cups (315 ml/10 fl oz) cream
1 tablespoon icing sugar
2 tablespoons icing sugar, extra

1 Put the yeast, 1 teaspoon sugar and the milk in a small bowl and leave in a warm place for 10 minutes, or until bubbles appear on the surface. The mixture should be frothy and slightly increased in volume. If your yeast doesn't foam, it is dead and you will have to start again. Sift the flour into a large bowl, stir in the remaining sugar and ¹/₂ teaspoon salt.

Make a well and add the milk mixture and butter and mix to a dough, first with a wooden spoon, then your hands. Turn onto a lightly floured surface and knead for 10 minutes, or until smooth and elastic. Place in a lightly oiled bowl, cover with plastic wrap, and leave in a warm place for 1 hour, or until well risen.

2 Punch down the dough and turn onto a lightly floured surface, then knead for 2 minutes or until smooth. Divide into 12 pieces. Knead one portion at a time for 30 seconds on a lightly floured surface and then shape into a ball.

3 Preheat the oven to hot 210°C (415°F/ Gas 6– 7). Lightly grease two baking trays, dust lightly with flour and shake off any excess. Place balls of dough, evenly spaced, on the trays. Set aside, covered with plastic wrap, in a warm place for 15 minutes, or until well risen. Bake for 20 minutes or until well browned and cooked. Set aside for 5 minutes, then transfer to a wire rack to cool completely. Using a serrated knife, cut diagonally into each bun, to a depth of 5 cm (2 inches), from the top towards the base.

4 Spread jam over the cut base of each bun. Using electric beaters, beat the cream and sugar in a small bowl until firm peaks form. Spoon into a piping bag and pipe the whipped cream into the buns. Dust the tops with icing sugar.

YEAST

Yeast is available dried or fresh. Small amounts of fresh yeast can be bought from some health food stores and bakeries but the most convenient yeast is the dried granules which are readily available from the supermarket. It is packed in foil sachets and keeps for a long time. It is very reliable so can be added directly into the dry ingredients, or added to some liquid in the traditional way and left until it froths. The latter method is always used for fresh yeast to check that it is alive.

RIGHT: Cream buns

FINGER BUNS

Preparation time: 45 minutes
  + 1 hour 25 minutes rising
Total cooking time: 15 minutes
Makes 12

4 cups (500 g/1 lb) plain flour
1/3 cup (35 g/1 1/4 oz) full-cream milk powder
2 x 7 g (1/4 oz) sachets dried yeast
1/2 cup (125 g/4 oz) caster sugar
1/2 cup (80 g/2 3/4 oz) sultanas
60 g (2 oz) unsalted butter, melted
1 egg, lightly beaten
1 egg yolk, extra, to glaze

Glacé icing

1 1/4 cups (155 g/5 oz) icing sugar
20 g (3/4 oz) unsalted butter, melted
pink food colouring

1 Mix 3 cups (375 g/12 oz) of the flour with the milk powder, yeast, sugar, sultanas and 1/2 teaspoon salt in a large bowl. Make a well in the centre. Combine the butter, egg and 1 cup (250 ml/8 fl oz) warm water and add all at once to the flour. Stir for 2 minutes, or until well combined. Add enough of the remaining flour to make a soft dough.

2 Turn out onto a lightly floured surface. Knead for 10 minutes, or until the dough is smooth and elastic, adding more flour if necessary. Place in a large lightly oiled bowl and brush with oil. Cover with plastic wrap and leave in a warm place for 1 hour, or until well risen.

3 Lightly grease two large baking trays. Preheat the oven to moderate 180°C (350°F/Gas 4). Punch down the dough and knead for 1 minute. Divide into 12 pieces. Shape each into a 15 cm (6 inch) long oval. Put on the trays 5 cm (2 inches) apart. Cover with plastic wrap and set aside in a warm place for 20–25 minutes, or until well risen.

4 Mix the extra egg yolk with 1 1/2 teaspoons water and brush over the dough. Bake for 12–15 minutes, until firm and golden. Transfer to a wire rack to cool.

5 For the glacé icing, stir the icing sugar, melted butter and 2–3 teaspoons water together in a bowl until smooth. Mix in the food colouring and spread over the tops of the buns. Finger buns are delicious buttered.

ABOVE: Finger buns

39

ROCK CAKES

Preparation time: 15 minutes
Total cooking time: 15 minutes
Makes about 20

2 cups (250 g/8 oz) self-raising flour
90 g (3 oz) unsalted butter, chilled, cubed
1/2 cup (125 g/4 oz) caster sugar
1/2 cup (95 g/3 oz) mixed dried fruit
1/2 teaspoon ground ginger
1 egg
1/4 cup (60 ml/2 fl oz) milk

1 Preheat the oven to moderately hot 200°C (400°F/Gas 6). Grease two baking trays. Sift the flour into a large bowl and rub in the butter with your fingertips until the mixture resembles fine breadcrumbs. Stir in the sugar, fruit and ginger.
2 Whisk the egg into the milk in a bowl, add to the dry ingredients and mix to a stiff dough. Drop rough heaps of mixture, about 3 tablespoons at a time, onto the trays. Bake for 10–15 minutes, or until golden. Cool on a wire rack.

BUTTERFLY CAKES

Preparation time: 20 minutes
Total cooking time: 20 minutes
Makes 12

120 g (4 oz) unsalted butter, softened
2/3 cup (160 g/5 1/2 oz) caster sugar
1 1/2 cups (185 g/6 oz) self-raising flour
1/2 cup (125 ml/4 fl oz) milk
2 teaspoons vanilla essence
2 eggs
1/2 cup (125 ml/4 fl oz) cream,
   whipped to soft peaks
1/3 cup (105 g/3 1/2 oz) strawberry jam
icing sugar, to dust

1 Preheat the oven to moderate 180°C (350°F/Gas 4). Line a 12-hole shallow patty tin with paper cases. Put the butter, sugar, flour, milk, vanilla and eggs in a bowl and beat with electric beaters on low speed for 2 minutes, or until well mixed. Increase the speed and beat for 2 minutes, or until smooth and pale.

2 Divide the mixture evenly among the cases and bake for 20 minutes, or until cooked and golden. Transfer to a wire rack to cool completely.
3 Using a small sharp knife, cut shallow rounds from the top of each cake. Cut these in half. Spoon a half tablespoon of cream into the cavity in each cake, then top with a teaspoon of jam. Position two halves of the cake tops in the jam in each cake to resemble butterfly wings. Dust the cakes with icing sugar before serving.
NOTE: To make iced cup cakes, don't cut off the tops. Mix 1/2 cup (60 g/2 oz) sifted icing sugar, 1 teaspoon softened unsalted butter, 1/2 teaspoon vanilla essence and up to 3 teaspoons hot water to form a smooth paste, then spread icing on the cooled cakes.

ORANGE CUP CAKES

Preparation time: 15 minutes
Total cooking time: 20 minutes
Makes 12

120 g (4 oz) unsalted butter, softened
2/3 cup (160 g/5 1/2 oz) caster sugar
1 1/2 cups (185 g/6 oz) self-raising flour
1/2 cup (125 ml/4 fl oz) orange juice
2 teaspoons vanilla essence
2 eggs
3 tablespoons grated orange rind
shredded orange rind, to decorate, optional

Icing

60 g (2 oz) unsalted butter, softened
3/4 cup (90 g/3 oz) icing sugar
1 tablespoon orange juice

1 Preheat the oven to moderate 180°C (350°F/Gas 4). Line a deep 12-hole shallow patty tin with paper cases. Place the butter, sugar, flour, juice, vanilla and eggs in a bowl and beat with electric beaters on low speed for 2 minutes, or until well mixed. Increase the speed and beat for 2 minutes, or until smooth and pale. Stir in the orange rind. Divide among the cases and bake for 20 minutes, or until golden. Transfer to a wire rack to cool.
2 For the icing, beat the butter in a bowl with electric beaters until pale. Beat in half the icing sugar, the juice, then the remaining icing sugar. Spread over the cakes, then decorate if you like.

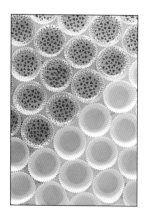

BUTTER

Butter is made by churning cream until it solidifies. Unsalted butter is also known as sweet butter and is used in baking and desserts as it has a good flavour. Cultured butter, also called Danish butter, when available, can be used for sweet baking. It has a bacteria added to give extra flavour and interest. Prior to refrigeration, salt was added to butter to help preserve it, but today salt is added to please the palate. Butter should always be covered, or well wrapped, and stored in the refrigerator because it very readily takes on other flavours. It freezes well.

OPPOSITE PAGE, FROM TOP: Rock cakes; Butterfly cakes; Orange cup cakes

CHELSEA BUNS

Spread the creamed butter and sugar all over the dough, leaving a small border on one long edge.

Arrange the slices close together with the seams facing inward.

CHELSEA BUNS

Preparation time: 30 minutes
  + 1 hour 40 minutes rising
Total cooking time: 25 minutes
Makes 24

★★

7 g (¹/4 oz) sachet dried yeast
1 teaspoon sugar
2¹/2 cups (310 g/10 oz) plain flour, sifted
¹/2 cup (125 ml/4 fl oz) milk, warmed
185 g (6 oz) unsalted butter, cubed
1 tablespoon sugar, extra
2 teaspoons grated lemon rind
1 teaspoon mixed spice
1 egg, lightly beaten
¹/4 cup (45 g/1¹/2 oz) soft brown sugar
1 cup (185 g/6 oz) mixed dried fruit
1 tablespoon milk, extra, for glazing
2 tablespoons sugar, extra, for glazing

Glacé icing

¹/2 cup (60 g/2 oz) icing sugar
1–2 tablespoons milk

ABOVE: Chelsea buns

1 Combine the yeast, sugar and 1 tablespoon of the flour in a small bowl. Add the milk and mix until smooth. Set aside in a warm place for 10 minutes, or until frothy. Place the remaining flour in a large bowl and rub in 125 g (4 oz) of the butter with your fingertips. Stir in the extra sugar, rind and half the mixed spice. Make a well, add the yeast mixture and egg and mix. Gather together and turn out onto a lightly floured surface.

2 Knead for 2 minutes, or until smooth, then shape into a ball. Place in a large, lightly oiled bowl, cover with plastic wrap and set aside in a warm place for 1 hour, or until well risen. Punch down and knead for 2 minutes, or until smooth.

3 Preheat the oven to hot 210°C (415°F/ Gas 6– 7). Lightly grease a baking tray. Beat the remaining butter with the brown sugar in a small bowl with electric beaters until light and creamy. Roll the dough out to a 40 x 25 cm (16 x 10 inch) rectangle. Spread the butter and sugar all over the dough to within 2 cm (³/4 inch) of the edge of one of the longer sides. Spread with the combined fruit and remaining spice. Roll the dough from the long side, firmly and evenly, to enclose the fruit. Use a sharp knife to cut the roll into eight slices about 5 cm (2 inch) wide. Arrange the slices, close together and with

the seams inwards, on the tray. Flatten slightly. Set aside, covered with plastic wrap, in a warm place for 30 minutes, or until well risen. Bake for 20 minutes, or until brown and cooked. When almost ready, stir the milk and sugar for glazing in a small saucepan over low heat until the sugar dissolves and the mixture is almost boiling. Brush over the hot buns. Cool.

4 Mix the icing sugar and milk, stir until smooth, then drizzle over the buns.

MADELEINES

Preparation time: 20 minutes
Total cooking time: 15 minutes
Makes 12

1 cup (125 g/4 oz) plain flour
2 eggs
³/4 cup (185 g/6 oz) caster sugar
185 g (6 oz) unsalted butter, melted and cooled
1 teaspoon finely grated orange rind
2 tablespoons icing sugar, to dust

1 Preheat the oven to moderate 180°C (350°F/ Gas 4). Lightly grease twelve madeleine holes in a madeleine tin (see Note). Lightly dust the madeleine tin with flour and shake off any excess.

2 Sift the flour three times onto baking paper. This process helps lighten the texture of the madeleines. Combine the eggs and sugar in a heatproof bowl. Place the bowl over a saucepan of simmering water and beat the mixture with a whisk or electric beaters until thick and pale yellow. Remove the bowl from the heat and continue to beat the mixture until cooled slightly and increased in volume.

3 Add the sifted flour, butter and orange rind to the bowl and fold in quickly and lightly with a metal spoon until just combined. Spoon the mixture carefully into the madeleine holes.

4 Bake for 10– 12 minutes, or until lightly golden. Carefully remove from the tin and place on a wire rack until cold. Dust with icing sugar before serving. Madeleines are best eaten on the day of baking.

NOTE: Madeleine tins (see page 21) are available from kitchenware speciality shops. However, if you prefer, you can cook the mixture in shallow patty tins instead.

MADELEINES

Place the bowl over a saucepan of simmering water and beat the mixture until thick and pale yellow.

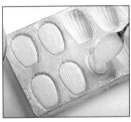

Carefully spoon the mixture into the lightly greased and floured madeleine holes.

LEFT: Madeleines

ECCLES CAKES

Preparation time: 20 minutes
Total cooking time: 20 minutes
Makes 27

1 cup (150 g/5 oz) currants
1/2 cup (95 g/3 oz) mixed peel
1 tablespoon brandy
1 tablespoon sugar
1/2 teaspoon ground cinnamon
500 g (1 lb) home-made or bought puff pastry
  (see page 150)
1 egg white
2 teaspoons sugar, extra

1 Preheat the oven to hot 210°C (415°F/ Gas 6– 7). Lightly grease two baking trays. Combine the currants, peel, brandy, sugar and cinnamon in a bowl.
2 Divide the pastry into three and roll each piece out to a thickness of 3 mm (1/8 inch). Using an 8 cm (3 inch) scone cutter, cut nine circles from each sheet of pastry. (Any remaining pastry can be frozen.) Place 2 level teaspoons of filling on each circle. Bring the edges of the rounds up together and pinch to seal. Turn seam-side-down and roll out to 1 cm (1/2 inch) thick ovals.
3 Place on the trays. Brush the tops with egg white and sprinkle with extra sugar. Make three slashes across the top of each cake. Bake for 15– 20 minutes, or until golden. Serve warm.

LAMINGTONS

Preparation time: 50 minutes
Total cooking time: 1 hour
Makes 16

⋆ ⋆

1 1/2 cups (185 g/6 oz) self-raising flour
1/3 cup (40 g/1 1/4 oz) cornflour
185 g (6 oz) unsalted butter, softened
1 cup (250 g/8 oz) caster sugar
2 teaspoons vanilla essence
3 eggs, lightly beaten
1/2 cup (125 ml/4 fl oz) milk
3/4 cup (185 ml/6 fl oz) thick (double) cream

ECCLES CAKES

These spicy currant pastries originated in the British town of Eccles in Lancashire. They were traditionally made during the *Eccles Wakes* festival and today are still a favourite. The puff pastry round is rolled thinly so that the enclosed filling will show through when the pastry is cooked. They can be made with shortcrust pastry but whichever pastry is used they are always sprinkled with sugar before baking and are best eaten warm straight from the oven.

RIGHT: Eccles cakes

Using a serrated knife, carefully cut the filled cake into 16 squares.

Use two forks to lower each piece of cake into the icing and roll it around to cover all sides.

Roll the iced cake in coconut to thoroughly cover it, then place on a wire rack.

Icing

4 cups (500 g/1 lb) icing sugar

1/3 cup (40 g/1 1/4 oz) cocoa powder

30 g (1 oz) unsalted butter, melted

2/3 cup (170 ml/5 1/2 fl oz) milk

3 cups (270 g/9 oz) desiccated coconut

1 Preheat the oven to moderate 180°C (350°F/ Gas 4). Lightly grease a shallow 23 cm (9 inch) square cake tin and line the base and sides with baking paper.

2 Sift the flour and cornflour into a large bowl. Add the butter, sugar, vanilla essence, eggs and milk. Using electric beaters, beat on low speed for 1 minute, or until the ingredients are just moistened. Increase the speed to high and beat for 3 minutes, or until free of lumps and increased in volume. Pour into the tin and smooth the surface. Bake for 50–55 minutes, or until a skewer comes out clean when inserted in the centre. Leave in the tin for 3 minutes before turning out onto a wire rack to cool.

3 Using a serrated knife, trim the top of the cake until flat. Trim the crusts from the sides, then cut the cake in half horizontally. Using electric beaters, beat the cream in a small bowl until stiff peaks form. Place the first layer of cake on a board and spread it evenly with cream. Place the remaining cake layer on top. Cut the cake into 16 squares.

4 For the icing, sift the icing sugar and cocoa into a heatproof bowl and add the butter and milk. Stand the bowl over a saucepan of simmering water, stirring, until the icing is smooth and glossy, then remove from the heat. Place 1 cup (90 g/3 oz) of the coconut on a sheet of baking paper. Using two forks, roll a piece of cake in chocolate icing, then hold the cake over a bowl and allow the excess to drain. (Add 1 tablespoon boiling water to the icing if it seems too thick.) Roll the cake in coconut, then place on a wire rack. Repeat with the remaining cake, adding extra coconut for rolling as needed.

NOTE: If you cook the cake a day ahead, it will be easier to cut and won't crumble as much. Lamingtons are not necessarily cream filled, so if you prefer, you can ice unfilled squares of cake.

ABOVE: Lamingtons

CAKES

Have you ever stopped to consider how much importance we place on cakes? They seem to pop up in almost every aspect of our lives. For example, we promote a diet rich in fruit and vegetables with banana cake and orange poppy seed cake, not to mention myriad dried fruit cakes and carrot cake. Our career opportunities are represented by the lumberjack cake. Hummingbird and mud cakes suggest an avid interest in nature, while the sponge cake clearly displays a healthy attitude towards cleanliness. Madeira cake, tipsy cakes and upside-down cakes? Well, perhaps they show a fondness for 'relaxation'.

PREPARING TINS

Preparation of cake tins varies according to the type of cake you are baking. Below

we outline which cakes require tins to be greased and lined and how it is done.

GREASING TINS Apply melted, unsalted butter or oil evenly and not too thickly, using a pastry brush. Vegetable sprays can be used—apply in a well-ventilated area away from any heat source.

LINING TINS Greaseproof paper and non-stick baking paper are both excellent for lining cake tins. If you use greaseproof, it will need to be greased, but non-stick baking paper does not need greasing.

DUSTING WITH FLOUR Let the greased tin or paper dry off a little before dusting with plain flour. Turn the tin to evenly coat the base and sides. Shake off any excess before spooning in the mixture.

LINING ROUND TINS Place the tin base on a square of baking paper, draw around it and cut out as marked. Cut a strip of baking paper the same length as the circumference of the tin and about

3 cm (1¼ inches) deeper than the height. Fold down a cuff about 2 cm (¾ inch) deep on one edge of the strip. Cut the folded cuff diagonally at 2 cm (¾ inch) intervals. Grease the tin. Place the baking paper strip in the tin with the folded side on the base. The cut strip will act like pleats and sit on the base. Press the baking paper into the base and side. Place the round of baking paper on the base over the pleats.

LINING SQUARE TINS Place the tin base on a square of baking paper, draw around the base, then cut out as marked. Cut a strip of baking paper the same length as the outside of the tin and about 1 cm (½ inch) deeper than the height.

Grease the base and sides of the tin. Place the square of baking paper in the base and the strip around the inside of the tin, pressing into the sides.

LINING SWISS ROLL TINS Place the tin base on a square of baking paper and draw around it. Measure the depth of the tin, add 2 cm (¾ inch), then measure that distance from the drawn line and cut at that distance all around. Crease the paper along the drawn lines, then cut a diagonal line from each outside corner to the nearest drawn corner. Lightly grease the tin. Press the paper down into the base and sides of the tin.

BUTTER CAKES AND CHOCOLATE CAKES For these cakes, you need to line both the base and sides of the tin. Many bakers only line the base of the tin for butter cakes and this will work in most cases. However, if you have the time, it is safer to line the sides as well to be sure the cake doesn't stick to the tin. Baba tins and kugelhopf tins need to be greased and lightly floured.

SPONGE CAKES For easy removal of the cooked sponge cake, the tins must be greased and the bases lined, then the whole tin dusted with flour.

RICH FRUIT CAKES These cakes need to be cooked in tins which have the base and sides lined with a double thickness of paper but it is generally not necessary to grease the paper. Lining fruit cake tins is fully explained on pages 84–85.

TO COLLAR A CAKE TIN Lightly grease a cake tin, then cut a strip of baking paper long enough to fit around the outside of the tin and tall enough to extend 5 cm (2 inches) above the top. Fold down one cuff, about 2 cm (¾ inch) deep, along the length of the strip. Make diagonal cuts up to the fold line about 1 cm (½ inch) apart. Fit the collar around the inside edge of the tin, with the cuts in the base, pressing the cuts out at right angles so they sit flat around the base. Cut a piece of paper to fit in the base, using the tin as a guide, and place in the tin over the cuts in the collar.

A collar extends the height of a cake and gives extra protection during cooking. As a general rule, a single layer of baking paper is enough for a collar on an average-sized cake. Larger cakes and fruit cakes need two layers of paper for the collar and base.

BUTTER CAKES

If you follow our helpful hints you will have no trouble making a beautiful butter

cake which can be stored for a couple of days, wrapped tightly in plastic wrap.

EQUIPMENT

It is crucial to use the correct-sized tin. For this basic butter cake you will need a 20 cm (8 inch) round tin. Lightly grease the base and side with melted unsalted butter or oil. Use a pastry brush to apply an even, not too thick, layer. Line the tin (see pages 48– 49) with baking paper or greaseproof and brush the paper evenly with melted unsalted butter or oil.

It is also essential to have a set of standard measuring cups and spoons and an accurate set of kitchen scales. As well, you need a small and large bowl, a metal spoon, a large sieve, a rubber spatula and an electric mixer. If the quantities are not too great, adequate results can be obtained using a hand-held electric beater or mixing by hand, but the mixing time increases considerably.

The butter, eggs and liquid should be at room temperature. The butter should be malleable, not melted or very soft.

OVEN

An accurate oven temperature is vital for successful cake making so it is a good idea to invest in an oven thermometer. The recipes in this book have all been tested in a conventional (not fan-forced) oven.

BUTTER CAKE

To make one cake, you will need
1½ cups (185 g/6 oz) self-raising flour,
½ cup (60 g/2 oz) plain flour, 185 g
(6 oz) chopped unsalted butter, softened,
¾ cup (185 g/6 oz) caster sugar, 3 lightly
beaten eggs, 1 teaspoon vanilla essence
and ¼ cup (60 ml/2 fl oz) milk. When
you have assembled all the ingredients
and the utensils you need, preheat your
oven to moderate 180°C (375°F/Gas 4).

This cake is made using the creaming
method, the most frequently used
technique in cake-making. The first step
is to sift the flours to aerate and separate
the particles. Cream the butter and sugar
in a small bowl by beating at moderate
speed until light and fluffy. The mixture
will almost double in volume and should
have no trace of the sugar granules.
Scrape the side of the bowl with a spatula
several times during the creaming process
to make sure the butter and sugar are
well incorporated. This initial creaming
process can take up to 8 minutes.

With the beaters still running,
gradually add the egg, a little at a time,
beating thoroughly after each addition.
Add the vanilla essence and beat well
to combine.

Transfer the mixture to a large bowl.
Using a large metal spoon, gently fold in
the sifted flour and the milk. Stir until
just combined and almost smooth. Take
care with this final stage, mixing the
ingredients lightly and evenly. Over-
enthusiastic beating can undo all your
previous good work and produce a
heavy, coarse-textured cake.

Next, gently spoon or pour the
mixture into the tin, spread out evenly
and smooth the surface. Check the oven
temperature. For best results when
baking a cake, position an oven rack in
the lower third of the oven so the top
of the cake is in the middle of the oven.
Centre the cake tin on the oven rack and
bake for 45 minutes. The cake is cooked
when it begins to shrink from the side
of the tin and is lightly golden. If gently
pressed with a finger, it should spring
back into shape. As a final check, insert a
fine skewer in the centre—it should come
out clean, without any moisture. Avoid
opening the oven door until at least two-
thirds of the way through baking.

A cake is quite fragile when removed
from the oven, so leave it in the tin for
10 minutes before turning out onto
a wire rack to cool. If the cake is stuck
to the tin, gently run a flat-bladed knife
around the side to release it. Remove
the paper lining immediately.

WHAT WENT WRONG?

BUTTER CAKES

PERFECT   TOP VIEW

PERFECT   SIDE VIEW

PERFECT

The texture is light, moist and even, with a golden brown crust. When a skewer is inserted into the centre of the cake, it comes out clean. The cake springs back when pressed lightly with a fingertip.

OVERCOOKED   TOP VIEW

OVERCOOKED   SIDE VIEW

OVERCOOKED

The top of the cake is very dark and the texture of the cake crumb quite dry. The cooking time may have been too long or the cooking temperature too high. It's also possible that the tin was the wrong size or that the cake was placed too high in the oven.

UNDERCOOKED AND SUNKEN   TOP VIEW

UNDERCOOKED AND SUNKEN   SIDE VIEW

UNDERCOOKED AND SUNKEN

The centre of the cake is sunken and when a skewer is inserted into the centre, it comes out sticky. The cake has a soggy, dense texture. The cooking time may have been too short or the oven temperature too low. Too little flour or too much butter may have been used in the recipe. The oven door may have been opened during the early stages of cooking.

UNDERMIXED   TOP VIEW

UNDERMIXED   SIDE VIEW

UNDERMIXED

The top crust of the cake has a mottled effect and the texture of the cake is rough with visible pockets of flour and raising agents. The mixture has not been beaten enough or the flour has not been sifted. The mixture may not have been mixed to combine the ingredients properly.

FRUIT CAKES

PERFECT TOP VIEW

PERFECT SIDE VIEW

PERFECT
The crust is an even, deep golden brown. When a skewer is inserted into the centre of the cake, it comes out clean. The texture of the cake is moist and the fruit is evenly distributed.

OVERCOOKED TOP VIEW

OVERCOOKED SIDE VIEW

OVERCOOKED
The oven temperature may have been too high or the cooking time too long. The mixture might have had too little fat or too much raising agent. Too much sugar may cause a dark crust. If the cake is colouring too quickly and the oven temperature is correct, then the top can be protected by covering with foil or a double layer of baking paper.

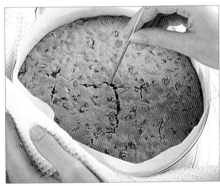

UNDERCOOKED AND SUNKEN TOP VIEW

UNDERCOOKED AND SUNKEN SIDE VIEW

UNDERCOOKED AND SUNKEN
The baking time may have been too short or the oven temperature too low. There might be too much fruit or too little raising agent. The cake may have been placed too low in the oven. The tin needs to be placed in the middle of the oven.

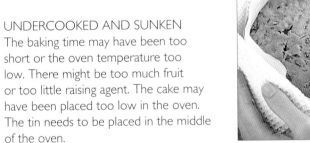

FRUIT SUNKEN TOP VIEW

FRUIT SUNKEN SIDE VIEW

FRUIT SUNKEN
When cut, a dense layer of fruit is visible at the base of the cake. This may be caused by the oven temperature being too low, or too little raising agent being used, or the batter not being mixed well enough. Careful mixing is very important to combine the many ingredients.

1 Preheat the oven to moderate 180°C (350°F/ Gas 4). Lightly grease a 20 cm (8 inch) square cake tin and line with baking paper.
2 Cream the butter and sugars in a small bowl with electric beaters until light and fluffy. Add the eggs gradually, beating thoroughly after each addition. Beat in the vanilla and jam. Transfer to a large bowl. Using a metal spoon, gently fold in the combined sifted flour, cocoa and soda alternately with the milk. Stir until the mixture is just combined and almost smooth.
3 Pour into the tin and smooth the surface. Bake for 45 minutes, or until a skewer comes out clean. Leave in the tin for 15 minutes before turning onto a wire rack to cool completely.
4 For the buttercream, stir the ingredients in a small pan over low heat until smooth and glossy. Spread over the top with a flat-bladed knife.

CINNAMON TEACAKE

Preparation time: 20 minutes
Total cooking time: 30 minutes
Makes 1

60 g (2 oz) unsalted butter, softened
1/2 cup (125 g/4 oz) caster sugar
1 egg, lightly beaten
1 teaspoon vanilla essence
3/4 cup (90 g/3 oz) self-raising flour
1/4 cup (30 g/1 oz) plain flour
1/2 cup (125 ml/4 fl oz) milk

Topping

20 g (3/4 oz) unsalted butter, melted
1 tablespoon caster sugar
1 teaspoon ground cinnamon

1 Preheat the oven to moderate 180°C (350°F/ Gas 4). Grease a 20 cm (8 inch) round shallow cake tin and line the base with baking paper.
2 Cream the butter and sugar in a small bowl with electric beaters until light and fluffy. Gradually add the egg, beating well after each addition. Beat in the vanilla, then transfer to a large bowl. Using a metal spoon, fold in the sifted flours alternately with the milk. Stir until smooth. Spoon into the tin and bake for 30 minutes, or until a skewer comes out clean. Leave in the tin for 5 minutes before turning out onto a wire rack. Brush the warm cake with butter and sprinkle with sugar and cinnamon.

CHOCOLATE CAKE

Preparation time: 25 minutes
Total cooking time: 50 minutes
Makes 1

125 g (4 oz) unsalted butter, softened
1/2 cup (125 g/4 oz) caster sugar
1/3 cup (40 g/1 1/4 oz) icing sugar, sifted
2 eggs, lightly beaten
1 teaspoon vanilla essence
1/4 cup (80 g/2 3/4 oz) blackberry jam
1 1/4 cups (155 g/5 oz) self-raising flour
1/2 cup (60 g/2 oz) cocoa powder
1 teaspoon bicarbonate of soda
1 cup (250 ml/8 fl oz) milk

Chocolate buttercream

50 g (1 3/4 oz) dark chocolate, finely chopped
25 g (3/4 oz) unsalted butter
3 teaspoons cream
1/4 cup (30 g/1 oz) icing sugar, sifted

ABOVE: Chocolate cake

GINGER CAKE

Preparation time: 30 minutes
Total cooking time: 1 hour
Makes 1

125 g (4 oz) unsalted butter

1/2 cup (175 g/6 oz) black treacle

1/2 cup (175 g/6 oz) golden syrup

1 1/2 cups (185 g/6 oz) plain flour

1 cup (125 g/4 oz) self-raising flour

1 teaspoon bicarbonate of soda

3 teaspoons ground ginger

1 teaspoon mixed spice

1/4 teaspoon ground cinnamon

3/4 cup (165 g/5 1/2 oz) firmly packed
    soft brown sugar

1 cup (250 ml/8 fl oz) milk

2 eggs, lightly beaten

glacé ginger, optional, to decorate

Lemon and ginger icing

2 cups (250 g/8 oz) icing sugar

1 teaspoon ground ginger

30 g (1 oz) unsalted butter, melted

3 teaspoons milk

3 teaspoons lemon juice

1 teaspoon lemon rind

1 Preheat the oven to moderate 180°C (350°F/ Gas 4). Lightly grease a deep 20 cm (8 inch) square cake tin and line the base with baking paper.

2 Combine the butter, treacle and golden syrup in a saucepan and stir over low heat until the butter has melted. Remove from the heat.

3 Sift the flours, bicarbonate of soda and spices into a large bowl, add the sugar and stir until well combined. Make a well in the centre. Add the butter mixture to the well, then pour in the combined milk and eggs. Stir with a wooden spoon until the mixture is smooth and well combined. Pour into the tin and smooth the surface. Bake for 45– 60 minutes, or until a skewer comes out clean when inserted in the centre of the cake. Leave in the tin for 20 minutes before turning out onto a wire rack to cool.

4 For the lemon and ginger icing, sift the icing sugar into a small heatproof bowl and stir in the ground ginger, butter, milk, lemon juice and rind until the mixture forms a smooth paste.

Stand the bowl over a saucepan of simmering water, making sure the base of the bowl does not touch the water. Stir until smooth and glossy, then remove from the heat. Spread over the cake with a flat-bladed knife. Decorate the top with glacé ginger, if desired.

NOTES: If black treacle is unavailable, you can substitute the same amount of golden syrup.

This delicious ginger cake can be served the day it is baked but it is best served two or three days after baking so the flavours have time to develop. It will store well for up to a week in an airtight container, or can be frozen, un-iced, for up to three months. It can also be served un-iced and decorated by lightly dusting the top with sifted icing sugar.

BELOW: Ginger cake

CARROT CAKE

Preparation time: 40 minutes
Total cooking time: 1 hour 30 minutes
Makes 1

1 cup (125 g/4 oz) self-raising flour
1 cup (125 g/4 oz) plain flour
2 teaspoons ground cinnamon
1 teaspoon ground ginger
1/2 teaspoon ground nutmeg
1 teaspoon bicarbonate of soda
1 cup (250 ml/8 fl oz) oil
1 cup (185 g/6 oz) soft brown sugar
4 eggs
1/2 cup (175 g/6 oz) golden syrup
2 1/2 cups (400 g/13 oz) grated carrot
1/2 cup (60 g/2 oz) chopped pecans or walnuts

Lemon icing

175 g (6 oz) cream cheese, softened
60 g (2 oz) butter, softened
1 1/2 cups (185 g/6 oz) icing sugar
1 teaspoon vanilla essence
1–2 teaspoons lemon juice

1 Preheat the oven to warm 160°C (315°F/Gas 2–3). Lightly grease a 23 cm (9 inch) round cake tin and line the base and side with baking paper.
2 Sift the flours, spices and soda into a large bowl and make a well in the centre.
3 Whisk together the oil, sugar, eggs and golden syrup in a jug until combined. Add this mixture to the well in the flour and gradually stir into the dry ingredients with a metal spoon until smooth. Stir in the carrot and nuts, then spoon into the tin and smooth the surface. Bake for 1 hour 30 minutes, or until a skewer comes out clean when inserted into the centre of the cake.
4 Leave the cake in the tin for at least 15 minutes before turning out onto a wire rack to cool completely.
5 For the lemon icing, beat the cream cheese and butter with electric beaters until smooth. Gradually add the icing sugar alternately with the vanilla and lemon juice, beating until light and creamy. Spread the icing over the cooled cake using a flat-bladed knife. Can be sprinkled with freshly grated nutmeg.
NOTE: If you prefer, you can cut the cake in half horizontally, then sandwich the layers together with half the icing.

ORANGE CAKE

Preparation time: 15 minutes
Total cooking time: 50 minutes
Makes 1

2 cups (250 g/8 oz) self-raising flour
1/3 cup (40 g/1 1/4 oz) custard powder
1 1/3 cups (340 g/11 oz) caster sugar
80 g (2 3/4 oz) unsalted butter, chopped and softened
3 eggs
2 teaspoons finely grated orange rind
1 cup (250 ml/8 fl oz) orange juice

Orange buttercream

3/4 cup (90 g/3 oz) icing sugar
125 g (4 oz) unsalted butter, softened
1 tablespoon orange juice
1 teaspoon finely grated orange rind

1 Preheat the oven to moderate 180°C (350°F/Gas 4). Lightly grease the base and side of a 23 cm (9 inch) round cake tin and line the base with baking paper.
2 Sift the flour and custard powder into a large bowl and add the sugar, butter, egg, orange rind and juice. Beat with electric beaters for 4 minutes, or until the mixture is smooth.
3 Spoon the mixture into the tin and smooth the surface. Bake for 50 minutes, or until a skewer comes out clean when inserted into the centre of the cake.
4 Leave the cake in the tin for 5 minutes before turning out onto a wire rack to cool completely.
5 For the orange buttercream, beat all the ingredients in a small bowl with electric beaters until smooth and creamy. Spread evenly over the cooled cake.
NOTE: You can also make a cream cheese topping for this cake. Mix 125 g (4 oz) of softened cream cheese with 2 tablespoons icing sugar until well blended and spread over the top of the cake.

CITRUS RIND
The rind from any citrus fruit, including oranges, lemons and limes, is also known as the zest. It contains essential oils that impart an intense flavour. The rind is removed with a fine grater or zester. Remove the coloured area only as the white pith just under the rind has a bitter flavour. You can also extract the citrus oils by rubbing a sugar cube firmly over the fruit until the sugar cube becomes moist and coloured with the oils.

OPPOSITE PAGE: Carrot cake (top); Orange cake

BANANA CAKE

Preparation time: 20 minutes
Total cooking time: 1 hour
Makes 1

125 g (4 oz) unsalted butter, softened
1/2 cup (125 g/4 oz) caster sugar
2 eggs, lightly beaten
1 teaspoon vanilla essence
4 ripe medium bananas, mashed
1 teaspoon bicarbonate of soda
1/2 cup (125 ml/4 fl oz) milk
2 cups (250 g/8 oz) self-raising flour, sifted
1/2 teaspoon ground mixed spice

Butter frosting

125 g (4 oz) unsalted butter, softened
3/4 cup (90 g/3 oz) icing sugar
1 tablespoon lemon juice
1/4 cup (15 g/1/2 oz) flaked coconut, toasted

1 Preheat the oven to moderate 180°C (350°F/ Gas 4). Lightly grease a 20 cm (8 inch) round cake tin and line the base with baking paper.
2 Cream the butter and sugar in a small bowl with electric beaters until light and fluffy. Add the egg gradually, beating thoroughly after each addition. Add the vanilla and banana and beat until combined. Transfer to a large bowl.
3 Dissolve the soda in the milk. Using a metal spoon, gently fold the sifted flour and mixed spice alternately with the milk into the banana mixture. Stir until all the ingredients are just combined and the mixture is smooth. Spoon into the prepared tin and smooth the surface. Bake for 1 hour, or until a skewer comes out clean when inserted into the centre of the cake.
4 Leave the cake in the tin for 10 minutes before turning out onto a wire rack to cool completely.
5 For the frosting, beat the butter, icing sugar and lemon juice with electric beaters until smooth and creamy. Spread over the cooled cake using a flat-bladed knife and sprinkle with toasted coconut flakes.
NOTE: Very ripe bananas are best for this recipe as they have the most developed flavour.

BANANAS

Native to Southeast Asia, bananas are now grown in many other places that have a warm climate. There are many varieties but the most common are Cavendish and Lady Finger. Bananas can be purchased green and will slowly ripen. If you need to hurry up the ripening process, place the green bananas in a brown paper bag with a ripe banana or apple. For baking purposes a very ripe, or even an over-ripe banana, is very useful. An over-ripe banana adds an intense banana flavour to baked cakes, muffins and ice cream.

RIGHT: Banana cake

MADEIRA CAKE

Preparation time: 20 minutes
Total cooking time: 50 minutes
Makes 1

185 g (6 oz) unsalted butter, softened

3/4 cup (185 g/6 oz) caster sugar

3 eggs, lightly beaten

2 teaspoons finely grated orange
    or lemon rind

1¼ cups (155 g/5 oz) self-raising flour,
    sifted

1 cup (125 g/4 oz) plain flour

2 tablespoons milk

1 Preheat the oven to warm 160°C (315°F/ Gas 2–3). Lightly grease a loaf tin with a base measuring 20 x 10 x 7 cm (8 x 4 x 2¾ inches) and line the base and sides with baking paper.

2 Cream the butter and sugar in a small bowl with electric beaters until light and fluffy. Add the egg gradually, beating thoroughly after each addition. Add the rind and beat until combined. Transfer to a large bowl. Using a metal spoon, fold in the flour and milk. Stir until smooth.

3 Spoon into the loaf tin and smooth the surface. Bake for 50 minutes, or until a skewer comes out clean when inserted in the centre of the cake. Cool the cake in the tin for 10 minutes before turning out onto a wire rack to cool completely.

NOTE: This cake keeps well in an airtight container for up to a week.

MADEIRA CAKE

This rich butter cake was popular in Victorian England. It was often served with a glass of Madeira, hence the name. It is a moist tender cake due to the high butter content. Often, citrus rind is added, or a slice of candied citrus peel is placed on top as a decoration, but usually it is kept fairly plain so as not to mask the delicious buttery flavour.

ABOVE: Madeira cake

CHOCOLATE MUD CAKE

Preparation time: 30 minutes
Total cooking time: 2 hours
Makes 1

☆

250 g (8 oz) unsalted butter
250 g (8 oz) dark chocolate, chopped
2 tablespoons instant coffee powder
150 g (5 oz) self-raising flour
150 g (5 oz) plain flour
1/2 cup (60 g/2 oz) cocoa powder
1/2 teaspoon bicarbonate of soda
2 1/4 cups (550 g/1 lb 2 oz) caster sugar
4 eggs, lightly beaten
2 tablespoons oil
1/2 cup (125 ml/4 fl oz) buttermilk

Icing

150 g (5 oz) unsalted butter, chopped
150 g (5 oz) dark chocolate, chopped

ABOVE: Chocolate mud cake

1 Preheat the oven to warm 160°C (315°F/ Gas 2–3). Lightly grease a deep 22 cm (9 inch) round cake tin and line with baking paper, making sure the paper around the side extends at least 5 cm (2 inches) above the top edge.
2 Put the butter, chocolate and coffee in a pan with 3/4 cup (185 ml/6 oz) hot water and stir over low heat until smooth. Remove from the heat.
3 Sift the flours, cocoa and bicarbonate of soda into a large bowl. Stir in the sugar and make a well in the centre. Add the combined eggs, oil and buttermilk and, using a large metal spoon, slowly stir into the dry ingredients. Gradually stir in the butter mixture.
4 Pour the mixture (it will be quite wet) into the tin and bake for 1 3/4 hours. Test the centre with a skewer—the skewer may be slightly wet. Remove the cake from the oven. If the top looks raw, bake for another 5–10 minutes, then remove. Leave in the tin until completely cold, then turn out and wrap in plastic wrap.
5 For the icing, combine the butter and chocolate in a saucepan and stir over low heat until the butter and chocolate are melted. Remove and cool slightly. Pour over the cake and allow it to run down the side.
NOTE: Refrigerate in an airtight container for up to three weeks or in a cool dry place for up to a week. Freeze for up to two months. For a 20 cm (8 inch) round cake, bake for 2 hours.

APPLE AND SPICE TEACAKE

Preparation time: 30 minutes
Total cooking time: 1 hour
Makes 1

180 g (6 oz) unsalted butter, softened
1/2 cup (95 g/3 oz) soft brown sugar
2 teaspoons finely grated lemon rind
3 eggs, lightly beaten
1 cup (125 g/4 oz) self-raising flour
1/2 cup (75 g/2 1/2 oz) wholemeal flour
1/2 teaspoon ground cinnamon
1/2 cup (125 ml/4 fl oz) milk
410 g (13 oz) can pie apple
1/4 teaspoon ground mixed spice
1 tablespoon soft brown sugar, extra
1/4 cup (25 g/3/4 oz) flaked almonds

1 Preheat the oven to moderate 180°C (350°F/Gas 4). Grease the base and side of a 20 cm (8 inch) springform pan, and line the base with baking paper.
2 Cream the butter and sugar in a small bowl with electric beaters until light and fluffy. Beat in the lemon rind. Add the eggs gradually, beating thoroughly after each addition.
3 Transfer the mixture to a large bowl. Using a metal spoon, fold in the sifted flours and cinnamon alternately with the milk. Stir until the mixture is just combined and almost smooth.
4 Spoon half the mixture into the tin, top with three-quarters of the pie apple, then the remaining cake mixture. Press the remaining pie apple around the edge of the top. Combine the mixed spice, extra sugar and flaked almonds and sprinkle over the cake.
5 Bake for 1 hour, or until a skewer comes out clean when inserted into the centre of the cake. Leave in the tin for 15 minutes before turning out onto a wire rack to cool.
NOTE: Pie apricots can be used instead of apples, if preferred.

APPLE AND SPICE TEACAKE

Cream the butter and sugar, then add the grated lemon rind.

Spoon apple onto half the batter and then top with the remaining batter.

The cake is cooked when a skewer inserted into the centre comes out clean.

LEFT: Apple and spice teacake

POUND CAKE

This fine-textured, buttery cake, dating back to the eighteenth century, is made in a loaf tin and was originally based on pound (pre-metric) measures of one pound each of butter, sugar, eggs and flour. The butter and sugar are well creamed before beating in the eggs and folding in the flour. Vanilla or grated citrus rind are added for extra flavour. Ground almonds and dried fruit such as sultanas are sometimes added but this is not traditional.

OPPOSITE PAGE: Lemon cake with crunchy topping (left); Pound cake

LEMON CAKE WITH CRUNCHY TOPPING

Preparation time: 25 minutes
Total cooking time: 1 hour 20 minutes
Makes 1

250 g (8 oz) unsalted butter, softened
200 g (6½ oz) caster sugar
2 teaspoons finely grated lemon rind
4 eggs, lightly beaten
2 cups (250 g/8 oz) self-raising flour
1 teaspoon baking powder
2 tablespoons lemon juice

Topping

½ cup (125 g/4 oz) sugar
¼ cup (60 ml/2¾ fl oz) lemon juice

1 Preheat the oven to warm 170°C (325°F/ Gas 3). Lightly grease a 22 cm (9 inch) square tin and line the base with baking paper.
2 Cream the butter and sugar in a small bowl with electric beaters until the mixture is light and fluffy. Beat in the lemon rind, then add the egg gradually, beating thoroughly after each addition. Transfer the mixture to a large bowl. Using a large metal spoon, fold in the combined sifted flour, baking powder and ¼ teaspoon salt, as well as the lemon juice. Stir until the mixture is just combined and almost smooth.
3 Spoon the mixture into the tin and smooth the surface. Bake for 1 hour 20 minutes, or until a skewer comes out clean when inserted into the centre of the cake. Remove from the tin and turn out onto a wire rack.
4 For the topping, mix together the sugar and lemon juice (do not dissolve the sugar), and quickly brush over the top of the warm cake. The juice will sink into the cake, and the sugar will form a crunchy topping. Leave to cool.

POUND CAKE

Preparation time: 25 minutes
Total cooking time: 1 hour
Makes 1

375 g (12 oz) unsalted butter, softened
1½ cups (375 g/12 oz) caster sugar
1 teaspoon vanilla essence
6 eggs, lightly beaten
3 cups (375 g/12 oz) plain flour, sifted
1 teaspoon baking powder
¼ cup (60 ml/4 fl oz) milk
icing sugar, to dust

1 Preheat the oven to moderate 180°C (350°F/ Gas 4). Lightly grease the base and side of a 22 cm (9 inch) round cake tin and line the base with baking paper.
2 Cream the butter and sugar in a small bowl with electric beaters until the mixture is light and fluffy. Beat in the vanilla essence, then add the eggs gradually, beating thoroughly after each addition. Transfer to a large bowl. Using a metal spoon, fold in the sifted flour and baking powder alternately with the milk. Do this in three or four lots. Stir until the mixture is just combined and almost smooth.
3 Spoon the mixture into the tin and smooth the surface. Bake for 1 hour, or until a skewer comes out clean when inserted into the centre of the cake. Leave in the tin for 10 minutes before turning out onto a wire rack to cool. Lightly dust the top with icing sugar just before serving.
NOTES: This cake can be used as a base to make many variations in flavour.
  To make orange pound cake, add 2 tablespoons finely grated orange rind to the butter and use ¼ cup (60 ml/2 fl oz) orange juice instead of the milk.
  To make coconut pound cake, add 1 cup (90 g/3 oz) desiccated coconut before folding in the flour and milk.
  To make hazelnut pound cake, add 125 g (4 oz) chopped toasted hazelnuts before folding in the flour. Dissolve 2 teaspoons instant coffee powder in the milk.

SOUR CREAM

Traditional sour cream is non-pasteurized cream skimmed from the top of the milk and left at room temperature until it has soured due to the natural bacteria present. Today however, the process is more controlled as the cream, by law, has to be pasteurized. A special culture is added and results in a slightly soured and thick cream. It has a tenderizing effect when used in baking, resulting in a soft-crumbed cake.

SOUR CREAM COFFEE CAKE

Preparation time: 25 minutes
Total cooking time: 40 minutes
Makes 1

125 g (4 oz) unsalted butter, softened

1 cup (250 g/8 oz) caster sugar

3 eggs, lightly beaten

1 teaspoon vanilla essence

1 tablespoon instant coffee powder

3/4 cup (90 g/3 oz) plain flour

1/2 cup (60 g/2 oz) self-raising flour

1/3 cup (90 g/3 oz) sour cream

Coffee icing

2 teaspoons coffee powder

1 cup (125 g/4 oz) icing sugar

20 g (3/4 oz) unsalted butter, melted

ABOVE: Sour cream coffee cake

1 Preheat the oven to warm 160°C (315°F/ Gas 2– 3). Lightly grease a shallow 28 x 18 cm (11 x 7 inch) cake tin and line with baking paper.
2 Cream the butter and sugar in a small bowl with electric beaters until light and fluffy. Add the egg gradually, beating thoroughly after each addition. Dissolve the vanilla and coffee powder in 1 tablespoon warm water and beat into the mixture until combined. Transfer to a large bowl. Using a metal spoon, fold in the sifted flours alternately with the sour cream. Stir until the mixture is just combined and almost smooth.
3 Spoon the mixture into the tin and smooth the surface. Bake for 30– 40 minutes, or until a skewer comes out clean when inserted into the centre of the cake. Leave the cake in the tin for 5 minutes before turning out onto a wire rack to cool completely.
4 For the icing, dissolve the coffee powder in 1– 2 tablespoons warm water in a small bowl. Add the icing sugar and butter, mix until well combined, then spread over the cooled cake.

COCONUT
This fruit of tropical coconut palms contains a milky drinkable liquid surrounded by soft white flesh or 'meat'. The latter is often used in baking, confectionery and sweet meats. It can be used freshly grated or dried as desiccated or shredded coconut. If dried, it can be lightly toasted and used to decorate cakes. Coconut milk and cream are liquid extracted from the flesh and can also be used in baking. The cream is the oily surface that forms on the milk when it has separated after chilling. The milk and cream are available in cans.

LEMON COCONUT CAKE

Preparation time: 20 minutes
Total cooking time: 40 minutes
Makes 1

1¹/2 cups (185 g/6 oz) self-raising flour
¹/2 cup (45 g/1¹/2 oz) desiccated coconut
1 tablespoon grated lemon rind
1 cup (250 g/8 oz) caster sugar
125 g (4 oz) unsalted butter, melted
2 eggs
1 cup (250 ml/8 fl oz) milk

Coconut icing

1¹/2 cups (185 g/6 oz) icing sugar, sifted
1 cup (90 g/3 oz) desiccated coconut
¹/2 teaspoon grated lemon rind
¹/4 cup (60 ml/2 fl oz) lemon juice

1 Preheat the oven to moderate 180°C (350°F/ Gas 4). Lightly grease a deep 20 cm (8 inch) round cake tin and line with baking paper.
2 Sift the flour into a large bowl and add the coconut, lemon rind, sugar, butter, eggs and milk. Mix well with a wooden spoon until smooth. Pour into the tin and smooth the surface. Bake for 40 minutes, or until a skewer comes out clean when inserted in the centre of the cake.
3 Leave the cake in the tin for 5 minutes before turning onto a wire rack to cool completely.
4 For the coconut icing, combine the icing sugar and coconut in a bowl, then add the lemon rind and enough lemon juice to make a stiff but spreadable icing. Spread the icing over the cold cake.

ABOVE: Lemon coconut cake

ORANGE POPPY SEED CAKE

Preparation time: 30 minutes
Total cooking time: I hour
Makes I

1 ½ cups (185 g/6 oz) self-raising flour

⅓ cup (60 g/2 oz) ground almonds

¼ cup (40 g/1 ¼ oz) poppy seeds

185 g (6 oz) unsalted butter

⅔ cup (160 g/5 ½ oz) caster sugar

¼ cup (80 g/2 ¾ oz) apricot jam or marmalade

2– 3 teaspoons finely grated orange rind

⅓ cup (80 ml/2 ¾ fl oz) orange juice

3 eggs, lightly beaten

orange rind, optional, to decorate

Cream cheese icing

100 g (3 ½ oz) unsalted butter, softened

100 g (3 ½ oz) cream cheese, softened

1 cup (125 g/4 oz) icing sugar, sifted

1 teaspoon lemon juice or vanilla essence

1 Preheat the oven to moderate 180°C (350°F/ Gas 4). Lightly grease a deep 20 cm (8 inch) round cake tin and line with baking paper. Sift the flour into a bowl and add the almonds and poppy seeds. Make a well in the centre.

2 Place the butter, sugar, jam, orange rind and juice in a pan. Stir over low heat until the butter has melted and the mixture is smooth. Gradually add the butter mixture to the dry ingredients, stirring with a whisk until smooth. Add the eggs and whisk until combined. Pour into the tin and bake for 50– 60 minutes, or until a skewer comes out clean when inserted into the centre of the cake. Leave in the tin for 15 minutes before turning onto a wire rack to cool.

3 For the cream cheese icing, beat the butter and cream cheese until smooth. Add the icing sugar and lemon juice or vanilla essence gradually and beat until thick and creamy. Spread the icing over the cooled cake. You can decorate with strips of orange rind.

ABOVE: Orange poppy seed cake

LUMBERJACK CAKE

Preparation time: 30 minutes
Total cooking time: 1 hour 15 minutes
Makes 1

200 g (6½ oz) fresh dates, pitted and chopped
1 teaspoon bicarbonate of soda
125 g (4 oz) unsalted butter, softened
1 cup (250 g/8 oz) caster sugar
1 egg
1 teaspoon vanilla essence
2 Granny Smith apples, peeled, cored, grated
1 cup (125 g/4 oz) plain flour
½ cup (60 g/2 oz) self-raising flour
icing sugar, optional, to dust

Topping

75 g (2½ oz) unsalted butter
½ cup (95 g/3 oz) soft brown sugar
⅓ cup (80 ml/2¾ oz) milk
1 cup (60 g/2 oz) shredded coconut

1 Grease a 20 cm (8 inch) round springform cake tin and line the base with baking paper. Preheat the oven to moderate 180°C (350°F/Gas 4).
2 Put the dates in a small saucepan with 1 cup (250 ml/8 fl oz) water and bring to the boil. Stir in the bicarbonate of soda, then remove from the heat. Set aside until just warm.
3 Cream the butter and sugar in a small bowl with electric beaters until light and fluffy. Add the egg and vanilla and beat until combined. Stir in the date mixture and the apple, then fold in the sifted flours until just combined and almost smooth. Spoon into the tin and smooth the surface. Bake for 40 minutes.
4 Meanwhile, combine all the topping ingredients in a small saucepan and stir over low heat until the butter is melted and the ingredients well combined. Remove the cake from the oven and carefully spread the topping over the cake. Return the cake to the oven for 20–30 minutes, or until the topping is golden and the cake is cooked through.
5 Remove from the oven and leave the cake in the tin to cool completely, then turn out and place on a serving plate. The cake can be dusted with icing sugar just before serving.

LUMBERJACK CAKE

Cream the butter and sugar together until light and fluffy.

Fold the flour into the date and apple mixture until almost smooth.

Spoon the mixture into the cake tin and smooth the surface with the back of a spoon.

Remove the cake from the oven and gently spread the topping over it.

LEFT: Lumberjack cake

1 Preheat the oven to moderate 180°C (350°F/ Gas 4). Lightly grease a 20 cm (8 inch) square cake tin and line with baking paper.
2 Place the banana, pineapple and sugar in a large bowl. Add the sifted flour and cinnamon or mixed spice. Stir together with a wooden spoon until well combined.
3 Whisk together the oil, juice and eggs in a jug. Pour onto the banana mixture and stir until combined and the mixture is smooth.
4 Spoon into the tin and smooth the surface. Bake for 1 hour, or until a skewer comes out clean when inserted into the centre of the cake. Leave in the tin for 15 minutes before turning out onto a wire rack to cool.
5 For the icing, beat the butter and cream cheese with electric beaters until smooth. Gradually add the icing sugar alternately with the juice. Beat until thick and creamy.
6 Spread the icing thickly over the top of the cooled cake, or thinly over the top and side.
NOTE: If you are unable to buy crushed pineapple, use pineapple rings chopped very finely. Buy the fruit in natural juice rather than syrup, reserve the juice when draining to use in the recipe.

SEED CAKE

Preparation time: 20 minutes
Total cooking time: 50 minutes
Makes 1

125 g (4 oz) unsalted butter, softened
1/2 cup (125 g/4 oz) caster sugar
3 eggs, lightly beaten
3 teaspoons caraway seeds
1 1/4 cups (155 g/5 oz) self-raising flour
2 tablespoons milk

1 Preheat the oven to moderate 180°C (350°F/ Gas 4). Lightly grease the base and side of an 18 cm (7 inch) round cake tin, and line the base with baking paper.
2 Cream the butter and sugar in a small bowl with electric beaters until light and fluffy. Gradually add the egg, beating thoroughly after each addition.
3 Transfer the mixture to a large bowl. Using a metal spoon, fold in the caraway seeds and sifted flour alternately with the milk. Stir until the mixture is just combined and almost smooth. Spoon into the tin and smooth the surface.

HUMMINGBIRD CAKE

Preparation time: 30 minutes
Total cooking time: 1 hour
Makes 1

2 ripe medium bananas, mashed
1/2 cup (125 g/4 oz) drained crushed pineapple
1 1/4 cups (310 g/10 oz) caster sugar
1 2/3 cups (210 g/7 oz) self-raising flour
2 teaspoons ground cinnamon or mixed spice
2/3 cup (170 ml/5 1/2 fl oz) oil
1/4 cup (60 ml/2 fl oz) pineapple juice
2 eggs

Icing

60 g (2 oz) unsalted butter, softened
125 g (4 oz) cream cheese, softened
1 1/2 cups (185 g/6 oz) icing sugar
1–2 teaspoons lemon juice

ABOVE: Hummingbird cake

Bake for 50 minutes, or until a skewer comes out clean when inserted in the centre of the cake. Leave the cake in the tin for 20 minutes before turning onto a wire rack to cool completely. Can be served plain or dusted with sifted icing sugar.

NOTE: Seed cake will keep for up to a week in an airtight container, or, if you prefer, you can freeze it for three months. It is a traditional English cake made to celebrate the end of the Spring crop sowing.

CHERRY CAKE

Preparation time: 30 minutes
Total cooking time: 40 minutes
Makes 1

1 cup (210 g/7 oz) glacé cherries
2/3 cup (85 g/3 oz) plain flour
90 g (3 oz) unsalted butter, softened
2/3 cup (160 g/5 1/2 oz) caster sugar
2 eggs, lightly beaten
1 teaspoon vanilla essence
1 cup (125 g/4 oz) self-raising flour
1/3 cup (80 ml/2 3/4 fl oz) milk

Icing

1 cup (125 g/4 oz) icing sugar
20 g (3/4 oz) unsalted butter
pink food colouring

1 Preheat the oven to moderate 180°C (350°F/ Gas 4). Grease a 20 cm (8 inch) kugelhopf tin. Dust with flour, then shake off any excess. Rinse and dry the glacé cherries and cut each in half. Toss them in a little of the flour.
2 Cream the butter and sugar in a small bowl with electric beaters until light and fluffy. Add the eggs gradually, beating thoroughly after each addition. Beat in the vanilla. Transfer to a large bowl. Using a large metal spoon, fold in the sifted flours alternately with the milk. Stir in the cherries. Spoon into the tin and smooth the surface. Bake for 35 minutes, or until a skewer comes out clean when inserted into the centre of the cake. Leave in the tin for 10 minutes before turning onto a wire rack to cool completely.
3 For the icing, combine the sifted icing sugar, butter and 1–2 tablespoons water in a small heatproof bowl. Stand the bowl over a saucepan of simmering water, ensuring the base doesn't touch the water. Stir the mixture until the butter has melted and the icing is glossy and smooth. Stir in a couple of drops of colouring. Drizzle over the cake, allowing it to run down the sides.

GLACE CHERRIES
To help prevent glacé cherries from sinking to the base of a cake during cooking, remove the syrup by rinsing the cherries under cold water, then pat dry and toss in a little of the flour before stirring into the batter. It is also a good idea to cut each cherry in half.

LEFT: Cherry cake

SEMOLINA LIME SYRUP CAKE

Preparation time: 30 minutes
Total cooking time: 55 minutes
Makes 1

150 g (5 oz) unsalted butter, softened
3/4 cup (185 g/6 oz) caster sugar
2 eggs, lightly beaten
2 teaspoons finely grated lime rind
1 1/2 cups (185 g/6 oz) finely ground
   semolina
1 cup (95 g/3 oz) ground almonds
1 1/2 teaspoons baking powder
1/4 cup (60 ml/2 oz) milk

Lime syrup

1/4 cup (60 ml/2 fl oz) lime juice
1/4 cup (60 ml/2 fl oz) lemon juice
1 teaspoon finely grated lime rind
1/2 cup (125 g/4 oz) caster sugar

*BELOW: Semolina
lime syrup cake*

1 Preheat the oven to moderate 180°C (350°F/ Gas 4). Lightly grease a deep 23 cm (9 inch) fluted ring tin, dust it lightly with flour, then shake off any excess.
2 Cream the butter and sugar in a small bowl with electric beaters until light and fluffy. Gradually add the egg, beating thoroughly after each addition. Beat in the lime rind, then transfer to a large bowl.
3 Using a metal spoon, fold in the combined semolina, almonds and baking powder alternately with the milk. Stir until just combined and almost smooth.
4 Spoon into the tin and smooth the surface. Bake for 45– 50 minutes, or until a skewer comes out clean when inserted into the centre of the cake. Leave in the tin for 5 minutes before turning out onto a serving plate.
5 For the lime syrup, combine the juices, rind and sugar in a small saucepan. Stir over medium heat, without boiling, until the sugar has dissolved. Bring to the boil, reduce the heat and simmer for 5 minutes. Cool slightly. Brush the warm syrup over the top and sides of the warm cake, then leave to cool.

ORANGE AND LEMON SYRUP CAKE

Preparation time: 40 minutes
Total cooking time: 1 hour 50 minutes
Makes 1

one butter cake (see page 51)
1 teaspoon grated orange rind
2 oranges
2 lemons
610 g (1 1/4 lb) caster sugar

1 Preheat the oven to moderate 180°C (350°F/ Gas 4). Lightly grease a 20 cm (8 inch) kugelhopf tin. Dust lightly with flour.
2 Follow the instructions for the butter cake recipe on page 51, folding in the orange rind with the flour. Spoon the mixture into the tin and cook for 1 hour 5 minutes, or until a skewer comes out clean.
3 While the cake is cooking, cut the oranges and lemons into thin slices, without peeling them. Place 250 g (8 oz) of the sugar in a heavy-based frying pan with 80 ml (2 3/4 fl oz) water.

Stir over low heat until the sugar has completely dissolved. Bring to the boil, then reduce the heat and simmer. Add a quarter of the sliced fruit to the syrup and leave to simmer for 5– 10 minutes, or until transparent and toffee-like. Lift out the fruit with tongs and cool on a wire rack.
4 Add an extra 90 g (3 oz) of sugar to the syrup and stir gently to dissolve—the juice from the fruit breaks down the concentrated syrup and the fruit won't candy properly unless you add the sugar. Now you are ready to simmer the second batch of sliced fruit. Add 90 g (3 oz) of sugar to the syrup before cooking each batch.
5 When all the fruit has been candied, turn the cake out onto a wire rack over a tray and pour the hot syrup over the warm cake, allowing it to soak in—if the syrup is too thick, thin it with a little orange juice. Put the cake on a serving plate. When the fruit slices have firmed, arrange them on top of the cake (you can cut and twist some of the slices).
NOTE: The candied fruit can be kept between layers of baking paper in an airtight container for up to two days. The cake should be served within a few hours of decorating. If you prefer, you can bake this cake in a 20 cm (8 inch) round tin.

SUGAR SYRUPS
Sugar syrup is made by stirring sugar and water in a saucepan over low heat, without boiling, until the sugar is completely dissolved. The heat is increased and the syrup allowed to boil rapidly to form a concentrated syrup. There are several stages a sugar syrup goes through, from a soft, sticky ball to a hard crack stage, before finally turning into a caramel syrup. Each stage is used for different purposes, from a simple syrup used to poach fresh fruit, to making crème caramel, confectionery and spun sugar.

ABOVE: Oranges and lemons syrup cake

CREAM

Cream is used extensively in baking either as part of the baking mixture, or whipped to use as a decoration. It adds richness, moistness and flavour to the finished product. Cream needs to contain at least thirty per cent fat to be whipped successfully. When whipping cream, have the cream cold straight from the fridge. Ideally, pour it into a cold metal bowl and beat over a basin of cold water. Use ice cubes in the water in hot weather. Beat until stiff but take care not to overbeat or the cream will curdle. If you like, you can flavour beaten cream with a teaspoon each of icing sugar and vanilla.

ABOVE: Classic sponge

CLASSIC SPONGE

Preparation time: 20 minutes
Total cooking time: 25 minutes
Makes 1 layered sponge

75 g (2¹/₂ oz) plain flour
150 g (5 oz) self-raising flour
6 eggs
220 g (7 oz) caster sugar
¹/₂ cup (160 g/5¹/₂ oz) strawberry jam
1 cup (250 ml/8 fl oz) cream
icing sugar, for dusting

1 Preheat the oven to moderate 180°C (350°F/ Gas 4). Lightly grease two 22 cm (9 inch) sandwich tins or round cake tins and line the bases with baking paper. Dust the tins with a little flour, shaking off any excess.
2 Sift the flours together three times onto a sheet of greaseproof paper. Beat the eggs in a large bowl with electric beaters for 7 minutes, or until thick and pale. Gradually add the sugar to the egg, beating well after each addition. Using a large metal spoon, quickly and gently fold in the sifted flour and 2 tablespoons boiling water.
3 Spread the mixture evenly into the tins and bake for 25 minutes, or until the sponges are lightly golden and shrink slightly from the sides of the tins. Leave the sponges in their tins for 5 minutes before turning out onto a wire rack to cool.
4 Spread jam over one of the sponges. Beat the cream in a small bowl until stiff, then spoon into a piping bag and pipe rosettes over the jam. Place the other sponge on top. Dust with icing sugar.
NOTES: The secret to making a perfect sponge lies in the folding technique. A beating action, or using a wooden spoon, will cause loss of volume in the egg mixture and result in a flat, heavy cake.

Unfilled sponges can be frozen for up to one month—freeze in separate freezer bags. Thaw at room temperature for about 20 minutes. Once a sponge is filled it is best served immediately.

GENOISE SPONGE

Preparation time: 25 minutes
Total cooking time: 25 minutes
Makes 1

2¹/₃ cups (290 g/10 oz) plain flour
8 eggs
220 g (7 oz) caster sugar
100 g (3¹/₂ oz) unsalted butter, melted

1 Preheat the oven to moderate 180°C (350°F/ Gas 4). Lightly grease one 25 cm (10 inch) Genoise tin or two shallow 22 cm (9 inch) round cake tins with melted butter. Line the base with baking paper, then grease the paper. Dust the tin with a little flour, shaking off any excess.

2 Sift the flour three times onto baking paper. Mix the eggs and sugar in a large heatproof bowl. Place the bowl over a pan of simmering water, making sure the base doesn't touch the water, and beat with electric beaters for 8 minutes, or until the mixture is thick and fluffy and a ribbon of mixture drawn in a figure of eight doesn't sink immediately. Remove from the heat and beat for 3 minutes, or until slightly cooled.

3 Add the cooled butter and sifted flour. Using a large metal spoon, fold in quickly and lightly until the mixture is just combined.

4 Spread the mixture evenly into the tin. Bake for 25 minutes, or until the sponge is lightly golden and has shrunk slightly from the side of the tin. Leave the cake in the tin for 5 minutes before turning out onto a wire rack to cool. The top can be lightly dusted with sifted icing sugar just before serving.

GENOISE SPONGE
The Genoise sponge is traditionally made in a tin with sloping sides and served dusted with icing sugar. However, it is often baked to be used for a decorated gateau or celebration cake, in which case it is generally baked in two sandwich tins. In this case, you can ensure you have exactly half the mixture in each tin by weighing each tin first, then dividing the mixture between the tins before weighing the tins again to make sure they are equal.

LEFT: Genoise sponge

CHOCOLATE SWISS ROLL

Preparation time: 25 minutes
+ 30 minutes chilling
Total cooking time: 12 minutes
Makes 1

★ ★

3 eggs
1/2 cup (125 g/4 oz) caster sugar
1/4 cup (30 g/1 oz) plain flour
2 tablespoons cocoa powder
1 cup (250 ml/8 fl oz) cream
1 tablespoon icing sugar, plus extra, to dust
1/2 teaspoon vanilla essence

1 Preheat the oven to moderately hot 200°C (400°F/Gas 6). Lightly grease the base and sides of a 30 x 25 x 2 cm (12 x 10 x 3/4 inch) swiss roll tin. Line the base with baking paper, extending over the two long sides.
2 Beat the eggs and 1/3 cup (90 g/3 oz) caster sugar in a small bowl with electric beaters until thick and creamy. Using a metal spoon, gently fold in the combined sifted flour and cocoa.
3 Spread the mixture into the tin and smooth the surface. Bake for 10–12 minutes, or until the cake is just set. Meanwhile, place a clean tea towel on a work surface, cover with baking paper and sprinkle with the remaining caster sugar. When the cake is cooked, turn it out immediately onto the sugar. Roll the cake up from the short side, rolling the paper inside the roll and using the tea towel as a guide. Stand the rolled cake on a wire rack for 5 minutes, then carefully unroll and allow the cake to cool to room temperature. Trim the ends with a knife.
4 Beat the cream, icing sugar and vanilla essence until stiff peaks form. Spread the cream over the cooled cake, leaving a 1 cm (1/2 inch) border all around. Re-roll the cake, using the paper as a guide. Place the roll, seam-side-down, on a tray. Refrigerate, covered, for 30 minutes. Lightly dust the top of the swiss roll with icing sugar before cutting into slices to serve.

BELOW: Chocolate swiss roll

SWISS ROLL

Preparation time: 25 minutes
Total cooking time: 12 minutes
Makes 1

★

3/4 cup (90 g/3 oz) self-raising flour
3 eggs, lightly beaten
3/4 cup (185 g/6 oz) caster sugar
1/2 cup (160 g/51/2 oz) strawberry jam

1 Preheat the oven to moderately hot 190°C (375°F/Gas 5). Lightly grease a shallow 30 x 25 x 2 cm (12 x 10 x 3/4 inch) swiss roll tin and line the base with baking paper, extending over the two long sides. Sift the flour three times onto baking paper.
2 Beat the eggs with electric beaters in a small bowl for 5 minutes, or until thick and pale. Add 1/2 cup (125 g/4 oz) of the sugar gradually, beating constantly until the mixture is pale and glossy.
3 Transfer to a large bowl. Using a metal spoon, fold in the flour quickly and lightly. Spread into the tin and smooth the surface. Bake for 10–12 minutes, or until lightly golden and springy to touch. Meanwhile, place a clean tea towel on a work surface, cover with baking paper and lightly sprinkle with the remaining caster sugar. When the cake is cooked, turn it out immediately onto the sugar.

Add the sugar gradually to the eggs, beating until pale and glossy.

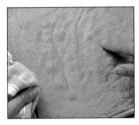

Bake the cake until lightly golden on top and springy to touch.

Roll up the cake with baking paper, using the tea towel as a guide.

4 Using the tea towel as a guide, carefully roll the cake up from the short side, rolling the paper inside the roll. Stand the rolled cake on a wire rack for 5 minutes, then carefully unroll and allow the cake to cool to room temperature. Spread with the jam and re-roll. Trim the ends with a knife.

NOTE: To make the jam easier to spread, beat it in a bowl with a fork for 30 seconds, or microwave briefly in a small heatproof bowl.

HONEY CREAM ROLL

Preparation time: 40 minutes
Total cooking time: 12 minutes
Makes 1

 ✷ ✷

3/4 cup (90 g/3 oz) self-raising flour

2 teaspoons mixed spice

3 eggs

2/3 cup (125 g/4 oz) soft brown sugar

1/4 cup (25 g/3/4 oz) desiccated coconut

Honey cream

125 g (4 oz) unsalted butter, softened

1/3 cup (40 g/1 1/4 oz) icing sugar

2 tablespoons honey

1 Preheat the oven to moderately hot 190°C (375°F/Gas 5). Lightly grease a 30 x 25 x 2 cm (12 x 10 x 3/4 inch) swiss roll tin and line the base with baking paper, extending over the two long sides. Sift the flour and mixed spice three times onto a sheet of baking paper.

2 Beat the eggs with electric beaters in a large bowl for 5 minutes, or until thick, frothy and pale. Add the sugar gradually, beating constantly until the sugar is dissolved and the mixture is pale and glossy. Using a metal spoon, fold in the flour quickly and lightly. Spread into the tin and smooth the surface. Bake for 10–12 minutes, or until the cake is lightly golden and springy to touch. Meanwhile, place a clean tea towel on a work surface, cover with baking paper and sprinkle the paper with coconut. Turn the cooked cake out onto the coconut.

3 Using the tea towel as a guide, carefully roll the cake, along with the paper, up from the short side. Leave until cool.

4 Beat the honey cream ingredients with electric beaters in a bowl until the mixture is light and creamy and the sugar has dissolved. Unroll the cake and discard the paper. Spread with the honey cream and re-roll. Trim the ends with a knife.

NOTE: Swiss roll mixtures contain little fat so they dry out quickly. They need a moist filling, usually made with cream or buttercream. The filling can be flavoured with citrus zest, essences, or fruit and melted chocolate.

ABOVE: Honey cream roll

DEVIL'S FOOD CAKE

This is rich, moist and chocolaty, quite the opposite to the angel food cake. The dark colour contrasts with the white of the angel food cake. The devil's food cake is supposedly sinful because it is so rich. It is filled in the centre and coated, either on top or all over, with whipped cream or a white or chocolate icing. This cake always contains bicarbonate of soda which helps darken the cake.

ABOVE: Devil's food cake

DEVIL'S FOOD CAKE

Preparation time: 30 minutes
Total cooking time: 35 minutes
Makes 1 layered cake

1¹/₂ cups (280 g/9 oz) soft brown sugar

¹/₃ cup (40 g/1¹/₄ oz) cocoa powder

1 cup (250 ml/8 fl oz) milk

90 g (3 oz) dark chocolate, chopped

125 g (4 oz) unsalted butter, softened

1 teaspoon vanilla essence

2 eggs, separated

1¹/₂ cups (185 g/6 oz) plain flour

1 teaspoon bicarbonate of soda

Chocolate icing

50 g (1³/₄ oz) dark chocolate, chopped

30 g (1 oz) unsalted butter

1 tablespoon icing sugar

Filling

1 cup (250 ml/8 fl oz) cream

1 tablespoon icing sugar

1 teaspoon vanilla essence

1 Preheat the oven to warm 160°C (315°F/ Gas 2–3). Lightly grease two deep 20 cm (8 inch) round cake tins and line the bases with baking paper. Combine a third of the brown sugar with the cocoa and milk in a small saucepan. Stir over low heat until the sugar and cocoa have dissolved. Remove from the heat and stir in the chocolate, stirring until it is melted. Cool.

2 Cream the remaining brown sugar with the butter in a small bowl with electric beaters until light and fluffy. Beat in the vanilla and egg yolks and the cooled chocolate mixture. Transfer to a large bowl, and stir in the sifted flour and bicarbonate of soda.

3 Beat the egg whites in a small bowl until soft peaks form. Fold into the chocolate mixture. Divide the mixture evenly between the tins. Bake for 35 minutes, or until a skewer inserted in the centre of the cakes comes out clean.

Leave in the tins for 5 minutes before turning out onto a wire rack to cool.

4 For the icing, put the chocolate and butter in a heatproof bowl. Place the bowl over a pan of simmering water, making sure it does not touch the water, and stir until the mixture is melted and smooth. Gradually add the sifted icing sugar and stir until smooth.

5 For the filling, whip the cream, icing sugar and vanilla in a small bowl with electric beaters until stiff peaks form. Spread over one of the cold cakes, top with the second cake and spread with icing, over the top or top and sides.

ANGEL FOOD CAKE

Preparation time: 30 minutes
Total cooking time: 40 minutes
Makes 1

1 cup (125 g/4 oz) self-raising flour
1 1/2 cups (375 g/12 oz) caster sugar
12 egg whites
1 1/2 teaspoons cream of tartar

1/2 teaspoon vanilla essence
1/4 teaspoon almond essence
icing sugar, to dust
fresh fruit, sliced or chopped, for serving

1 Preheat the oven to moderate 180°C (350°F/ Gas 4). Have an ungreased angel food tin (see page 21) ready. Sift the flour and 3/4 cup (185 g/6 oz) sugar together four times.

2 Using electric beaters, beat the egg whites with the cream of tartar and 1/4 teaspoon salt until stiff peaks form. Beat in the remaining sugar, 1 tablespoon at a time. Fold in the vanilla and almond essences. Sift a quarter of the flour and sugar mixture onto the egg white and, using a spatula, gradually fold in. Repeat with the remaining flour and sugar.

3 Spoon the mixture into the angel food tin and bake for 35– 40 minutes, or until puffed and golden, and a skewer inserted in the centre comes out clean. Turn upside-down on a wire rack and leave in the tin until cool. Gently shake to remove the cake. Lightly dust with icing sugar and serve with fruit.

NOTE: Angel food cake can be served with fresh fruit and whipped or thick (double) cream as a dessert cake.

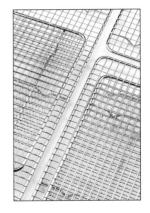

ANGEL FOOD CAKE
This is a classic vanilla-flavoured sponge that was devised in America. It is made in a special high central-tubed tin, called an angel food tin, which is available at speciality kitchenware shops. Due to the high egg white content, the cake has a very light texture and is white. Traditionally, the cake is pulled apart with two forks into portions, rather than cutting. The cake is so light it is often difficult to cut neatly. The cake does not freeze well as it contains no fat and will therefore toughen on defrosting. The defrosted cake or leftover stale cake, however, is delicious sliced and toasted.

LEFT: Angel food cake

WHOLE ORANGE AND ALMOND CAKE

Preparation time: 20 minutes
+ cooling oranges
Total cooking time: 2 hours
Makes 1

★

2 large oranges
5 eggs
250 g (8 oz) ground almonds
220 g (7 oz) sugar
1 teaspoon baking powder
icing sugar, to dust

1 Lightly grease a 22 cm (9 inch) springform tin and line the base with baking paper.
2 Scrub the orange skins under warm running water with a soft bristle brush to remove the wax coating. Put the whole oranges in a saucepan, cover with water and boil for 1 hour. Remove from the water and set aside to cool.
3 Preheat the oven to moderate 180°C (350°F/Gas 4). Using a plate to catch any juice, cut the cooled oranges into quarters and remove any seeds. Blend the orange quarters, including the skin, in a food processor or blender until they turn to a pulp.
4 Beat the eggs in a large bowl with electric beaters until light and fluffy. Add the orange pulp and any reserved juice, almonds, sugar and baking powder to the bowl, mix thoroughly, then pour into the tin. Bake for 1 hour, or until the cake is firm to touch and lightly golden. Cook the cake a little longer if it is still wet. Cool in the tin before turning out onto a wire rack to cool completely. Dust with sifted icing sugar before serving.

BELOW: Whole orange and almond cake

SACHER TORTE

Preparation time: 40 minutes
Total cooking time: 50 minutes
Makes 1

★ ★

1 cup (125 g/4 oz) plain flour
1/4 cup (30 g/1 oz) cocoa powder
1 cup (250 g/8 oz) caster sugar
100 g (3 1/2 oz) unsalted butter
1/4 cup (80 g/2 3/4 oz) strawberry jam
4 eggs, separated

Ganache topping

2/3 cup (170 ml/5 1/2 fl oz) cream
1/3 cup (90 g/3 oz) caster sugar
200 g (6 1/2 oz) dark chocolate, chopped

 Preheat the oven to moderate 180°C (350°F/ Gas 4). Lightly grease a 20 cm (8 inch) round cake tin and line with baking paper.

2 Sift the flour and cocoa into a large bowl and make a well. Combine the sugar, butter and half the jam in a small saucepan. Stir over low heat until the butter is melted and the sugar has dissolved, then add to the flour with the lightly beaten egg yolks and stir until just combined.

3 Beat the egg whites in a small bowl with electric beaters until soft peaks form. Stir a third of the egg white into the cake mixture, then fold in the rest in two batches. Pour into the tin and smooth the surface. Bake for 40–45 minutes, or until a skewer comes out clean when inserted into the centre. Leave in the tin for 15 minutes before turning out onto a wire rack to cool.

4 To make the topping, stir the cream, sugar and chocolate in a small saucepan over low heat until the mixture is melted and smooth.

5 Trim the top of the cake so that it is flat, then turn it upside down on a wire rack over a tray. Melt the remaining jam and brush it over the cake. Pour most of the topping over the cake and tap the tray to flatten the surface. Place the remaining mixture in a piping bag and pipe 'Sacher' on the top of the cake.

SACHER TORTE
Vienna's most famous torte was created in 1832 by Franz Sacher, a pastry cook from a famous family of restaurateurs and hoteliers. The cake is brushed with warm jam before being covered with the rich chocolate glaze. It is usually served with lashings of whipped cream and it is traditional to write the word *Sacher* in chocolate across the top.

ABOVE: Sacher torte

PINEAPPLE UPSIDE-DOWN CAKE

Put the pineapple rings on the butter and sugar at the base of the tin.

Fold in the flours, coconut and pineapple juice with a large metal spoon.

Spoon the cake mixture into the tin and indent the centre slightly with the back of a spoon.

ABOVE: Pineapple upside-down cake

PINEAPPLE UPSIDE-DOWN CAKE

Preparation time: 30 minutes
Total cooking time: 1 hour
Makes 1

90 g (3 oz) unsalted butter, melted

1/2 cup (95 g/3 oz) soft brown sugar

440 g (14 oz) can pineapple rings in natural juice

6 red glacé cherries

125 g (4 oz) unsalted butter, extra, softened

3/4 cup (185 g/6 oz) caster sugar

2 eggs, lightly beaten

1 teaspoon vanilla essence

1 1/2 cups (185 g/6 oz) self-raising flour

1/2 cup (60 g/2 oz) plain flour

1/3 cup (30 g/1 oz) desiccated coconut

1 Preheat the oven to moderate 180°C (350°F/ Gas 4). Pour the melted butter into a 20 cm (8 inch) round tin, brushing some of it up the side, but leaving most on the base. Sprinkle the brown sugar over the base.

2 Drain the pineapple, reserving 1/2 cup (125 ml/4 fl oz) of the juice. Arrange the pineapple rings over the base of the tin (five on the outside and one in the centre) and put a cherry in the centre of each ring.

3 Cream the butter and sugar in a small bowl with electric beaters until light and fluffy. Add the egg gradually, beating thoroughly after each addition. Add the vanilla essence and beat until combined.

4 Transfer to a large bowl. Using a metal spoon, fold in the sifted flours, then add the coconut and reserved pineapple juice. Stir until the mixture is just combined and almost smooth.

5 Spoon the mixture into the tin over the pineapple rings and smooth the surface. Indent the centre slightly with the back of a spoon to ensure the cake has a reasonably flat base. Bake for 50–60 minutes, or until a skewer comes out clean when inserted into the centre of the cake. Leave the cake in the tin for 10 minutes before turning out onto a plate to cool.

RHUBARB AND APPLE UPSIDE-DOWN CAKE

Preparation time: *40 minutes*
Total cooking time: *55 minutes*
Makes 1

⭐

1 cup (250 g/8 oz) sugar

250 g (8 oz) rhubarb, chopped
    into 2 cm (³/4 inch) pieces

1 small Granny Smith apple, peeled,
    cored and chopped

2 eggs

¹/3 cup (40 g/1 ¹/4 oz) icing sugar

¹/2 teaspoon vanilla essence

100 g (3¹/2 oz) unsalted butter,
    melted and cooled

1 cup (125 g/4 oz) self-raising flour

1 Preheat the oven to moderate 180°C (350°F/ Gas 4). Lightly grease a deep 20 cm (8 inch) round cake tin and line the base with baking paper.

2 Put the sugar in a small saucepan with ¹/3 cup (80 ml/2³/4 fl oz) water and heat gently, shaking occasionally, until the sugar has dissolved. Increase the heat and cook until a pale caramel colour—it will turn a deeper colour in the oven. Pour into the tin and then press the rhubarb and apple into the caramel.

3 Beat the eggs, icing sugar and vanilla essence in a small bowl with electric beaters until the mixture is frothy. Fold in the melted butter. Sift the flour over the top and stir (the mixture will be soft). Spoon gently over the fruit, being careful not to dislodge it.

4 Bake for about 45 minutes, or until set on top. Run a knife around the side of the cake and turn out very carefully onto a rack or plate. Be sure to do this straight away, otherwise the caramel will cool and stick to the tin. Serve warm.

NOTES: This can be served as a teacake, or served warm with cream as a dessert.

Fresh plums can be substituted for the apple and rhubarb in this recipe. The plums should be halved and cored, then sliced and pressed into the caramel in a decorative spiral pattern, or randomly. Bake the cake as for the original recipe and serve either warm or cold.

Cook the sugar syrup until it turns a pale caramel colour.

Pour the caramel into the cake tin and press the chopped rhubarb and apple into the caramel.

BELOW: Rhubarb and apple upside-down cake

BLACK FOREST CAKE

Preparation time: I hour
Total cooking time: I hour
Makes I

200 g (6¹/2 oz) unsalted butter, softened
³/4 cup (185 g/6 oz) caster sugar
3 eggs, lightly beaten
I teaspoon vanilla essence
I²/3 cups (210 g/7 oz) self-raising flour
¹/3 cup (40 g/1¹/4 oz) plain flour
³/4 cup (90 g/3 oz) cocoa powder
I tablespoon instant coffee powder
¹/2 teaspoon bicarbonate of soda
¹/2 cup (125 ml/4 fl oz) buttermilk
¹/3 cup (80 ml/2³/4 fl oz) milk
I¹/4 cups (315 ml/10 fl oz) cream, whipped
425 g (14 oz) can pitted cherries, drained
chocolate curls, for decoration

Chocolate topping

300 g (10 oz) dark chocolate, chopped
375 g (12 oz) unsalted butter, softened

I Preheat the oven to moderate 180°C (350°F/ Gas 4). Grease a 23 cm (9 inch) round cake tin and line the base and side with baking paper.
2 Cream the butter and sugar in a small bowl with electric beaters until light and fluffy. Add the egg gradually, beating thoroughly after each addition. Add the vanilla essence and beat until well combined.
3 Transfer the mixture to a large bowl. Using a metal spoon, fold in the sifted flours, cocoa, coffee and soda alternately with the combined buttermilk and milk. Stir until the mixture is just combined and almost smooth.
4 Pour the mixture into the tin and smooth the surface. Bake for 40– 50 minutes, or until a skewer comes out clean when inserted into the centre of the cake. Leave the cake in the tin for 20 minutes before turning out onto a wire rack to cool.
5 For the chocolate topping, bring a saucepan of water to the boil and remove from the heat. Place the chocolate in a heatproof bowl and sit the bowl over the pan, making sure the bowl is not touching the water. Allow to stand, stirring occasionally, until the chocolate has melted. Beat the butter in a small bowl until light and creamy. Add the chocolate, beating for 1 minute, or until the mixture is glossy and smooth.

6 Turn the cake upside down and cut into three layers horizontally. Place the first layer on a serving plate. Spread evenly with half the whipped cream, then top with half the cherries. Continue layering with the remaining cake, cream and cherries, ending with the cake on the top. Spread the chocolate topping over the top and side, using a flat-bladed knife. Using a piping bag, pipe swirls with the remaining topping around the cake rim. Decorate with chocolate curls.
NOTE: This cake and its filling are best assembled and eaten on the day that it is made.

FLOURLESS CHOCOLATE CAKE

Preparation time: 20 minutes
Total cooking time: I hour 5 minutes
Makes I

★

250 g (8 oz) dark cooking chocolate, chopped
100 g (3¹/2 oz) caster sugar
100 g (3¹/2 oz) unsalted butter, cubed
I tablespoon coffee-flavoured liqueur
125 g (4 oz) ground hazelnuts
5 eggs, separated
icing sugar, to decorate

I Preheat the oven to moderate 180°C (350°F/ Gas 4). Grease a 23 cm (9 inch) springform tin and line the base with baking paper.
2 Place the cooking chocolate, sugar, butter and liqueur in a heatproof bowl. Bring a small saucepan of water to the boil, then reduce the heat to a gentle simmer. Sit the bowl over the saucepan, making sure the base of the bowl does not touch the water. Stir occasionally to ensure even melting. When fully melted, remove from the heat and mix thoroughly.
3 Transfer the chocolate mixture to a large bowl. Stir in the hazelnuts, then beat in the egg yolks one at a time, mixing well after each addition. In a dry bowl, whisk the egg whites until they form medium stiff peaks. Stir a tablespoonful of the whisked whites into the chocolate, then gently fold in the rest using a large metal spoon or rubber spatula.
4 Pour the mixture into the tin and bake for 50– 60 minutes, or until a skewer comes out clean when inserted into the centre of the cake. Leave to cool completely in the tin, before turning out and dusting with icing sugar.

DARK CHOCOLATE

The seeds from the beans of the cacao tree, native to Central America, are fermented, dried, roasted and then formed into a solidified paste known as bitter unsweetened chocolate. The more bitter the chocolate, the more intense the flavour. Bitter-sweet and semi-sweet chocolates have some sugar added. Couverture chocolate, though very expensive, is considered the best baking chocolate as it is very high quality due to its high cocoa butter content.

OPPOSITE PAGE:
Black forest cake (top);
Flourless chocolate cake

FRUIT CAKES With a little careful

attention to the lining of the tin, you will be assured of that special feeling of

fulfilment when lifting a freshly baked fruit cake out of the oven.

FUNDAMENTALS

Fruit cakes are generally made by the creaming method so it is recommended you read the detailed description of creaming butter and sugar on page 51.

Before you begin, read through your recipe, checking you have all the right equipment and ingredients at hand. Leave plenty of time as fruit cakes take a little longer to prepare than simple cakes and also take a few hours to cook.

Before you mix your cake, line the tin and make sure the oven rack is positioned so the cake will sit in the centre of the oven, then preheat the oven.

LINING THE TIN

Lightly grease the cake tin. Fruit cakes need a double layer of baking paper for the collar and base. Cut two circles of baking paper, using the base as a guide. A collar gives extra protection during

cooking. For the collar, cut a double strip of baking paper long enough to fit around the outside of the tin and tall enough to extend 5 cm (2 inches) above the top of the tin. Fold a 2 cm (3/4 inch) deep cuff along the length of the strip, then make diagonal cuts up to the fold line about 1 cm (1/2 inch) apart. Fit in the tin, with the cuts on the base, pressing them out at right angles so they sit flat around the base. Place the circles over the cuts.

Because of the long cooking time, fruit cakes require extra protection, both around the side and under the base. This is why we wrap layers of newspaper around the outside of the tin, and sit the tin on layers of newspaper in the oven. Because the oven temperature is low, this is quite safe.

MAKING THE CAKE

Weigh all the ingredients in your recipe and complete preparations such as softening butter, sifting flour and spices, blanching nuts, tossing fruit in flour or marinating fruit, if required. Dried fruit is sold ready for use and does not usually need to be washed. Dates and prunes may have stones that need to be removed. Glacé fruit such as cherries, pineapple or ginger are better if cut into small pieces as they are heavy and may sink. If peel is large, cut or chop into smaller pieces.

Following the methods described in making a creamed butter cake, beat the butter and sugar with electric beaters until light and fluffy. Gradually add the eggs, beating thoroughly after each addition. Add any essences, rind, juice, jam, syrup or molasses as specified. Transfer to a large bowl and add the specified dried or glacé fruit. Mix with a large metal spoon until combined. Next, using a large metal spoon, fold in the sifted dry ingredients. Alcohol, if specified, can also be added at this time. Stir until just combined and almost smooth. Spoon evenly into the tin, spread into the corners and smooth the top. Some fruit cakes are decorated at this stage by placing blanched almonds in a pattern on the top. Check that the oven temperature is correct. Wrap layers of newspaper around the tin, coming up as high as the collar, and secure with string or paper clips. Some people like to finish

with a layer of brown paper. Place a few layers of newspaper on the rack in the oven and place the tin on top. Slow cooking is vital for dense cakes heavy with fruit. If the cake browns before it is cooked, cover it loosely with foil.

WHEN IS IT READY?

As ovens vary, check the cake about 20 minutes before the specified time. If it is cooked, a skewer should come out clean when inserted into the centre. The cake should shrink from the side of the tin. Cool the cake completely in the tin, preferably overnight, before removing. Fruit cakes improve if kept for a few weeks wrapped in baking paper and foil, or kept in an airtight container, before decorating or cutting. Un-iced fruit cakes can be refrigerated for up to 3 months. They can be fed alcohol by inserting holes with a skewer and pouring in brandy or whisky.

BAKING PAPER

Baking paper, now an essential item in the kitchen, is a silicone-coated paper that is used to line cake tins. The paper is non-stick and easy to use. Greasing the tin before lining with baking paper allows the paper to sit firmly on the base of the tin and not slip around.

SULTANA CAKE

Preparation time: 20 minutes
Total cooking time: 1 hour 30 minutes
Makes 1

250 g (8 oz) unsalted butter, softened
1 cup (250 g/8 oz) caster sugar
3 eggs, lightly beaten
2 teaspoons grated lemon rind
1 teaspoon vanilla essence
2 cups (320 g/11 oz) sultanas
3 cups (375 g/12 oz) plain flour
1 1/2 teaspoons baking powder
2/3 cup (170 ml/5 1/2 fl oz) buttermilk

1 Preheat the oven to warm 160°C (315°F/ Gas 2– 3). Lightly grease and line a 20 cm (8 inch) square cake tin (see page 84).
2 Cream the butter and sugar in a small bowl with electric beaters until light and fluffy. Gradually add the egg, beating thoroughly after each addition. Beat in the rind and vanilla. Transfer to a large bowl. Using a metal spoon, fold in the sultanas and sifted flour and baking powder, alternately with the buttermilk. Spoon into the tin and smooth the surface. Bake for 1 1/4– 1 1/2 hours, or until a skewer comes out clean when inserted in the centre. Cool in the tin for 20 minutes, then turn out onto a wire rack.

LIGHT FRUIT CAKE

Preparation time: 35 minutes
Total cooking time: 3 hours 30 minutes
Makes 1

250 g (8 oz) unsalted butter, softened
1 cup (250 g/8 oz) caster sugar
4 eggs, lightly beaten
1 teaspoon vanilla essence
1 kg (2 lb) mixed dried fruit
1 1/2 cups (185 g/6 oz) plain flour
1/2 cup (60 g/2 oz) self-raising flour
1/2 cup (125 ml/4 fl oz) sherry
125 g (4 oz) assorted glacé fruits, to decorate
60 g (2 oz) walnut halves, to decorate

RIGHT: Sultana cake

1 Preheat the oven to warm 160°C (315°F/ Gas 2– 3). Lightly grease and line a deep 20 cm (8 inch) round cake tin (see page 84).

2 Cream the butter and sugar in a small bowl with electric beaters until light and fluffy. Gradually add the egg, beating thoroughly after each addition. Add the vanilla and beat well.

3 Transfer to a large bowl and add the dried fruit. Using a metal spoon, fold in the sifted flours alternately with the sherry. Stir until the mixture is just combined and almost smooth.

4 Spoon into the tin, then smooth the surface and decorate. Wrap the outside of the tin (see page 85) and sit the tin on several layers of newspaper in the oven. Bake for 3– 3½ hours, or until a skewer comes out clean when inserted into the centre of the cake. Cool in the tin overnight.

NOTE: Light fruit cake can be stored, covered with several layers of plastic wrap in the refrigerator, for up to a month. You can use any combination of dried and glacé fruits to the same weight as stated in the recipe. The type of alcohol and nuts that you include can also be varied.

DUNDEE CAKE

Preparation time: 30 minutes
Total cooking time: 2 hours 30 minutes
Makes 1

250 g (8 oz) unsalted butter

1 cup (230 g/7½ oz) firmly packed soft
   brown sugar

4 eggs, lightly beaten

1 cup (160 g/5½ oz) raisins

1 cup (160 g/5½ oz) sultanas

1⅓ cups (185 g/6 oz) currants

⅓ cup (60 g/2 oz) combined orange and
   lemon peel

¼ cup (60 g/2 oz) glacé cherries,
   chopped

1 cup (95 g/3 oz) almond meal

¾ cup (90 g/3 oz) slivered almonds

1½ cups (185 g/6 oz) plain flour

½ cup (60 g/2 oz) self-raising flour

2 tablespoons rum

100 g (3½ oz) blanched whole almonds,
   to decorate

1 Preheat the oven to slow 150°C (300°F/Gas 2). Lightly grease and line a 20 cm (8 inch) round cake tin (see page 84).

2 Cream the butter and sugar in a small bowl with electric beaters until light and fluffy. Gradually add the egg, beating well after each addition. Transfer to a large bowl and add the fruits, peel and nuts. Using a metal spoon, fold in the sifted flours alternately with the rum. Stir to just combine. Do not overbeat.

3 Spoon into the tin and smooth the surface. Arrange the whole almonds in a pattern over the top of the cake. Wrap the outside of the tin (see page 85) and sit the cake tin on several layers of newspaper in the oven. Bake for 2– 2½ hours, or until a skewer comes out clean when inserted into the centre of the cake. Leave the cake in the tin for at least 4 hours before turning out.

NOTE: Store, wrapped in several layers of plastic wrap, in the refrigerator for up to two months.

DUNDEE CAKE

This fruit cake, named after the town of Dundee in Scotland, is lighter than the traditional Christmas cake and is made as a general eating cake rather than for special occasions. The top is always covered closely with blanched whole almonds.

ABOVE: Dundee cake

GLACE FRUITS

These are also known as candied fruit. They are stoned fruit that have been preserved in a very high concentration of sugar syrup, resulting in dense, very sweet, moist and sticky fruit. The fruit is usually chopped for adding to fruit cakes to give colour and flavour, and is also used whole to decorate cakes. Mostly available from health food stores, glacé fruits should be bought in small amounts, as you need them, although any unused fruits can be refrigerated until the use-by date.

ABOVE: Golden fruit cake

GOLDEN FRUIT CAKE

Preparation time: 25 minutes
Total cooking time: 2 hours
Makes 1

½ cup (110 g/3½ oz) chopped glacé pears

1 cup (240 g/7½ oz) chopped glacé apricots

1 cup (220 g/7 oz) chopped glacé pineapple

⅓ cup (60 g/2 oz) chopped mixed peel

½ cup (95 g/3 oz) chopped glacé orange slices

½ cup (80 g/2¾ oz) blanched almonds, coarsely chopped

1½ cups (185 g/6 oz) plain flour

½ cup (60 g/2 oz) self-raising flour

250 g (8 oz) unsalted butter, softened

1 tablespoon finely grated orange rind

1 tablespoon finely grated lemon rind

1 cup (250 g/8 oz) caster sugar

4 eggs

¼ cup (60 ml/2 fl oz) sweet sherry

1 Preheat the oven to warm 160°C (315°F/ Gas 2–3). Lightly grease and line a deep 20 cm (8 inch) square tin (see page 84).

2 Combine the fruits and almonds in a bowl and toss with ¼ cup (30 g/1 oz) of the plain flour to help keep the fruits separate. Sift together the remaining flours.

3 Beat the butter and grated rind in a small bowl with electric beaters, gradually adding the sugar, until light and fluffy. Beat in the eggs, one at a time, beating well after each addition. Transfer the mixture to a large bowl, stir in the flour alternately with the sherry, then fold in the fruit, nut and flour mixture.

4 Spread evenly into the tin and wrap paper around the outside of the tin (see page 85). Sit the cake tin on several layers of newspaper in the oven. Bake for about 1¾–2 hours, or until cooked when a skewer inserted in the centre comes out clean. Leave in the tin for 20 minutes before turning out onto a wire rack to cool. Store in an airtight container for up to a month.

GLACE FRUIT AND NUT LOAF

Preparation time: 30 minutes
Total cooking time: 1 hour 45 minutes
Makes 1

✩ ✩

50 g (1³/₄ oz) unsalted butter, softened
¹/₃ cup (60 g/2 oz) soft brown sugar
2 tablespoons breakfast marmalade
2 eggs, lightly beaten
1 cup (125 g/4 oz) plain flour
1 teaspoon baking powder
1 teaspoon ground nutmeg
1¹/₄ cups (225 g/7 oz) pitted dates, chopped
1¹/₂ cups (240 g/7¹/₂ oz) raisins
1 cup (155 g/5 oz) brazil nuts
²/₃ cup (140 g/4¹/₂ oz) red, yellow
   and green glacé cherries
¹/₂ cup (110 g/3¹/₂ oz) chopped glacé
   pear or pineapple
¹/₂ cup (120 g/4 oz) chopped glacé apricots
¹/₂ cup (120 g/4 oz) chopped glacé peaches
¹/₃ cup (120 g/4 oz) chopped glacé figs
1 cup (100 g/3¹/₂ oz) walnut halves
²/₃ cup (100 g/3¹/₂ oz) blanched almonds

Topping

2 teaspoons gelatine
2 tablespoons breakfast marmalade
150 g (5 oz) glacé pineapple or
   pear rings
100 g (3¹/₂ oz) red, yellow and green
   glacé cherries
¹/₄ cup (40 g/1¹/₄ oz) blanched almonds

1 Preheat the oven to slow 150°C (300°F/ Gas 2). Lightly grease and line a 20.5 x 8 x 7 cm (8 x 3 x 2³/₄ inch) bar tin (see page 84).
2 Cream the butter, sugar and marmalade in a small bowl with electric beaters until pale and fluffy. Add the egg gradually, beating thoroughly after each addition.
3 Sift the flour, baking powder and nutmeg into a large bowl. Add the fruit and nuts and mix until each piece is coated in the flour mixture. Add to the egg mixture and mix to combine well.
4 Spoon the mixture into the tin, pushing well into each corner. Wrap the outside of the tin (see page 85) and sit the cake tin on several layers of newspaper in the oven. Bake for 1¹/₂– 1³/₄ hours, or until a skewer inserted into the centre comes out clean. Cool in the tin for 30 minutes, then turn out onto a wire rack to cool.
5 For the topping, sprinkle the gelatine over the marmalade and 2 tablespoons water in a small heatproof bowl. Bring a saucepan of water to the boil, then remove from the heat. Stand the bowl in the pan and stir until the gelatine has dissolved. Brush the top of the cake with some of the gelatine mixture and arrange the pineapple, cherries and almonds over the top. Brush or drizzle with more gelatine mixture and allow to set.
NOTE: You can toast the blanched almonds for the topping to add colour to them. To do this, spread them in a single layer on a baking tray and bake in a moderate 180°C (350°F/Gas 4) oven for 7 minutes, or until lightly golden.

BELOW: Glacé fruit and nut loaf

BOILED FRUIT CAKE

Preparation time: 30 minutes
Total cooking time: 1 hour 30 minutes
Makes 1

★★

250 g (8 oz) unsalted butter
1 cup (185 g/6 oz) soft brown sugar
1 kg (2 lb) mixed dried fruit
1/2 cup (125 ml/4 fl oz) sweet sherry
1/2 teaspoon bicarbonate of soda
1 1/2 cups (185 g/6 oz) self-raising flour
1 cup (125 g/4 oz) plain flour
1 teaspoon mixed spice
4 eggs, lightly beaten

1 Preheat the oven to moderate 180°C (350°F/ Gas 4). Lightly grease and line a 22 cm (9 inch) round cake tin (see page 84).
2 Put the butter, sugar, mixed fruit, sherry and 3/4 cup (185 ml/6 fl oz) water in a saucepan. Stir over low heat until the butter has melted and the sugar has dissolved. Bring to the boil, then reduce the heat and simmer for 10 minutes. Remove from the heat, stir in the bicarbonate of soda and cool.
3 Sift the flours and spice into a large bowl and make a well. Add the egg to the fruit, mix well, then pour into the well and mix thoroughly.

Pour into the tin and smooth the surface. Wrap the outside of the tin (see page 85) and sit the cake tin on several layers of newspaper in the oven. Bake for 1–1 1/4 hours, or until a skewer comes out clean when inserted into the centre of the cake. Leave in the tin for at least an hour before turning out. The flavour improves after standing for 3 days.

NOTE: Can be kept for up to two months. The cake colour will depend on the fruit. For a dark cake, use raisins, currants and sultanas. For a lighter colour, mix in chopped glacé fruit.

RICH FRUIT CAKE

Preparation time: 30 minutes
  + overnight soaking
Total cooking time: 3 hours 15 minutes
Makes 1

★★

500 g (1 lb) sultanas
375 g (12 oz) raisins, chopped
250 g (8 oz) currants
250 g (8 oz) glacé cherries, quartered
1 cup (250 ml/8 fl oz) brandy or rum, plus
  1 tablespoon to glaze
250 g (8 oz) unsalted butter
230 g (7 1/2 oz) soft dark brown sugar

FRUIT CAKES

Traditionally, rich fruit cakes are baked for celebrations such as Christmas, weddings and anniversaries. For special occasions, they are usually iced with a marzipan or almond paste covering the whole cake, then often decorated with piped and moulded icing. A good fruit cake should be made well in advance to give the flavour time to develop. The addition of sherry, rum or brandy adds to the flavour and helps to keep the cake moist.

RIGHT: Boiled fruit cake

2 tablespoons apricot jam

2 tablespoons treacle or syrup

1 tablespoon grated lemon or orange rind

4 eggs

350 g (11 oz) plain flour

1 teaspoon ground ginger

1 teaspoon mixed spice

1 teaspoon ground cinnamon

1 Put the fruit in a bowl with the brandy and soak overnight.

2 Preheat the oven to slow 150°C (300°F/Gas 2). Lightly grease and line a deep 22 cm (9 inch) round cake tin (see page 84).

3 Beat the butter and sugar in a large bowl with electric beaters to just combine. Beat in the jam, treacle and rind. Add the eggs one at a time, beating after each addition.

4 Stir the fruit and the combined sifted flour and spices alternately into the mixture.

5 Spoon into the tin and smooth the surface. Tap the tin on the bench to remove any air bubbles. Level the surface with wet hands. Wrap the outside of the tin (see page 85). Sit the cake tin on several layers of newspaper in the oven and bake for 3– 3¼ hours, or until a skewer comes out clean when inserted into the centre. Brush with the extra tablespoon of brandy. Cover the top of the cake with paper and wrap in a tea towel. Cool completely in the tin.

NOTES: This cake can be kept, tightly wrapped in plastic wrap, in a cool dry place for up to eight months, or frozen for twelve months. You can cook the mixture in the following tins, changing the cooking time as stated:

For one 23 cm (9 inch) square cake, 3 hours.

For one 18 x 25 cm (7 x 10 inch) oval cake, 3½ hours.

For one 15 cm (6 inch) and one 30 cm (12 inch) round cake, use 2 quantities of mixture and bake for 2 hours 40 minutes and 3 hours 10 minutes respectively.

For one 12 cm (5 inch) and one 25 cm (10 inch) square cake, use 2 quantities of mixture and bake for 2 hours 50 minutes and 3½ hours respectively.

For one 16 cm (6½ inch) and one 30 cm (12 inch) square cake, use 3 quantities of mixture and bake for 3 hours and 4 hours 40 minutes respectively.

ABOVE: Rich fruit cake

BISCUITS

It's one thing to staunchly honour the diet and refuse a whole piece of cake, but biscuits are another matter entirely. They're so little and innocent, surely one couldn't do any harm? Especially straight out of the oven. There must be some reward after the tantalising aroma of freshly baked biscuits has been following you around the house, merciless in its pursuit. Dear little jam drops with their oozy centre, the crunchy gingernut, the rich melt-in-the-mouth sweetness of Scottish shortbread. You know you can't resist — that's just the way the cookie crumbles . . .

BASIC BISCUITS

Nothing beats the heavenly aroma of freshly baked biscuits. Biscuits are made using

several methods, each giving special characteristics to the biscuits.

CREAMING METHOD

With the following recipe, which uses the creaming method, you can make a basic butter biscuit and variations. To make about 30 biscuits, line two trays with baking paper or lightly grease with melted butter. Allow 125 g (4 oz) butter to soften to room temperature, then cut it into cubes. This will make it is easier to work with. Preheat the oven to hot 210°C (415°F/Gas 6– 7) and check the racks are near the centre. Cream the softened butter with ½ cup (125 g/4 oz) caster sugar in a small bowl with electric beaters, or by hand, until light and fluffy. This will take about 3– 5 minutes with electric beaters, or 10 minutes by hand. Scrape down the side of the bowl occasionally with a spatula. The mixture should look pale and be quite smooth. The sugar should be almost dissolved. Add ¼ cup (60 ml/2 fl oz) milk and ¼ teaspoon vanilla essence and beat until combined. Add 1½ cups (185 g/6 oz) self-raising flour and ½ cup (60 g/2 oz) custard powder and use a flat-bladed knife to bring to a soft dough. Rotate the bowl as you work and use a cutting motion to incorporate the dry ingredients. Don't overwork the dough or you will end up with tough biscuits. Roll level teaspoons into balls and place on the trays, leaving 5 cm (2 inches) between

each biscuit. Flatten the balls lightly with your fingertips, then press with a fork. The biscuits should be about 5 cm (2 inches) in diameter. Bake for 15– 18 minutes, until lightly golden. Avoid opening the oven door until at least two-thirds of the way through baking. Cool on the trays for 3 minutes before transferring to a wire rack to cool completely. Store in an airtight container for up to a week. To freeze, place in freezer bags and seal, label and date. Unfilled and un-iced cooked biscuits can be frozen for up to two months. After thawing, refresh them in a moderate 180°C (350°F/Gas 4) oven for a few minutes, then cool and decorate, as desired, before serving. Uncooked biscuit dough freezes well. To do this, wrap it in plastic wrap, place in a plastic bag and seal. When ready to use, thaw at room temperature and bake as directed. Plain cooked biscuits can be decorated with

sifted icing sugar just before serving. Or they can be iced, or drizzled with melted chocolate from a plastic bag which has the corner snipped off. Below are some variations on the basic biscuit.

CITRUS
Omit the vanilla essence, add 2 teaspoons orange or lemon rind to the creamed butter and sugar and proceed with the recipe. When cool, combine 2 cups (250 g/8 oz) sifted icing sugar, 20 g (3/4 oz) softened butter and 1 tablespoon lemon or orange juice in a small bowl and use to ice the biscuits.

NUTTY
Mix 1/2 cup (55 g/2 oz) finely chopped walnuts or pecans into the basic mixture before adding the flour. Press a nut onto each biscuit, instead of pressing with a fork, and bake as above.

Biscuits can also be made using the following methods:

MELT AND MIX
This quick method involves mixing the dry ingredients, then mixing in the melted butter (and any other ingredients in the recipe) with a wooden spoon until the dry ingredients are well moistened.

RUBBING IN
This involves cutting cold butter into small pieces and rubbing it into the flour with your fingertips until the mixture is crumbly and resembles fine breadcrumbs. Then almost all the liquid is added and cut into the dry ingredients with a knife, adding the remaining liquid if necessary to bring the mixture together. Do not add the liquid all at once as flour varies a great deal so the full amount of liquid may not be required.

WHAT WENT WRONG?

DROP BISCUITS

PERFECT The biscuit has even golden colouring on both the top and base and has even thickness.

UNEVENLY SPREAD The mixture may have been placed too close together on the tray, not allowing enough room to spread. Make sure the baking tray is at room temperature before spooning the biscuits onto the tray. The mixture may have been too wet or may contain too much fat or sugar. The mixture may have needed chilling before baking.

UNDERCOOKED, STICKING These biscuits are pale and the tops soft to touch. This indicates that the cooking time may have been too short, leaving the mixture undercooked and sticky. Alternatively, the oven temperature may have been too low or the oven insufficiently preheated.

OVERCOOKED These biscuits are too darkly coloured indicating that the oven temperature may have been too high or the cooking time may have been too long. The biscuit may have too much sugar, which causes biscuits to darken. Be sure to only rest the biscuits for a couple of minutes on the tray after cooking because they will continue to cook if left on the tray. Transfer them to a wire rack to cool completely.

OTHER PROBLEMS

Biscuit mixture should be put on a baking tray that is at room temperature. When re-using baking trays, don't put the biscuit mixture on a hot tray because the biscuits will spread too much and lose their shape. Don't use trays or tins that have high sides, otherwise the heat distribution during cooking will not be even. Most biscuits are best baked in or close to the centre of the oven.

STORING BISCUITS

Most biscuits can be kept for up to four days if stored correctly. They should be allowed to cool completely after baking, then stored in an airtight container in a cool place. Moisture is absorbed easily by biscuits so they lose their crispness if not in an airtight jar. It is best not to store different types of biscuits in the same jar and biscuits should definitely not be stored in the same container as cakes. Biscuits that are to be filled should be stored without their filling and then filled just before you want to use them. If you store biscuits after filling them, they tend to soften.

MIXTURE ROLLED OUT AND CUT INTO SHAPES

PERFECT The biscuit has a light golden colouring and even thickness.

THIN, OVERCOOKED The mixture may have been rolled too thinly or the oven may have been too hot, or perhaps the biscuits cooked too long.

TOO THICK The mixture was rolled and cut too thickly. This biscuit, although probably too thick, would need extra baking time.

MIXTURE SHAPED BY HAND OR PIPED

PERFECT The biscuit has even, golden colouring on both the top and base. It is also the correct thickness.

UNDERCOOKED The biscuit is a pale colour. The oven temperature may have been too low, the oven not preheated, or the biscuits not cooked long enough.

OVERCOOKED AND SPREAD TOO MUCH The oven may have been too hot or the biscuits cooked too long.

MERINGUES

PERFECT The meringue is firm and dry, and still very white and pale in colour, both on the top and base. The inside of the meringue is crisp.

WEEPING The meringue is wet and weeping and the inside may look sticky. The mixture may have been under- or over-beaten before or after the addition of the sugar.

OVERCOOKED The meringue should be white. The oven temperature was probably too high, or the cooking time may have been too long.

JAM DROPS

Preparation time: 20 minutes
Total cooking time: 15 minutes
Makes 32

80 g (2³/4 oz) unsalted butter, softened
¹/3 cup (90 g/3 oz) caster sugar
2 tablespoons milk
¹/2 teaspoon vanilla essence
1 cup (125 g/4 oz) self-raising flour
¹/3 cup (40 g/1¹/4 oz) custard powder
¹/3 cup (100 g/3¹/2 oz) raspberry jam

1 Preheat the oven to moderate 180°C (350°F/ Gas 4). Line two baking trays with baking paper.
2 Cream the butter and sugar in a small bowl with electric beaters until light and fluffy. Add the milk and vanilla and beat until combined. Add the sifted flour and custard powder and mix to form a soft dough. Roll heaped teaspoons of the mixture into balls and place on the trays.
3 Make an indentation in each ball using the end of a wooden spoon. Fill each hole with a little jam. Bake for 15 minutes, cool slightly on the trays, then transfer to a wire rack to cool.

CHOCOLATE BISCUITS

Preparation time: 20 minutes
 + 30 minutes refrigeration
Total cooking time: 12 minutes
Makes 25

125 g (4 oz) dark chocolate, chopped
125 g (4 oz) unsalted butter, cubed
1 egg
1 cup (185 g/6 oz) soft brown sugar
1¹/2 cups (185 g/6 oz) self-raising flour

1 Preheat the oven to moderate 180°C (350°F/ Gas 4). Line two baking trays with baking paper.
2 Place the chocolate and butter in a heatproof bowl. Bring a saucepan of water to the boil, then remove from the heat. Sit the bowl over the saucepan, making sure the base of the bowl does not sit in the water. Stir occasionally until the chocolate and butter have melted.
3 Break the egg into a large bowl, add the sugar and beat lightly for 2 minutes, or until combined. Mix in the melted chocolate, and stir in the sifted flour until just combined. Cover and refrigerate for 30 minutes, or until firm.
4 Roll tablespoons of dough into balls and

place on the trays, leaving room for spreading. Press down gently with the back of a spoon. Bake for 10–12 minutes, or until firm to touch and cracked on top. Cool slightly on the trays before transferring to a wire rack to cool completely. When completely cold, store in an airtight container.

CHOCOLATE CHOC CHIP COOKIES

Preparation time: 20 minutes
Total cooking time: 10 minutes
Makes 40

1¹/₂ cups (185 g/6 oz) plain flour
³/₄ cup (90 g/3 oz) cocoa powder
1¹/₂ cups (280 g/9 oz) soft brown sugar
180 g (6 oz) unsalted butter, cubed
150 g (5 oz) dark chocolate, chopped
3 eggs, lightly beaten
1¹/₂ cups (265 g/8 oz) choc bits

1 Preheat the oven to moderate 180°C (350°F/ Gas 4). Line two baking trays with baking paper.
2 Sift the flour and cocoa powder into a large bowl, add the soft brown sugar and make a well in the centre.
3 Combine the butter and dark chocolate in a small heatproof bowl. Bring a saucepan of water to the boil, then remove the pan from the heat. Sit the heatproof bowl over the saucepan, making sure the base of the bowl does not sit in the water. Stir occasionally until the chocolate and butter have melted and are smooth. Mix well.
4 Add the butter and chocolate mixture and the eggs to the dry ingredients. Stir with a wooden spoon until well combined, but do not overbeat. Stir in the choc bits. Drop tablespoons of the mixture onto the trays, allowing room for spreading. Bake for 7–10 minutes, until firm to touch. Cool on the trays for 5 minutes before transferring to a wire rack to cool completely. When the cookies are completely cold, store in an airtight container.
NOTE: When dropping the dough onto the tray, it is easier and less messy to use two tablespoons, one to measure accurately and the other to push the dough off the spoon onto the tray.

COOKIES
This is an American term for 'biscuits'. Originally biscuits were small flat dry cakes, rather like rusks, that were baked twice to keep them crisp and long-lasting. Today the terms biscuit and cookie cover a wide range of small baked goods, from crispy to chewy, made in a variety of flavours and shapes. The basic ingredients usually include butter, sugar, eggs and flour. Flavours such as chocolate, nuts, dried fruits and essences are added, according to taste.

LEFT: Chocolate choc chip cookies

ANZACS

These famous biscuits were developed at the time of the First World War and sent in food parcels to the ANZAC troops (Australia and New Zealand Army Corps). They are an economical, crisp, long-lasting biscuit made without eggs (which were in short supply at that time). The recipe is still popular, having been handed down through the generations.

BELOW: Anzac biscuits

ANZAC BISCUITS

Preparation time: 15 minutes
Total cooking time: 25 minutes
Makes 26

1 cup (125 g/4 oz) plain flour
2/3 cup (160 g/5 1/2 oz) sugar
1 cup (100 g/3 1/2 oz) rolled oats
1 cup (90 g/3 oz) desiccated coconut
125 g (4 oz) unsalted butter, cubed
1/4 cup (90 g/3 oz) golden syrup
1/2 teaspoon bicarbonate of soda

1 Preheat the oven to moderate 180°C (350°F/ Gas 4). Line two baking trays with baking paper.
2 Sift the flour into a large bowl. Add the sugar, oats and coconut and make a well in the centre.
3 Put the butter and golden syrup together in a small saucepan and stir over low heat until the butter has melted and the mixture is smooth. Remove from the heat. Dissolve the bicarbonate of soda in 1 tablespoon boiling water and add immediately to the butter mixture. It will foam up instantly. Pour into the well in the dry ingredients and stir with a wooden spoon until well combined.
4 Drop level tablespoons of mixture onto the trays, allowing room for spreading. Gently flatten each biscuit with your fingertips. Bake for 20 minutes, or until just browned, leave on the tray to cool slightly, then transfer to a wire rack to cool completely. Store in an airtight container.

GINGERNUTS

Preparation time: 15 minutes
Total cooking time: 15 minutes
Makes 50

2 cups (250 g/8 oz) plain flour
1/2 teaspoon bicarbonate of soda
1 tablespoon ground ginger
1/2 teaspoon mixed spice
125 g (4 oz) unsalted butter, chopped
1 cup (185 g/6 oz) soft brown sugar
1/4 cup (60 ml/2 fl oz) boiling water
1 tablespoon golden syrup

1 Preheat the oven to moderate 180°C (350°F/ Gas 4). Line two baking trays with baking paper.
2 Sift the flour, bicarbonate of soda, ginger and mixed spice into a large bowl. Add the butter and sugar and rub into the flour with your fingertips until the mixture resembles fine breadcrumbs.
3 Pour the boiling water into a small heatproof jug, add the golden syrup and stir until dissolved. Add to the flour and mix to a soft dough with a flat-bladed knife.
4 Roll into balls using 2 heaped teaspoons of mixture at a time. Place on the trays, allowing room for spreading, and flatten out slightly with your fingertips. Bake for 15 minutes, or until well-coloured and firm. Cool on the trays for 10 minutes before transferring to a wire rack to cool completely. Repeat with the remaining mixture. When cold, store in an airtight jar.
NOTE: If you want to dress the biscuits up, make icing by combining 2–3 teaspoons lemon juice, 1/2 cup (60 g/2 oz) sifted icing sugar and 10 g (1/4 oz) melted butter in a bowl. Mix until smooth, then spread over the biscuits and allow to set.

Measure level tablespoons of the mixture onto the baking tray, allowing room for spreading.

Spread the chocolate over the tops of the biscuits with a palette knife.

AFGHANS

Preparation time: 20 minutes
Total cooking time: 20 minutes
Makes 25

150 g (5 oz) unsalted butter, softened
1/3 cup (60 g/2 oz) soft brown sugar
1 egg, lightly beaten
1 teaspoon vanilla essence
1 cup (125 g/4 oz) plain flour
2 tablespoons cocoa powder
1/3 cup (30 g/1 oz) desiccated coconut
1 1/2 cups (45 g/1 1/2 oz) lightly crushed
    cornflakes
1/2 cup (90 g/3 oz) dark choc bits

1 Preheat the oven to moderate 180°C (350°F/ Gas 4). Line two baking trays with baking paper.
2 Cream the butter and sugar in a large bowl with electric beaters until light and fluffy. Add the egg and vanilla essence and beat thoroughly.
3 Add the sifted flour and cocoa to the bowl with the coconut and cornflakes. Stir with a metal spoon until the ingredients are just combined. Put level tablespoons of mixture on the trays, allowing room for spreading.

Bake for 20 minutes or until lightly browned, then leave on the tray to cool completely.
4 Place the choc bits in a small heatproof bowl. Bring a saucepan of water to the boil, then remove from the heat. Sit the bowl over the pan, making sure the base of the bowl does not sit in the water. Stir until the chocolate has melted and the mixture is smooth. Spread the biscuits thickly with chocolate and allow to set.

COCONUT MACAROONS

Preheat the oven to warm 160°C (315°F/ Gas 2–3). Line two baking trays with baking paper. Beat 3 egg whites in a dry bowl with electric beaters until soft peaks form. Gradually add 1 1/4 cups (310 g/10 oz) caster sugar, beating constantly until thick and glossy and the sugar has dissolved. Add 1 teaspoon grated lemon rind and 1/2 teaspoon coconut essence and beat until just combined. Add 2 tablespoons sifted cornflour and 3 cups (270 g/9 oz) desiccated coconut and stir gently with a metal spoon. Drop heaped teaspoons onto the trays, about 3 cm (1 1/4 inches) apart. Bake for 15–20 minutes, until golden. Transfer to a wire rack to cool. Repeat with the remaining mixture. Makes 60.

ABOVE: Afghans

STORAGE OF BISCUITS

Biscuits usually have a reasonably high butter, egg and sugar content, making them sweet and moist. Because they are moist, they do not usually have a long shelf life as exposure to moisture makes them soften and go stale quickly. After cooking and cooling completely on a wire rack, store them in an airtight container. Refrigerate if the weather is hot. If a batch lasts long enough in your household before being consumed, you can freeze half of them in an airtight container for up to a month. Layer them in the container between sheets of baking paper. If biscuits have softened, they can be refreshed by placing them, in a single layer on a baking tray, in a warm 160°C (315°F/ Gas 2–3) oven for about 5 minutes. Cool them on a wire rack.

ABOVE: Cornflake cookies

CORNFLAKE COOKIES

Preparation time: 15 minutes
Total cooking time: 20 minutes
Makes 36

★

125 g (4 oz) unsalted butter, softened
3/4 cup (185 g/6 oz) sugar
2 eggs, lightly beaten
1 teaspoon vanilla essence
2 tablespoons currants
1 1/2 cups (135 g/4 1/2 oz) desiccated coconut
1/2 teaspoon bicarbonate of soda
1/2 teaspoon baking powder
2 cups (250 g/8 oz) plain flour
3 cups (90 g/3 oz) cornflakes, lightly crushed

1 Preheat the oven to moderate 180°C (350°F/ Gas 4). Line two baking trays with baking paper.

2 Cream the butter and sugar in a small bowl with electric beaters until light and fluffy. Gradually add the egg, beating thoroughly after each addition. Add the vanilla essence and beat until combined.

3 Transfer the mixture to a large bowl and stir in the currants and coconut. Fold in the sifted bicarbonate of soda, baking powder and flour with a metal spoon and stir until the mixture is almost smooth. Put the cornflakes in a shallow dish, drop level tablespoons of mixture onto the cornflakes and roll into balls. Arrange on the trays, allowing room for spreading.

4 Bake for 15–20 minutes, or until crisp and golden. Cool slightly on the tray, then transfer to a wire rack to cool. When completely cold, store in an airtight container.

NOTE: A mess-free method for crushing cornflakes is to put them in a plastic bag and loosely seal them in. Lightly crush with your hands or use a rolling pin.

FAMILY-STYLE GINGERBREAD PEOPLE

Preparation time: 40 minutes
  + 15 minutes refrigeration
Total cooking time: 10 minutes
Makes 16

125 g (4 oz) unsalted butter, softened
1/3 cup (60 g/2 oz) soft brown sugar
1/4 cup (90 g/3 oz) golden syrup
1 egg, lightly beaten
2 cups (250 g/8 oz) plain flour
1/4 cup (30 g/1 oz) self-raising flour
1 tablespoon ground ginger
1 teaspoon bicarbonate of soda
1 tablespoon currants

Icing

1 egg white
1/2 teaspoon lemon juice
1 1/4 cups (155 g/5 oz) icing sugar, sifted
assorted food colourings

1 Preheat the oven to moderate 180°C (350°F/ Gas 4). Line two baking trays with baking paper.

2 Cream the butter, sugar and golden syrup in a small bowl with electric beaters until light and fluffy. Add the egg gradually, beating well after each addition. Transfer to a large bowl. Sift the dry ingredients onto the butter mixture and mix with a knife until just combined. Combine the dough with well-floured hands. Turn onto a well-floured surface and knead for 1–2 minutes, or until smooth. Roll out the dough on a chopping board, between two sheets of baking paper, to 5 mm (1/4 inch) thick. Refrigerate on the board for 15 minutes to firm.

3 Cut the dough into shapes with a 13 cm (5 inch) gingerbread person cutter. Press the remaining dough together and re-roll. Cut out shapes and place the biscuits on the trays. Place currants as eyes and noses. Bake for 10 minutes, or until lightly browned. Cool completely on the trays.

4 For the icing, beat the egg white with electric beaters in a small, clean, dry bowl until foamy. Gradually add the lemon juice and icing sugar and beat until thick and creamy. Divide the icing among several bowls. Tint the mixture with food colourings and spoon into small paper icing bags. Seal the open ends, snip the tips off the bags and pipe on faces and clothing.

NOTE: When the icing is completely dry, store the biscuits in an airtight container in a cool, dry place for up to three days.

FAMILY-STYLE GINGERBREAD PEOPLE

Mix the dry ingredients into the butter mixture with a knife until just combined.

Cut the dough into shapes with a gingerbread person cutter.

Snip the tip off the end of the piping bag and pipe on faces and clothing.

LEFT: Family-style gingerbread people

TOLLHOUSE COOKIES

Preparation time: 20 minutes
Total cooking time: 10 minutes
Makes 40

180 g (6 oz) unsalted butter, softened
³/4 cup (140 g/4¹/2 oz) soft brown
   sugar
¹/2 cup (125 g/4 oz) sugar
2 eggs, lightly beaten
1 teaspoon vanilla essence
2¹/4 cups (310 g/10 oz) plain flour
1 teaspoon bicarbonate of soda
2 cups (350 g/11 oz) dark chocolate bits
1 cup (100 g/3¹/2 oz) pecans,
   roughly chopped

BELOW: Tollhouse cookies

1 Preheat the oven to moderately hot 190°C (375°F/Gas 5). Line two baking trays with baking paper.
2 Cream the butter and sugars in a large bowl with electric beaters until light and fluffy. Gradually add the egg, beating well after each addition. Stir in the vanilla, then the sifted flour and bicarbonate of soda until just combined. Mix in the chocolate bits and pecans.
3 Drop tablespoons of mixture onto the trays, leaving room for spreading. Bake the cookies for 8– 10 minutes, or until lightly golden. Cool slightly on the trays before transferring to a wire rack to cool completely. When completely cold, store in an airtight container.
NOTE: You can use any nuts such as walnuts, almonds or hazelnuts.

PEANUT BISCUITS

Preparation time: 30 minutes
  + 15 minutes refrigeration
Total cooking time: 20 minutes
Makes 30

185 g (6 oz) unsalted butter, softened
2 cups (370 g/12 oz) soft brown sugar
¹/2 cup (140 g/4¹/2 oz) smooth peanut butter
1 teaspoon vanilla essence
1 egg
1¹/2 cups (185 g/6 oz) plain flour
¹/2 teaspoon baking powder
1¹/4 cups (125 g/4 oz) rolled oats
³/4 cup (120 g/4 oz) raw peanuts

1 Preheat the oven to moderate 180°C (350°F/ Gas 4). Line two baking trays with baking paper.
2 Cream the butter, sugar, peanut butter and vanilla essence in a small bowl with electric beaters until light and fluffy. Add the egg and beat until smooth. Transfer to a large bowl and mix in the combined sifted flour and baking powder. Fold in the oats and peanuts and mix until smooth. Chill for 15 minutes, or until firm.
3 Roll heaped tablespoons of the mixture into balls and place on the trays, leaving room for spreading. Press down gently with a floured fork to make a crisscross pattern. Bake for 15– 20 minutes, or until golden. Cool slightly on the trays before transferring to a wire rack to cool completely. When cold, store in an airtight container.

DIGESTIVE BISCUITS

Preparation time: 15 minutes
 + 1 hour 20 minutes refrigeration
Total cooking time: 12 minutes
Makes 16

★★

125 g (4 oz) unsalted butter, softened
1/3 cup (60 g/2 oz) soft brown sugar
1 tablespoon malt extract
1 egg, lightly beaten
1 cup (125 g/4 oz) plain flour
1 cup (150 g/5 oz) wholemeal plain flour
1/2 cup (35 g/1 1/4 oz) unprocessed bran
1 teaspoon baking powder

1 Line two baking trays with baking paper.
Cream the butter, sugar and malt in a small bowl
with electric beaters until light and fluffy.

Gradually add the egg, beating well after each
addition. Transfer to a large bowl.
2 Sift the flours, bran and baking powder into
a small bowl, returning the husks to the bowl.
Using a large metal spoon, fold in the dry
ingredients in three portions and mix to a firm
dough. Cover and refrigerate for at least 1 hour.
3 Preheat the oven to moderate 180°C (350°F/
Gas 4). Roll out half the dough between two
sheets of baking paper to 5 mm (1/4 inch) thick.
Cut out rounds using a 7 cm (2 3/4 inch) plain
cutter and place the rounds on the trays. Repeat
with the remaining dough and re-roll any scraps.
Refrigerate for 20 minutes to firm.
4 Bake for 12 minutes, or until golden brown
and firm. Leave on the trays to cool slightly
before transferring to a wire rack to cool
completely. When the biscuits are cold, store
in an airtight container.
NOTE: Digestives can be eaten plain but are
delicious buttered or served with cheese. They
can also be drizzled with melted chocolate.

DIGESTIVE BISCUITS
These popular biscuits are
made from a pastry-like
dough, usually using a
coarse flour. Although
their name implies that
your digestion may be
improved if you eat them,
they actually have no
special digestive properties
at all. They are also known
as 'wheatmeal' biscuits.

ABOVE: Digestive biscuits

SCOTTISH SHORTBREAD

Preparation time: 25 minutes
  + 20 minutes refrigeration
Total cooking time: 35 minutes
Makes two large rounds

250 g (8 oz) unsalted butter, softened
1/2 cup (125 g/4 oz) caster sugar
2 cups (250 g/8 oz) plain flour
2/3 cup (115 g/4 oz) rice flour
1 teaspoon sugar, to decorate

1 Preheat the oven to warm 160°C (315°F/ Gas 2–3). Line two baking trays with baking paper. Mark a 20 cm (8 inch) circle on the paper on each tray and turn the paper over.
2 Cream the butter and sugar in a small bowl with electric beaters until light and fluffy. Add the sifted flours and a pinch of salt and mix with a knife, using a cutting action, to form a soft dough. Gather together and divide into 2 portions. Refrigerate in plastic wrap for 20 minutes.
3 Place one dough portion on each tray and press into a round, using the drawn circle as a guide. Pinch and flute the edges decoratively and prick the surface with a fork. Use a sharp knife to mark each circle into twelve segments. Sprinkle with sugar and bake for 30–35 minutes, until firm and pale golden. Cool on the trays. When cold, store in an airtight container.
NOTE: Usually, no liquid is used, but if the mixture is very crumbly, moisten with not more than 1 tablespoon of milk or cream.

GINGER SHORTBREAD

Preparation time: 25 minutes
Total cooking time: 45 minutes
Makes 36

250 g (8 oz) unsalted butter, softened
1/2 cup (60 g/2 oz) icing sugar
2 cups (250 g/8 oz) plain flour
1 teaspoon ground ginger
1/3 cup (75 g/2 1/2 oz) chopped crystallized
  ginger

1 Preheat the oven to slow 150°C (300°F/ Gas 2). Line a 23 cm (9 inch) square tin or a baking tray with baking paper.

2 Cream the butter and sugar in a small bowl with electric beaters until light and fluffy. Sift the flour into the bowl with the ground ginger. Add the chopped ginger and mix with a knife, using a cutting motion, to form a soft dough. Gently gather together and press into the tin, or shape into a round about 1 cm (1/2 inch) thick on a baking tray. Pierce all over with a fork and score into fingers or wedges.
3 Bake for 40–45 minutes, or until lightly golden. While still warm, cut into the fingers or wedges. Cool in the tin or on the tray for about 3 minutes, then transfer to a wire rack to cool completely. When cold, store in an airtight container.

BROWN SUGAR SHORTBREAD

Preparation time: 25 minutes
  + 20 minutes refrigeration
Total cooking time: 20 minutes
Makes 50

250 g (8 oz) unsalted butter, softened
3/4 cup (140 g/4 1/2 oz) soft brown sugar
2 cups (250 g/8 oz) plain flour
1/2 cup (90 g/3 oz) rice flour
1/2 teaspoon mixed spice

1 Preheat the oven to warm 160°C (315°F/ Gas 2–3). Line two baking trays with baking paper.
2 Cream the butter and sugar in a small bowl with electric beaters until light and fluffy. Add the sifted flours, spice and a pinch of salt and mix with a knife, using a cutting action, to a soft dough. Gather together and gently knead for 1 minute. Refrigerate in plastic wrap for 20 minutes.
3 Divide the mixture into four, then gently knead and roll a portion onto a lightly floured surface to a thickness of 5 mm (1/4 inch). Cut out shapes with a 4–5 cm (1 1/2–2 inch) biscuit cutter, or cut into 5 cm (2 inch) rounds. Re-roll the trimmings and repeat the kneading, rolling and cutting with the remaining portions of dough.
4 Place the shortbreads on the trays and bake for 15–20 minutes, or until lightly golden and firm to touch. Remove from the oven and leave on the trays to cool for 2 minutes before transferring to a wire rack to cool completely. When the shortbreads are completely cold, store in an airtight container.

SHORTBREAD
Shortbread has a long Scottish history, where it is eaten especially at New Year. However, it has become a traditional snack at Christmas time in many parts of the world. The name comes from the high butter (shortening) content. The butter when mixed thoroughly with the gluten, the protein content of the flour, has the ability to shorten the flour protein strands and results in a tender melt-in-the-mouth biscuit. Rice flour, semolina or cornflour are often added to help this tenderizing process. The first two add texture as well. Shortbread should not be overcooked and dark. It should be pale and lightly golden. If allowed to brown too much, it will taste of slightly bitter and burnt butter.

OPPOSITE PAGE, FROM TOP: Scottish shortbread; Ginger shortbread; Brown sugar shortbread

2 Cream the butter and icing sugar in a bowl with electric beaters until light and fluffy, then beat in the vanilla essence. Sift in the flour and custard powder and mix with a knife, using a cutting motion, to form a soft dough.
3 Roll level tablespoons of dough into balls (you should have 28) and place on the trays, leaving room for spreading. Flatten slightly with a floured fork. Bake for 20 minutes, or until lightly golden. Cool slightly on the trays before transferring to a wire rack to cool completely.
4 For the passionfruit filling, beat the butter and sugar in a bowl with electric beaters until light and creamy, then beat in the passionfruit pulp. Use to sandwich the biscuits together. Leave to firm before serving.
NOTE: The biscuits will keep for up to four days in an airtight container. You can vary the flavour of the filling. For a coffee flavour, for example, dissolve 2 teaspoons of instant coffee in 2 teaspoons water and add to the butter and sugar mixture. Beat until well combined.

GREEK SHORTBREAD

Preparation time: 40 minutes
Total cooking time: 15 minutes
Makes 38

200 g (6¹/2 oz) unsalted butter, softened
1 cup (125 g/4 oz) icing sugar, sifted
1 teaspoon finely grated orange rind
1 egg
1 egg yolk
2¹/2 cups (310 g/10 oz) plain flour
1¹/2 teaspoons baking powder
1 teaspoon ground cinnamon
250 g (8 oz) blanched almonds, toasted, finely chopped
1 cup (125 g/4 oz) icing sugar, extra, to dust

1 Preheat the oven to warm 160°C (315°F/ Gas 2– 3). Line two baking trays with baking paper.
2 Cream the butter, icing sugar and orange rind in a small bowl with electric beaters until light and fluffy. Add the egg and egg yolk and beat until thoroughly combined. Transfer the mixture to a large bowl.
3 Using a metal spoon, fold in the sifted flour, baking powder, cinnamon and almonds, and mix until well combined.

MELTING MOMENTS

Preparation time: 40 minutes
Total cooking time: 20 minutes
Makes 14

250 g (8 oz) unsalted butter, softened
¹/3 cup (40 g/1¹/4 oz) icing sugar
1 teaspoon vanilla essence
1¹/2 cups (185 g/6 oz) self-raising flour
¹/2 cup (60 g/2 oz) custard powder

Passionfruit filling

60 g (2 oz) unsalted butter
¹/2 cup (60 g/2 oz) icing sugar
1¹/2 tablespoons passionfruit pulp

1 Preheat the oven to moderate 180°C (350°F/ Gas 4). Line two baking trays with baking paper.

ABOVE: Melting moments

4 Shape level tablespoons of mixture into crescent shapes and place on the trays. Bake for 15 minutes, or until lightly golden. Cool on the trays for 5 minutes, then transfer to a wire rack to cool completely. While still warm, dredge with icing sugar. Just before serving, dust heavily again with icing sugar.

NOTE: After dusting the Greek shortbreads heavily with icing sugar, store them in an airtight container. They will keep for a week.

VIENNESE FINGERS

Preparation time: 20 minutes
Total cooking time: 12 minutes
Makes 20

100 g (3¹/₂ oz) unsalted butter, softened
¹/₃ cup (40 g/1¹/₄ oz) icing sugar
2 egg yolks
1¹/₂ teaspoons vanilla essence
1 cup (125 g/4 oz) plain flour
100 g (3¹/₂ oz) dark cooking chocolate, chopped
30 g (1 oz) unsalted butter, extra, for icing

1 Preheat the oven to moderate 180°C (350°F/ Gas 4). Line two baking trays with baking paper.
2 Cream the butter and icing sugar in a small bowl with electric beaters until light and fluffy. Gradually add the egg yolks and vanilla and beat thoroughly. Transfer to a large bowl, then sift in the flour. Using a knife, mix until the ingredients are just combined and the mixture is smooth.
3 Spoon the mixture into a piping bag fitted with a fluted 1 cm (¹/₂ inch) piping nozzle and pipe the mixture into wavy 6 cm (2¹/₂ inch) lengths on the trays. Bake for 12 minutes, or until golden brown. Cool slightly on the trays, then transfer to a wire rack to cool completely.
4 Place the chocolate and extra butter in a small heatproof bowl. Half fill a saucepan with water and bring to the boil, then remove from the heat. Sit the bowl over the pan, making sure the base of the bowl does not sit in the water. Stir occasionally until the chocolate and butter have melted and the mixture is smooth. Dip half of each biscuit into the melted chocolate mixture and leave to set on greaseproof paper or foil. Store in an airtight container for up to two days.
NOTE: To make piping easier, fold down the bag by about 5 cm (2 inches) before spooning the mixture in, then unfold. The top will be clean and easy to twist, thereby stopping the mixture from squirting out the top.

SHORTBREAD SHAPES
Shortbread-type mixtures can be made into a variety of shapes and sizes. A traditional Scottish shortbread is sometimes pressed into a special-purpose wooden mould, usually decorated with a Scottish thistle design. Petticoat shortbread is pressed into a circle and fluted on the edges with your fingers to represent a petticoat edge. The mixture can also be piped, as with the Viennese fingers shown here, or simply rolled and shaped into rounds, triangles, rectangles or squares.

LEFT: Viennese fingers

LANGUES DE CHAT

Preparation time: 25 minutes
Total cooking time: 7 minutes
Makes 24

★ ★

75 g (2¹/₂ oz) unsalted butter, softened
¹/₃ cup (90 g/3 oz) caster sugar
2 egg whites
75 g (2¹/₂ oz) plain flour, sifted

1 Preheat the oven to hot 220°C (425°F/Gas 7). Line two baking trays with baking paper.
2 Cream the butter and sugar in a small bowl with electric beaters until light and fluffy. Whisk the egg whites in a small bowl with a fork until frothy, then gradually add to the butter mixture, beating well after each addition. Lightly fold in the sifted flour and a pinch of salt until well combined.

3 To make even-sized langues de chat draw with a pencil 8 cm (3 inch) wide lines on the baking paper. Turn the paper over. Use the lines as a guide to pipe the mixture, leaving a space for expansion. You will be able to fit two 8 cm (3 inch) lines on each tray and pipe 12 biscuits per tray. If your trays are small, cook in batches. Spoon the mixture into a piping bag fitted with a 1 cm (¹/₂ inch) plain tube and pipe 8 cm (3 inch) lengths onto the trays. Bake for 6– 7 minutes, or until cooked through and lightly brown around the edges. Cool on the trays for 2 minutes, then transfer to a wire rack to cool completely.
NOTE: Langues de chat translates from French as cats' tongues, obviously referring to the shape of the biscuit. These thin, narrow and delicate biscuits are often served with ice creams, sorbets, and other iced or soft desserts such as mousses and sabayons. They are also served as a snack with tea and coffee. They will keep, stored in an airtight container in the refrigerator, for up to a week.

RIGHT: Langues de chat

Use a knife to mix the dry ingredients into the melted butter mixture.

Dip one half of each biscuit into the melted chocolate and place onto a tray lined with baking paper.

LEBKUCHEN

Preparation time: 25 minutes
Total cooking time: 30 minutes
Makes 35

2¹/₃ cups (290 g/10 oz) plain flour

¹/₂ cup (60 g/2 oz) cornflour

2 teaspoons cocoa powder

1 teaspoon mixed spice

1 teaspoon ground cinnamon

¹/₂ teaspoon ground nutmeg

100 g (3¹/₂ oz) unsalted butter, cubed

³/₄ cup (260 g/8 oz) golden syrup

2 tablespoons milk

150 g (5 oz) white chocolate melts

¹/₄ teaspoon mixed spice, extra

1 Preheat the oven to moderate 180°C (350°F/Gas 4). Line two baking trays with baking paper.
2 Sift the flours, cocoa and spices into a large bowl and make a well in the centre.

3 Place the butter, golden syrup and milk in a small saucepan, and stir over low heat until the butter has melted and the mixture is smooth. Remove from the heat and add to the dry ingredients. Using a knife, mix with a cutting motion until the mixture comes together in small beads. Gather together with your hands and turn out onto a sheet of baking paper.
4 Roll the dough out to 7 mm (³/₈ inch) thick. Cut into heart shapes using a 6 cm (2¹/₂ inch) biscuit cutter. Place on the trays and bake for 25 minutes, or until lightly browned. Leave on the trays to cool slightly, then transfer to a wire rack to cool completely.
5 Place the chocolate in a small heatproof bowl. Bring a saucepan of water to the boil, then remove from the heat. Sit the bowl over the pan, making sure the base of the bowl does not touch the water. Stir occasionally until the chocolate has melted.
6 Dip one half of each biscuit into the chocolate and place on a sheet of baking paper until the chocolate has set. Sprinkle with mixed spice. These biscuits can be stored in an airtight container for up to five days.

ABOVE: Lebkuchen

REFRIGERATOR BISCUITS

Preparation time: 30 minutes
+ 30 minutes refrigeration
Total cooking time: 15 minutes
Makes about 60

180 g (6 oz) unsalted butter, softened
1 cup (185 g/6 oz) soft brown sugar
1 teaspoon vanilla essence
1 egg
2¹/4 cups (280 g/9 oz) plain flour
1 teaspoon baking powder

1 Cream the butter and sugar in a small bowl with electric beaters until light and fluffy. Add the vanilla essence and egg and beat until well combined. Transfer to a large bowl and add the sifted flour and baking powder. Using a knife, mix to a soft dough. Gather together, then divide the mixture into two portions.
2 Place one portion of the dough on a sheet of baking paper and press lightly until the dough is 30 cm (12 inches) long and 4 cm (1¹/2 inches) thick. Fold the paper around the dough and roll neatly into a log shape. Twist the edges of the paper to seal. Repeat the process with the other portion. Refrigerate for 30 minutes, or until firm.
3 Preheat the oven to moderate 180°C (350°F/ Gas 4). Line two baking trays with baking paper.
4 Cut the logs into slices about 1 cm (¹/2 inch) thick. Place on the prepared trays, leaving 3 cm (1¹/4 inches) between each slice. Bake for 10– 15 minutes, or until golden. Cool on the trays for 3 minutes before transferring to a wire rack to cool completely. When cold, store in an airtight container.
NOTE: Variations of the basic recipe can be made as suggested.

VARIATIONS:

SPICY FRUIT
Add 1 teaspoon mixed spice and ¹/2 teaspoon ground ginger with the sifted flour. Divide the dough into two, roll one portion out on a sheet of baking paper to a rectangle about 2 mm (¹/8 inch) thick and trim the edges. Refrigerate until just firm. Spread with ¹/2 cup (95 g/3 oz) fruit mince, and then carefully roll up swiss-roll-style. Repeat the process with the other portion of dough. Refrigerate, slice and bake as above.

MOCHA SPIRALS
Divide the dough into two portions. Add 2 teaspoons of cocoa powder to one portion and 2 teaspoons of instant coffee powder to the other and knead each lightly. Divide both doughs in half again. Roll two of the different coloured portions separately to even rectangles about 2 mm (¹/8 inch) thick, and then place one layer on top of the other on a sheet of baking paper. Trim the edges and roll up swiss-roll-style. Repeat with the remaining dough portions. Refrigerate and slice as above.

MAPLE AND PECAN
Add ¹/4 cup (60 ml/2 fl oz) maple syrup to the creamed butter and sugar mixture. Roll the logs in 1 cup (125 g/4 oz) finely chopped pecans before refrigerating. Press a whole nut into the top of each biscuit before baking as above.

MACADAMIA
Add ¹/2 cup (45 g/1¹/2 oz) desiccated coconut and ¹/2 cup (70 g/2¹/4 oz) toasted chopped macadamia nuts with the flour. Using a ruler as a guide, shape the logs into a triangle shape. Refrigerate, slice and bake as above. When the log is cut, the biscuits will be in the shape of triangles.

MARBLED
Replace the brown sugar with caster sugar. Divide the creamed butter and egg mixture into three bowls. Add a few drops of red food colouring to one and 50 g (1³/4 oz) melted dark chocolate, 1 tablespoon cocoa powder and 2 teaspoons milk to another. Leave one plain. Add ³/4 cup (90 g/3 oz) sifted flour and ¹/4 teaspoon baking powder to each bowl. Mix each to a soft dough, divide in half and roll into thin logs. Twist the 3 colours together to create a marbled effect, then shape the combined dough into 2 logs. Refrigerate, slice and bake as above.

VANILLA BEANS OR PODS
These are the seed pod of a climbing orchid plant that is native to South America. The pods are dried and cured and are available at delicatessens. Pure vanilla extract is an aromatic, rich liquid made from the bean. It is very concentrated and should be used sparingly. Good-quality vanilla essence is is also extracted from the vanilla pod but is a thinner liquid. It has a strong flavour and is often used in cookery for convenience. Imitation vanilla essence is a much cheaper synthetic product.

OPPOSITE PAGE:
Refrigerator biscuits, from top: Plain; Spicy fruit; Mocha spirals; Maple and pecan; Macadamia; Marbled

BISCOTTI

Preparation time: 25 minutes
Total cooking time: 50 minutes
Makes 45

★ ★

2 cups (250 g/8 oz) plain flour
1 teaspoon baking powder
1 cup (250 g/8 oz) caster sugar
3 eggs
1 egg yolk
1 teaspoon vanilla essence
1 teaspoon grated orange rind
3/4 cup (110 g/3 1/2 oz) pistachio nuts

1 Preheat the oven to moderate 180°C (350°F/ Gas 4). Line two baking trays with baking paper and lightly dust with flour.
2 Sift the flour and baking powder into a large bowl. Add the sugar and mix well. Make a well in the centre and add 2 whole eggs, the egg yolk, vanilla essence and orange rind. Using a large metal spoon, stir until just combined. Mix in the pistachios. Knead for 2– 3 minutes on a lightly floured surface. The dough will be stiff at first. Sprinkle a little water onto the dough at this stage. Divide the mixture into two portions and roll each into a log about 25 cm (10 inches) long and 8 cm (3 inches) wide. Slightly flatten the tops.
3 Place the logs on the baking trays, allowing room for spreading. Beat the remaining egg and brush over the logs to glaze. Bake for 35 minutes, then remove from the oven.
4 Reduce the oven to slow 150°C (300°F/Gas 2). Allow the logs to cool slightly and cut each into 4 mm (1/4 inch) slices. Place them flat-side-down on the trays and bake for another 8 minutes. Turn them over and cook for 8 minutes, or until slightly coloured and crisp and dry. Transfer to a wire rack to cool. Store in an airtight container.
NOTE: You can make chocolate and macadamia nut biscotti using the same basic recipe. Remove the vanilla and pistachio nuts and replace 1/3 cup (40 g/1 1/4 oz) of the flour with 1/3 cup (40 g/ 1 1/4 oz) sifted cocoa (add to the flour). Stir 1/2 cup (70 g/2 1/4 oz) lightly toasted, roughly chopped macadamia nuts and 1/2 cup (90 g/3 oz) dark chocolate bits into the mixture until just combined. Divide into two portions and roll each into a log 25 x 8 cm (10 x 3 inches). Flatten the tops slightly. Bake and slice as above.

ABOVE: Biscotti

AMARETTI

Preparation time: 15 minutes + 1 hour standing
Total cooking time: 20 minutes
Makes 40

1 tablespoon plain flour
1 tablespoon cornflour
1 teaspoon ground cinnamon
2/3 cup (160 g/5 1/2 oz) caster sugar
1 teaspoon grated lemon rind
1 cup (95 g/3 oz) ground almonds
2 egg whites
1/4 cup (30 g/1 oz) icing sugar

1 Line two baking trays with baking paper. Sift the flour, cornflour, cinnamon and half the caster sugar into a large bowl, then add the lemon rind and ground almonds.

2 Beat the egg whites in a clean, dry bowl with electric beaters until firm peaks form. Gradually add the remaining caster sugar, beating constantly until the mixture is thick and glossy and all the sugar has dissolved. Using a metal spoon, fold the egg white mixture into the dry ingredients and stir until the ingredients are just combined.

3 Roll 2 level teaspoons of mixture at a time with oiled or wetted hands into balls and arrange on the trays, allowing room for spreading. Set the trays aside, uncovered, for 1 hour.

4 Preheat the oven to moderate 180°C (350°F/ Gas 4). Sift icing sugar liberally over the biscuits, then bake for 15– 20 minutes, or until crisp and lightly browned. Transfer to a wire rack and leave to cool completely. These biscuits can be stored in an airtight container for up to two days.

AMARETTI
Amaretti are light crisp Italian biscuits, similar to the macaroon, with an almond flavour. They are an especially good biscuit to accompany coffee but can also be crushed and used as a flavoursome filling for fruits, particularly cored apples and halved stoned peaches. The crushed biscuits are made into a paste with sugar and butter then stuffed into the apples or spooned onto the peaches. The fruit are then baked in a little wine which adds to the flavour.

LEFT: Amaretti

FLORENTINES

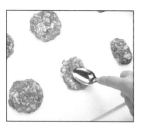

Add the almonds, apricots, glacé cherries, mixed peel and flour to the pan.

Flatten the mixture slightly, then reshape into rounds.

Use a fork to make a wavy pattern on the chocolate before it sets.

FLORENTINES

Preparation time: 25 minutes
Total cooking time: 15 minutes
Makes 12

55 g (2 oz) unsalted butter
1/4 cup (45 g/1 1/2 oz) soft brown sugar
2 teaspoons honey
1/4 cup (25 g/3/4 oz) flaked almonds, roughly chopped
2 tablespoons chopped dried apricots
2 tablespoons chopped glacé cherries
2 tablespoons mixed peel
1/3 cup (40 g/1 1/4 oz) plain flour, sifted
120 g (4 oz) dark chocolate

1 Preheat the oven to moderate 180°C (350°F/ Gas 4). Line two large baking trays with baking paper. Place the butter, sugar and honey in a saucepan and stir over low heat until the butter is melted and all the ingredients are combined. Remove from the heat and add the almonds, apricots, glacé cherries, mixed peel and flour. Mix well.

2 Place level tablespoons of the mixture well apart on the trays. Flatten the biscuits into 5 cm (2 inch) rounds, then gently reshape before cooking.

3 Bake for 10 minutes, or until lightly browned. Cool slightly on the tray, then transfer to a wire rack to cool completely.

4 To melt the dark chocolate, break it up into small pieces and put it in a heatproof bowl. Bring a small saucepan of water to the boil, remove from the heat and place the bowl over the saucepan, making sure the base of the bowl doesn't sit in the water. Stir the chocolate occasionally to ensure even melting. Spread on the base of each florentine and, using a fork, make a wavy pattern on the chocolate before it sets. Let the chocolate set before serving.
NOTE: If preferred, you can use white chocolate to decorate the underneath of the florentines instead of dark chocolate.

RIGHT: Florentines

ALMOND BREAD

Preparation time: 30 minutes + cooling
Total cooking time: 45 minutes
Makes 50

125 g (4 oz) blanched almonds
3 egg whites
1/2 cup (125 g/4 oz) caster sugar
3/4 cup (90 g/3 oz) plain flour

1 Preheat the oven to moderate 180°C (350°F/Gas 4). Lightly grease a 26 x 8 x 4.5 cm (10 1/2 x 3 x 1 3/4 inch) bar tin and line with baking paper. Make sure the paper extends up the two long sides.

2 Spread the almonds on a baking tray and toast in the oven for 2– 3 minutes, then allow to cool. Place the egg whites in a clean, dry bowl and beat until stiff peaks form. Gradually add the sugar, beating constantly until the mixture is thick and glossy and all the sugar has dissolved.

3 Add the sifted flour and almonds. Using a metal spoon, gently fold the ingredients together until combined. Spread into the tin and smooth the surface. Bake for 25 minutes. Remove from the oven and cool completely in the tin.

4 Preheat the oven to warm 160°C (315°F/Gas 2– 3). Using a serrated knife, cut the loaf into 5 mm (1/4 inch) slices and place on baking trays. Bake for 15 minutes, turning once halfway through, or until lightly golden and crisp. Serve almond bread with coffee or a dessert wine.

NOTES: Almond bread will keep for up to a month in an airtight container.

Blanched almonds simply means almonds with their brown skins removed. If you can't buy blanched almonds and so you need to remove the skin, place the nuts in a bowl, cover with boiling water, leave them for 5 minutes then drain and press the softened skin away from the nuts with your fingers.

ALMONDS
These originated in the Middle East and are used extensively in the cuisines of that region for both sweet and savoury dishes. Almonds are now grown world-wide, the largest producer being California. They are used especially in the baking of biscuits and cakes and either chopped or ground in desserts. They also marry beautifully with chicken and trout and are especially good when lightly toasted and served with chocolate and poached fruits.

ABOVE: Almond bread

MERINGUES

Just two ingredients are all that you require to make a basic mixture for meringues. When egg white and sugar are beaten together, then baked, they miraculously turn into crunchy, delicate delights.

BASIC MERINGUE RECIPE

Preheat the oven to slow 150°C (300°F/ Gas 2) and line two biscuit or baking trays with baking paper. Beat 2 egg whites into stiff peaks in a small dry bowl with electric beaters. Add ½ cup (125 g/4 oz) caster sugar, 1 tablespoon at a time, beating well after each addition. Beat until the mixture is thick and glossy and the sugar has dissolved (this will take up to 10 minutes). Spoon into a piping bag and pipe small shapes onto the trays. Bake for 20–25 minutes, or until pale and dry. Turn off the oven, leave the door ajar and cool the meringues in the oven. When cold, store in an airtight jar. Makes 30.

CUSTARD DISCS

Prepare the basic meringue mixture until it is thick and glossy, then beat in 1 tablespoon custard powder. Spoon the mixture into a piping bag with a plain 5 mm (¼ inch) or 1 cm (½ inch) nozzle. Pipe spirals onto trays and bake as above. Dust with icing sugar. Makes 40.

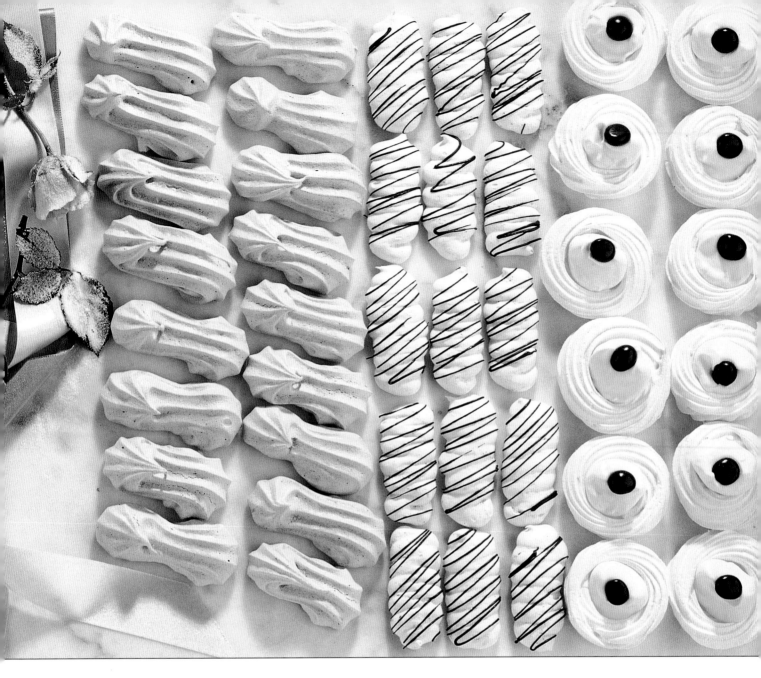

COFFEE KISSES

Prepare the basic meringue mixture until it is thick and glossy, then beat in 2–3 teaspoons instant coffee powder. Spoon the mixture into a piping bag fitted with a small star nozzle and pipe onto the trays. Bake as for the basic recipe. Coffee kisses are delicious if served as is or sandwiched together with 60 g (2 oz) melted chocolate. Makes 30.

CHOCOLATE FINGERS

Prepare the basic meringue mixture until it is thick and glossy, then beat in 1 tablespoon sifted cocoa powder. Spoon the mixture into a piping bag fitted with a plain round nozzle and pipe fine 8 cm (3 inch) lengths onto

lined trays, allowing room for spreading. Bake as for the basic recipe and serve as they are, or drizzled with melted chocolate or lightly dusted with dark cocoa powder combined with a little icing sugar. Makes 40.

HAZELNUT SNAILS

Prepare the basic meringue mixture until it is thick and glossy. Gently beat in 2 tablespoons ground hazelnuts. Spoon the mixture into a piping bag fitted with a plain 1 cm (½ inch) nozzle and pipe in fine short zigzag lengths onto the trays. Bake as for the basic recipe. These can be served lightly dusted with a mixture of icing sugar and ground cinnamon, or drizzled with melted chocolate. Makes 30.

MERINGUE NESTS

Prepare the basic meringue mixture until it is thick and glossy. Spoon into a piping bag fitted with a star nozzle and pipe into nests on the trays. Bake as for the basic recipe. Meringue nests are delicious if filled with whipped cream flavoured with coffee or chocolate liqueur, topped with a chocolate-coated coffee bean. They can also be filled with a chocolate truffle mixture and topped with a slice of strawberry. Makes 40.

LEFT, FROM TOP: Basic meringues; Custard discs; Coffee kisses; Basic meringues ABOVE, FROM LEFT: Chocolate fingers; Hazelnut snails; Meringue nests

BRANDY SNAPS

Drop 3 level teaspoons of the mixture onto the lined trays, leaving plenty of room for spreading.

While the biscuits are still hot, lift off the tray and wrap around the handle of a thin wooden spoon.

Dip both ends of the brandy snaps in the melted chocolate and leave to dry on a foil-lined tray.

BRANDY SNAPS

Preparation time: 30 minutes
Total cooking time: 15 minutes
Makes 15

★★

60 g (2 oz) unsalted butter
2 tablespoons golden syrup
1/3 cup (60 g/2 oz) soft brown sugar
1/4 cup (30 g/1 oz) plain flour
1 1/2 teaspoons ground ginger
60 g (2 oz) dark chocolate, chopped

1 Preheat the oven to moderate 180°C (350°F/ Gas 4). Line two baking trays with baking paper.
2 Place the butter, golden syrup and sugar in a small saucepan and stir over low heat until the butter has melted and the sugar has dissolved. Remove from the heat and add the sifted flour and ground ginger to the saucepan. Use a wooden spoon to stir the mixture until the ingredients are well combined, taking care not to overbeat.

3 Using 3 level teaspoons of the mixture for each brandy snap, drop the mixture onto the trays about 12 cm (5 inches) apart. Bake for 5– 6 minutes, or until lightly browned. Leave the biscuits on the trays for 30 seconds then, while still hot, lift one biscuit off the tray, using a large flat knife or spatula, and wrap around the handle of a thin wooden spoon. Slide the biscuit off the spoon and set aside to cool while you curl the remaining brandy snaps. Repeat to use all the mixture.
4 Put the chopped chocolate in a heatproof bowl. Bring a saucepan of water to the boil, remove from the heat and place the bowl over the water, making sure the base of the bowl doesn't sit in the water. Stir occasionally until the chocolate has melted.
5 Dip both ends of each brandy snap in the melted chocolate and leave to dry on a foil-lined tray.
NOTE: There is a real art to working with these biscuits: work quickly, as they harden and crack when cooled. If they cool too much, return them to the oven for a few minutes to warm, then try again.

ABOVE: Brandy snaps

CHOCOLATE PEPPERMINT CREAMS

Preparation time: 40 minutes
  + 15 minutes refrigeration
Total cooking time: 20 minutes
Makes 20

65 g (2¼ oz) unsalted butter
¼ cup (60 g/2 oz) caster sugar
½ cup (60 g/2 oz) plain flour
⅓ cup (40 g/1¼ oz) self-raising flour
2 tablespoons cocoa powder
2 tablespoons milk

Peppermint cream

1 egg white
1¾ cups (215 g/7 oz) icing sugar, sifted
2– 3 drops peppermint essence or oil, to taste

Chocolate topping

150 g (5 oz) dark chocolate, chopped
150 g (5 oz) dark chocolate melts

1 Preheat the oven to moderate 180°C (350°F/ Gas 4). Line two baking trays with baking paper.
2 Cream the butter and sugar in a small bowl with electric beaters until light and fluffy. Add the sifted flours and cocoa alternately with the milk. Mix with a knife until the mixture forms a soft dough. Turn out onto a floured surface and gather together into a rough ball. Cut the dough in half. Roll each half between two sheets of baking paper to 2 mm (⅛ inch) thick. Slide onto a tray and refrigerate for 15 minutes, or until firm. Cut the dough into rounds using a 4 cm (1½ inch) round cutter, re-rolling the dough scraps and cutting more rounds. Place on the trays, allowing room for spreading. Bake for 10 minutes, or until firm. Transfer to a wire rack to cool completely.
3 For the peppermint cream, put the egg white in a small, clean, dry bowl. Beat in the icing sugar 2 tablespoons at a time, using electric beaters on low speed. Add more icing sugar, if necessary, until a soft dough forms.
4 Turn the dough onto a surface dusted with icing sugar and knead in enough icing sugar so that the dough is not sticky. Knead in the peppermint essence.
5 Roll a teaspoon of peppermint cream into a ball, and flatten slightly. Sandwich between 2 chocolate biscuits, pressing together to spread the peppermint to the edges. Repeat with the remaining filling and chocolate biscuits, keeping the filling covered as you work.
6 For the topping, put the chopped chocolate and the chocolate melts in a heatproof bowl. Half fill a saucepan with water and bring to the boil. Remove from the heat and place the bowl over the pan, making sure it is not touching the water. Stir occasionally until the chocolate is melted. Remove from the heat and allow to cool slightly. Use a fork to dip the biscuits into the chocolate and allow any excess to drain away. Place on a baking paper-lined tray to set.

COCOA POWDER
This is the powder that is ground from the dried solids left when cocoa butter, or fat, is removed from the processed cacao tree seeds. The powder is used extensively in baking. It is usually sifted in with the dry ingredients so it is distributed evenly. Cocoa is sweetened and sold as drinking chocolate. Dutch cocoa is considered the best quality as it has a rich flavour and a dark colour. It is available at some delicatessens.

LEFT: Chocolate peppermint creams

FORTUNE COOKIES

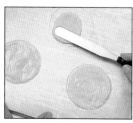

Use a flat-bladed knife to spread mixture over each marked circle.

Fold each cookie in half, then in half again.

BELOW: Fortune cookies

FORTUNE COOKIES

Preparation time: 45 minutes
+ 15 minutes standing
Total cooking time: 50 minutes
Makes 30

★ ★

3 egg whites
1/2 cup (60 g/2 oz) icing sugar, sifted
45 g (1 1/2 oz) unsalted butter, melted
1/2 cup (60 g/2 oz) plain flour

1 Preheat the oven to moderate 180°C (350°F/ Gas 4). Lightly grease a baking tray. Draw three 8 cm (3 inch) circles on a sheet of baking paper, turn over and use to line the tray.
2 Place the egg whites in a clean, dry bowl and whisk until just frothy. Add the icing sugar and butter and stir until smooth. Add the flour, mix until smooth and leave for 15 minutes. Using a flat-bladed knife, spread 2 level teaspoons of mixture over each circle. Bake for 5 minutes, or until slightly brown around the edges.
3 Working quickly, remove from the trays by sliding a flat-bladed knife under each round. Place a written fortune message in each cookie. Fold in half, then in half again, over the edge of a bowl or a palette knife. Keep a tea towel handy to use when folding the cookies. The tray is hot and you need to work fast, so take care not to burn your hands. Cool on a wire rack. Cook the remaining mixture the same way. Make two or three cookies at a time, otherwise they will harden too quickly and break when folding.
NOTE: These were originated by Chinese Americans. Each biscuit contains a message, usually a proverb or horoscope, or more recently a joke. The biscuits are served at the end of a Chinese meal to wish good fortune. They keep for two days in an airtight container.

MONTE CREAMS

Preparation time: 30 minutes
Total cooking time: 20 minutes
Makes 25

★

125 g (4 oz) unsalted butter
1/2 cup (125 g/4 oz) caster sugar
3 tablespoons milk
1 1/2 cups (185 g/6 oz) self-raising flour
1/4 cup (30 g/1 oz) custard powder
1/3 cup (30 g/1 oz) desiccated coconut

Filling

75 g (2 1/2 oz) unsalted butter, softened
2/3 cup (85 g/3 oz) icing sugar
2 teaspoons milk
1/3 cup (105 g/3 1/2 oz) strawberry jam

1 Preheat the oven to moderate 180°C (350°F/ Gas 4). Line two baking trays with baking paper.
2 Cream the butter and sugar in a small bowl with electric beaters until light and fluffy. Add the milk and beat until combined. Sift the flour and custard powder and add to the bowl with the coconut. Mix to form a soft dough.
3 Roll two teaspoons of the mixture into balls. Place on the trays and press with a fork. Dip the fork in the custard powder occasionally to prevent it from sticking. Bake for 15–20 minutes, or until just golden. Transfer to a wire rack to cool completely before filling.
4 For the filling, beat the butter and icing sugar in a small bowl with electric beaters until light and creamy. Beat in the milk. Spread one biscuit with half a teaspoon of the filling and one with half a teaspoon of jam, then press them together.
NOTE: These will keep for up to four days in an airtight container.

FIG NEWTONS

Preparation time: 30 minutes
+ 2 hours refrigeration
Total cooking time: 1 hour 10 minutes
Makes 24

 ✷ ✷

75 g (2¹/₂ oz) unsalted butter, softened
2 tablespoons sour cream
³/₄ cup (140 g/4¹/₂ oz) soft brown sugar
1 teaspoon vanilla essence
2 eggs, lightly beaten
3 cups (375 g/12 oz) plain flour
2 teaspoons baking powder
¹/₂ teaspoon bicarbonate of soda
¹/₂ teaspoon ground cinnamon

Fig filling

370 g (12 oz) dried figs, stems removed
¹/₃ cup (90 g/3 oz) caster sugar
1 teaspoon grated lemon rind

1 Cream the butter, sour cream, sugar and vanilla in a small bowl with electric beaters until light and fluffy. Gradually add the egg, beating well after each addition. The mixture will appear curdled.

2 Transfer to a large bowl and fold in the combined sifted flour, baking powder, bicarbonate of soda and cinnamon. The mixture will be very soft. Wrap in a sheet of floured plastic wrap and refrigerate for at least 2 hours.

3 For the filling, place the figs and 1 cup (250 ml/8 fl oz) water in a large saucepan. Bring to the boil, then reduce the heat and simmer, covered, for 30 minutes, or until the figs have softened. Add the sugar and lemon rind, and simmer for another 10 minutes. Cool, then drain off any remaining syrup and chop the figs in a food processor until smooth. Set aside to cool.

4 Preheat the oven to moderate 180°C (350°F/ Gas 4). Line a baking tray with baking paper. Divide the dough into three portions. Refrigerate two and roll the other portion on a floured surface to measure 12 x 28 cm (5 x 11 inches). Spread a third of the filling lengthways along one half of the pastry, leaving a 2 cm (³/₄ inch) border on that side and on the ends. Brush the border with water. Fold the unfilled half over the filling and press around the edges. Trim 1 cm (¹/₂ inch) from the side and ends to neaten. Lift onto the tray and refrigerate. Repeat with the remaining portions of dough. Lay the three rolls on the tray, allowing room for spreading. Bake for 25 minutes, or until cooked and golden. Cool for 5 minutes on a wire rack, then trim the ends and cut each roll at 2 cm (³/₄ inch) intervals. When cold, store in an airtight container.

FIG NEWTONS

Spread the prepared fig filling lengthways along one side of the pastry leaving a border.

Place the three rolls on a large baking tray lined with baking paper.

ABOVE: Fig newtons

123

GRAHAM CRACKERS

Preparation time: 25 minutes
+ 30 minutes refrigeration
Total cooking time: 10 minutes
Makes 12

2¹/₃ cups (350 g/11 oz) wholemeal plain flour
¹/₂ cup (60 g/2 oz) cornflour
¹/₄ cup (60 g/2 oz) caster sugar
150 g (5 oz) butter
³/₄ cup (185 ml/6 fl oz) cream

1 Sift the flours into a bowl, stir in the sugar and ¹/₂ teaspoon salt. Rub in the butter with your fingertips until the mixture resembles breadcrumbs. Mix in the cream with a knife, using a cutting motion, to make a pliable dough.
2 Gather the dough together and shape into a disc. Wrap in plastic wrap and refrigerate for 30 minutes.
3 Preheat the oven to moderately hot 200°C (400°F/Gas 6). Line two baking trays with baking paper.
4 Roll out the dough to a rectangle measuring 30 x 24 cm (12 x 9 inches). Cut the dough into 12 rectangles with a pastry wheel or sharp knife. Place the rectangles on the baking trays, allowing a little room for spreading.
5 Bake for 7–10 minutes, or until firm and golden brown. Leave to cool on the trays for 2–3 minutes, then transfer to a wire rack to cool completely. When the crackers are cold, store in an airtight container.

OATCAKES

Preparation time: 15 minutes
Total cooking time: 25 minutes
Makes 14

2 cups (250 g/8 oz) medium oatmeal
¹/₂ teaspoon baking powder
2 teaspoons soft brown sugar
60 g (2 oz) butter, melted
oatmeal, extra, for sprinkling

1 Preheat the oven to moderate 180°C (350°F/Gas 4). Line two baking trays with baking paper.
2 Combine the oatmeal, baking powder, sugar and a pinch of salt in a large bowl. Make a well in the centre and add the melted butter and ¹/₂ cup (125 ml/4 fl oz) hot water.
3 Using a flat-bladed knife, mix to form a dough. Gather the dough together and turn onto a surface lightly sprinkled with extra oatmeal, then press into a flattish round.
4 Roll the dough out to a thickness of 5 mm (¹/₄ inch), sprinkling with extra oatmeal. Cut the dough into 6 cm (2¹/₂ inch) rounds with a biscuit cutter. Place on the baking trays, leaving room for spreading. Bake for 25 minutes, or until lightly golden. Allow to cool on the trays for 5 minutes before transferring to a wire rack to cool completely. When the oatcakes are cold, store them in an airtight container.

CHEESE BISCUITS

Preparation time: 10 minutes
+ 30 minutes freezing
Total cooking time: 10 minutes
Makes 45

125 g (4 oz) butter, chopped
125 g (4 oz) Cheddar, grated
2 tablespoons grated Parmesan
1 cup (125 g/4 oz) plain flour
2 tablespoons self-raising flour
pinch of cayenne pepper
2 teaspoons lemon juice

1 Place the butter, cheeses, flours, cayenne pepper, lemon juice and a pinch of salt in a food processor. Process for 60 seconds, or until the mixture comes together and forms a ball.
2 Gently knead the mixture for 2 minutes on a lightly floured surface. Form the dough into a sausage shape about 3 cm (1¹/₄ inches) in diameter. Wrap in plastic wrap, then in foil and freeze for 30 minutes. Remove and leave at room temperature for 5 minutes.
3 Preheat the oven to moderate 180°C (350°F/Gas 4). Line two baking trays with baking paper.
4 Slice the dough into thin slices, about 3 mm (¹/₈ inch) thick, and place on the trays, allowing a little room for spreading. Bake the biscuits for 9–10 minutes, or until golden. Allow to cool on the trays.
NOTE: Cheese biscuits are best eaten on the day of baking. They are delicious served as an accompaniment to drinks at a cocktail party.

GRAHAM CRACKERS
In the United States the word 'graham' means any bread, biscuit or cake that is made from wholemeal flour, including the bran. Graham flour was developed and promoted by Dr Sylvester Graham in the early nineteenth century. He was an ardent advocate of unrefined foods and vegetarianism. Graham bread, Graham crackers and Graham rusks all denote that the baked products have been made with wholemeal or wholewheat flour.

OPPOSITE PAGE:
Cheese biscuits (top);
Graham crackers

TWO-SEED CRACKERS

Preparation time: 20 minutes
Total cooking time: 25 minutes
Makes 30

2 cups (250 g/8 oz) plain flour

1 teaspoon baking powder

2 tablespoons poppy seeds

2 tablespoons sesame seeds

60 g (2 oz) butter, chilled and chopped

1/2 cup (125 ml/4 fl oz) iced water

1 Preheat the oven to moderate 180°C (350°F/ Gas 4). Line two baking trays with baking paper.
2 Sift the flour, baking powder and 1/2 teaspoon salt into a bowl. Stir in the seeds and some pepper. Rub the butter into the flour with your fingertips until the mixture resembles fine breadcrumbs.
3 Make a well in the centre and add almost all the water. Mix together with a flat-bladed knife using a cutting action, adding the remaining water if necessary, until the mixture comes together in soft beads. Gather together into a rough ball. Handle the dough gently and do not knead it at any stage. Divide the dough into two portions. Place one portion between two sheets

ABOVE: Two-seed crackers

of baking paper and roll out to 2 mm (1/8 inch) thick. Cover the other portion with plastic wrap.
4 Using a 6 cm (2 1/2 inch) round cutter, cut rounds from the dough. Prick all over with a fork and transfer to the trays. Repeat with the remaining dough. Pile any dough trimmings together (do not knead) and gently re-roll. Cut out more rounds. Bake for 20– 25 minutes, or until golden. Cool completely on a wire rack.
NOTE: Store in an airtight container for up to five days. Can be re-crisped in a moderate oven for 2– 3 minutes, then allowed to cool.

WATER CRACKERS

Preparation time: 15 minutes
Total cooking time: 10 minutes
Makes 50

2 cups (250 g/8 oz) self-raising flour

50 g (2 oz) unsalted butter, chopped

1 Preheat the oven to hot 220°C (425°F/Gas 7). Line two baking trays with baking paper.
2 Sift the flour and 1/2 teaspoon salt into a bowl. Cut the butter into the flour with a knife, and

then rub in with your fingertips. Knead in enough water (you may need about ³/4 cup/185 ml/ 6 fl oz) to make a fairly stiff dough. Lightly knead the dough for a few minutes until smooth.

3 On a large floured board, roll the dough out until it is as thin as a wafer. Cut into large rounds (you can cut a small hole in the centre of each for decoration) and bake batches for 8– 10 minutes each batch, or until the biscuits bubble and brown. Transfer to a wire rack to cool completely.

CRISPBREAD

Preparation time: 20 minutes
  + 30 minutes standing
Total cooking time: 30 minutes
Makes 24

1 cup (250 ml/8 fl oz) lukewarm milk
2 x 7 g (¹/4 oz) sachets dried yeast
¹/4 teaspoon dried fennel seeds
250 g (8 oz) stoneground flour
200 g (6¹/2 oz) coarse rye meal

1 Line two baking trays with baking paper. Put the milk in a bowl, add the yeast and stir until dissolved. Leave in a warm place for 10 minutes, or until bubbles appear on the surface. The mixture should be frothy and slightly increased in volume. If your yeast doesn't foam, it is dead and you will have to discard it and start again.

2 Mix the fennel, flour, rye meal and 1 teaspoon salt in a bowl. Make a well in the centre and add the yeast mixture. Gather together and knead on a floured surface for 5 minutes, adding a little water if necessary. Divide into four portions.

3 Divide each portion into six pieces and shape each into a ball. Cover and leave in a warm place for 20 minutes, or until doubled in size.

4 Preheat the oven to moderate 180°C (350°F/ Gas 4). Roll out each ball of dough to make a circle about 13 cm (5 inches) in diameter. Cut out the centre of each circle with a round 2 cm (³/4 inch) biscuit cutter. Discard the centre, then prick each crispbread with a fork and place on a baking tray. You will have to cook the crispbread in batches, so just fit as many as you can on a tray. Bake each batch for 10 minutes, or until firm and dry and slightly coloured. When cold, store in an airtight container.

CRISPBREAD

Mix the dry ingredients, make a well in the centre and add the yeast, then gather the mixture together.

Shape small portions of the mixture into a ball and leave in a warm place, until doubled in size.

LEFT: Crispbread

SLICES

Crunchy, gooey, sticky, fruity, spongy, fudgy, chewy, creamy, nutty, chocolaty — whatever your culinary craving, a slice can satisfy it simply and completely. Loved by children and grown-ups alike, slices grow up with you, becoming more sophisticated as your tastes develop (or not, as the case may be!). The beauty of slices is that they can be as simple or as richly exotic as you like. Easily transportable, they can accompany you to school, to work, to a picnic, or even as far as the sitting room with a cup of coffee and a good book. Cut a piece as little or as large as you like and indulge yourself.

STRAWBERRIES

These delicious red vine fruits are related to the rose, which accounts for the beautiful fragrant aroma and flavour. The strawberry is unusual in that the seeds or small pips are on the outside of the fruit rather than in the centre as with other fruits. When at the height of the season, in summer, they are often served just as they are or sweetened and eaten with cream or ice cream. Strawberries make beautiful tart and cake fillings and, of course, jam. Sweetened and puréed, they make a simple sauce called a coulis.

COCONUT JAM SLICE

Preparation time: 30 minutes
  + 10 minutes refrigeration
Total cooking time: 45 minutes
Makes 20 pieces

1 cup (125 g/4 oz) plain flour
1/2 cup (60 g/2 oz) self-raising flour
150 g (5 oz) unsalted butter, cubed
1/2 cup (60 g/2 oz) icing sugar
1 egg yolk
1/2 cup (150 g/5 oz) strawberry jam
1/2 cup (125 g/4 oz) caster sugar
3 eggs
3 cups (270 g/9 oz) desiccated coconut

1 Preheat the oven to moderate 180°C (350°F/ Gas 4). Lightly grease a shallow 23 cm (9 inch) square tin and line with baking paper, leaving the paper hanging over on two opposite sides. This makes it easy to lift the cooked slice out of the tin.

2 Put the flours, butter and icing sugar together in a food processor and mix in short bursts until the mixture is fine and crumbly. Add the egg yolk and process until the mixture just comes together. Alternatively, put the flour and icing sugar in a bowl and rub in the butter with your fingertips until the mixture is fine and crumbly. Mix in the egg yolk and then gather together. Press the dough into the tin and refrigerate for 10 minutes.

3 Bake for 15 minutes, or until golden brown. Allow to cool, then spread the jam evenly over the pastry.

4 Beat the caster sugar and eggs together in a small bowl until creamy, then stir in the coconut. Spread the mixture over the jam, gently pressing down with the back of a spoon. Bake for another 25–30 minutes, or until lightly golden. Leave to cool in the tin, then lift the slice out, using the paper as handles. Cut the slice into pieces. When cold, store in an airtight container for up to four days.

RIGHT: Coconut jam slice

CHOCOLATE PEPPERMINT SLICE

Preparation time: 25 minutes
  + 30 minutes refrigeration
Total cooking time: 20 minutes
Makes 24 pieces

²/₃ cup (90 g/3 oz) self-raising flour

¹/₄ cup (30 g/1 oz) cocoa powder

¹/₂ cup (45 g/1¹/₂ oz) desiccated coconut

¹/₄ cup (60 g/2 oz) sugar

140 g (4¹/₂ oz) unsalted butter, melted

1 egg, lightly beaten

Peppermint filling

1¹/₂ cups (185 g/6 oz) icing sugar, sifted

30 g (1 oz) Copha (white vegetable shortening), melted

2 tablespoons milk

¹/₂ teaspoon peppermint essence

Chocolate topping

185 g (6 oz) dark chocolate, chopped

30 g (1 oz) Copha (white vegetable shortening)

1 Preheat the oven to moderate 180°C (350°F/ Gas 4). Lightly grease a shallow tin measuring 18 x 28 cm (7 x 11 inches) and line with baking paper, leaving the paper hanging over on the two long sides. This makes it easy to lift the cooked slice out of the tin.

2 Sift the flour and cocoa into a bowl. Stir in the coconut and sugar, then add the butter and egg and mix well. Press the mixture firmly into the tin. Bake for 15 minutes, then press down with the back of a spoon and leave to cool.

3 For the peppermint filling, sift the icing sugar into a bowl. Stir in the Copha, milk and peppermint essence. Spread over the base and refrigerate for 5– 10 minutes, or until firm.

4 For the chocolate topping, put the chocolate and Copha in a heatproof bowl. Half fill a saucepan with water, bring to the boil, then remove from the heat. Sit the bowl over the saucepan, making sure the base of the bowl does not touch the water. Stir occasionally until the chocolate and Copha have melted and combined. Spread evenly over the filling. Refrigerate the slice for 20 minutes, or until the chocolate topping is firm. Carefully lift the slice from the tin, using the paper as handles. Cut into pieces with a warm knife to give clean edges. Store in an airtight container in the refrigerator.

PEPPERMINT ESSENCE
Peppermint is a herb belonging to the mint family. The herb can be used fresh and as a herb tea. In baking, the oil that is extracted from the peppermint is used. This comes from its leaves and flowers and is sold as peppermint essence. Its concentrated flavour is added in small amounts to confectionery, chocolates, chocolate fillings and icings. The liqueur, crème de menthe, is flavoured with the oil.

ABOVE: Chocolate peppermint slice

VANILLA SLICE

Preparation time: 40 minutes
Total cooking time: 15 minutes
Makes 9 pieces

★ ★

500 g (1 lb) home-made or bought
   puff pastry (see page 150)
1 cup (250 g/8 oz) caster sugar
3/4 cup (90 g/3 oz) cornflour
1/2 cup (60 g/2 oz) custard powder
1 litre cream
60 g (2 oz) unsalted butter, cubed
2 teaspoons vanilla essence
3 egg yolks

Icing

1 1/2 cups (185 g/6 oz) icing sugar
1/4 cup (60 g/2 oz) passionfruit pulp
15 g (1/2 oz) unsalted butter, melted

1 Preheat the oven to hot 210°C (415°F/
Gas 6– 7). Grease two baking trays with oil. Line
the base and side of a shallow 23 cm (9 inch)
square cake tin with foil, leaving the foil hanging

over on two opposite sides (the foil makes this
heavy slice easy to lift from the tin). Divide
the pastry in half, roll each piece to a 25 cm
(10 inch) square about 3 mm (1/8 inch) thick
and place each one on a prepared tray. Prick
all over with a fork and bake for 8 minutes,
or until golden. Trim each pastry sheet to a
23 cm (9 inch) square. Place one sheet top-side-
down in the cake tin.

2 Combine the sugar, cornflour and custard
powder in a saucepan. Gradually add the cream
and stir until smooth. Place over medium heat
and stir constantly for 2 minutes, or until the
mixture boils and thickens. Add the butter and
vanilla essence and stir until smooth. Remove
from the heat and whisk in the egg yolks until
combined. Spread the custard over the pastry
in the tin and cover with the remaining pastry,
top-side-down. Allow to cool.

3 For the icing, combine the icing sugar,
passionfruit pulp and butter in a small bowl
and stir together until smooth.

4 Lift the slice out, using the foil as handles,
spread the icing over the top and leave it to
set before carefully cutting into squares with
a serrated knife.

ABOVE: Vanilla slice

APPLE CUSTARD STREUSEL SLICE

Preparation time: 30 minutes
  + 20 minutes refrigeration
Total cooking time: 1 hour 15 minutes
Makes 16 pieces

1¼ cups (155 g/5 oz) plain flour

1 tablespoon caster sugar

80 g (2¾ oz) unsalted butter, melted
  and cooled

1 egg yolk

Apple custard topping

3 green apples

20 g (¾ oz) unsalted butter

4 tablespoons caster sugar

2 eggs

¾ cup (185 ml/6 fl oz) thick (double) cream

1 teaspoon vanilla essence

Crumble topping

½ cup (60 g/2 oz) plain flour

2 tablespoons dark brown sugar

⅓ cup (40 g/1¼ oz) finely chopped walnuts

60 g (2 oz) unsalted butter, cubed

1 Lightly grease an 18 x 28 cm (7 x 11 inch) shallow tin and line with baking paper, leaving the paper hanging over on the two long sides.
2 Sift the flour and sugar into a bowl. Add the butter, egg yolk and 2– 3 tablespoons water and mix to form a ball. Roll out the dough between two sheets of baking paper and fit in the base of the tin. Refrigerate for 20 minutes. Preheat the oven to moderately hot 190°C (375°F/Gas 5).
3 Line the pastry with baking paper, fill with baking beads or uncooked rice and bake for 15 minutes. Remove the paper and rice, reduce the oven to 180°C (350°F/Gas 4) and bake the pastry for 5 minutes, or until golden. Cool.
4 Peel, core and chop the apples and place in a saucepan with the butter, half the sugar and 2 tablespoons water. Cover and cook over low heat for 15 minutes, or until soft. Uncover and simmer for another 5 minutes, to reduce the liquid. Use a wooden spoon to break down the apples until they have a smooth texture. Cool.
5 Whisk together the eggs, cream, remaining sugar and vanilla essence. Spread the cooled apple over the pastry, then carefully pour on the cream mixture. Bake for 20 minutes, or until the custard has half set.
6 For the crumble, mix the flour, sugar and walnuts and rub in the butter until the mixture is crumbly. Sprinkle over the custard and bake for 15 minutes. Cool in the tin before slicing. These will refrigerate for up to a week.

STREUSEL
This is an American term for a crumble topping, which usually consists of flour or breadcrumbs with sugar and spices, on baked cakes and desserts. The butter is rubbed in until it forms a rough crumble. Often chopped nuts or rolled oats are added for extra flavour and texture. The adaptation came from a European yeast cake, called a Streusel cake, which has a spiced crumble mix baked onto it.

LEFT: Apple custard streusel slice

CARAMEL SLICE

Preparation time: 30 minutes
  + 20 minutes refrigeration
Total cooking time: 30 minutes
Makes 20 pieces

1 cup (125 g/4 oz) self-raising flour
1 cup (90 g/3 oz) desiccated coconut
½ cup (125 g/4 oz) caster sugar
125 g (4 oz) unsalted butter, melted

Caramel filling

400 g (13 oz) can sweetened condensed
  milk
20 g (¾ oz) unsalted butter
2 tablespoons golden syrup

Chocolate topping

150 g (5 oz) dark chocolate, chopped
20 g (¾ oz) Copha (white vegetable
  shortening)

1 Preheat the oven to moderate 180°C (350°F/ Gas 4). Lightly grease an 18 x 28 cm (7 x 11 inch) shallow tin and line with baking paper, leaving the paper hanging over on the two long sides.
2 Sift the flour into a bowl, then mix in the coconut and sugar. Add the melted butter to the bowl and stir through thoroughly. Press firmly into the tin and bake for 12– 15 minutes, or until lightly coloured. Allow to cool.
3 For the caramel filling, place all the ingredients in a small saucepan over low heat. Slowly bring to the boil, stirring constantly, then boil gently, stirring, for 4– 5 minutes, or until lightly caramelized. Quickly pour over the cooled base, spreading evenly. Bake for 10 minutes, then set aside to cool.
4 For the chocolate topping, place the dark chocolate and Copha in a heatproof bowl. Half fill a saucepan with water and bring to the boil. Remove from the heat and sit the bowl over the saucepan, making sure the bowl does not sit in the water. Stir occasionally until the chocolate and Copha have melted. Spread over the caramel. You can make a decorative effect with the side of a knife. Refrigerate for 20 minutes, or until set. Lift the slice from the tin, using the paper as handles. Cut into pieces with a hot, dry knife.

CONDENSED MILK
Condensed milk is sold canned or in a tube. It is a sweetened evaporated milk. The whole full-fat milk is evaporated by about forty per cent and then about forty per cent sugar is added. The high density of sugar acts as a preservative. Condensed milk will keep indefinitely but, after opening, it should be refrigerated. It is used to sweeten desserts, cakes, slices and sauces, and for making caramels.

RIGHT: Caramel slice

MUESLI SLICE

Preparation time: 20 minutes
  + 2 hours refrigeration
Total cooking time: 50 minutes
Makes 18 pieces

250 g (8 oz) unsalted butter, cubed

1 cup (250 g/8 oz) caster sugar

2 tablespoons honey

2¹/2 cups (250 g/8 oz) rolled oats

³/4 cup (65 g/2¹/4 oz) desiccated coconut

1 cup (30 g/1 oz) cornflakes, lightly crushed

¹/2 cup (45 g/1¹/2 oz) flaked almonds

1 teaspoon mixed spice

¹/2 cup (45 g/1¹/2 oz) finely chopped dried apricots

1 cup (185 g/6 oz) dried mixed fruit

1 Preheat the oven to warm 160°C (315°F/ Gas 2– 3). Lightly grease a shallow tin measuring 20 x 30 cm (8 x 12 inches) and line with baking paper, leaving the paper hanging over on the two long sides. This makes it easy to lift the cooked slice out of the tin.

2 Put the butter, sugar and honey in a small saucepan and stir over low heat for 5 minutes, or until the butter has melted and the sugar has dissolved.

3 Mix the remaining ingredients together in a bowl and make a well in the centre. Pour in the butter mixture and stir well, then press into the tin. Bake for 45 minutes, or until golden. Cool completely in the tin, then refrigerate for 2 hours, to firm.

4 Lift the slice from the tin, using the paper as handles, before cutting into pieces. This slice will keep for up to three days stored in an airtight container.

MIXED SPICE
This is a blend of freshly ground spices, usually including cloves, nutmeg, cinnamon and allspice, and sometimes ginger. It adds a lightly spiced flavour to puddings, spice cakes, biscuits and fruit cakes. It is often added when apples are being cooked as they seem to complement each other very well. As with all spices, mixed spice should be bought in small amounts and kept in an airtight container in a dark place. Spices can be frozen for up to six months.

ABOVE: Muesli slice

CHOCOLATE BROWNIES

Preparation time: 20 minutes
+ 2 hours refrigeration
Total cooking time: 50 minutes
Makes 24 pieces

1/3 cup (40 g/1 1/4 oz) plain flour
1/2 cup (60 g/2 oz) cocoa powder
2 cups (500 g/1 lb) sugar
1 cup (125 g/4 oz) chopped pecans or walnuts
250 g (8 oz) good-quality dark chocolate, chopped into small pieces
250 g (8 oz) unsalted butter, melted
2 teaspoons vanilla essence
4 eggs, lightly beaten

1 Preheat the oven to moderate 180°C (350°F/ Gas 4). Lightly grease a 20 x 30 cm (8 x 12 inch) cake tin and line with baking paper, leaving the paper hanging over on the two long sides.
2 Sift the flour and cocoa into a bowl and add the sugar, nuts and chocolate. Mix together and make a well in the centre.
3 Pour the butter into the dry ingredients with the vanilla and eggs and mix well. Pour into the tin, smooth the surface and bake for 50 minutes (the mixture will still be a bit soft on the inside). Chill for at least 2 hours before lifting out, using the paper as handles, and cutting into pieces.

MACADAMIA BLONDIES

Preparation time: 20 minutes
Total cooking time: 45 minutes
Makes 25 pieces

100 g (3 1/2 oz) unsalted butter, cubed
100 g (3 1/2 oz) white chocolate, chopped
1/2 cup (125 g/4 oz) caster sugar
2 eggs, lightly beaten
1 teaspoon vanilla essence
1 cup (125 g/4 oz) self-raising flour
1/2 cup (80 g/2 3/4 oz) macadamia nuts, roughly chopped

1 Preheat the oven to moderate 180°C (350°F/ Gas 4). Lightly grease a 20 cm (8 inch) square tin and line with baking paper, leaving the paper hanging over on two opposite sides.

2 Place the butter and white chocolate in a heatproof bowl. Half fill a saucepan with water and bring to the boil. Remove from the heat. Place the bowl over the saucepan, making sure the base of the bowl does not sit in the water. Stir occasionally until the butter and chocolate have melted and are smooth.
3 Add the caster sugar to the bowl and gradually stir in the eggs. Add the vanilla, fold in the flour and macadamia nuts, then pour into the tin. Bake for 35– 40 minutes. If the top starts to brown too quickly, cover lightly with a sheet of foil. When cooked, cool in the tin before lifting out, using the paper as handles, and cutting into squares. Can be drizzled with melted white chocolate.

JAFFA TRIPLE-CHOC BROWNIES

Preparation time: 20 minutes
Total cooking time: 45 minutes
Makes 25 pieces

125 g (4 oz) unsalted butter, cubed
350 g (11 oz) dark chocolate, roughly chopped
1 cup (185 g/6 oz) soft brown sugar
3 eggs
2 teaspoons grated orange rind
1 cup (125 g/4 oz) plain flour
1/4 cup (30 g/1 oz) cocoa powder
100 g (3 1/2 oz) milk chocolate bits
100 g (3 1/2 oz) white chocolate bits

1 Preheat the oven to moderate 180°C (350°F/ Gas 4). Lightly grease a 23 cm (9 inch) square shallow tin and line with baking paper, leaving the paper hanging over on two opposite sides.
2 Place the butter and 250 g (8 oz) of the dark chocolate in a heatproof bowl. Half fill a saucepan with water, bring to the boil, then remove from the heat. Sit the bowl over the saucepan, making sure the base of the bowl does not sit in the water. Stir occasionally until the butter and chocolate have melted. Cool.
3 Beat the sugar, eggs and rind in a bowl until thick and fluffy. Fold in the chocolate mixture.
4 Sift the flour and cocoa into a bowl, then stir into the chocolate mixture. Stir in the remaining dark chocolate and all the chocolate bits. Spread into the tin and bake for 40 minutes, or until just cooked. Cool in the tin before lifting out, using the paper as handles, and cutting into squares. Can be drizzled with melted dark chocolate.

MACADAMIAS
These are also called Queensland nuts because they are native to north-east Australia, although the Hawaiians cultivated the seeds and have become large producers of the nuts. The creamy nut is enclosed in an extremely hard shell, which needs to be cracked with a hammer or special-purpose clamp. The nut can be used raw or roasted and is usually chopped. It is used in the baking of brownies, cakes and biscuits. Buy unsalted nuts for cooking.

OPPOSITE PAGE:
Chocolate brownies;
Macadamia blondies;
Jaffa triple-choc brownies

BERRIES

There are many berries which are wonderful to eat ripe off the vine but have multiple uses in baking. The most common varieties, depending on the region and climate, are sold from spring to early autumn. They include blackberries, raspberries, strawberries, blueberries, mulberries, cranberries, currants and gooseberries. Berries are used a lot in baking and are made into desserts such as pies, puddings and tarts, as well as being used to flavour slices, cakes, muffins, friands and biscuits.

ABOVE: Berry almond slice

BERRY ALMOND SLICE

Preparation time: 25 minutes
Total cooking time: 1 hour 15 minutes
Makes 15 pieces

1 sheet ready-rolled puff pastry, thawed
150 g (5 oz) unsalted butter
3/4 cup (185 g/6 oz) caster sugar
3 eggs, lightly beaten
2 tablespoons grated lemon rind
2/3 cup (125 g/4 oz) ground almonds
2 tablespoons plain flour
150 g (5 oz) raspberries
150 g (5 oz) blackberries
icing sugar, for dusting

1 Preheat the oven to moderately hot 200°C (400°F/Gas 6). Lightly grease a 23 cm (9 inch) square shallow tin and line with baking paper, leaving the paper hanging over on two opposite sides.

2 Place the pastry on a baking tray lined with baking paper. Prick the pastry all over with a fork and bake for 15 minutes, or until golden. Ease into the tin, trimming the edges if necessary. Reduce the oven to moderate 180°C (350°F/Gas 4).

3 Cream the butter and sugar in a small bowl with electric beaters until light and fluffy. Gradually add the egg, beating after every addition, then the lemon rind. Fold in the almonds and flour, then spread the mixture over the pastry.

4 Scatter the fruit on top and bake for 1 hour, or until lightly golden. Cool in the tin, then lift out, using the paper as handles. Cut into pieces and dust with icing sugar to serve.

ROCKY ROAD SLICE

Preparation time: 15 minutes
+ 30 minutes cooling
Total cooking time: 25 minutes
Makes 24 pieces

150 g (5 oz) unsalted butter, cubed, softened
1/2 cup (125 g/4 oz) sugar
1 egg, lightly beaten
50 g (1 3/4 oz) dark chocolate, melted
1 cup (125 g/4 oz) self-raising flour
2 tablespoons cocoa powder
250 g (8 oz) dark chocolate, chopped, extra
25 g (3/4 oz) unsalted butter, extra
1/2 cup (105 g/3 1/2 oz) glacé cherries, halved
50 g (1 3/4 oz) mini marshmallows
1/2 cup (80 g/2 3/4 oz) unsalted peanuts

1 Preheat the oven to moderate 180°C (350°F/ Gas 4). Lightly grease two 26 x 8 x 4.5 cm (10 1/2 x 3 x 1 3/4 inch) bar tins and line with baking paper, leaving the paper hanging over on the two long sides.

2 Cream the butter and sugar in a small bowl with electric beaters until light and fluffy. Beat in the egg and melted chocolate and transfer to a large bowl. Using a metal spoon, fold in the combined sifted flour and cocoa and mix well. Divide the mixture between the tins, smoothing the surface. Bake for 20–25 minutes. Gently press down the outer edges of the slice, using the back of a spoon, to make the surface level. Leave to cool in the tins for 30 minutes.

3 Place the extra chocolate and butter in a heatproof bowl. Half fill a saucepan with water, bring to the boil, then remove from the heat. Sit the bowl over the saucepan, making sure the base of the bowl does not sit in the water. Stir occasionally until the mixture has melted and is smooth. Spread melted chocolate over the bases, using about a third of the chocolate altogether. Top each randomly with cherries, marshmallows and peanuts, then spoon the remaining chocolate evenly over the tops. Tap the tins on a bench to distribute the chocolate evenly. Leave to set, lift out using the paper as handles, then cut into 2 cm (3/4 inch) wide fingers for serving. These will keep in an airtight container in a cool, dark place for up to four days.

FLOUR
Flour made from wheat is the most common type used for baking. It provides structure to bread doughs, cakes mixtures, pastries and batters. During manufacture, the whole grain is processed or milled until it is finely ground to a powder. Plain white flour is also known as all-purpose flour. Self-raising flour is the same product but with the addition of baking powder. The baking powder acts as a leavener or raising agent in baked products. Wholemeal plain and wholemeal self-raising flours are also available. They are less refined, so they have a coarser texture.

LEFT: Rocky road slice

CRUNCHY PEANUT MERINGUE SLICE

Preparation time: 20 minutes
  + cooling
Total cooking time: 35 minutes
Makes 20 pieces

1 cup (125 g/4 oz) plain flour
2 teaspoons icing sugar
80 g (2¾ oz) unsalted butter, cubed
⅓ cup (100 g/3½ oz) apricot jam

Nut meringue

1½ cups (240 g/7½ oz) unsalted peanuts,
  roughly chopped
¾ cup (185 g/6 oz) caster sugar
⅓ cup (30 g/1 oz) desiccated coconut
1 egg white

1 Preheat the oven to moderate 180°C (350°F/Gas 4). Lightly grease a shallow tin measuring 18 x 28 cm (7 x 11 inches) and line with baking paper, leaving the paper hanging over on the two long sides.
2 Put the flour, icing sugar and butter in a food processor and mix in short bursts until fine and crumbly. Add 1 tablespoon iced water and process until the mixture just comes together.
3 Turn the dough out onto a floured surface, gather into a smooth ball, then press out evenly, using floured hands or the base of a floured glass, to cover the base of the tin. Prick well and bake for 15 minutes, or until golden. Cool for 10 minutes before spreading jam evenly over the surface.
4 For the nut meringue, put all the ingredients in a large saucepan and stir with a wooden spoon over low heat until the mixture is just lukewarm. Spread over the slice, then bake for 20 minutes, or until the topping is golden and crisp. When cool, lift out, using the paper as handles, and cut into pieces for serving.

PEANUTS

Peanuts are not nuts at all, but a legume or bean, which grows underground. They are highly nutritious and are eaten raw or roasted and are also ground into butter and oil. The peanut can be used in all these forms in baking, except the oil, which is too strong in flavour and is better used for frying savoury foods. For baking, use unsalted peanuts. If they are not available, you can wash the salt off the whole nuts, then dry thoroughly before using.

RIGHT: Crunchy
peanut meringue slice

PARKIN

Preparation time: 20 minutes
Total cooking time: 45 minutes
Makes 25 pieces

150 g (5 oz) unsalted butter, cubed
3/4 cup (140 g/4 1/2 oz) dark brown sugar
1/2 cup (175 g/6 oz) treacle
2 cups (200 g/6 1/2 oz) rolled oats
1 cup (125 g/4 oz) plain flour
1 teaspoon bicarbonate of soda
1 tablespoon ground ginger
2 teaspoons mixed spice
1/2 cup (125 ml/4 fl oz) milk
2 tablespoons rolled oats, extra
2 tablespoons raw sugar

1 Preheat the oven to moderate 180°C (350°F/ Gas 4). Lightly grease a shallow 23 cm (9 inch) square tin and line with baking paper, leaving the paper hanging over on two opposite sides.
2 Put the butter, brown sugar and treacle in a saucepan and stir over low heat until the butter and sugar have melted. Remove from the heat.

3 Coarsely chop the oats in a food processor, then transfer to a large bowl. Add the sifted flour, bicarbonate of soda, ginger and mixed spice. Stir in the treacle mixture and milk and mix well. Pour into the tin. Mix the extra rolled oats with the raw sugar and sprinkle over the top.
4 Bake for 40 minutes, or until a skewer inserted into the centre comes out clean. Leave in the tin for 5 minutes before lifting out onto a wire rack to cool completely. Cut into pieces for serving. Store for up to a week in an airtight container.

MUESLI CHEWS

Preheat the oven to moderate 180°C (350°F/ Gas 4). Line an 18 x 28 cm (7 x 11 inch) swiss roll tin with baking paper, leaving the paper hanging over the two long sides. In a large bowl, combine 4 crushed wheat breakfast biscuits, 1 cup (100 g/3 1/2 oz) rolled oats, 1/2 cup (45 g/1 1/2 oz) desiccated coconut and 1/2 cup (95 g/3 oz) soft brown sugar. Stir in 125 g (4 oz) melted butter and 1 tablespoon honey. Press firmly into the tin. Bake for 15 minutes, or until golden. Cool in the tin, then lift out and cut into squares with a sharp knife. Makes 20.

PARKIN

This is a moist, dense type of ginger cake, containing oats and sweetened with treacle. It is commonly baked in Yorkshire in the north of England. After baking, parkin is often left to mature for a week or so before serving. It is traditionally served on Guy Fawkes Day (bonfire night) each year.

ABOVE: Parkin

RASPBERRIES

Like the strawberry, the raspberry is a member of the rose family, hence the beautiful fragrant flavour and aroma. Originally from Europe, they are now grown world-wide in cooler climates. They have a short season, only lasting from summer to early autumn. They are highly perishable and will only last a couple of days, so take care when buying them. Check both the top and bottom of the punnet for signs of mould or juices leaching out. Raspberries should be refrigerated if not being used immediately and should never be washed.

ABOVE: Princess fingers

PRINCESS FINGERS

Preparation time: 35 minutes
Total cooking time: 35 minutes
Makes 24 pieces

125 g (4 oz) unsalted butter, cubed, softened
1/3 cup (90 g/3 oz) caster sugar
1 teaspoon vanilla essence
2 egg yolks
2 cups (250 g/8 oz) plain flour
1 teaspoon baking powder
1 tablespoon milk
1/2 cup (160 g/5 1/2 oz) raspberry jam
1/3 cup (40 g/1 1/4 oz) chopped walnuts
1/3 cup (80 g/2 3/4 oz) chopped red glacé cherries

Coconut meringue

2 egg whites
1/2 cup (125 g/4 oz) caster sugar
1 tablespoon grated orange rind
1/2 cup (45 g/1 1/2 oz) desiccated coconut
1 cup (30 g/1 oz) puffed rice cereal

1 Preheat the oven to moderate 180°C (350°F/ Gas 4). Lightly grease a 20 x 30 cm (8 x 12 inch) shallow tin and line with baking paper, leaving the paper hanging over on the two long sides.
2 Cream the butter, sugar and vanilla with electric beaters until light and fluffy. Add the egg yolks one at a time, beating well after each addition.
3 Sift the flour and baking powder into a bowl, then fold into the creamed mixture with a metal spoon. Fold in the milk, then press evenly and firmly into the tin. Spread the jam over the surface and sprinkle with the chopped walnuts and cherries.
4 For the coconut meringue, beat the egg whites in a small dry bowl until stiff peaks form. Fold in the sugar and orange rind with a metal spoon, then fold in the coconut and puffed rice cereal. Spread over the slice with a metal spatula.
5 Bake for 30–35 minutes, or until firm and golden brown. Cool the slice in the tin before lifting out, using the paper as handles, and cutting into fingers. This slice can be kept for up to four days in an airtight container.

PECAN COFFEE SLICE

Preparation time: 30 minutes
+ refrigeration
Total cooking time: 30 minutes
Makes 20 pieces

✯ ✯

125 g (4 oz) whole pecans
170 g (5 1/2 oz) blanched almonds
2 tablespoons plain flour
3/4 cup (185 g/6 oz) sugar
7 egg whites

Coffee cream

200 g (6 1/2 oz) unsalted butter, cubed, softened
150 g (5 oz) dark chocolate, melted
3– 4 teaspoons instant coffee powder

1 Preheat the oven to moderate 180°C (350°F/ Gas 4). Lightly grease a shallow 23 cm (9 inch) square tin and line with baking paper, leaving the paper hanging over on two opposite sides.
2 Roast the pecans and almonds on a baking tray for 5– 10 minutes, or until golden. Cool slightly, then chop in a food processor until finely ground. Transfer to a bowl, add the flour and 1/2 cup (125 g/4 oz) sugar and mix well.

Beat the egg whites in a large dry bowl until soft peaks form. Gradually add the remaining sugar, beating until the mixture is thick and glossy and the sugar has dissolved. Gradually fold the nut mixture into the meringue, a third at a time, using a metal spoon. Spoon into the tin and smooth the surface. Bake for 20 minutes, or until springy when touched. Leave in the tin for 5 minutes, then lift out, using the paper as handles, and place on a wire rack to cool completely.
3 For the coffee cream, beat the butter in a small bowl with electric beaters until light and creamy. Gradually pour in the cooled melted chocolate and beat well. Mix the coffee with 2 teaspoons water until dissolved, then add to the chocolate and mix well. Refrigerate for 5– 10 minutes to thicken slightly.
4 Cut the slice in half horizontally with a sharp serrated knife. Carefully remove the top layer and spread half the coffee cream over the base. Replace the top and spread evenly with the remaining cream. Run a palette knife backwards and forwards across the top to create a lined pattern, or use an icing comb to create swirls. Refrigerate until firm. Trim the edges and cut into squares or fingers. Serve at room temperature or cold, dusted with dark cocoa powder or decorated with chocolate-coated or plain coffee beans, if desired. The slice can be refrigerated for up to five days.

BELOW: Pecan coffee slice

FRUIT MINCE SLICE

Preparation time: 20 minutes
+ 15 minutes refrigeration
Total cooking time: 40 minutes
Makes 15 pieces

2 cups (250 g/8 oz) plain flour
1/2 cup (60 g/2 oz) icing sugar
185 g (6 oz) unsalted butter, cubed
1 egg
410 g (13 oz) jar fruit mince
150 g (5 oz) pitted prunes, chopped
100 g (3 1/2 oz) glacé ginger, chopped
1 egg, lightly beaten
icing sugar, to dust

1 Preheat the oven to moderately hot 190°C (375°F/Gas 5). Lightly grease a shallow 28 x 18 cm (11 x 7 inch) tin and line the base with baking paper, leaving the paper hanging over the two long sides. This makes it easy to lift the cooked slice out of the tin.
2 Sift the flour and icing sugar into a large bowl. Rub in the butter with your fingertips until the mixture resembles fine breadcrumbs. Make a well in the centre and add the egg. Mix with a flat-bladed knife, using a cutting action, until the mixture comes together. Turn onto a lightly floured surface and press together until smooth.
3 Divide the dough in half and press one portion into the tin. Bake for 10 minutes, then leave to cool. Roll the remaining pastry out on a piece of baking paper and refrigerate for 15 minutes. Spread the fruit mince evenly over the baked pastry, topping with the prunes and ginger. Cut the rolled pastry into thin strips with a sharp knife or fluted pastry wheel. Arrange on top of the fruit in a diagonal lattice pattern. Brush with beaten egg. Bake for 30 minutes, or until golden. Cool in the tin, then lift out, using the paper as handles, and cut into squares or fingers. Serve dusted with icing sugar. The slice can be kept for up to four days if stored in an airtight container in a cool place, or in the refrigerator.
NOTE: Although this slice is thought of as a traditional Christmas treat, it can be made any time of the year as the fruit mince in jars is readily available.

PRUNES
These are the whole dried fruit from certain varieties of plum trees. After being dehydrated, they take on a dark wrinkled appearance and have a very sweet flavour. They are suitable to eat on their own or to be used in cakes, slices and puddings. Sold in sealed packets or cans, they should be refrigerated in hot weather. Although mostly used as a sweet addition they are also combined with meats such as rabbit, pork and game. They have been used for centuries by Arab countries in both sweet and savoury dishes.

RIGHT: Fruit mince slice

PLUM AND ALMOND SLICE

Preparation time: 30 minutes
Total cooking time: 1 hour 10 minutes
Makes 9 pieces

160 g (5½ oz) unsalted butter, cubed
  and softened
²/3 cup (160 g/5½ oz) caster sugar
2 eggs
½ cup (60 g/2 oz) plain flour
⅓ cup (40 g/1¼ oz) cornflour
2 tablespoons rice flour
1½ tablespoons thinly sliced glacé ginger
825 g (1 lb 11 oz) can plums in syrup,
  drained, seeded and halved
1 cup (100 g/3½ oz) flaked almonds
1 tablespoon warmed honey

1 Preheat the oven to moderate 180°C (350°F/ Gas 4). Lightly grease a 20 cm (8 inch) square tin with baking paper, leaving the paper hanging over the top edge of the tin on all sides. Leaving the paper hanging over makes it easy to lift the cooked slice out of the tin.

2 Cream the butter and sugar in a small bowl with electric beaters until light and fluffy. Add the eggs one at a time, beating well after each addition. Sift the flours over the mixture and fold into the mixture with the ginger. Spread into the tin. Arrange the plum halves on top, pressing them in. Scatter with the flaked almonds, pressing in gently, then drizzle with the honey.

3 Bake for 1 hour 10 minutes, or until firm and golden. Cover with foil if the slice starts to brown too much. Cool in the tin, then lift out, using the paper as handles, before cutting into pieces. The slice can be kept for up to four or five days if stored in an airtight container in the refrigerator.

NOTE: If they are in season, you can use 7 ripe blood plums. They may bleed more than the canned plums.

HONEY
Honey is the oldest food-sweetening substance and was used hundreds of years before sugar. It has a long tradition in baking. The ancient Greeks and Romans made breads and honey spice cakes. Many ancient recipes are still made today, such as the German Lebkuchen and English gingerbread. There are also nougats, baklava and halva, all based on honey and almonds. There are many flavours of honey depending on the type of nectar taken by the bees from the flowers.

ABOVE: Plum and almond slice

145

SWEET PIES AND PASTRIES

To the uncertain cook, pastry can be a scary thing, so many of us find ourselves reaching for the frozen ready-made stuff or worse, avoiding recipes involving pastry altogether. By doing this we really miss out — the thin, flimsy little pies and pastries sold in supermarket freezers cannot compare to the aroma and flavour of a home-made masterpiece. In the following pages, we take the mystery out of pastry and talk you through the potential pitfalls so you can proceed with confidence. You'll soon find making pastry as easy as . . . well . . . pie!

SHORTCRUST The secret to making

good shortcrust pastry is to work the dough quickly and lightly, in a cool room if

possible, on a cool surface, and preferably not on a hot day.

If you don't have a marble slab, rest a tray of iced water on the work surface for a while before you start. Use *real* unsalted butter for pastry, not margarine or softened butter blends.

Unsweetened pastry works well with sweet fillings, giving a good contrast of flavours. To make a sweet pastry, add 2 tablespoons of caster sugar to the flour. Some recipes contain egg yolks to enrich the pastry and give good colour.

SHORTCRUST PASTRY

To make enough to line a 23 cm (9 inch) tin, use 2 cups (250 g/8 oz) plain flour, 150 g (5 oz) chilled, chopped unsalted butter and 2–4 tablespoons chilled water. This makes about 500 g (1 lb) pastry.

1 Sift the flour into a large bowl and add the butter. Using just your fingertips, rub the butter into the flour until the mixture resembles fine breadcrumbs.

2 Make a well in the centre, then add 2–4 tablespoons water and mix with a flat-bladed knife. Use a cutting action, rather than stirring, and turn the bowl with your free hand. The mixture will come together in small beads of dough. To test if you need more water, pinch a little dough between your fingers. If it doesn't hold together, add a little more water. If the pastry is too dry, it will fall apart when you roll it, and if too wet it will be sticky and shrink when baked.

3 Gently gather the dough together with your hand and lift out onto a sheet of baking paper or a floured work surface.
4 Press, don't knead, the dough together into a ball. Handle gently, keeping your actions light and to a minimum.
5 Press the dough into a flat disc, wrap in plastic wrap and refrigerate for 20 minutes. Roll out between two sheets of baking paper or plastic wrap, or on a lightly floured surface. Always roll from the centre outwards, rotating the dough, rather than backwards and forwards.
6 If you used baking paper to roll out the pastry, remove the top sheet, carefully invert the pastry over the tin (make sure you centre the pastry, as it can't be moved once in place), and then peel away the paper. If you rolled out on a lightly floured surface, roll the pastry back over the rolling pin so it is hanging, and ease it into the tin.

7 Once the pastry is in the tin, quickly lift up the sides so they don't break over the edges of the tin, which can be sharp, particularly in metal tart tins. Use a small ball of excess dough to help ease and press the pastry shell into the side of the tin. Allow the excess to hang over the side and, if using a tart tin, roll the rolling pin over the top of the tin to cut off the excess pastry. If you are using a glass or ceramic pie dish, use a small sharp knife to cut away the excess pastry.
8 However gently you handle dough, it is bound to shrink a little, so let it sit a little above the side of the tin. If you rolled off the excess pastry with a rolling pin, you may find it has 'bunched' down the sides. Gently press the sides of the pastry with your thumbs to flatten and lift it a little. Refrigerate the pastry in the tin for 15 minutes to relax it and prevent or minimize shrinkage. Preheat the oven.

BLIND BAKING
If pastry is to have a moist filling, it will probably require partial blind baking to prevent the base becoming soggy. If it is not cooked again after filling, it will need to be fully blind baked. This means baking the pastry without the filling, but with some weight on it to prevent it rising. Line the shell with crumpled greaseproof or baking paper. Pour in baking beads, dried beans or uncooked rice (these can be used again). Bake for the given time, then lift out the filled paper. Return the pastry to the oven to dry it and colour a little. When cooked, it should look dry with no greasy patches. Small pastry shells can just be pricked with a fork to prevent them rising or bubbling, but only do this if specified, as the filling may run through.

Cool pastry completely before filling. Cooked filling should also be cooled before adding, to prevent soggy pastry.

PUFF PASTRY This is made by layering

dough with butter and folding to create hundreds of layers. The butter melts and

the dough produces steam, forcing the layers apart and making the pastry rise.

For perfect pastry which rises evenly, the edges must be cut cleanly with a sharp knife or cutter, not torn. Egg glazes give a shine but must be applied carefully—any drips down the side may glue the layers together and stop them rising evenly. The pastry should be chilled for at least 30 minutes before baking, to relax it.

Always bake puff pastry at a very high temperature—it should rise evenly so, if your oven has areas of uneven heat, turn

the pastry around when it has set. If you have an oven with a bottom element, cook your pastry on the bottom shelf. When puff pastry is cooked, the top and base should be browned, with only a small amount of underbaked dough inside, and the layers should be visible. Puff pastry is not always perfect—it may fall over or not rise to quite the heights you had imagined— but provided you don't burn it, and it is well cooked, it will still be delicious.

MAKING PUFF PASTRY
We've given a range of butter quantity. If you've never made puff pastry before, you'll find it easier to use the lower amount. This recipe makes about 500 g (1 lb) pastry. You will need 200–250 g (6½– 8 oz) unsalted butter, 2 cups (250 g/8 oz) plain flour, ½ teaspoon salt and ⅔ cup (170 ml/5½ fl oz) chilled water.
1 Melt 30 g (1 oz) of the butter in a saucepan. Sift the flour and salt onto

a work surface and make a well in the centre. Add the melted butter and water to the centre and blend with your fingertips, gradually drawing in the flour. You should end up with a crumb mixture—if it seems a little dry, add extra drops of water before bringing it all together to form a dough.

2 Cut the dough with a pastry scraper, using a downward cutting action, then turn the dough and repeat in the opposite direction. The dough should now come together to form a soft ball. Score a cross in the top to prevent shrinkage, wrap and refrigerate for 15–20 minutes.

3 Soften the remaining butter by pounding it between two sheets of baking paper with a rolling pin. Then, still between the sheets of baking paper, roll it into a 10 cm (4 inch) square. The butter must be the same consistency as the dough or they will not roll out the

same amount and the layers will not be even. If the butter is too soft, it will squeeze out of the sides. Too hard and it will break through the dough and disturb the layers.

4 Put the pastry on a well-floured surface. Roll it out to form a cross, leaving the centre slightly thicker than the arms. Place the butter in the centre of the cross and fold over each of the arms to make a parcel. Turn the dough so that it looks like a book with the hinge side to the left. Tap and roll out the dough to form a 15 x 45 cm (6 x 18 inch) rectangle. Make this as neat as possible, squaring off the corners—otherwise, every time you fold, the edges will become less neat and the layers will not be even.

5 Fold the dough like a letter, the top third down and the bottom third up, to form a square, brushing off any excess flour between the layers. Turn the

dough 90° to bring the hinge side to your left and press the seam sides down with the rolling pin to seal them. Re-roll and fold as before to complete two turns and mark the dough by gently pressing into the corner with your fingertip for each turn—this will remind you where you're up to. Wrap the dough in plastic wrap and chill again for at least 30 minutes.

6 Re-roll and fold twice more and then chill, and then again to complete six turns. If it is a very hot day, you may need to chill for 30 minutes between each turn, rather than doing a double turn as described above. The pastry should now be an even yellow and is ready to use—if it looks a little streaky, roll and fold once more. The aim is to ensure that the butter is evenly distributed throughout so that the pastry rises and puffs up evenly when baked. Refrigerate until required.

CHOUX PASTRY

This is most often used to make profiteroles, eclairs, gougères and the French wedding cake called 'croquembouche'.

MAKING CHOUX PASTRY

Choux pastry is easy to make but the process is different from pastries such as shortcrust that have the butter rubbed into the flour. Instead, you melt the butter and water together, then beat the flour into the mixture and cook the mixture until it is no longer sticky. Then the mixture is cooled slightly and lightly beaten eggs are very gradually added and

beaten in. The dough should be stiff enough to shape.

Before you begin, you should read the recipe and assemble all the necessary ingredients, weighing and measuring them carefully. Preheat the oven to hot 210°C (415°F/Gas 6–7). Sift 1½ cups (185 g/6 oz) plain flour and ¼ teaspoon salt onto a sheet of baking paper. Place 100 g (3½ oz) chopped unsalted butter

in a large heavy-based saucepan with 1½ cups (375 ml/12 fl oz) water and stir over medium heat. Once the butter has melted, increase the heat to bring the water to the boil. Remove from the heat immediately: prolonged boiling will evaporate enough water to alter the proportions of the ingredients. Add the flour and salt all at once and quickly beat it into the water using hand-held beaters

or a wooden spoon. Return to the heat and continue beating until the mixture forms a ball and leaves the side of the saucepan. Transfer to a large clean bowl and cool slightly. Beat the mixture to release any heat. Lightly beat 6 eggs in a bowl, then gradually add to the butter mixture, about 3 teaspoons at a time. Beat well after each addition. When all the egg has been added the mixture should be thick and glossy—a wooden spoon should stand up in it. If the mixture is too runny, the egg has been added too quickly. To correct this, beat for several more minutes, or until thickened. The pastry is now ready to use and may be piped, spooned or shaped according to the recipe you are following. The pastry is cooked when it is golden and hollow sounding when tapped on the base. Turn off the oven and leave inside to dry out.

PROFITEROLES OR PUFFS

Lightly sprinkle three baking trays with water. Spoon the mixture onto the trays, leaving plenty of room for spreading. One small puff is equal to 1 heaped teaspoon of mixture. Bake for 20–30 minutes or until golden. Remove from the oven and make a small hole in the base of each one to assist drying. Return them to the oven for 5 minutes to dry out. Cool on a wire rack. Cooked puffs can be frozen for up to 2 months. Reheat in a moderate 180°C (350°F/Gas 4) oven for 5 minutes.

HELPFUL TIPS

It helps to sprinkle the baking tray with water before placing the dough on it as this creates steam in the oven, helping the shapes to rise. You may need to prepare and cook them in two or more batches, especially if making a croquembouche.

MAKING GOUGERES

By adding a touch of cheese, such as Emmenthal or Gruyère, to choux pastry dough, you can make gougères. These delicately flavoured puffs originated in Burgundy and are a great idea to have as starters. To make them, substitute half the water with the same quantity of milk and follow the procedure for choux pastry. After all the eggs have been incorporated, add 1/2 cup (65 g/ 2 1/4 oz) grated cheese. Using a piping bag fitted with a plain tube, pipe 6 cm (2 1/2 inch) rounds (or smaller for parties) onto a baking tray lined with baking paper. Lightly beat an egg yolk and lightly brush over the gougères. Scatter with more grated cheese, using about 1/4 cup (35 g/1 1/4 oz). Bake as for regular choux pastry. This quantity will make about 12 large or 24 small gougères.

WHAT WENT WRONG?

SHORTCRUST PASTRY

PERFECT Pastry is even and lightly golden. The sides are cooked evenly and shrunk slightly from the sides of the tin. The base is crisp, golden and dry.

OVERCOOKED The cooking time was too long, or the oven too hot. The pastry may have been placed either too high or too low in the oven.

STUCK TO BASE The pastry may have had too much liquid added, or may not have been chilled before rolling. The tin may not have been greased, or was not clean.

OTHER PROBLEMS

SHORTCRUST PASTRY
If there are holes in the pastry case, the pastry was rolled out too thinly or the pastry case has shrunk and split during cooking due to being overworked or not being chilled before cooking. If the fork marks are too large, this can cause holes.

If the pastry is tough, the pastry dough may have been overworked during mixing or rolling, or there was too much water added to the pastry dough.

PASTRY SHRUNK TOO MUCH The pastry was overworked or not chilled before baking. The weights may have been pressed too firmly against the sides of the pastry case, or removed too early.

UNDERCOOKED The cooking temperature was too low, or the cooking time not long enough. The pastry case may have been rolled out too thickly. The tin should be put on a preheated baking tray.

PUFF PASTRY

PERFECT The pastry is well and evenly risen with pastry layers visible. The pastry is deep golden brown and the texture is light and flaky.

UNEVENLY RISEN WHEN COOKED The edges were not trimmed with a sharp knife. The glaze has dripped down the sides, gluing the layers together.

OVERCOOKED The oven may have been too hot, or the cooking time too long, or the pastry may have been placed too high in the oven.

FILO PASTRY

PERFECT The filo pastry is dry, crisp, flaky and puffed and golden brown.

UNDERCOOKED The pastry is pale and soggy. There are many things that can cause this. The filling may be heavy and too moist or there may be too many layers of filo. The cooking temperature may have been too low or the cooking time too short. Excessive amounts of butter or oil may have been brushed on the layers of filo.

OVERCOOKED The pastry is unevenly coloured and too dark in some areas. The oven temperature may have been too high or the layers unevenly brushed with butter or oil. The tin may have been placed too high in the oven.

OTHER PROBLEMS

FILO PASTRY
If the filling leaks, there may be too much filling, or not enough filo layers. The oven may have been too hot or the filling too moist. Otherwise, the parcels were not shaped and secured well enough or were rolled too tightly.

CHOUX PASTRY

PERFECT The choux pastry is crisp and puffy, hollow inside and has a deep golden colour. To assist in drying and to release steam, make a small hole in the base of each puff with a skewer.

POORLY RISEN The pastry is not puffed and dense inside. Too little egg was added (the more eggs you add the more the dough will puff). Otherwise, the oven temperature was not hot enough or the oven was opened too soon during baking. Also, the cooking time may have been too short.

NOTE:
Spraying the inside of the oven with water, as well as sprinkling the baking tray with water, helps create steam which aids in the rising of choux pastry.

OTHER PROBLEMS

PUFF PASTRY
There are three pointers for success:
1 Chilling the pastry both during the making and prior to the baking.
2 Ensuring that the sides of the pastry are trimmed with a sharp knife and that glaze does not dribble over the sides.
3 Checking that the oven is hot during the initial cooking stages to ensure that the layers separate adequately.

If puff pastry is soggy and undercooked, the cooking time may have been too short, or the cooking temperature too low, so the pastry was not dried out sufficiently in the last stages of cooking.

If puff is unevenly risen, it may have been unevenly rolled or the oven heat may have been uneven. The butter may not have been incorporated evenly.

If shrunken and poorly risen, the pastry may have been overworked, or not rested and chilled before baking.

4– 5 tablespoons iced water

2 tablespoons marmalade

I egg, lightly beaten

I tablespoon sugar

I Lightly grease a 23 cm (9 inch) pie plate. Peel, core and cut the apples into wedges. Place in a saucepan with the sugar, lemon rind, cloves and 2 tablespoons water. Cover and cook over low heat for 8 minutes, or until the apples are just tender, shaking the pan occasionally. Drain and cool completely.

2 Sift the flours into a bowl and rub in the butter, using your fingertips, until the mixture resembles fine breadcrumbs. Stir in the sugar, then make a well in the centre. Add almost all the water and mix with a flat-bladed knife, using a cutting action, until the mixture comes together in beads. Add more water if the dough is too dry. Gather together and lift out onto a lightly floured surface. Press into a ball and divide into two, making one half a little bigger. Cover with plastic wrap and refrigerate for 20 minutes.

3 Preheat the oven to moderately hot 200°C (400°F/Gas 6). Roll out the larger piece of pastry between two sheets of baking paper to line the base and side of the pie plate. Line the pie plate with the pastry. Use a small sharp knife to trim away any excess pastry. Brush the marmalade over the base and spoon the apple into the shell. Roll out the other pastry between the baking paper until large enough to cover the pie. Brush water around the rim, then place the top on. Trim off any excess pastry, pinch the edges and cut a round hole or a couple of steam slits in the top.

4 Re-roll the pastry scraps and cut into leaves for decoration. Lightly brush the top with egg, then sprinkle with sugar. Bake for 20 minutes, then reduce the oven temperature to moderate 180°C (350°F/Gas 4) and bake for another 15– 20 minutes, or until golden.

APPLE PIE

Preparation time: 45 minutes
  + 20 minutes refrigeration
Total cooking time: 50 minutes
Serves 6

✹ ✹

Filling

6 large Granny Smith apples

2 tablespoons caster sugar

I teaspoon finely grated lemon rind

pinch of ground cloves

2 cups (250 g/8 oz) plain flour

1/4 cup (30 g/1 oz) self-raising flour

150 g (5 oz) unsalted butter, chilled, cubed

2 tablespoons caster sugar

LEMON MERINGUE PIE

Preparation time: I hour
  + 15 minutes refrigeration
Total cooking time: 45 minutes
Serves 6

✹ ✹

1 1/2 cups (185 g/6 oz) plain flour

125 g (4 oz) unsalted butter, chilled, cubed

2 tablespoons icing sugar

2– 3 tablespoons iced water

ABOVE: Apple pie

Lemon filling

1/4 cup (30 g/1 oz) cornflour

1/4 cup (30 g/1 oz) plain flour

1 cup (250 g/8 oz) caster sugar

3/4 cup (185 ml/6 fl oz) lemon juice

3 teaspoons grated lemon rind

40 g (1 1/4 oz) unsalted butter

6 egg yolks

Meringue topping

6 egg whites

1 1/2 cups (375 g/12 oz) caster sugar

1/2 teaspoon cornflour

1 Lightly grease a deep 23 cm (9 inch) pie plate. Sift the flour into a bowl and rub in the butter, using your fingertips, until the mixture resembles fine breadcrumbs. Stir in the icing sugar, then make a well in the centre. Add 2 tablespoons water and mix with a flat-bladed knife, using a cutting action, until the mixture comes together in beads. Add the remaining water if the dough is too dry.

2 Gather the dough together and roll between two sheets of baking paper until large enough to line the base and side of the pie plate. Line the plate with the pastry. Trim off any excess pastry. Fork the edge and refrigerate for 15 minutes.

3 Preheat the oven to moderate 180°C (350°F/Gas 4). Line the pastry shell with crumpled baking paper and pour in some baking beads or uncooked rice. Bake for 10– 15 minutes, then remove the paper and beads. Return the pastry to the oven for 10 minutes, or until cooked through. Cool completely. Increase the oven temperature to hot 220°C (425°F/Gas 7).

4 For the lemon filling, put the flours and sugar in a saucepan. Whisk in the lemon juice, rind and 1 1/2 cups (375 ml/12 fl oz) water. Whisk continually over medium heat until the mixture boils and thickens, then reduce the heat and cook for 1 minute. Remove from the heat, then whisk in the butter, then egg yolks, one at a time. Cover the surface with plastic wrap and cool. Spread the filling into the pastry shell.

5 For the meringue topping, put the egg whites and sugar in a clean, dry bowl. Beat with electric beaters on high for 10 minutes, or until the sugar is almost completely dissolved and the meringue is thick and glossy. Beat in the cornflour. Spread the meringue over the top, making peaks by drawing the meringue up with a knife, piling it high towards the centre. Bake for 5– 10 minutes, or until lightly browned. Cool before serving.

MERINGUES

A soft meringue is a mixture of stiffly beaten egg white and sugar, usually in a proportion of 1 egg white to 60 g (2 oz) sugar. The sugar is gradually added to the beaten egg white until the sugar is dissolved and the mixture is smooth and glossy. Soft meringues are used as swirled topping on various sweet pies such as lemon meringue pie and fruit pies. The meringue is piled high onto the pie filling, then lightly browned in the oven. The pie should be eaten soon after browning as the meringue topping will start to 'weep' and lose volume if it stands too long.

LEFT: Lemon meringue pie

PECAN PIE

Preparation time: 30 minutes
  + 40 minutes refrigeration
Total cooking time: 1 hour 15 minutes
Serves 6

★★

Shortcrust pastry

1 1/2 cups (185 g/6 oz) plain flour
100 g (3 1/2 oz) unsalted butter, chilled, cubed
2– 4 tablespoons iced water

Filling

2 cups (200 g/6 1/2 oz) whole pecans
3 eggs
60 g (2 oz) unsalted butter, melted
2/3 cup (125 g/4 oz) soft brown sugar
2/3 cup (170 ml/5 1/2 fl oz) corn syrup
1 teaspoon vanilla essence

1 Lightly grease a 23 cm (9 inch) pie plate. Sift the flour into a bowl and rub in the butter, using your fingertips, until the mixture resembles fine breadcrumbs. Make a well in the centre, add almost all the water and mix with a flat-bladed knife, using a cutting action, until the mixture comes together in small beads, adding water if the dough is too dry. Gather together, cover with plastic wrap and refrigerate for 20 minutes.

2 Roll the dough out between two sheets of baking paper to 3 mm (1/8 inch) thick. It should be large enough to line the pie plate and leave some for decorating. Line the pie plate with pastry and trim any excess pastry with a sharp knife. Gather the scraps together and roll out to 3 mm (1/8 inch) thick. Using small cutters, cut shapes from the pastry (score veins into the leaf shapes). Lightly brush the pastry rim with water and attach the shapes. Refrigerate for 20 minutes. Preheat the oven to moderate 180°C (350°F/Gas 4).

3 Cover the decorative edge of the pastry with wide strips of foil. Line the pastry shell with crumpled baking paper, and fill with baking beads or uncooked rice. Bake for 15 minutes, then remove the beads and paper and bake for another 15 minutes, or until the base is lightly golden and dry. Remove the foil and set aside to cool completely before filling.

4 Place the pecans on the pastry base. Whisk together the eggs, butter, sugar, corn syrup, vanilla and 1/4 teaspoon salt in a bowl and pour the mixture over the pecans. Place the dish on a baking tray and bake for 45 minutes, or until the filling is set. Serve warm or cold.

PECANS

The pecan is native to America and is related to the walnut. It has a mild, creamy and less bitter flavour than the walnut but the walnut does make an adequate substitute. The pecan is known as a dessert nut as it is used mostly in the baking of desserts and pies, in confectionery and ice cream. The most famous of the dessert pies is the traditional American Pecan Pie, popular in the southern states. The distinctive flavour is due to corn syrup which is a by-product of sweet corn and can be bought in bottles from health food stores and delicatessens.

RIGHT: Pecan pie

Roll the dough between two sheets of baking paper to a 28 cm (11 inch) circle.

Pour the rhubarb filling into a pie plate and smooth the surface.

Place the latticed pastry on top of the pie and trim the edges with a sharp knife.

RHUBARB LATTICE PIE

Preparation time: 35 minutes
+ 40 minutes refrigeration
Total cooking time: 1 hour
Serves 4–6

✿ ✿

Rhubarb filling

500 g (1 lb) rhubarb, trimmed, leaves discarded
1/2 cup (125 g/4 oz) caster sugar
5 cm (2 inch) piece orange rind, pith removed
1 tablespoon orange juice
410 g (13 oz) can pie apples

1 1/4 cups (155 g/5 oz) plain flour
1/4 teaspoon baking powder
90 g (3 oz) unsalted butter, chilled, cubed
1 tablespoon caster sugar
3–4 tablespoons iced water
milk, for glazing
demerara sugar, for decoration

 For the rhubarb filling, preheat the oven to moderate 180°C (350°F/Gas 4). Cut the rhubarb into 3 cm (1 1/4 inch) lengths and combine in a large casserole dish with the sugar, orange rind and juice. Cover the dish with a lid or foil and bake for 30 minutes, or until the rhubarb is just tender. Drain away any excess juice and discard the rind. Cool, then stir in the apple. Add more sugar, to taste.

2 While the rhubarb is cooking, sift the flour and baking powder into a bowl and rub in the butter, using your fingertips, until the mixture resembles fine breadcrumbs. Stir in the sugar. Make a well and add almost all the water. Mix with a flat-bladed knife, using a cutting action, until the mixture comes together in beads, adding more water if necessary. Gather together, wrap in plastic wrap and chill for 20 minutes.

3 Roll the pastry out between two sheets of baking paper to a 28 cm (11 inch) circle. Cut the pastry into 1.5 cm (5/8 inch) strips, using a sharp knife or a fluted cutter. Lay half the strips on a sheet of baking paper, leaving a 1 cm (1/2 inch) gap between each strip. Interweave the remaining strips to form a lattice. Cover with plastic wrap and refrigerate, flat, for 20 minutes.

4 Increase the oven to 210°C (415°F/Gas 6–7). Pour the filling into a 20 cm (8 inch) pie plate and smooth the surface. Place the pastry on the pie and trim. Bake for 10 minutes. Remove from the oven, brush with milk and sprinkle with sugar. Reduce the oven to 180°C (350°F/Gas 4) and bake the pie for 20 minutes, or until the pastry is golden and the filling is bubbling.

ABOVE: Rhubarb lattice pie

CUSTARD TARTS

Preparation time: 30 minutes
+ 20 minutes refrigeration
Total cooking time: 45 minutes
Makes 12

 ☆

2 cups (250 g/8 oz) plain flour
1/3 cup (60 g/2 oz) rice flour
1/4 cup (30 g/1 oz) icing sugar
120 g (4 oz) unsalted butter, chilled, cubed
1 egg yolk
3 tablespoons iced water
1 egg white, lightly beaten

Custard filling

3 eggs
1 1/2 cups (375 ml/12 fl oz) milk
1/4 cup (60 g/2 oz) caster sugar
1 teaspoon vanilla essence
1/2 teaspoon ground nutmeg

1 Sift the flours and icing sugar into a large bowl and rub in the butter, using your fingertips, until the mixture resembles fine breadcrumbs. Make a well and add the egg yolk and almost all the water. Mix with a flat-bladed knife, using a cutting action, until the mixture comes together in small beads, adding more water if the dough is too dry. Gather together and roll out between two sheets of baking paper. Divide the dough into 12 equal portions and roll each portion out to fit the base and side of a 10 cm (4 inch) loose-based fluted tart tin. Line the tins with the pastry and roll the rolling pin over the tins to cut off any excess pastry. Refrigerate for 20 minutes.
2 Preheat the oven to moderate 180°C (350°F/ Gas 4). Line each pastry-lined tin with crumpled baking paper. Fill with baking beads or uncooked rice. Place the tins on two large baking trays and bake for 10 minutes. Remove the baking paper and beads and return the trays to the oven. Bake for 10 minutes, or until the pastry is lightly golden. Cool. Brush the base and side of each pastry case with beaten egg white. Reduce the oven temperature to slow 150°C (300°F/Gas 2).
3 For the filling, whisk the eggs and milk in a bowl to combine. Add the sugar gradually, whisking to dissolve completely. Stir in the vanilla essence. Strain into a jug, then pour into the cooled pastry cases. Sprinkle with nutmeg and bake for 25 minutes, or until the filling is just set. Serve at room temperature.

APPLE TARTE TATIN

Preparation time: 30 minutes
+ 30 minutes refrigeration
Total cooking time: 50 minutes
Serves 6

 ☆

1 2/3 cups (210 g/7 oz) plain flour
125 g (4 oz) unsalted butter, chilled, cubed
2 tablespoons caster sugar
1 egg, lightly beaten
2 drops vanilla essence
8 medium Granny Smith apples
1/2 cup (125 g/4 oz) sugar
40 g (1 1/4 oz) unsalted butter, chopped, extra

1 Sift the flour into a bowl and rub in the butter, using your fingertips, until the mixture resembles fine breadcrumbs. Stir in the caster sugar, then make a well in the centre. Add the egg and vanilla essence and mix with a flat-bladed knife, using a cutting action, until the mixture comes together in beads. Gather the dough together, then turn out onto a lightly floured surface and shape into a disc. Wrap in plastic wrap and refrigerate for at least 30 minutes, to firm.
2 Peel and core the apples and cut each into eight slices. Place the sugar and 1 tablespoon water in a heavy-based 25 cm (10 inch) frying pan that has a metal or removable handle, so that it can safely be placed in the oven. Stir over low heat for 1 minute, or until the sugar has dissolved. Increase the heat to medium and cook for 4– 5 minutes, or until the caramel turns golden. Add the extra butter and stir to incorporate. Remove from the heat.
3 Place the apple slices in neat circles to cover the base of the frying pan. Return the pan to low heat and cook for 10– 12 minutes, until the apples are tender and caramelized. Remove the pan from the heat and leave to cool for 10 minutes.
4 Preheat the oven to hot 220°C (425°F/Gas 7). Roll the pastry out on a lightly floured surface to a circle 1 cm (1/2 inch) larger than the frying pan. Place the pastry over the apples to cover them completely, tucking it down firmly at the edges. Bake for 30– 35 minutes, or until the pastry is cooked. Leave for 15 minutes before turning out onto a plate. Serve warm or cold with cream or ice cream.
NOTE: Special high-sided tatin tins are available for making this dessert. Look for them at speciality kitchenware shops.

TARTE TATIN
This is traditionally an upside-down apple, or sometimes pear, tart. The fruit is cooked in an ovenproof dish or tin and the rolled pastry cooked on top in the oven. The pie is then inverted to show off the caramelized, juicy cooked fruit. The name commemorates the Tatin sisters who lived in the Loire Valley in the early twentieth century and made their living selling it. The French call it *tarte des demoiselles Tatin* or 'the tart of two unmarried women named Tatin'.

OPPOSITE PAGE:
Custard tarts (top);
Apple tarte tatin

SUMMER BERRY TART

Preparation time: 35 minutes
  + 20 minutes refrigeration
Total cooking time: 35 minutes
Serves 4– 6

1 cup (125 g/4 oz) plain flour
90 g (3 oz) unsalted butter, chilled, cubed
2 tablespoons icing sugar
1– 2 tablespoons iced water

Filling

3 egg yolks
2 tablespoons caster sugar
2 tablespoons cornflour
1 cup (250 ml/8 fl oz) milk
1 teaspoon vanilla essence
250 g (8 oz) strawberries, halved
125 g (4 oz) blueberries
125 g (4 oz) raspberries
1– 2 tablespoons baby apple gel

1 Preheat the oven to moderate 180°C (350°F/ Gas 4). Lightly grease a 20 cm (8 inch) round, loose-based, fluted tart tin. Sift the flour into a bowl and rub in the butter, using your fingertips, until the mixture resembles fine breadcrumbs. Mix in the sugar. Make a well in the centre and add almost all the water. Mix with a flat-bladed knife, using a cutting action, until the mixture comes together in beads, adding more water if the dough is too dry.

2 Roll out the pastry between two sheets of baking paper to fit the base and side of the tart tin. Line the tin with the pastry and trim away any excess. Refrigerate for 20 minutes. Line the tin with baking paper and pour in baking beads or uncooked rice. Bake for 15 minutes, then remove the paper and beads. Bake the pastry for another 15 minutes, or until golden.

3 For the filling, place the egg yolks, sugar and cornflour in a bowl and whisk until pale. Heat the milk in a small saucepan until almost boiling, then remove from the heat and add gradually to the egg mixture, beating constantly. Strain into the pan. Stir constantly over low heat for 3 minutes, or until the mixture boils and thickens. Remove from the heat and add the vanilla essence. Transfer to a bowl, cover with plastic wrap and set aside to cool.

4 Spread the filling in the pastry shell and top with berries. Heat the apple gel in a heatproof bowl in a saucepan of simmering water, or in the microwave, until it liquefies. Brush over the fruit with a pastry brush. Allow to set before cutting.

ABOVE: Summer berry tart

TREACLE TART

Preparation time: 30 minutes
  + 20 minutes refrigeration
Total cooking time: 35 minutes
Serves 4– 6

Shortcrust pastry

1½ cups (185 g/6 oz) plain flour
90 g (3 oz) unsalted butter, chilled, cubed
3– 4 tablespoons iced water
1 egg, beaten, to glaze

Filling

1 cup (350 g/11 oz) golden syrup
25 g (¾ oz) unsalted butter
1 teaspoon ground ginger
1¾ cups (140 g/4½ oz) fresh white
  breadcrumbs

1 Sift the flour into a large bowl and rub in the butter, using your fingertips, until the mixture resembles fine breadcrumbs. Make a well in the centre and add almost all the water. Mix together with a flat-bladed knife, using a cutting action, until the mixture comes together in small beads, adding the remaining water if necessary.

2 Gently gather the dough together and roll out between two sheets of baking paper to a circle to fit the base and side of a 20 cm (8 inch) round, loose-based, fluted tart tin. Line the tin with the pastry and roll the rolling pin over the top of the tin to cut off any excess pastry.

3 Re-roll the trimmings on the baking paper into a rectangle 20 x 10 cm (8 x 4 inches). Using a sharp knife or fluted pastry wheel, cut into long 1 cm (½ inch) wide strips. Cover with plastic wrap and refrigerate, along with the pastry-lined tin, for 20 minutes.

4 Preheat the oven to moderate 180°C (350°F/ Gas 4). Combine the golden syrup, butter and ginger in a small saucepan and stir over low heat until the butter has melted. Stir in the breadcrumbs, then pour into the pastry case.

5 Lay half the pastry strips on a sheet of baking paper, leaving a 1 cm (½ inch) gap between each strip. Interweave the remaining strips to form a lattice pattern, then place on top of the pie. Brush the lattice with beaten egg. Bake for 30 minutes, or until the pastry is lightly golden. Serve warm or at room temperature. The tart can be lightly dusted with icing sugar just before serving.

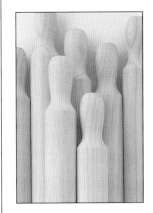

TARTS
A tart has a shallow-sided pastry crust without an enclosing pastry top. The filling can be sweet or savoury. Sweet tarts usually have a custard base and are decorated with fruit or nuts. Savoury tarts often have a cheesy filling or savoury custard with meats or vegetables. Small tarts are called 'tartlets' and are suitable as appetizers or, if bite-sized, for party food. Special tart tins can be bought from speciality kitchenware shops. They come in various sizes either with straight or fluted sides. Most tart tins have a loose base so that the cooked tart can be easily removed from the tin.

LEFT: Treacle tart

PLUMS

There are many varieties of this stone fruit. Most have a shiny skin and they range in colour from deep purple to green, yellow and red. They are available only for a short period during summer. Buy plums that are firm and plump and leave them to fully ripen at room temperature. Refrigerate them once they have ripened. They can be used in pies, tarts and puddings and are also suitable for poaching and serving as an accompaniment to rich cakes. Plums make a beautiful jam as well as sweet and savoury sauces and chutneys. They are also available canned, which is useful when fresh plums are out of season. When dried, they are sold as prunes.

OPPOSITE PAGE:
Citron tart (top); Plum tart

CITRON TART

Preparation time: 1 hour
+ 30 minutes refrigeration
Total cooking time: 1 hour 45 minutes
Serves 6–8

✧ ✧

1 cup (125 g/4 oz) plain flour
75 g (2 1/2 oz) unsalted butter, softened
1 egg yolk
2 tablespoons icing sugar, sifted

Citron filling

3 eggs
2 egg yolks
3/4 cup (185 g/6 oz) caster sugar
1/2 cup (125 ml/4 fl oz) cream
3/4 cup (185 ml/6 fl oz) lemon juice
1 1/2 tablespoons finely grated lemon rind
2 small lemons
2/3 cup (160 g/5 1/2 oz) sugar

1 For the pastry, sift the flour and a pinch of salt into a large bowl. Make a well in the centre and add the butter, egg yolk and icing sugar. Work together the butter, yolk and sugar with your fingertips, then slowly incorporate the flour. Bring together into a ball—you may need to add a few drops of chilled water. Flatten the ball slightly, cover with plastic wrap and refrigerate for 20 minutes.
2 Lightly grease a loose-based, fluted tart tin, about 2 cm (3/4 inch) deep and 21 cm (8 1/2 inches) in diameter. Preheat the oven to moderately hot 200°C (400°F/Gas 6).
3 Roll out the pastry between two sheets of baking paper to 3 mm (1/8 inch) thick, to fit the base and side of the tin. Line the tin and use a small sharp knife to trim away any excess pastry. Refrigerate for 10 minutes. Line the pastry shell with baking paper and pour in some baking beads or uncooked rice, then bake for 10–15 minutes. Remove the paper and beads and bake for another 10 minutes, or until the pastry looks dry all over. Set the tart tin aside to allow the pastry to cool. Reduce the oven to slow 150°C (300°F/Gas 2).
4 For the citron filling, whisk the eggs, egg yolks and sugar together in a small bowl, add the cream and lemon juice and mix well. Strain into a jug, then add the lemon rind. Place the tart tin on a baking tray on the middle shelf of the oven and carefully pour in the filling right to the top.

Bake for 40 minutes, or until just set—it should wobble in the centre when the tin is firmly tapped. Cool the tart before removing from the tin.
5 Wash and scrub the lemons well, then cut them into very thin slices (about 2 mm/ 1/8 inch). Combine the sugar and 3/4 cup (185 ml/6 fl oz) water in a small frying pan and stir over low heat until the sugar has dissolved. Add the lemon slices and simmer over low heat for 40 minutes, or until the peel is very tender and the pith looks transparent. Lift the slices out of the syrup and drain on baking paper. If serving the tart immediately, cover the surface with the lemon slices. If not, keep the slices covered and use to decorate the tart when ready to serve. Serve warm or chilled, with a little cream.

PLUM TART

Preparation time: 20 minutes
Total cooking time: 35 minutes
Serves 6

✧

500 g (1 lb) home-made or bought puff pastry (see page 150)

Topping

1 tablespoon plum jam
5 large plums, very thinly sliced
1 tablespoon brandy
1 tablespoon sugar

1 Preheat the oven to moderately hot 200°C (400°F/Gas 6). Roll out the pastry on a lightly floured surface to make an irregular rectangular shape, about 20 x 30 cm (8 x 12 inches) and 4 mm (1/4 inch) thick.
2 Place the pastry on a greased baking tray. Heat the plum jam with 2 teaspoons of water in a small saucepan over low heat until the jam is softened and spreadable. Brush the jam over the pastry base, leaving a 2 cm (3/4 inch) border. Lay the plum slices along the pastry, leaving a 2 cm (3/4 inch) border all around. Lightly brush the fruit with the brandy and sprinkle with the sugar. Bake for 30 minutes, or until the pastry is puffed and golden. Cut into slices and serve warm with cream or ice cream.
NOTE: This tart can also be made using four very thinly sliced large nectarines and substituting apricot jam for the plum jam.

PUMPKIN PIE

Preparation time: 20 minutes
  + 20 minutes refrigeration
Total cooking time: 1 hour 10 minutes
Serves 8

★ ★

Filling

500 g (1 lb) pumpkin
2 eggs, lightly beaten
3/4 cup (140 g/4 1/2 oz) soft brown sugar
1/3 cup (80 ml/2 3/4 fl oz) cream
1 tablespoon sweet sherry
1 teaspoon ground cinnamon
1/2 teaspoon ground nutmeg
1/2 teaspoon ground ginger

BELOW: Pumpkin pie

Pastry

1 1/4 cups (155 g/5 oz) plain flour
100 g (3 1/2 oz) unsalted butter, cubed
2 teaspoons caster sugar
1/3 cup (80 ml/2 3/4 fl oz) iced water
1 egg yolk, lightly beaten, for glazing
1 tablespoon milk, for glazing

1 Lightly grease a 23 cm (9 inch) round pie plate. Chop the pumpkin for the filling into small chunks and steam or boil for 10 minutes, or until the pumpkin is just tender. Drain the pumpkin thoroughly, then mash and set aside to cool.

2 For the pastry, sift the flour into a large bowl and rub in the butter, using your fingertips, until the mixture resembles fine breadcrumbs. Stir in the caster sugar. Make a well in the centre, add almost all the water and mix with a flat-bladed knife, using a cutting action, until the mixture comes together in beads, adding the remaining water if the dough is too dry.

3 Gather the dough together and roll out between two sheets of baking paper until large enough to cover the base and side of the pie plate. Line the dish with pastry, trim away excess pastry and crimp the edges. Roll out the pastry trimmings to 2 mm (1/8 inch) thick. Using a sharp knife, cut out leaf shapes of different sizes and score vein markings onto the leaves. Refrigerate the pastry-lined dish and the leaf shapes for about 20 minutes.

4 Preheat the oven to moderate 180°C (350°F/ Gas 4). Cut baking paper to cover the pastry-lined dish. Spread baking beads or uncooked rice over the paper. Bake for 10 minutes, then remove the paper and beads. Return the pastry to the oven for 10 minutes, or until lightly golden. Meanwhile, place the leaves on a baking tray lined with baking paper, brush with the combined egg yolk and milk and bake for 10– 15 minutes, or until lightly golden. Set aside to cool.

5 For the filling, whisk the eggs and brown sugar in a large bowl. Add the cooled mashed pumpkin, cream, sherry, cinnamon, nutmeg and ginger to the bowl and stir to combine thoroughly. Pour the filling into the pastry shell, smooth the surface with the back of a spoon, then bake for 40 minutes, or until set. If the pastry edges begin to brown too much during cooking, cover the edges with foil. Allow the pie to cool to room temperature and then decorate the top with the leaves. Pumpkin pie can be served with ice cream or whipped cream.

FREE-FORM BLUEBERRY PIE

Preparation time: 20 minutes
  + 10 minutes refrigeration
Total cooking time: 35 minutes
Serves 4

1¹/2 cups (185 g/6 oz) plain flour

¹/2 cup (60 g/2 oz) icing sugar, plus extra
  for dusting

125 g (4 oz) unsalted butter, chilled and
  cut into cubes

¹/4 cup (60 ml/2 fl oz) lemon juice

500 g (1 lb) blueberries

¹/4 cup (30 g/1 oz) icing sugar

1 teaspoon finely grated lemon rind

¹/2 teaspoon ground cinnamon

1 egg white, lightly beaten

1 Preheat the oven to moderate 180°C (350°F/ Gas 4). Sift the flour and icing sugar into a bowl and rub in the butter, using your fingertips, until the mixture resembles fine breadcrumbs. Make a well in the centre and add almost all the juice. Mix together with a flat-bladed knife, using a cutting action, until the mixture comes together in beads, adding the remaining juice if necessary.
2 Gently gather the dough together and lift onto a sheet of baking paper. Roll out to a circle about 30 cm (12 inches) in diameter. Cover with plastic wrap and refrigerate for 10 minutes.
3 Place the blueberries in a bowl and sprinkle them with icing sugar, rind and cinnamon.
4 Place the pastry (still on baking paper) on a baking tray. Brush the centre of the pastry lightly with egg white. Pile the blueberry mixture onto the pastry in a 20 cm (8 inch) diameter circle, then fold the edges of the pastry over the filling, leaving the centre uncovered. Bake for 30–35 minutes. Dust with icing sugar before serving. Cut into wedges and serve warm with whipped cream or ice cream.

BLUEBERRIES
These are native to North America but are now grown all over the world. However, America, where blueberry is called huckleberry, is still the major producer. They are available in the warmer months. The small purplish-blue berry is grown on an evergreen shrub related to heather. Purchase firm, dry and unblemished blueberries with their natural whitish 'bloom' still evident. Store them unwashed and in their container. They can be refrigerated for up to two days and can be used for pies, tarts and muffins, as well as for jam and in berry fruit salads.

ABOVE: Free-form blueberry pie

FRUIT MINCE PIES

Preparation time: 30 minutes
Total cooking time: 25 minutes
Makes 24

Fruit mince

1/3 cup (55 g/2 oz) raisins, chopped
1/3 cup (60 g/2 oz) soft brown sugar
1/4 cup (40 g/1 1/4 oz) sultanas
1/4 cup (45 g/1 1/2 oz) mixed peel
1 tablespoon currants
1 tablespoon chopped almonds
1 small apple, grated
1 teaspoon lemon juice
1/2 teaspoon finely grated orange rind
1/2 teaspoon finely grated lemon rind
1/2 teaspoon mixed spice
pinch of ground nutmeg
25 g (3/4 oz) unsalted butter, melted
1 tablespoon brandy

2 cups (250 g/8 oz) plain flour
150 g (5 oz) unsalted butter, chilled, cubed
2/3 cup (85 g/3 oz) icing sugar
2– 3 tablespoons iced water
icing sugar, to dust

1 For the fruit mince, combine the ingredients in a bowl, spoon into a sterilized jar and seal. You can use the fruit mince straight away but the flavours develop if kept for a while. Keep it in a cool dark place for up to 3 months. (Use ready-made fruit mince if you are short of time.)
2 Preheat the oven to moderate 180°C (350°F/ Gas 4). Lightly grease two 12-hole shallow patty tins. Sift the flour into a bowl, add the butter and rub into the flour with your fingertips until the mixture resembles fine breadcrumbs. Stir in the sugar and make a well in the centre. Add almost all the water and mix with a flat-bladed knife, using a cutting action, until the mixture comes together in beads, adding the remaining water if necessary. Turn out onto a lightly floured surface and gather into a ball. Roll out two thirds of the pastry and cut out 24 rounds, slightly larger than the holes in the patty tins, with a round fluted cutter. Fit the rounds into the tins.
3 Divide the fruit mince among the pastry cases. Roll out the remaining pastry, a little thinner than before, and cut 12 rounds with the same cutter. Using a smaller fluted cutter, cut 12 more rounds. Place the large circles on top of half the pies and press the edges to seal. Place the smaller circles on the remainder. Bake for 25 minutes, or until golden. Leave in the tins for 5 minutes, then lift out with a knife and cool on wire racks. Dust lightly with icing sugar.

PITHIVIER

Preparation time: 20 minutes
Total cooking time: 20 minutes
Makes 1

375 g (12 oz) home-made or bought
 puff pastry (see page 150)
1 egg, lightly beaten

Filling

90 g (3 oz) unsalted butter, softened
2/3 cup (85 g/3 oz) icing sugar
2 egg yolks
1 1/4 cups (135 g/4 1/2 oz) ground almonds
2 teaspoons almond essence

1 Preheat the oven to hot 210°C (415°F/ Gas 6– 7). Lightly grease a large baking tray, line with baking paper, then place in the hot oven to heat.
2 Divide the pastry in half and roll out each piece between two sheets of baking paper to 3 mm (1/8 inch) thick. Using cake tins as a guide, cut a 20 cm (8 inch) round from one sheet of pastry and an 18 cm (7 inch) round from the other. Place the smaller round on the baking tray to form the base.
3 For the filling, beat the butter and icing sugar in a bowl with electric beaters until light and creamy. Add the egg yolks and beat until combined. Add the almonds and almond essence and stir together.
4 Carefully spread the filling over the pastry base, leaving a 2.5 cm (1 inch) border. Place the remaining pastry round over the top and press slightly on the border to seal. Mark into eight curved wedges, being careful not to cut all the way through. Make deep cuts around the border at 2 cm (3/4 inch) intervals and make indentations with the back of a floured knife. Brush the beaten egg all over the top of the pastry. Bake the pithivier for about 20 minutes, or until the puff pastry is puffed and golden brown.

Spread the almond filling evenly over the pastry base, leaving a border.

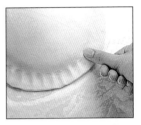

Press the pastry edges together all the way around to seal.

Mark the top into eight curved wedges, being careful not to cut all the way through.

OPPOSITE PAGE: Fruit mince pies (top); Pithivier

BAKEWELL TART

In the mid-nineteenth century, in Bakewell, a town in Derbyshire, this tart made its first appearance as *Bakewell Pudding*. The famous recipe writer Eliza Action made reference to it in her 'Modern Cookery' book in 1845. The idea of puddings with a jam layer topped with fruit and a sugar, butter and egg mixture was part of early British cooking. However, the pastry base, a feature of the Bakewell, was not common. Almond flavour was also added, firstly with drops of almond essence and later with ground almonds, which changed the texture.

ABOVE: Bakewell tart

BAKEWELL TART

Preparation time: 25 minutes
  + 20 minutes refrigeration
Total cooking time: 55 minutes
Serves 6

★ ★

1 cup (125 g/4 oz) plain flour
90 g (3 oz) unsalted butter, chilled, cubed
2 teaspoons caster sugar
2 tablespoons iced water

Filling

90 g (3 oz) unsalted butter
1/3 cup (90 g/3 oz) caster sugar
2 eggs, lightly beaten
3 drops almond essence
2/3 cup (70 g/2 1/4 oz) ground almonds
1/3 cup (40 g/1 1/4 oz) self-raising flour
1/2 cup (155 g/5 oz) raspberry jam

1 Preheat the oven to moderate 180°C (350°F/ Gas 4). Lightly grease a 20 cm (8 inch) round, loose-based, fluted tart tin. Sift the flour into a large bowl and rub in the butter, using your fingertips, until the the mixture resembles fine breadcrumbs. Stir in the sugar. Make a well in the centre, add almost all the water and mix with a flat-bladed knife, using a cutting action, until the mixture comes together in beads, adding more water if the dough is too dry.

2 Gently gather the dough together and roll out between two sheets of baking paper to cover the base and side of the tin. Line the tin with the pastry, trim the edges and refrigerate for 20 minutes. Line the pastry with baking paper and pour in some baking beads or uncooked rice. Bake for 10 minutes, remove the paper and beads, then bake the pastry for another 7 minutes, or until golden. Set aside to cool.

3 For the filling, beat the butter and sugar in a small bowl with electric beaters until light and creamy. Gradually add the egg, beating thoroughly after each addition. Add the almond essence and beat until combined. Transfer to a large bowl and fold in the ground almonds and sifted flour with a metal spoon.

4 Spread the jam over the pastry, then spoon the almond mixture on top and smooth the surface. Bake for 35 minutes, or until risen and golden.

NEENISH TARTS

Preparation time: 1 hour
  + 30 minutes refrigeration
Total cooking time: 15 minutes
Makes 12

★ ★ ★

2 tablespoons plain flour
²/₃ cup (60 g/2 oz) ground almonds
¹/₂ cup (60 g/2 oz) icing sugar, sifted
1 egg white, lightly beaten

Creamy filling

1 tablespoon plain flour
¹/₂ cup (125 ml/4 fl oz) milk
2 egg yolks
60 g (2 oz) unsalted butter, softened
2 tablespoons caster sugar
¹/₄ teaspoon vanilla essence

Icing

1 cup (125 g/4 oz) icing sugar
2 tablespoons milk, extra
1 tablespoon cocoa powder

1 Lightly grease a 12-hole shallow patty tin. Sift the flour into a bowl and stir in the ground almonds and icing sugar. Make a well in the centre, add the beaten egg white and mix with a flat-bladed knife, using a cutting action, until the mixture comes together in beads and forms a stiff paste. Turn onto a lightly floured surface and gently gather into a ball. Wrap in plastic wrap and refrigerate for 30 minutes, to firm.

2 Preheat the oven to moderately hot 190°C (375°F/Gas 5). Roll out the dough between two sheets of baking paper to 2–3 mm (¹/₈ inch) thick. Cut the pastry into 12 circles with a 7 cm (2³/₄ inch) fluted cutter. Press the pastry circles into the greased patty tin and prick evenly with a fork. Bake for 10 minutes, or until lightly golden.

3 For the creamy filling, stir the flour and milk in a saucepan until smooth, then stir over medium heat for 2 minutes, or until the mixture boils and thickens. Remove from the heat, then quickly stir in the egg yolks until smooth. Cover the surface with plastic wrap and set aside to cool. Using electric beaters, beat the butter, sugar and vanilla essence in a bowl until light and creamy. Gradually add the cooled egg mixture and beat until smooth.

Spoon some of the mixture into each pastry shell and gently smooth the tops with the back of a spoon.

4 For the icing, combine the icing sugar and milk in a heatproof bowl, place over a saucepan of simmering water and stir until smooth and glossy. Remove, transfer half the icing to a small bowl, add the cocoa and stir until smooth.

5 Using a small, flat-bladed knife, spread plain icing over half of each tart, starting from the centre and making a straight line with the icing, then pushing the icing out to the edge. Allow to set. Reheat the chocolate icing and ice the other half of each tart. Allow the icing to set completely before serving.

ABOVE: Neenish tarts

DEEP DISH APPLE PIE

Preparation time: 1 hour
+ 40 minutes refrigeration
Total cooking time: 1 hour
Serves 8

✫ ✫

2 cups (250 g/8 oz) plain flour
1/4 cup (30 g/1 oz) self-raising flour
150 g (5 oz) unsalted butter, chilled, cubed
2 tablespoons caster sugar
4– 5 tablespoons iced water
1 egg, extra, lightly beaten, for glazing

Filling

8 large Granny Smith apples
2 thick strips lemon rind
6 whole cloves
1 cinnamon stick
1/2 cup (125 g/4 oz) sugar

BELOW: Deep dish apple pie

1 Lightly grease a deep 20 cm (8 inch) diameter springform tin. Line the base with baking paper and grease the paper, then dust lightly with flour and shake off the excess.
2 Sift the flours into a bowl and rub in the butter with your fingertips until the mixture resembles fine breadcrumbs. Mix in the sugar, then make a well in the centre. Add almost all the water and mix with a flat-bladed knife, using a cutting action, until the mixture comes together in beads. Add more water if necessary. Gather together on a floured surface. Wrap in plastic wrap and refrigerate for 20 minutes.
3 Roll two thirds of the pastry between two sheets of baking paper until large enough to cover the base and side of the tin. Line the tin with the pastry. Roll out the remaining pastry between the baking paper sheets to fit the top of the tin. Refrigerate the pastry for 20 minutes.
4 Peel and core the apples and cut each apple into 12 wedges. Combine with the lemon rind, cloves, cinnamon, sugar and 2 cups (500 ml/ 16 fl oz) water in a large saucepan. Cover and simmer for 10 minutes, or until tender. Drain well and set aside until cold. Discard the rind, cloves and cinnamon.
5 Preheat the oven to moderate 180°C (350°F/ Gas 4). Spoon the apple into the pastry shell. Cover with the pastry top. Brush the pastry edges with beaten egg and trim with a sharp knife, crimping the edges to seal. Prick the top with a fork and brush with beaten egg. Bake for 50 minutes, or until the pastry is cooked. Leave in the tin for 10 minutes before removing.

LINZERTORTE

Preparation time: 30 minutes
+ 40 minutes refrigeration
Total cooking time: 30 minutes
Makes 1

✫ ✫

2/3 cup (100 g/3 1/2 oz) blanched almonds
1 1/2 cups (185 g/6 oz) plain flour
1/2 teaspoon ground cinnamon
90 g (3 oz) unsalted butter, chilled, cubed
1/4 cup (60 g/2 oz) caster sugar
1 egg yolk
2– 3 tablespoons lemon juice or water
1 cup (315 g/10 oz) raspberry jam
1 egg yolk, extra
1/4 cup (80 g/2 3/4 oz) apricot jam

LINZERTORTE
This beautiful tart originally came from Linz in Austria but is now well known all over the world. Mrs Beeton's famous *Book of Household Management* mentions the tart as far back as 1906. The pastry is rich and contains ground almonds and spices. The base is traditionally spread with jam, always raspberry, and the top is decoratively latticed with pastry and glazed with egg yolk to give it a rich dark crust.

1 Grind the almonds in a food processor until they are the consistency of a medium coarse meal. Place the flour and cinnamon in a bowl and rub in the butter with your fingertips until the mixture resembles fine breadcrumbs. Stir in the caster sugar and almonds.

2 Make a well in the centre and add the egg yolk and lemon juice. Mix with a flat-bladed knife, using a cutting action until the mixture comes together in beads. Turn onto a lightly floured surface and knead briefly until smooth. Wrap in plastic wrap and refrigerate for at least 20 minutes to firm.

3 Roll two thirds of the pastry out between two sheets of baking paper into a circle to fit a 20 cm (8 inch) round, loose-based, fluted tart tin. Press into the tin and trim away any excess pastry. Spread the raspberry jam over the base.

4 Roll out the remaining pastry, including any scraps, to a thickness of 3 mm (1/8 inch). Cut it into 2 cm (3/4 inch) strips with a fluted cutter.

Lay half the strips on a sheet of baking paper, leaving a 1 cm (1/2 inch) gap between each strip. Interweave the remaining strips to form a lattice pattern. Place on top of the tart and trim the edges with a sharp knife. Cover with plastic wrap and refrigerate for 20 minutes.

5 Preheat the oven to moderate 180°C (350°F/ Gas 4). Place a baking tray in the oven to heat. Combine the extra egg yolk with 1 teaspoon water and brush over the tart. Place the tin on the heated tray and bake for 25– 30 minutes, or until the pastry is golden brown.

6 Meanwhile, heat the apricot jam with 1 tablespoon of water, then strain the jam and brush over the tart while hot. Leave to cool in the tin, then remove and cut into wedges.

NOTE: Fluted cutters or special lattice cutters are available from speciality kitchenware stores. If you cannot obtain these, simply cut straight lines instead.

ABOVE: Linzertorte

CHERRY AND CREAM CHEESE STRUDEL

Brush the filo pastry with melted butter, then sprinkle with the combined crumbs, almonds and sugar.

Roll the pastry from a long side and fold in the ends as you roll.

OPPOSITE PAGE:
Pear and almond flan (top); Cherry and cream cheese strudel

PEAR AND ALMOND FLAN

Preparation time: 15 minutes
+ 2 hours 30 minutes refrigeration
Total cooking time: 1 hour 10 minutes
Serves 8

 ✶ ✶

1¼ cups (155 g/5 oz) plain flour
90 g (3 oz) unsalted butter, chilled, cubed
¼ cup (60 g/2 oz) caster sugar
2 egg yolks, lightly beaten

Filling

165 g (5½ oz) unsalted butter, softened
⅔ cup (160 g/5½ oz) caster sugar
3 eggs
1¼ cups (135 g/4½ oz) ground almonds
1½ tablespoons plain flour
2 very ripe pears

1 Lightly grease a shallow 24 cm (9½ inch) round, loose-based, fluted tart tin. Sift the flour into a bowl and rub in the butter with your fingertips until the mixture resembles fine breadcrumbs. Stir in the caster sugar and mix together. Make a well in the centre, add the egg yolks and mix with a flat-bladed knife, using a cutting action, until the mixture comes together in beads. Turn out onto a lightly floured surface and gather into a ball. Wrap in plastic wrap and refrigerate for 30 minutes.
2 Preheat the oven to moderate 180°C (350°F/ Gas 4). Roll out the pastry between two sheets of baking paper until large enough to line the base and side of the tin. Line the tin with the pastry and trim off any excess. Sparsely prick the base with a fork. Line the base with baking paper, pour in some baking beads or uncooked rice and bake for 10 minutes. Remove the paper and beads and bake for another 10 minutes. Cool.
3 For the filling, beat the butter and sugar in a bowl with electric beaters for 30 seconds (don't cream the mixture). Add the eggs one at a time, beating after each addition. Fold in the ground almonds and flour and spread the filling smoothly over the cooled pastry base.
4 Peel the pears, halve lengthways and remove the cores. Cut crossways into 3 mm (⅛ inch) slices. Separate the slices slightly, then place each half on top of the tart to form a cross. Bake for about 50 minutes, or until the filling has set (the middle may still be a little soft). Cool in the tin, then refrigerate for at least 2 hours before serving. Can be dusted with icing sugar.

CHERRY AND CREAM CHEESE STRUDEL

Preparation time: 30 minutes
Total cooking time: 40 minutes
Serves 8

✶ ✶

250 g (8 oz) cream cheese, at
   room temperature
100 ml (3½ fl oz) cream
¼ cup (60 g/2 oz) caster sugar
1 tablespoon brandy or cherry brandy
1 teaspoon vanilla essence
10 sheets filo pastry
75 g (2½ oz) unsalted butter, melted
⅓ cup (35 g/1¼ oz) dry breadcrumbs
⅓ cup (35 g/1¼ oz) ground almonds
2 tablespoons caster sugar, extra
425 g (14 oz) can black pitted cherries,
   drained
icing sugar, to dust

1 Preheat the oven to moderately hot 200°C (400°F/Gas 6). Lightly grease a large baking tray. Put the cream cheese, cream, sugar, brandy and vanilla essence in a bowl and beat with electric beaters until smooth.
2 Take one sheet of filo pastry (keep the rest covered with a damp tea towel to prevent drying out), brush with some of the melted butter and sprinkle with some of the combined crumbs, almonds and sugar. Place another sheet of filo on top. Repeat brushing and sprinkling until all the filo sheets are used.
3 Spread the cream cheese mixture evenly over the pastry, leaving a 4 cm (1½ inch) border all around. Brush butter over the border. Arrange the cherries over the cream cheese.
4 Roll the pastry from one long side and fold in the ends as you roll. Form into a firm roll and place seam-side-down on the greased tray. Brush all over with the remaining butter. Bake for 10 minutes, then reduce the oven to moderate 180°C (350°F/Gas 4) and continue to bake for 30 minutes, or until crisp and golden. Place on a wire rack to cool. Dust liberally with icing sugar and cut into slices.

CHEESECAKES

Cheesecakes vary greatly from light and fluffy to dense and rich. The uncooked, lighter variety is set with gelatine and has a crushed biscuit base. However, the traditional European cheesecake has a pastry base and is baked. It is smooth, creamy and luscious. A variety of cheeses can be used, often a combination of cream cheese, ricotta, cottage cheese and sour cream. Eggs are added to bind and flavours such as sugar, grated citrus rind and essences are beaten in.

ABOVE: New York cheesecake

NEW YORK CHEESECAKE

Preparation time: 1 hour
 + 20 minutes refrigeration
Total cooking time: 1 hour 50 minutes
Serves 12

★ ★

1/2 cup (60 g/2 oz) self-raising flour
1 cup (125 g/4 oz) plain flour
80 g (2 3/4 oz) unsalted butter, chilled, cubed
1/4 cup (60 g/2 oz) caster sugar
1 teaspoon grated lemon rind
1 egg, lightly beaten
1 1/2 cups (375 ml/12 fl oz) cream, for serving

Filling

750 g (1 1/2 lb) cream cheese, softened
1 cup (250 g/8 oz) caster sugar
1/4 cup (30 g/1 oz) plain flour
2 teaspoons grated orange rind

2 teaspoons grated lemon rind
4 eggs
2/3 cup (170 ml/5 1/2 fl oz) cream

Candied rind

1 cup (250 g/8 oz) caster sugar
rind of 3 limes, 3 lemons and 3 oranges, shredded

1 Sift the flours into a bowl and rub in the butter with your fingertips until the mixture resembles fine breadcrumbs. Mix in the caster sugar and grated rind.
2 Make a well in the centre, add the egg and mix with a flat-bladed knife, using a cutting action, until the mixture comes together in beads. You may need to add a little iced water to bring the dough together. Turn onto a lightly floured surface, gather together and shape into a disc. Wrap in plastic wrap and refrigerate for 20 minutes, or until firm. Preheat the oven to hot 210°C (415°F/Gas 6–7).

3 Roll the pastry between two sheets of baking paper until large enough to fit the base and side of a greased 22 cm (9 inch) round springform cake tin. Remove the paper and put the pastry in the tin. Trim the edges. Line the pastry shell with crumpled baking paper and fill with baking beads or uncooked rice. Bake for 10 minutes, then remove the baking paper and beads, flatten the pastry lightly with the back of a spoon and bake for 5 minutes. Cool completely.

4 For the filling, reduce the oven to slow 150°C (300°F/Gas 2). Beat the cream cheese, sugar, flour and rinds until smooth. Add the eggs, one at a time, beating after each addition. Beat in the cream, pour the filling over the pastry and bake for 1 hour 25 minutes, or until almost set (it may take another 10 minutes). Cool, then refrigerate until ready to serve.

5 To make the candied rind, put the sugar in a saucepan with 1/4 cup (60 ml/2 fl oz) water and stir over low heat until dissolved. Add the rind, bring to the boil, reduce the heat and simmer for 5–6 minutes. Cool, then drain (you can save the syrup to serve with the cheesecake). Whip the cream, spoon over the cold cheesecake and top with candied rind. Cut into small wedges for serving.

JAM ROLY POLY

Preparation time: 20 minutes
Total cooking time: 35 minutes
Serves 4

★★

2 cups (250 g/8 oz) self-raising flour, sifted
125 g (4 oz) unsalted butter, chilled, cubed
2 tablespoons caster sugar
50 ml (1³/4 fl oz) milk
²/3 cup (210 g/7 oz) raspberry jam
1 tablespoon milk, extra

1 Preheat the oven to moderate 180°C (350°F/Gas 4) and line a baking tray with baking paper. Sift the flour into a large bowl and rub in the butter with your fingertips until the mixture resembles fine breadcrumbs. Stir in the sugar and make a well in the centre.

2 Add the milk and 50 ml (1³/4 fl oz) water to the well in the flour and mix with a flat-bladed knife, using a cutting action, until the mixture comes together in beads. Turn out onto a lightly floured surface and gather together to form a smooth dough. Roll out the dough, on a large sheet of baking paper, into a rectangle measuring about 33 x 23 cm (13 x 9 inches) and 5 mm (1/4 inch) thick. Spread with the raspberry jam, leaving a 5 mm (1/4 inch) border all around.

3 Roll up the dough lengthways like a swiss roll and place on the tray seam-side-down. Brush with the extra milk and bake for about 35 minutes, or until golden and cooked through. Leave for a few minutes before cutting into thick slices with a serrated knife. Serve warm with custard.

NOTE: During cooking, the jam will ooze out slightly from the pastry but this is fine.

BELOW: Jam roly poly

PORTUGUESE CUSTARD TARTS

Preparation time: 40 minutes
Total cooking time: 40 minutes
Makes 12

★ ★ ★

1 1/4 cups (155 g/5 oz) plain flour

25 g (3/4 oz) Copha (white vegetable shortening), chopped and softened

30 g (1 oz) unsalted butter, chopped and softened

1 cup (250 g/8 oz) sugar

2 cups (500 ml/16 fl oz) milk

1/4 cup (30 g/1 oz) cornflour

1 tablespoon custard powder

4 egg yolks

1 teaspoon vanilla essence

1 Sift the flour into a large bowl and add about 3/4 cup (185 ml/6 fl oz) water, or enough to form a soft dough. Gather the dough into a ball, then roll out on baking paper to form a 24 x 30 cm (9 1/2 x 12 inch) rectangle. Spread the vegetable shortening over the surface. Roll up from the short edge to form a log.

2 Roll the dough out into a rectangle again and spread with the butter. Roll up again into a roll and slice into 12 even pieces. Working from the centre outwards, use your fingertips to press each round out to a circle large enough to cover the base and side of 1/3 cup (80 ml/2 3/4 fl oz) muffin holes. Press into the holes and refrigerate while preparing the filling.

3 Put the sugar and 1/3 cup (80 ml/2 3/4 fl oz) water in a saucepan and stir over low heat until the sugar dissolves.

4 Stir a little of the milk with the cornflour and custard powder in a small bowl to form a smooth paste. Add to the pan with the remaining milk, egg yolks and vanilla. Stir over low heat until the mixture thickens. Transfer to a bowl, cover and cool.

5 Preheat the oven to hot 220°C (425°F/Gas 7). Divide the filling among the pastry bases and bake for 25–30 minutes, or until the custard is set and the tops have browned. Cool in the tins, then transfer to a wire rack.

BELOW: Portuguese custard tarts

Stir the apples occasionally until they are cooked and the mixture is golden.

Press the edges of the pastry together to seal.

Knock up the edges of the puff pastry with a knife to ensure that it rises during cooking.

JALOUSIE

Preparation time: 40 minutes
Total cooking time: 45 minutes
Serves 4–6

★★

30 g (1 oz) unsalted butter

¼ cup (45 g/1½ oz) soft brown sugar

500 g (1 lb) apples, peeled, cored and cubed

1 teaspoon grated lemon rind

1 tablespoon lemon juice

¼ teaspoon ground nutmeg

¼ teaspoon ground cinnamon

30 g (1 oz) sultanas

500 g (1 lb) home-made or bought
  puff pastry (see page 150)

1 egg, lightly beaten, to glaze

 Preheat the oven to hot 220°C (425°F/Gas 7). Lightly grease a baking tray and line it with baking paper.

2 Melt the butter and sugar in a frying pan. Add the apple, lemon rind and lemon juice. Cook over medium heat for 10 minutes, stirring occasionally, until the apples are cooked and the mixture is golden. Stir in the nutmeg, cinnamon and sultanas. Cool completely.

3 On a lightly floured surface, roll out one half of the pastry to a 24 x 18 cm (10 x 7 inch) rectangle. Spread the fruit mixture over the pastry, leaving a 2.5 cm (1 inch) border. Brush the edges lightly with some of the beaten egg.

4 Roll the second half of the pastry on a lightly floured surface to a 25 x 18 cm (10 x 7 inch) rectangle. Using a sharp knife, cut slashes in the pastry across its width, leaving a 2 cm (¾ inch) border around the edge. The slashes should open slightly and look like a venetian blind (jalousie in French). Place over the fruit and press the edges together. Trim away any extra pastry. Knock up the puff pastry (brush the sides upwards) with a knife to ensure rising during cooking. Glaze the top with the remaining beaten egg. Bake for 25–30 minutes, or until puffed and golden. Can be dusted with icing sugar.

ABOVE: Jalousie

slightly. Beat the mixture to release any remaining heat. Gradually add the egg, about 3 teaspoons at a time. Beat well after each addition until all the egg has been added and the mixture is glossy—a wooden spoon should stand upright. If it is too runny, the egg has been added too quickly. If this happens, beat for several more minutes, or until thickened.

3 Spoon the mixture into a piping bag fitted with a 1.5 cm (⅝ inch) plain nozzle. Sprinkle the baking trays lightly with water. Pipe 15 cm (6 inch) lengths onto the trays, leaving room for expansion. Bake for 10–15 minutes. Reduce the heat to moderate 180°C (350°F/Gas 4). Bake for another 15 minutes, or until golden and firm. Cool on a wire rack. Split each eclair, removing any uncooked dough. Fill the puffs with cream.

4 Put the chocolate in a heatproof bowl. Bring a saucepan of water to the boil and remove the pan from the heat. Sit the bowl over the pan, making sure the bowl is not touching the water. Allow to stand, stirring occasionally, until the chocolate has melted. Spread over the tops.

DANISH PASTRIES

Preparation time: 40 minutes
    + 1 hour 30 minutes rising
    + 4 hours 30 minutes refrigeration
Total cooking time: 25 minutes
Makes 12

★ ★ ★

7 g (¼ oz) sachet dried yeast
½ cup (125 ml/4 fl oz) warm milk
1 teaspoon caster sugar
2 cups (250 g/8 oz) plain flour
¼ cup (60 g/2 oz) caster sugar, extra
1 egg, lightly beaten
1 teaspoon vanilla essence
250 g (8 oz) unsalted butter, chilled

Pastry cream

2 tablespoons caster sugar
2 egg yolks
2 teaspoons plain flour
2 teaspoons cornflour
½ cup (125 ml/4 fl oz) hot milk

425 g (14 oz) can apricot halves, drained
1 egg, lightly beaten
40 g (1¼ oz) flaked almonds
¼ cup (80 g/2¾ oz) apricot jam, to glaze

CHOCOLATE ECLAIRS

Preparation time: 30 minutes
Total cooking time: 40 minutes
Makes 18

★ ★

125 g (4 oz) unsalted butter
1 cup (125 g/4 oz) plain flour, sifted
4 eggs, lightly beaten
300 ml (10 fl oz) cream, whipped
150 g (5 oz) dark chocolate, chopped

1 Preheat the oven to hot 210°C (415°F/Gas 6–7). Grease two baking trays. Combine the butter and 1 cup (250 ml/8 fl oz) water in a large heavy-based saucepan. Stir over medium heat until the butter melts. Increase the heat, bring to the boil, then remove from the heat.

2 Add the flour to the saucepan all at once and quickly beat into the water with a wooden spoon. Return to the heat and continue beating until the mixture leaves the side of the pan and forms a ball. Transfer to a large bowl and cool

ABOVE: Chocolate eclairs

1 Stir the yeast, milk and sugar together in a small bowl until dissolved. Leave in a warm place for 10 minutes, or until bubbles appear on the surface. The mixture should be frothy and slightly increased in volume. If not, the yeast is dead and you should start again.

2 Sift the flour and ½ teaspoon salt into a large bowl and stir in the extra sugar. Make a well in the centre and add the yeast mixture, egg and vanilla essence all at once. Mix to a firm dough. Turn out onto a floured surface and knead for 10 minutes to form a smooth, elastic dough.

3 Place the dough in a lightly greased bowl, cover and set aside in a warm place for 1 hour, or until doubled in size. Meanwhile, roll the cold butter between two sheets of baking paper to a 15 x 20 cm (6 x 8 inch) rectangle and then refrigerate until required.

4 Punch down the dough (give it one good punch with your fist) and knead for 1 minute. Roll out to a rectangle measuring 25 x 30 cm (10 x 12 inches). Place the butter in the centre of the dough and fold up the bottom and top of the dough over the butter to join in the centre. Seal the edges with a rolling pin.

5 Give the dough a quarter turn clockwise then roll out to a 20 x 45 cm (8 x 18 inch) rectangle. Fold over the top third of the pastry, then the bottom third and then give another quarter turn clockwise. Cover and refrigerate for 30 minutes. Repeat the rolling, folding, turning and chilling four more times. Wrap in plastic wrap and chill for at least another 2 hours before using.

6 For the pastry cream, place the sugar, egg yolks and flours in a saucepan and whisk to combine. Pour the hot milk over the flour and whisk until smooth. Bring to the boil over moderate heat, stirring all the time, until the mixture boils and thickens. Cover and set aside.

7 Preheat the oven to moderately hot 200°C (400°F/Gas 6) and line two baking trays with baking paper. On a lightly floured surface, roll the dough into a rectangle or square 3 mm (⅛ inch) thick. Cut the dough into 10 cm (4 inch) squares and place on the baking trays.

8 Spoon a tablespoon of pastry cream into the centre of each square and top with 2 apricot halves. Brush one corner with the beaten egg and draw up that corner and the diagonally opposite one to touch in the middle between the apricots. Press firmly in the centre. Leave in a warm place to prove for 30 minutes. Brush each pastry with the egg and sprinkle with the flaked almonds. Bake for 15–20 minutes, or until golden. Cool on wire racks.

9 Melt the apricot jam with 1 tablespoon water and then strain. Brush the tops of the apricots with the hot glaze and serve.

PASTRY CREAM

'Crème patissiere' is the French term for pastry cream. It is a delicious, thick custard based on milk, eggs and sugar and is thickened with flour or cornflour. It becomes firm once cooked and left to stand and is mostly used to fill choux, shortcrust and puff pastry products. The custard often has a praline of crushed toffee and nuts folded through for a different flavour. It is used extensively by French pastry cooks, often to fill elaborate pastries.

BELOW: Danish pastries

BAKLAVA

Mix the oil and melted butter and use to brush each filo sheet. Fold each sheet in half.

Place the oiled filo sheets in the greased tin.

Using a sharp knife, score the top of the baklava into four even strips.

Pour the cold syrup over the hot slice, then leave to soak in.

OPPOSITE PAGE: Baklava (top); Apple turnovers

BAKLAVA

Preparation time: 50 minutes
Total cooking time: 40 minutes
Makes 16 pieces

3¹/2 cups (375 g/12 oz) walnuts, finely chopped
1 cup (155 g/5¹/2 oz) almonds, finely chopped
¹/2 teaspoon ground cinnamon
¹/2 teaspoon mixed spice
1 tablespoon caster sugar
16 sheets filo pastry
1 tablespoon olive oil
200 g (6¹/2 oz) unsalted butter, melted

Syrup

2 cups (500 g/1 lb) sugar
3 whole cloves
3 teaspoons lemon juice

1 Preheat the oven to moderate 180°C (350°F/ Gas 4). Lightly grease the base and sides of an 18 x 28 cm (7 x 11 inch) shallow tin.
2 Mix together the walnuts, almonds, spices and sugar, then divide into three portions.
3 Work with one sheet of filo at a time, keeping the rest covered with a damp tea towel to prevent drying out. Place a sheet of pastry on a work surface. Mix the oil and melted butter and brush liberally over the pastry sheet. Fold the sheet in half crossways. Trim the edges so the pastry fits the base of the tin. Repeat with another three sheets of pastry, brushing each layer liberally with the butter mixture.
4 Sprinkle one portion of the nut filling over the pastry. Continue buttering the pastry, four sheets at a time as before, and layering with the nuts. Finish with pastry on top.
5 Trim the edges and brush the top with the remaining butter and oil. Score the slice lengthways into four even portions and bake for 30 minutes, or until golden and crisp.
6 For the syrup, put the sugar, cloves, lemon juice and 1¹/3 cups (330 ml/11 fl oz) water in a small saucepan and stir over low heat, without boiling, until the sugar has dissolved. Bring to the boil, then reduce the heat and simmer, without stirring, for 10 minutes, or until thickened. Remove from the heat and cool.
7 When the baklava is cooked, pour the cold syrup over the hot slice. The syrup should have the consistency of thick honey and will take a little while to soak in. Leave to cool and cut into diamonds when cold.

NOTES: The baklava can be stored for up to five days in an airtight container.
Filo pastry is a very fine pastry used in many sweet and savoury recipes from the Middle East and other parts of the world. It is available fresh or frozen.

APPLE TURNOVERS

Preparation time: 40 minutes
Total cooking time: 25 minutes
Makes 12 pieces

500 g (1 lb) home-made or bought puff pastry (see page 150)
1 egg white, lightly beaten
caster sugar, to sprinkle

Filling

1 cup (220 g/7 oz) pie or stewed apple
1– 2 tablespoons caster sugar, to taste
¹/4 cup (40 g/1¹/4 oz) raisins, chopped
¹/4 cup (30 g/1 oz) walnuts, chopped

1 Preheat the oven to hot 210°C (415°F/ Gas 6– 7). Lightly grease a baking tray. Roll the pastry on a lighty floured surface to 45 x 35 cm (18 x 14 inches). Cut out twelve 10 cm (4 inch) rounds.
2 For the apple filling, mix together the apple, sugar, raisins and walnuts.
3 Divide the filling among the pastry rounds, then brush the edges with water. Fold in half and pinch firmly together to seal. Use the back of a knife to push up the pastry edge at intervals. Brush the tops with egg white and sprinkle with caster sugar. Make 2 small slits in the top of each turnover. Bake for 15 minutes, then lower the oven to moderately hot 190°C (375°F/Gas 5) and bake for 10 minutes, or until golden. Delicious served warm.
NOTE: These delicious pastry treats are traditionally made as above using apple. However, you can make equally tasty turnovers by substituting the same quantity of cooked or canned pears or rhubarb for the apple. Fruit mince of the same quantity also makes an interesting substitute for the raisins and walnuts.

PROFITEROLES

Preparation: 30 minutes
Total cooking time: 50 minutes
Serves 10

★ ★ ★

Choux pastry

50 g (1³⁄₄ oz) unsalted butter
³⁄₄ cup (90 g/3 oz) plain flour, sifted twice
3 eggs, lightly beaten

Filling

1¹⁄₂ cups (375 ml/12 fl oz) milk
4 egg yolks
¹⁄₃ cup (90 g/3 oz) caster sugar
¹⁄₄ cup (30 g/1 oz) plain flour
1 teaspoon vanilla essence

110 g (3¹⁄₂ oz) good-quality dark chocolate
2 teaspoons oil

BELOW: Profiteroles

1 Preheat the oven to hot 210°C (415°F/ Gas 6– 7). Lightly grease two baking trays. Put the butter in a large heavy-based pan with ³⁄₄ cup (185 ml/6 fl oz) water and stir over medium heat until the mixture comes to the boil. Remove from the heat and quickly beat in the flour with a wooden spoon. Return to the heat and continue beating until the mixture comes together, forms a ball and leaves the side of the pan. Allow to cool slightly.

2 Transfer to a bowl and beat to release any remaining heat. Gradually add the beaten egg, about 3 teaspoons at a time, beating well after each addition, until all the egg has been added and the mixture is thick and glossy—a wooden spoon should stand upright in it. If it is too runny, the egg has been added too quickly. If this happens, beat for several more minutes, or until thickened.

3 Sprinkle the baking trays with water—this creates steam in the oven, helping the puffs to rise. Spoon heaped teaspoons of the mixture onto the baking trays, leaving room for spreading. Bake for 20– 30 minutes, or until browned and hollow sounding, then remove and make a small hole in the base of each puff with a skewer. Return to the oven for 5 minutes to dry out. Cool on a wire rack.

4 For the filling, put the milk in a small saucepan and bring to the boil. Set aside while quickly whisking the yolks and sugar in a bowl until combined. Whisk the flour into the egg mixture. Pour the hot milk slowly onto the egg mixture, whisking constantly. Wash out the pan, return the milk mixture and bring to the boil, stirring with a wooden spoon until the mixture comes to the boil and thickens. Transfer to a heatproof bowl and stir in the vanilla essence. Lay plastic wrap directly over the surface to prevent a skin forming, then refrigerate until cold.

5 Pipe the filling into the profiteroles through the hole in the base, using a piping bag fitted with a small nozzle.

6 Chop the chocolate and put it in a heatproof bowl with the oil. Bring a saucepan of water to the boil and remove the saucepan from the heat. Sit the bowl over the saucepan, making sure the bowl is not touching the water. Allow to stand, stirring occasionally, until the chocolate has melted. Stir until smooth and dip the profiterole tops in the chocolate. Allow to set completely before serving.

CROISSANTS

Preparation time: 40 minutes
  + 1 hour rising
  + overnight refrigeration
Total cooking time: 20 minutes
Makes 12

★ ★ ★

1¹/₃ cups (350 ml/11 fl oz) warm milk
7 g (¹/₄ oz) sachet dried yeast
¹/₄ cup (60 g/2 oz) caster sugar
3¹/₄ cups (405 g/13 oz) plain flour
1 teaspoon salt
250 g (8 oz) unsalted butter, at
  room temperature
1 egg

1 Combine the milk, yeast and 1 tablespoon of the sugar in a small bowl and stir until dissolved. Leave in a warm place for 10 minutes, or until bubbles appear on the surface. The mixture should be frothy and slightly increased in volume. If your yeast doesn't foam, it is dead, so you will have to discard it and start again.
2 Place the flour, salt and remaining sugar in a large bowl and make a well in the centre. Pour the yeast mixture into the well and mix to a rough dough with a wooden spoon. Turn out onto a floured surface and knead for 10 minutes, or until smooth and elastic. Add only a small amount of flour—just enough to stop the dough sticking.
3 Place in a greased large bowl, cover and set aside in a warm place for 1 hour, or until doubled in bulk.
4 Meanwhile, place the butter between two sheets of baking paper, cut in half lengthways and use a rolling pin to pat out to a 20 x 10 cm (8 x 4 inch) rectangle. Cover and refrigerate the butter.
5 Punch down the dough (hit once to expel the air). Knead briefly on a lightly floured surface then roll to a rectangle 45 x 12 cm (18 x 5 inches). Place the butter on the lower half of the dough and fold down the top half. Seal all around the edges using your fingertips to completely seal in the butter.
6 Turn the folded side of the dough to the right. Roll out the dough to a rectangle about 45 x 22 cm (18 x 8¹/₂ inches), then fold up the bottom third and fold down the top third. Wrap in plastic wrap for 20 minutes.
7 Roll again with the fold to the right. Chill for 20 minutes then repeat the process two more times. The butter should be completely incorporated—roll again if not incorporated.
8 Lightly brush two baking trays with melted butter. Cut the dough in half. Roll each half into a large rectangle and trim each to about 36 x 22 cm (14 x 8¹/₂ inches). Cut a cardboard triangular template 18 cm (7 inches) across the base and 14 cm (5¹/₂ inches) along each side. Cut each rectangle into six triangles. Stretch each triangle a little to extend its length. Roll each triangle into a crescent, starting from the base. Place well apart on the prepared tray, cover and refrigerate for a minimum of 4 hours, or overnight.
9 Preheat the oven to moderately hot 200°C (400°F/Gas 6). Lightly beat the egg with 2 teaspoons water in a small bowl. Brush the pastries with egg wash and set aside for 40 minutes, or until doubled in bulk. Brush again with egg wash. Bake for 15–20 minutes, or until crisp and golden.

CROISSANTS

Place the rectangle of butter on the lower half of the dough and fold down the top half.

Roll each triangle of dough into a crescent, starting from the base.

ABOVE: Croissants

PALMIERS

Fold the pastry inwards from the short edges so that they almost meet in the middle.

Fold in the same way again, so that the edges almost meet in the centre.

Arrange the palmiers, cut-side up on the trays, brush with melted butter and sprinkle with sugar mixture.

ABOVE: Sugar and spice palmiers

SUGAR AND SPICE PALMIERS

Preparation time: 20 minutes + 15 minutes refrigeration
Total cooking time: 20 minutes
Makes 32

500 g (1 lb) home-made or bought
  puff pastry (see page 150)
2 tablespoons sugar
1 teaspoon mixed spice
1 teaspoon ground cinnamon
40 g (1¼ oz) unsalted butter, melted
icing sugar, to dust

1 Preheat the oven to hot 210°C (415°F/ Gas 6–7). Lightly grease two baking trays, then line with baking paper. Roll out the pastry between two sheets of baking paper to make a 30 cm (12 inch) square 3 mm (⅛ inch) thick. Combine the sugar and spices in a small bowl. Cut the sheet of pastry in half, then brush each pastry sheet with melted butter. Sprinkle with the sugar mixture, reserving 2 teaspoons.

2 Fold the short edges of pastry inwards, so that the edges almost meet in the centre. Fold the same way once more, then fold over and place both rolls on a tray. Refrigerate for 15 minutes. Using a small, sharp knife, cut into 32 slices.

3 Arrange the palmiers, cut-side up, on the prepared trays, brush with butter and sprinkle lightly with the reserved sugar mixture. Bake for 20 minutes, until golden. Leave to cool on a wire rack. Lightly dust with sifted icing sugar before serving.

NOTE: These palmiers can be stored for up to a day in an airtight container. If you wish, you can re-crisp them in a moderate 180°C (350°F/Gas 4) oven for 5 minutes.

MILLEFEUILLE

Preparation time: 30 minutes
 + 20 minutes refrigeration
Total cooking time: 45 minutes
Serves 4

★★★

Passionfruit curd

3 eggs
60 g (2 oz) unsalted butter
1/2 cup (125 g/4 oz) passionfruit pulp
1/2 cup (125 g/4 oz) sugar

500 g (1 lb) home-made or bought
 puff pastry (see page 150)
300 ml (10 fl oz) cream
2 tablespoons icing sugar
1 teaspoon vanilla essence
1 large ripe mango, thinly sliced
sifted icing sugar, to sprinkle

1 For the passionfruit curd, beat the eggs well, then strain into a heatproof bowl and stir in the remaining ingredients. Place the bowl over a saucepan of simmering water and stir with a wooden spoon for 15–20 minutes, or until the butter has melted and the mixture has thickened slightly and coats the back of the wooden spoon. Cool, then transfer to a bowl, cover with plastic wrap and chill until required.

2 To make the millefeuille, preheat the oven to moderately hot 200°C (400°F/Gas 6). Line a large baking tray with baking paper. Roll the pastry to a 30 x 35 cm (12 inch x 14 inch) rectangle and transfer to the tray. Cover and refrigerate for 20 minutes. Sprinkle lightly with water and prick all over with a fork. Cook for 25 minutes, or until puffed and golden. Cool completely on a wire rack.

3 Whisk the cream with the icing sugar and vanilla until firm peaks form. Carefully trim the pastry sheet and cut into three even-sized strips lengthways. Spread one layer of pastry with half the passionfruit curd, spreading evenly and to the edges. Top this with half of the whipped cream and then top with half of the mango flesh. Place a second sheet of pastry on top and repeat the process. Top with the remaining pastry sheet and sprinkle liberally with icing sugar. Carefully transfer to a serving plate. Use a serrated knife to cut into slices.

NOTE: Instead of making one long millefeuille, you might prefer to make four individual ones.

MILLEFEUILLE

Trim the cooked pastry and cut lengthways into three even-sized strips.

Spread the passionfruit curd evenly over one of the pastry strips.

LEFT: Millefeuille

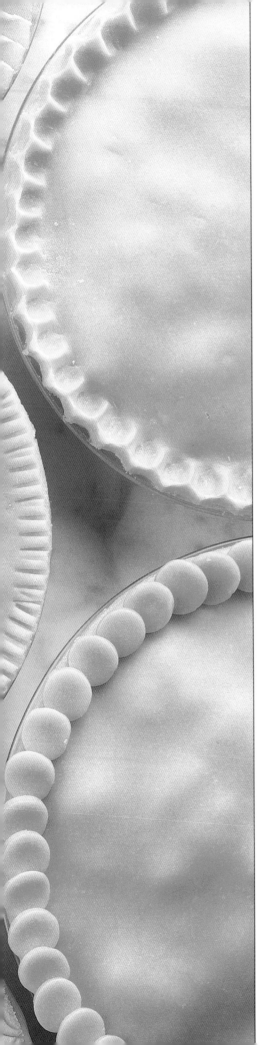

SAVOURY PIES AND PASTRIES

You'd be hard pressed to find someone who doesn't love savoury pies: the flaky, melt-in-the-mouth pastry, the scrumptious filling, the rich gravy. Intensely satisfying to eat, they are equally satisfying to make. As well as family pies, we've included recipes for individual pies and pastries because (and let's be honest here) there are times when you simply don't feel like sharing, and want to savour every bite at your own pace. So whether you're at the dinner table or watching a game, these golden pastries will sort out even the most ferocious appetites.

PIES AND TARTS

A simple decoration on pastry somehow makes a pie or tart seem more appealing,

so take the opportunity to make full use of your creative skills.

Traditionally, savoury pies were decorated to differentiate them from sweet pies when both were served at a meal. These days we use trimmings mainly for decorative effect.

Pies and tarts come in many shapes and sizes but pies are usually double-crusted (a pastry base and top) or with just a lid on top, whereas tarts are generally open with no pastry top. As well as giving pies a finished touch,

decorating can be very practical. Not only can you use up pastry trimmings but it helps seal the edges of a double-crusted pie so the lid remains securely in place.

DECORATIVE EDGES

FORK PRESSED Press a lightly floured fork around the edge of the pie crust.
FLUTED Press the pastry between your thumb and forefinger for a rippled effect.
CRIMPED Press the pastry between the

thumb and forefinger, while indenting with the other forefinger.
SCALLOPED Press an upturned teaspoon on the pastry edges to mark semi-circles.
CHECKERBOARD Make cuts in the pastry edge. Bend every second square inward.
LEAVES Cut out leaf shapes with a cutter or the point of a sharp knife and mark veins using the back of a knife. Attach to the lip of the pie using a little water or egg glaze.

PLAIT Cut three long strips 5 mm (¼ inch) wide. Plait together and attach to the lip of the pie using a little water or egg, pressing gently in place.

ROPE Twist two long sausages of pastry together and attach to the edge with a little water or egg.

FEATHERING Lift the pastry off the lip so that it stands upright and snip diagonally into the edge of the pie. Push one point inwards and one outwards.

DECORATIVE TOPS

There are endless shapes and forms you can use to decorate pies, from cherries and stars to abstract patterns, or simple initials. Alternatively, you can buy small biscuit cutters in various shapes. When rolling out the pastry trimmings, don't make the shapes too thick or they won't cook through. To attach them, first brush the pie lid with an egg glaze, then arrange the decorations and glaze them as well.

You can decorate an open tart with pastry shapes, either around the edge or on top. However, if the filling is quite liquid, cook the shapes separately and arrange on the middle of the tart after it is baked and the filling has set.

Another impressive finish for a pie is a lattice top which is shown on some of the pies in this book. This type of pastry top is surprisingly simple to make. Roll the pastry out on a sheet of baking paper to a square a little larger than the pie. Using a fluted pastry wheel or a small sharp knife, cut strips of pastry about 1.5 cm (⅝ inch) wide. On another sheet of baking paper, lay half the strips vertically, 1 cm (½ inch) apart. Fold back alternate strips of pastry and lay a strip of pastry horizontally across the unfolded strips, then fold the vertical strips back into place. Next, fold the lower strips back and lay another piece horizontally. Repeat with all the strips. Refrigerate until firm then invert the lattice onto the pie and remove the baking paper. Press the edges to seal and trim off the excess pastry.

You can vary not only the width of the pastry strips but also the spacing, to create a tightly woven lattice or one with just three or four strips.

Alternatively, you can make life very simple and buy a lattice cutter. Just roll out the pastry and roll over it with the cutter. Gently open the lattice out, lift it onto your pie and then trim the edges.

CLOKWISE, FROM TOP LEFT:
Rope; Scalloped; Crimped; Leaves; Plait;
Decorative top; Checkerboard; Fork pressed

CHICKEN AND LEEK PIE

Preparation time: 20 minutes
Total cooking time: 40 minutes
Serves 4

50 g (1¾ oz) butter
2 large leeks, thinly sliced
4 spring onions, sliced
1 clove garlic, crushed
¼ cup (30 g/1 oz) plain flour
1½ cups (375 ml/12 fl oz) chicken stock
½ cup (125 ml/4 fl oz) cream
1 barbecued chicken, chopped
375 g (12½ oz) home-made or bought
   puff pastry (see page 150)
¼ cup (60 ml/2 fl oz) milk

BELOW: Chicken and leek pie

1 Preheat the oven to moderately hot 200°C (400°F/Gas 6). Lightly grease a 20 cm (8 inch) pie plate.
2 Melt the butter in a saucepan and add the leek, spring onion and garlic. Cook over low heat for 6 minutes, or until the leek is soft but not browned. Sprinkle with the flour and mix well. Gradually pour in the stock and cook, stirring, until the mixture is thick and smooth.
3 Stir in the cream and add the chicken. Put the mixture in the pie dish and set aside to cool.
4 Divide the pastry into two pieces and roll each piece between two sheets of baking paper to a thickness of 3 mm (⅛ inch). Cut a circle out of one of the sheets of pastry to cover the top of the pie. Brush the rim of the pie plate with a little milk. Put the pastry on top and press to seal around the edge. Trim off any excess pastry and crimp the edge with the back of a fork. Cut the other sheet into 1 cm (½ inch) strips and roll each strip up loosely like a snail. Arrange on top of the pie, starting from the centre and leaving a gap between each one. The spirals may not cover the whole surface of the pie. Make a few small holes between the spirals to let out any steam, and brush the top of the pie lightly with milk.
5 Bake for 25– 30 minutes, or until the top is brown and crispy. Make sure the spirals look well cooked and are not raw in the middle.
NOTE: Make small pies by dividing the mixture among 4 greased 1¼ cup (315 ml/10 fl oz) round ovenproof dishes. Cut the pastry into 4 rounds to fit. Bake for 15 minutes, or until the pastry is crisp.

BEEF PIE

Preparation time: 35 minutes
   + 30 minutes refrigeration
Total cooking time: 2 hours 30 minutes
Serves 6

Filling

2 tablespoons oil
1 kg (2 lb) trimmed chuck steak, cubed
1 large onion, chopped
1 large carrot, finely chopped
2 cloves garlic, crushed
2 tablespoons plain flour
1 cup (250 ml/8 fl oz) beef stock
2 teaspoons fresh thyme
1 tablespoon Worcestershire sauce

Pastry

2 cups (250 g/8 oz) plain flour

150 g (5 oz) butter, chilled, cubed

1 egg yolk

2– 3 tablespoons iced water

1 egg yolk, extra

1 tablespoon milk

1 Lightly grease a 23 cm (9 inch) pie plate. For the filling, heat half the oil in a large frying pan and brown the meat in batches. Remove from the pan. Heat the remaining oil, add the onion, carrot and garlic and brown over medium heat.

2 Return the meat to the pan and stir in the flour. Cook for 1 minute, then remove from the heat and slowly stir in the stock, mixing the flour in well. Add the thyme and Worcestershire sauce, and bring to the boil. Season, to taste.

3 Reduce the heat to very low, cover and simmer for 1½– 2 hours, or until the meat is tender. During the last 15 minutes of cooking, remove the lid and allow the liquid to reduce so that the sauce is very thick and suitable for filling a pie. Allow to cool completely.

4 For the pastry, sift the flour into a large bowl and rub in the butter with your fingertips until it resembles fine breadcrumbs. Add the egg yolk and 2 tablespoons of the water and mix with a knife, using a cutting action, until the mixture comes together in beads, adding more water if the dough is too dry. Turn out onto a lightly floured surface and gather together to form a smooth dough. Wrap in plastic wrap and refrigerate for 30 minutes.

5 Preheat the oven to moderately hot 200°C (400°F/Gas 6). Divide the pastry in half and roll out one piece between two sheets of baking paper until large enough to line the pie plate. Line the plate, fill with the cold filling and roll out the remaining pastry to cover the pie plate. Brush the pastry edges with water. Lay the pastry over the pie and gently press or pinch to seal. Trim any excess pastry. Re-roll the scraps to make decorative shapes and press on the pie.

6 Cut a few steam holes in the top of the pastry. Beat together the egg yolk and milk and brush over the top of the pie. Bake for 20– 30 minutes, or until the pastry is golden and the filling is hot.

ABOVE: Beef pie

BEEF AND RED WINE PIES

Preparation time: 50 minutes
Total cooking time: 2 hours 40 minutes
Makes 6

✷✷

¼ cup (60 ml/2 fl oz) oil

1.5 kg (3 lb) chuck steak, cubed

2 onions, chopped

1 clove garlic, crushed

¼ cup (30 g/1 oz) plain flour

1¼ cups (315 ml/10 fl oz) good-quality
  dry red wine

2 cups (500 ml/16 fl oz) beef stock

2 bay leaves

2 sprigs fresh thyme

2 carrots, chopped

500 g (1 lb) home-made or bought
  shortcrust pastry (see page 148)

*ABOVE: Beef
and red wine pies*

500 g (1 lb) home-made or bought puff pastry
  (see page 150)
1 egg, lightly beaten

1 Lightly grease six metal pie tins measuring 9 cm (3½ inches) along the base and 3 cm 1¼ inches) deep.
2 Heat 2 tablespoons of the oil in a large frying pan and brown the meat in batches. Remove from the pan. Heat the remaining oil in the same pan, add the onion and garlic and stir over medium heat until golden brown. Add the flour and stir over medium heat for 2 minutes, or until well browned. Remove from the heat and gradually stir in the combined wine and stock.
3 Return to the heat and stir until the mixture boils and thickens. Return the meat to the pan, add the bay leaves and thyme and simmer for 1 hour. Add the carrot and simmer for another 45 minutes, or until the meat and carrot are tender and the sauce has thickened. Season, then remove the bay leaves and thyme. Allow to cool.
4 Preheat the oven to moderately hot 200°C (400°F/Gas 6). Divide the shortcrust into six and roll out each piece between two sheets of baking paper to a 25 cm (10 inch) square, 3 mm (⅛ inch) thick. Cut a circle from each shortcrust sheet big enough to line the base and side of a pie tin. Place in the tins and trim the edges. Line each pastry shell with baking paper and fill with baking beads or uncooked rice. Place on a baking tray and bake for 8 minutes. Remove the paper and beads and bake for another 8 minutes, or until the pastry is lightly browned. Allow to cool.
5 Divide the puff pastry into six portions and roll each piece between two sheets of baking paper to a square. Cut circles from the squares of dough, to fit the tops of the pie tins. Spoon some of the filling into each pastry case and brush the edge with some of the beaten egg. Cover with a pastry round and trim any excess pastry, pressing the edges with a fork to seal. Cut a slit in the top of each pie. Brush the pie tops with the remaining beaten egg and bake for 20– 25 minutes, or until the pastry is cooked and golden brown.
NOTES: You can make a family-sized pie using the same ingredients, but substituting a 23 cm (9 inch) metal pie tin. Bake in a moderately hot 200°C (400°F/Gas 6) oven for 30– 35 minutes. Any remaining pastry can be rolled and used to decorate the pie, or frozen for later use.

The alcohol content of the red wine dissipates on heating. While it adds a distinct flavour, you can use all stock if you don't like to use wine.

ONION TART

Preparation time: 40 minutes
 + 40 minutes refrigeration
Total cooking time: 1 hour 30 minutes
Serves 4– 6

Shortcrust pastry

1¼ cups (155 g/5 oz) plain flour

90 g (3 oz) butter, chilled, cubed

2– 3 tablespoons iced water

Filling

25 g (¾ oz) butter

7 onions, sliced

1 tablespoon Dijon mustard

3 eggs, lightly beaten

½ cup (125 g/4 oz) sour cream

¼ cup (25 g/¾ oz) grated Parmesan

1 Lightly grease a round 23 cm (9 inch) fluted tart plate. Sift the flour into a bowl and rub in the butter with your fingertips until the mixture resembles fine breadcrumbs. Make a well, add almost all the water and mix with a flat-bladed knife, using a cutting action, until the mixture comes together in beads, adding more water if the dough is too dry.

2 Gather the dough together and lift out onto a lightly floured surface. Press together until smooth, cover with plastic wrap and chill for 20 minutes. Roll out between two sheets of baking paper to cover the base and side of the tart plate. Place the pastry in the tin and trim any excess pastry. Cover with plastic wrap and chill for 20 minutes.

3 Preheat the oven to moderate 180°C (350°F/ Gas 4). Line the pastry shell with a piece of crumpled baking paper and pour in some baking beads or uncooked rice. Bake for 10 minutes, remove the paper and beads and return to the oven for another 10 minutes, or until lightly golden. Cool completely.

4 For the filling, melt the butter in a large heavy-based frying pan. Add the onion, cover and cook over medium heat for 25 minutes. Uncover and cook for another 10 minutes, stirring often, until soft and golden. Cool.

5 Spread the mustard over the base of the pastry, then spread the onion over the mustard. Whisk together the eggs and sour cream and pour over the onion. Sprinkle with Parmesan and bake for 35 minutes, or until set and golden.

ONIONS

The common dry onion comes in a wide range of varieties, shapes, flavours and sizes. The most readily available are the white, brown and red (Spanish), all of which are inter-changeable in cooking. The red onion is milder in flavour and can be used raw in salads. High heat will burn onions and give them a bitter flavour so, as a general rule, the longer and slower the chopped or sliced onion is cooked in butter or oil, the sweeter it becomes. Do not buy onions if they have started to sprout. Always buy dry-skinned firm onions and store in a wire basket so air can circulate to keep them dry. They will keep for a month if stored this way.

LEFT: Onion tart

RIGHT: Country vegetable pies

COUNTRY VEGETABLE PIES

Preparation time: 50 minutes
+ 30 minutes refrigeration
Total cooking time: 45 minutes
Serves 6

★

2 cups (250 g/8 oz) plain flour
125 g (4 oz) butter, chilled and cubed
2 egg yolks
2– 3 tablespoons iced water

Filling

2 new potatoes, cubed
350 g (11 oz) butternut pumpkin, cubed
100 g (3¹/2 oz) broccoli, cut into small florets
100 g (3¹/2 oz) cauliflower, cut into small florets
1 zucchini, grated
1 carrot, grated
3 spring onions, chopped
3/4 cup (90 g/3 oz) grated Cheddar
1/2 cup (125 g/4 oz) ricotta
1/2 cup (50 g/1 3/4 oz) grated Parmesan
3 tablespoons chopped fresh parsley
1 egg, lightly beaten

1 Sift the flour into a bowl and rub in the butter with your fingertips until the mixture resembles fine breadcrumbs. Make a well in the centre, add the egg yolks and 3 tablespoons of the water and mix with a flat-bladed knife, using a cutting action, until the mixture comes together in beads. Add more water if the dough is too dry. Gently gather the dough together and lift out onto a lightly floured work surface. Press into a ball, cover with plastic wrap and refrigerate for at least 15 minutes.

2 For the filling, steam or boil the potato and pumpkin for 10– 15 minutes, or until just tender. Drain well and place in a large bowl to cool. Gently fold in the broccoli, cauliflower, zucchini, carrot, spring onion, cheeses, parsley and beaten egg. Season, to taste, with salt and cracked black pepper.

3 Preheat the oven to moderately hot 190°C (375°F/Gas 5). Grease six 10 cm (4 inch) pie tins. Divide the pastry into 6 and roll each portion into a rough 20 cm (8 inch) circle. Place the pastry in the tins, leaving the excess overhanging.

4 Divide the filling among the tins. Fold over the overhanging pastry, gently folding or pleating as you go. Place on a baking tray, cover and refrigerate for 15 minutes. Bake for 25– 30 minutes, or until the pastry is cooked and golden brown. Serve hot.

STEAK AND KIDNEY PIE

Preparation time: 20 minutes
Total cooking time: 1 hour 50 minutes
Serves 6

★★

750 g (1½ lb) round steak

4 lamb kidneys

2 tablespoons plain flour

1 tablespoon oil

1 onion, chopped

30 g (1 oz) butter

1 tablespoon Worcestershire sauce

1 tablespoon tomato paste (tomato purée)

½ cup (125 ml/4 fl oz) red wine

1 cup (250 ml/8 fl oz) beef stock

125 g (4 oz) button mushrooms,
  sliced

½ teaspoon dried thyme

4 tablespoons chopped fresh parsley

500 g (1 lb) home-made or bought
  puff pastry (see page 150)

1 egg, lightly beaten

1 Trim the meat of excess fat and sinew and cut into 2 cm (¾ inch) cubes. Peel the skin from the kidneys. Quarter the kidneys and trim away any fat or sinew. Place the flour in a plastic bag with the meat and kidneys and toss gently.

2 Heat the oil in a frying pan, add the onion and cook for 5 minutes, or until soft. Remove from the pan with a slotted spoon. Add the butter to the pan, brown the meat and kidneys in batches and then return all the meat, kidneys and onion to the pan.

3 Add the Worcestershire sauce, tomato paste, wine, stock, mushrooms, thyme and parsley to the pan. Bring to the boil, reduce the heat and simmer, covered, for 1 hour or until the meat is tender. Season, to taste, and allow to cool. Spoon into a 1.5 litre pie plate.

4 Preheat the oven to hot 210°C (415°F/ Gas 6–7). Roll the puff pastry between two sheets of baking paper, so that it is 4 cm (1½ inches) larger than the pie plate. Cut thin strips from the edge of the pastry and press onto the rim of the plate, sealing the joins. Place the pastry on the pie, trim the edges and cut two steam holes in the pastry. Decorate the pie with leftover pastry and brush the top with egg. Bake for 35–40 minutes or until the pastry is golden.

STEAK AND KIDNEY PIE
This is a traditional British pie. Sometimes oysters, boiled eggs and potatoes are added. The cooled mixture is placed in a casserole dish and topped with a pastry crust. If the pie dish is deep, a decorative funnel, often in the shape of a bird, is placed in the centre of the pie to support the pastry and act as a steam vent during the long cooking. Another traditional dish, known as steak and kidney pudding, uses the same ingredients but they are placed, uncooked, in a pudding basin that is lined with suet pastry. The pudding is then steamed or baked.

ABOVE: Steak and kidney pie

BACON

Bacon is meat from the side and back of a pig. It is cured by dry-salting and then smoked to give the distinctive taste. Bacon is usually sold in thin slices called rashers. The middle cut, sometimes called the prime cut, contains the least fat and most meat. Streaky bacon is cut from the tail end of the loin and is streaked with more fat.

ABOVE: Bacon and egg pie

BACON AND EGG PIE

Preparation time: 20 minutes
  + 20 minutes refrigeration
Total cooking time: 1 hour
Serves 4– 6

★

2 tablespoons oil
4 rashers bacon, chopped
250 g (8 oz) home-made or bought
  shortcrust pastry (see page 148)
250 g (8 oz) home-made or bought
  puff pastry (see page 150)
5 eggs, lightly beaten
¼ cup (60 ml/2 fl oz) cream
1 egg, extra, lightly beaten

1 Lightly grease a 20 cm (8 inch) loose-based pie tin. Heat the oil in a frying pan. Add the bacon and cook over medium heat for a few minutes, or until lightly browned. Drain on paper towels and allow to cool slightly.
2 Roll out the shortcrust pastry between two sheets of baking paper until slightly larger than the tin. Place in the tin and roll a rolling pin over the tin to trim off any excess pastry. Refrigerate for 20 minutes. Preheat the oven to hot 210°C (415°F/Gas 6– 7).
3 Line the pastry shell with a piece of baking paper and pour in some baking beads or uncooked rice. Bake for 10 minutes, then remove the paper and beads and cook for another 10 minutes, or until the pastry is dry and golden. Allow to cool.
4 Roll out the puff pastry between two sheets of baking paper to a circle large enough to cover the top of the pie. Arrange the bacon over the cooled pastry base and pour the combined egg and cream over the top. Cover the pie with the puff pastry and press on firmly to seal. Trim the pastry edges and decorate the top with shapes cut from the pastry scraps. Brush with the extra egg and bake for 30– 35 minutes, or until the pastry is puffed and golden. Serve warm or at room temperature.
NOTE: Bacon and egg pie is excellent for taking on picnics. It can be made a day ahead and refrigerated overnight. Allow to come to room temperature before serving.

CORNISH PASTIES

Preparation time: 35 minutes
+ 20 minutes refrigeration
Total cooking time: 45 minutes
Makes 6

★ ★

Shortcrust pastry

2¹/₂ cups (310 g/10 oz) plain flour
125 g (4 oz) butter, chilled and cubed
4– 5 tablespoons iced water

160 g (5¹/₂ oz) round steak,
   finely chopped
I small potato, finely chopped
I small onion, finely chopped
I small carrot, finely chopped
I– 2 teaspoons Worcestershire sauce
2 tablespoons beef stock
I egg, lightly beaten

I Lightly grease a baking tray. Sift the flour and a pinch of salt into a large bowl and rub in the butter with your fingertips until the mixture resembles fine breadcrumbs. Make a well in the centre and add almost all the water. Mix together with a flat-bladed knife, using a cutting action, until the mixture comes together in small beads, adding more water if the dough is too dry. Turn out onto a floured surface and form into a ball. Cover with plastic wrap and refrigerate for 20 minutes.

2 Preheat the oven to hot 210°C (415°F/Gas 6– 7). Mix together the steak, potato, onion, carrot, Worcestershire sauce and stock in a bowl and season well.

3 Divide the dough into 6 portions. Roll out each portion to 3 mm (¹/₈ inch) thick. Using a 16 cm (6¹/₂ inch) diameter plate as a guide, cut 6 circles. Divide the filling among the circles.

4 Brush the edges with beaten egg and bring the pastry together to form a semi-circle. Pinch the edges into a frill and place on the tray. Brush the pastry with egg and bake for 15 minutes. Reduce the oven to moderate 180°C (350°F/Gas 4) and cook for 25– 30 minutes, or until golden.

CORNISH PASTIES

Mix together the steak, potato, onion, carrot, Worcestershire sauce and beef stock.

Lift both sides of the pastry up to enclose the filling. Pinch the edges to seal.

LEFT: Cornish pasties

QUICHES All these quiches are equally delicious

whether served hot or cold. The quantities are suitable to serve up to six people.

A fresh green salad makes a perfect accompaniment for any of the quiches.

PASTRY FOR QUICHES

Sift 1¾ cups (215 g/7 oz) plain flour into a bowl and add 100 g (3½ oz) chopped chilled butter. Rub the butter into the flour with your fingertips until it resembles fine breadcrumbs. Make a well in the centre and add 2 tablespoons iced water. Mix with a flat-bladed knife, using a cutting action, until the mixture comes together in beads. Add a little more water if the dough is too dry. Turn out onto a lightly floured surface and gather into a ball. Cover with plastic wrap and refrigerate for 20 minutes. Preheat the oven to moderately hot 190°C (375°F/ Gas 5). Roll out the pastry between two sheets of baking paper to fit a shallow loose-based 25 cm (10 inch) tart tin. Lift the pastry into the tin and press it well into the sides. Trim off any excess by rolling a rolling pin across the top of the tin. Refrigerate the pastry for 20 minutes. Cover the shell with baking paper, fill evenly with baking beads or uncooked rice and bake for 15 minutes, or until the pastry is dried out and golden. Cool slightly before filling with one of these fillings. For all these quiches, bake the pastry, then reduce the oven temperature to moderate 180°C (350°F/Gas 4).

FILLINGS

QUICHE LORRAINE Melt 30 g (1 oz) butter in a frying pan and cook 1 finely chopped onion and 3 finely chopped bacon rashers over medium heat for 10 minutes. Cool, then spread over the cooled pastry. Whisk together 3 eggs, ¾ cup (185 ml/ 6 fl oz) cream and 40 g (1¼ oz) grated Gruyère. Season. Pour over the onion and sprinkle with 40 g (1¼ oz) grated Gruyère and ¼ teaspoon nutmeg. Bake for 30 minutes, or until just firm.

SALMON Drain and flake a 415 g (13 oz) can red salmon and spread over the cooled pastry. Mix 4 lightly beaten eggs, ½ cup (60 g/2 oz) grated Cheddar, ½ cup (125 ml/4 fl oz) each of milk and cream, 4 sliced spring onions and 4 tablespoons chopped fresh parsley. Pour over the salmon. Bake for 30 minutes or until set.

CRAB Make the pastry using the basic pastry recipe, then line two greased 12 cm (5 inches) round, 4 cm (1½ inches) deep tart tins with the dough. Bake the pastry as described above and then set aside to cool slightly. Heat 20 g (¾ oz) of butter in a small frying pan and cook 1 thinly sliced onion until just soft. Remove from the pan and drain on paper towels. Drain a 200 g (6½ oz) can crab meat and squeeze out any excess moisture. Spread the onion and crab over the cooled pastry. Mix 3 eggs, ¾ cup (185 ml/6 fl oz) cream and ¾ cup (90 g/3 oz) grated Cheddar in a bowl. Pour into the pastry case and, if you like, top with some fresh dill sprigs. Bake for 40 minutes, or until lightly golden and set.

ASPARAGUS AND ARTICHOKE Trim 155 g (5 oz) asparagus, cut into bite-sized pieces and blanch the pieces in a saucepan of boiling salted water. Drain, then refresh in ice-cold water. Lightly beat together 3 eggs, ½ cup (125 ml/4 fl oz) cream and ⅓ cup (40 g/1¼ oz) grated Gruyère, then season with salt and black pepper. Cut 140 g (4½ oz) marinated artichoke hearts into quarters and spread over the cooled pastry, along with the asparagus. Pour on the egg and cream mixture and sprinkle with ½ cup (60 g/2 oz) grated Cheddar. Bake for 25 minutes, or until the filling is set and golden. Cover with foil if the pastry becomes too brown before the filling is fully set.

QUICHES, FROM TOP LEFT:
Quiche Lorraine; Salmon; Crab (2);
Asparagus and artichoke

RAISED PORK PIE

Cover the outside of the tin with the pastry, working quickly so that the pastry does not set.

The greased paper collar should fit snugly around the outside of the pastry.

Cut a small hole in the top of the pie to allow the gelatine to be poured in.

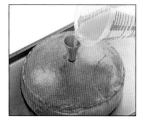

Gradually pour the gelatine into the cooked and cooled pie until it is full.

RAISED PORK PIE

Preparation time: 50 minutes
+ 10 minutes cooling
+ overnight setting
Total cooking time: 1 hour 10 minutes
Serves 8

⋆ ⋆ ⋆

1.2 kg (1 lb 6½ oz) pork mince

⅔ cup (100 g/3½ oz) pistachio nuts, shelled and chopped

2 green apples, peeled and finely chopped

6 fresh sage leaves, finely chopped

4 cups (500 g/1 lb) plain flour

150 g (5 oz) lard

2 eggs, lightly beaten

1 egg yolk

200 ml (6½ fl oz) vegetable stock

200 ml (6½ fl oz) unsweetened apple juice

2 teaspoons gelatine

1 Preheat the oven to moderately hot 200°C (400°F/Gas 6). Put the pork, pistachio nuts, apple and sage leaves in a bowl, mix well and season. Fry a piece of the mixture, to taste, and adjust the seasoning. Cover and refrigerate until ready to use. Wrap plastic wrap around a 6 cm (2½ inch) high, 20 cm (8 inch) straight-sided tin, then turn the tin over, and grease the outside base and side of the tin.

2 Sift the flour and 1 teaspoon salt into a bowl and make a well in the centre. Put the lard in a saucepan with 210 ml (7 fl oz) water, bring to the boil and add to the flour with the eggs.
Mix with a wooden spoon until combined, then turn out onto a work surface and bring the mixture together to form a smooth dough. Unlike any other kind of pastry, this hot water pastry must be kept warm. Cover with a cloth and leave in a warm place for 10 minutes until cool enough to handle.

3 When the pastry is just warm, set aside one third—do not refrigerate. Roll the remainder into a circle large enough to just cover the outside of the tin. Lift onto a rolling pin and place over the tin, working fast before the pastry sets. Refrigerate until the pastry hardens. Carefully pull out the tin and remove the plastic wrap. Attach a paper collar made of two layers of greased baking paper around the outside of the pastry so it fits snugly. Secure with string or a paper

RIGHT: Raised pork pie

clip at the top and bottom. Fill the pie with the mince mixture, then roll out the remaining pastry to form a lid. Attach it to the base with some water, pressing or crimping it to make it look neat. Cut a small hole in the top.

4 Put the pie on a baking tray, bake for 40 minutes and check the pastry top. If it is still pale, bake for another 10 minutes, then remove the paper. Brush with egg yolk mixed with 1 tablespoon water and bake for 15 minutes, or until the sides are brown. Cool completely.

5 Bring the stock and half the apple juice to the boil. Sprinkle the gelatine over the surface of the remaining apple juice in a jug and leave to go spongy, then pour into the stock and mix until the gelatine dissolves. Place a small funnel (piping nozzles work well) in the hole of the pie and pour in a little of the gelatine mixture, leave to settle and then pour in some more until the pie is full. Fill the pie completely so there will be no gaps when the gelatine sets. Refrigerate overnight.

NOTES: If wrapped tightly with plastic wrap, pork pies keep in the refrigerator for up to five days.

A raised pie is one made of hot pastry that is moulded around a tin or wooden mould. Hinged tins for raised pies are also available.

CREAMY SNAPPER PIE

Preparation time: 25 minutes
Total cooking time: 1 hour 20 minutes
Serves 6

★★

1 kg (2 lb) skinless snapper fillets
2 tablespoons olive oil
4 onions, thinly sliced
1 1/2 cups (375 ml/12 fl oz) fish stock
3 1/2 cups (875 ml/28 fl oz) cream
375 g (12 1/2 oz) home-made or bought puff
    pastry (see page 150)
1 egg, lightly beaten

 Cut the snapper fillets into large pieces. Heat the oil in a large deep-sided frying pan, add the onion and stir over medium heat for 20 minutes, or until the onion is golden brown and slightly caramelized.

2 Add the stock to the frying pan, bring to the boil and cook for 10 minutes, or until the liquid has nearly evaporated. Preheat the oven to hot 220°C (425°F/Gas 7).

3 Pour the cream into the frying pan and bring to the boil. Reduce the heat and simmer for about 20 minutes, until the liquid is reduced by half, or until it coats the back of a spoon.

4 Divide half the sauce among six 1 1/4 cup (315 ml/10 fl oz), deep ramekins. Put some fish in each ramekin, then top each with sauce.

5 Cut the pastry sheets into rounds slightly larger than the tops of the dishes. Brush the edges of the pastry with a little of the egg. Press onto the dishes. Brush lightly with the remaining beaten egg. Bake for 30 minutes, or until the pastry is crisp, golden and puffed.

NOTE: You can substitute bream, sea perch or garfish for the snapper fillets. When buying fresh fish, whether whole or filleted, make sure it looks plump and shiny, but not wet. If you are not using fish immediately after purchase, remove any plastic wrapping, place on a plate, cover loosely and refrigerate. Use it within a day. Purchase fish from a retailer where you know there is a high turnover of fish.

ABOVE: Creamy snapper pie

ABOVE: *Sausage rolls (left); Chicken rolls*

SAUSAGE ROLLS

Preparation time: 30 minutes
Total cooking time: 30 minutes
Makes 36

★

500 g (1 lb) home-made or bought puff pastry
(see page 150)
2 eggs, lightly beaten
750 g (1¹/₂ lb) sausage mince
1 onion, finely chopped
1 clove garlic, crushed
1 cup (80 g/2³/₄ oz) fresh breadcrumbs
3 tablespoons chopped fresh parsley
3 tablespoons chopped fresh thyme
¹/₂ teaspoon each of ground sage, nutmeg,
black pepper and cloves

1 Preheat the oven to moderately hot 200°C
(400°F/Gas 6). Lightly grease two oven trays.
2 If using home-made pastry, divide into thirds
and roll each piece between two sheets of baking
paper to form a 30 cm (12 inch) square, about
3 mm (¹/₈ inch) thick. Cut the pastry sheets in
half and lightly brush the edges with some of the
beaten egg.

3 Mix half the remaining egg with the
remaining ingredients in a large bowl, then
divide into six even portions. Pipe or spoon
the filling down the centre of each piece of
pastry, then brush the edges with some of the
egg. Fold the pastry over the filling, overlapping
the edges and placing the join underneath.
Brush the rolls with more egg, then cut each
into 6 short pieces.
4 Cut two small slashes on top of each roll, place
on the baking trays and bake for 15 minutes.
Reduce the oven temperature to moderate
180°C (350°F/Gas 4) and bake for another
15 minutes, or until puffed and golden.
NOTES: For a different flavour, make a chicken
filling for the pastry. Mix 750 g (1¹/₂ lb) chicken
mince, 4 finely chopped spring onions, 1 cup
(80 g/2³/₄ oz) fresh breadcrumbs, 1 finely
grated carrot, 2 tablespoons fruit chutney
and 1 tablespoon each of sweet chilli sauce
and grated fresh ginger. Sprinkle the pastry
with sesame seeds after glazing, then bake
as above.

You can cut the prepared uncooked rolls
into even smaller slices and cook for a few
minutes less. Small sausage rolls make an
excellent party food. Arrange them hot on
a tray with a bowl of your favourite dipping
sauce or tomato sauce.

COUNTRY BEEF WITH HERB SCONES

Preparation time: 30 minutes
Total cooking time: 2 hours 10 minutes
Serves 4

1/4 cup (30 g/1 oz) plain flour
1 kg (2 lb) chuck steak, trimmed and cut
  into 3 cm (1 1/4 inch) cubes
1/4 cup (60 ml/2 fl oz) oil
4 onions, roughly chopped
2 cloves garlic, crushed
1/3 cup (105 g/3 1/2 oz) plum jam
1/3 cup (80 ml/2 3/4 fl oz) brown vinegar
1 cup (250 ml/8 fl oz) beef stock
2 teaspoons sweet chilli sauce

Herb scones

2 cups (250 g/8 oz) self-raising flour
30 g (1 oz) butter, chilled and cubed
2 tablespoons snipped fresh chives
2 tablespoons chopped fresh parsley
3/4 cup (185 ml/6 fl oz) milk

1 Preheat the oven to moderate 180°C (350°F/ Gas 4). Put the flour in a plastic bag, add the meat and toss to coat. Shake off the excess.
2 Heat 2 tablespoons of the oil in a frying pan and brown the meat quickly in batches over medium heat. Drain on paper towels.
3 Heat the remaining oil in the same pan, add the onion and garlic and cook, stirring, for 3 minutes, or until soft. Transfer to a large bowl and combine with the meat. Mix in the plum jam, vinegar, stock and chilli sauce. Transfer to a 2-litre ovenproof dish. Cover and bake for 1 1/2 hours, or until the meat is tender.
4 For the herb scones, sift the flour into a bowl, rub in the butter until the mixture resembles fine breadcrumbs, then stir in the chives and parsley. Add the milk and stir until just combined. Turn onto a lightly floured surface and bring together until smooth. Press out to a 4 cm (1 1/2 inch) thick round and cut into rounds with a 5 cm (2 inch) cutter.
5 Increase the oven temperature to very hot 240°C (475°F/Gas 9). Place the herb scones on top of the meat and bake, uncovered, for 30 minutes or until the herb scones are cooked through and golden brown.
NOTE: This casserole can be cooked two days in advance, without the scones, and refrigerated. Reheat, then cook with the scone dough.

CUTS OF BEEF

For casseroles and stews, it is best to use the cheaper cuts of beef. They are full of flavour due to the higher fat content and the long, slow cooking tenderizes the meat fibres. Chuck, blade, round or topside are all suitable. However, it is important to seal in the meat juices by first pan-frying the meat cubes over high heat. Usually the meat is coated with a little flour before being quickly fried in batches. If you brown it all at once and overfill the frying pan, the meat may stew. Pan-frying first not only helps the browning process but adds colour and flavour to the finished dish. The more expensive cuts, such as rump and fillet, lack fat content and will toughen if cooked for a long time. These cuts are more suited to quick cooking methods such as grilling and barbecuing.

LEFT: Country beef with herb scones

POTATO PIES

Preparation time: 25 minutes
Total cooking time: 1 hour 5 minutes
Makes 6

1 kg (2 lb) floury potatoes, chopped
1 tablespoon oil
1 onion, finely chopped
1 clove garlic, crushed
500 g (1 lb) beef mince
2 tablespoons plain flour
2 cups (500 ml/16 fl oz) beef stock
2 tablespoons tomato paste (tomato purée)
1 tablespoon Worcestershire sauce
500 g (1 lb) home-made or bought shortcrust
   pastry (see page 148)
45 g (1½ oz) butter, softened
¼ cup (60 ml/2 fl oz) milk

1 Steam or boil the potatoes for 10 minutes, or until tender (pierce with the point of a small sharp knife and if the potato comes away easily it is ready). Drain thoroughly, then mash.

2 Preheat the oven to hot 210°C (415°F/ Gas 6– 7). Heat the oil in a frying pan, add the onion and cook for 5 minutes, or until soft. Add the garlic and cook for another minute. Add the mince and cook over medium heat for 5 minutes, or until browned, breaking up any lumps with a fork.

3 Sprinkle the flour over the meat and stir to combine. Add the stock, tomato paste, sauce and some salt and pepper to the pan and stir for 2 minutes. Bring to the boil, then reduce the heat slightly and simmer for 5 minutes, or until the mixture has reduced and thickened. Allow to cool completely.

4 Lightly grease six 11 cm (4½ inch) pie tins. Roll out the pastry between two sheets of baking paper and, using a plate as a guide, cut the pastry into 15 cm (6 inch) circles and line the pie tins. Cut baking paper to cover each tin, spread baking beads or uncooked rice over the paper and bake for 7 minutes. Remove the paper and beads and cook the pastry for another 5 minutes. Allow to cool.

5 Divide the meat filling among the pastry cases. Stir the butter and milk into the mashed potato and pipe or spread all over the top of the meat filling. Bake for 20 minutes, or until the potato is lightly golden.

WORCESTERSHIRE SAUCE

This condiment was developed in India by an Englishman. It was first bottled by a company called Lea and Perrins, in the town of Worcester in England, hence the name. Today it is still made by the same company. Widely available the world over, it is a piquant mixture of onions, garlic, tamarind, soy sauce, molasses, lime, anchovies and vinegar. It is used to add flavour to stews, gravies and soups, and is particularly famous as an essential ingredient in the cocktail called Bloody Mary.

RIGHT: Potato pies

When the salmon has cooled slightly, add the egg, dill and parsley and season, to taste.

Roll out the pastry and trim to a neat shape. Reserve the trimmings to decorate.

Spread the remaining rice over the other layers of filling.

Roll out the remaining pastry and place over the filling. Seal with beaten egg.

SALMON AND RICE PIE

Preparation time: 25 minutes
+ 30 minutes refrigeration
Total cooking time: 1 hour 40 minutes
Serves 4– 6

✷✷

1/3 cup (65 g/2 1/4 oz) brown rice

60 g (2 oz) butter

1 onion, finely chopped

200 g (6 1/2 oz) button mushrooms, sliced

2 tablespoons lemon juice

200 g (6 1/2 oz) salmon fillet, boned and cut into small pieces, or 220 g (7 oz) can red salmon

2 hard-boiled eggs, chopped

2 tablespoons chopped fresh dill

3 tablespoons chopped fresh parsley

1/4 cup (60 ml/2 fl oz) cream

500 g (1 lb) home-made or bought puff pastry (see page 150)

1 egg, lightly beaten

 Bring a large saucepan of water to a rapid boil. Add the brown rice and cook, uncovered, for 30– 40 minutes, stirring occasionally. Drain.
2 Grease a baking tray. Melt half the butter in a frying pan, add the onion and cook for 5 minutes until soft but not browned. Add the mushrooms and cook for 5 minutes, or until softened. Add the lemon juice, then remove from the pan.
3 Heat the remaining butter in the pan, add the salmon, stir and cook for 2 minutes. Remove from the heat, cool slightly and mix in the egg, dill, parsley and salt and pepper, to taste. Mix the rice and cream in a small bowl.
4 Roll out half the pastry to a 15 x 25 cm (6 x 10 inch) rectangle. Trim the pastry, saving the trimmings, and put on a greased baking tray.
5 Layer the filling onto the pastry, leaving a 3 cm (1 1/4 inch) border. Put half the rice on the pastry, then the salmon and egg, followed by the mushroom mixture. Top with the remaining rice. Brush the border with egg.
6 Roll out the remaining pastry to 20 x 30 cm (8 x 12 inches) and place over the filling. Seal the edges. Knock up the pastry by using the blunt edge of a floured knife to push into the edge at 2 cm (3/4 inch) intervals, leaving a scallop pattern. Make two slits in the top. Decorate with the pastry trimmings and chill for 30 minutes.
7 Preheat the oven to moderately hot 200°C (400°F/Gas 6). Lightly brush the pie with egg and bake for 15 minutes. Reduce the oven to moderate 180°C (350°F/Gas 4) and bake for 25– 30 minutes, or until golden brown. Serve with sour cream.

ABOVE: Salmon and rice pie

EMPANADAS

Preparation time: 1 hour 10 minutes
Total cooking time: 45 minutes
Serves 8

★★

3 tablespoons olive oil

250 g (8 oz) onions, finely diced

4 spring onions, thinly sliced

3 cloves garlic, crushed

200 g (6¹/₂ oz) beef mince

2 teaspoons ground cumin

2 teaspoons dried oregano

250 g (8 oz) potatoes, cut into small cubes

500 g (1 lb) home-made or bought puff pastry
    (see page 150)

100 g (3¹/₂ oz) black olives, pitted and
    cut into quarters

2 hard-boiled eggs, finely chopped

1 egg, separated

pinch of paprika

pinch of sugar

ABOVE: Empanadas

1 Heat 1 tablespoon oil in a frying pan, add the onion and spring onion and stir over low heat for 5 minutes. Stir in the garlic and cook for 3 minutes. Remove from the pan.

2 Heat another tablespoon of oil in the pan, add the mince and stir over medium heat until browned, breaking up any lumps with a fork. Return the onion and stir well. Add the cumin, oregano and a teaspoon each of salt and pepper, and stir for another 2 minutes. Transfer to a bowl and allow to cool. Wipe out the pan.

3 Heat the remaining oil in the pan, add the potato and stir over high heat for 1 minute. Reduce the heat to low and stir for 5 minutes, or until tender. Transfer to a plate to cool. Gently mix the potato into the beef mixture. Preheat the oven to moderately hot 200°C (400°F/Gas 6). Grease two baking trays.

4 Divide the pastry into two and roll out each piece on a lightly floured surface until 2.5 mm (¹/₈ inch) thick. Cut out rounds, using a 10 cm (4 inch) cutter.

5 Spoon the beef mixture onto one half of each pastry round, leaving a border all around. Place a few olive pieces and some chopped egg on top. Brush the pastry border with egg white. Fold each pastry over to make a half-moon shape, pressing firmly to seal. Press the edges with a floured fork, then transfer to the trays. Mix the egg yolk, paprika and sugar and brush over the empanadas. Bake for 15 minutes, or until golden.

CHICKEN AND BACON GOUGERE

Preparation time: 40 minutes
Total cooking time: 50 minutes
Serves 6

60 g (2 oz) butter
1– 2 cloves garlic, crushed
1 red onion, chopped
3 rashers bacon, chopped
1/4 cup (30 g/1 oz) plain flour
1 1/2 cups (375 ml/12 fl oz) milk
1/2 cup (125 ml/4 fl oz) cream
2 teaspoons wholegrain mustard
250 g (8 oz) cooked chicken, chopped
1/2 cup (30 g/1 oz) chopped fresh parsley

Choux pastry

1/2 cup (60 g/2 oz) plain flour
60 g (2 oz) butter, chilled and cut into cubes
2 eggs, lightly beaten
35 g (1 1/4 oz) grated Parmesan

1 Melt the butter in a frying pan, add the garlic, onion and bacon and cook for 5– 7 minutes, stirring occasionally, or until cooked but not brown. Stir in the flour and cook for 1 minute. Gradually add the milk and stir until thickened. Simmer for 2 minutes, then add the cream and mustard. Remove from the heat and fold in the chicken and parsley. Season with pepper.

2 For the choux pastry, sift the flour onto a piece of baking paper. Put the butter in a large saucepan with 1/2 cup (125 ml/4 fl oz) water and stir over medium heat until the mixture comes to the boil. Remove from the heat, add the flour in one go and quickly beat it into the water with a wooden spoon. Return to the heat and continue beating until the mixture forms a ball and leaves the side of the pan. Transfer to a large clean bowl and cool slightly. Beat the mixture to release any more heat. Gradually add the beaten eggs, about 3 teaspoons at a time. Beat well after each addition until all the egg has been added and the mixture is thick and glossy—a wooden spoon should stand up in it. If it is too runny, the egg has been added too quickly. If so, beat for several minutes more, or until thickened. Add the Parmesan.

3 Preheat the oven to hot 210°C (415°F/ Gas 6– 7). Grease a deep 23 cm (9 inch) ovenproof dish, pour in the filling and spoon heaped tablespoons of choux around the outside. Bake for 10 minutes, then reduce the oven to moderate 180°C (350°F/Gas 4). Bake for 20 minutes, or until the choux is puffed and golden. Sprinkle with a little more grated Parmesan if you wish.

MUSTARDS

Mustard is produced from three mustard plants that produce different coloured seeds: white or yellow, brown and black. Mustard has been used as a condiment for thousands of years in Europe, dating back to Greek and Roman times. The French have had exclusive rights to make Dijon mustard since 1634. English powdered mustard came into favour in the eighteenth century and was later produced commercially in Norfolk by Mr Colman. This company still makes the powder today. Most mustards are made with the seed left whole or crushed and mixed to a paste with vinegar or verjuice, citrus juices, herbs and seasonings. Most are mild in flavour although some English, Chinese and Japanese mustard pastes are hot and fiery.

LEFT: Chicken and bacon gougère

TARTLETS
These savoury tartlet recipes are simplicity itself and will provide you with ideas for very quick lunch or first course dishes. Most can be ready in under half an hour.

These delicious tartlets can be made with either home-made or bought puff pastry. They can be made as four individual serves or shaped into two rectangles to serve 4 people as a light meal.

You will need 500 g (1 lb) of home-made (see page 150) or bought puff pastry. The pastry should be divided into two and each portion rolled between two sheets of baking paper. If making four tartlets, cut out two 12 cm (5 inch) circles of pastry from each portion, or for two long tartlets roll each portion of pastry into a rectangle 12 x 25 cm (5 x 10 inches). The topping variations are placed on the pastry shapes, leaving a 1.5 cm (1/2 inch) border. The tartlets are then baked in the top half of a preheated moderately hot 200°C (400°F/Gas 6) oven. These tartlets are best served warm or hot. They are delicious accompanied by some dressed green salad leaves.

TOPPINGS

TAPENADE AND ANCHOVY Spread 1/2 cup (125 g/4 oz) tapenade evenly over the pastry, leaving a 1.5 cm (1/2 inch) border. Drain a 45 g (11/2 oz) can of anchovies, cut them into thin strips and arrange them over the top of the tapenade. Sprinkle 1/3 cup (35 g/11/4 oz) grated Parmesan and 1/2 cup (75 g/21/2 oz) grated mozzarella over the top and bake for 10 minutes, or until risen and golden.

MUSHROOM, ASPARAGUS AND FETA Heat 2 tablespoons oil in a frying pan, add 400 g (13 oz) sliced, small button mushrooms and 100 g (3½ oz) thin asparagus spears and stir until softened. Remove from the heat, add 2 tablespoons chopped fresh parsley and 200 g (6½ oz) chopped feta. Stir and season. Spoon onto the pastry bases, leaving a 1.5 cm (½ inch) border. Bake for 10– 15 minutes, until risen and brown.

FRIED GREEN TOMATO Thinly slice 2 green tomatoes. Heat 1 tablespoon oil in a frying pan, add ½ teaspoon cumin and 1 crushed clove garlic and cook for 1 minute. Add the tomatoes in two batches and cook for 2– 3 minutes each batch, adding more oil and garlic if needed, until slightly softened. Drain on paper towels. Combine ⅓ cup (90 g/3 oz) sour cream, 2 tablespoons chopped fresh basil and 2 tablespoons chopped fresh parsley and set aside. Using 1 cup (120 g/4 oz) grated Cheddar, sprinkle over the centre of the pastry bases, leaving a 1.5 cm (½ inch) border. Arrange the tomato over the cheese and bake for 10 minutes. Place a dollop of cream mixture in the middle and sprinkle the tarts with another tablespoon of shredded fresh basil.

ITALIAN SUMMER Heat 2 tablespoons olive oil in a saucepan over low heat, add 2 sliced red onions and cook, stirring occasionally, for 10 minutes. Add 1 tablespoon each of balsamic vinegar and soft brown sugar and cook for 10 minutes, or until soft and lightly browned. Remove from the heat, stir in 1 tablespoon chopped fresh thyme, then leave to cool. Spread evenly over the pastry, leaving a 1.5 cm (½ inch) border.

Bake for 10 minutes. Drain a 170 g (5½ oz) jar of quartered, marinated artichokes and arrange over the onion. Fill the spaces with 24 pitted black olives and 6 quartered slices of lightly rolled prosciutto. Drizzle with extra virgin olive oil and garnish with thyme.

CHERRY TOMATO AND PESTO Spread ½ cup (125 g/4 oz) pesto over the pastry shapes, leaving a 1.5 cm (½ inch) border. Top with cherry tomatoes (you will need about 375 g/12 oz) and 2 finely sliced spring onions. Season and bake for 10 minutes, or until golden. Drizzle with extra virgin olive oil and garnish with sliced spring onion.

FROM LEFT: Tapenade and anchovy (top); Mushroom, asparagus and feta (2); Fried green tomato (2); Italian summer (2); Cherry tomato and pesto (2)

SPINACH & FETA TRIANGLES

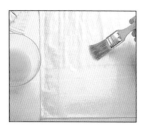

Lightly brush each sheet of pastry with the butter and oil mixture.

Lift the corner of the filo pastry and fold it over to enclose the spinach and form a triangle.

Continue folding the triangle over until you reach the end of the strip of filo pastry.

SPINACH AND FETA TRIANGLES

Preparation time: 30 minutes
Total cooking time: 45 minutes
Makes 8

✦ ✦

1 kg (2 lb) English spinach
1/4 cup (60 ml/2 fl oz) olive oil
1 onion, chopped
10 spring onions, sliced
4 tablespoons chopped fresh parsley
1 tablespoon chopped fresh dill
large pinch of ground nutmeg
1/3 cup (35 g/1 1/4 oz) freshly grated Parmesan
150 g (5 oz) crumbled feta
90 g (3 oz) ricotta
4 eggs, lightly beaten
40 g (1 1/4 oz) butter, melted
1 tablespoon olive oil, extra
12 sheets filo pastry

1 Trim any coarse stems from the spinach, then wash the leaves thoroughly, roughly chop them and place in a large saucepan with just a little water clinging to the leaves. Cover and cook over low heat for 5 minutes, or until the leaves have wilted. Drain well and allow to cool slightly before squeezing tightly to remove the excess water.

2 Heat the oil in a heavy-based frying pan. Add the onion and cook over low heat for 10 minutes, or until tender and golden. Add the spring onion and cook for another 3 minutes. Remove from the heat. Stir in the spinach, parsley, dill, nutmeg, Parmesan, feta, ricotta and egg. Season well.

3 Preheat the oven to moderate 180°C (350°F/Gas 4). Lightly grease two baking trays. Combine the butter with the extra oil. Work with three sheets of pastry at a time, keeping the rest covered with a damp tea towel. Brush each sheet with butter mixture and layer them and cut in half lengthways.

4 Place 4 tablespoons of the filling on an angle at the end of each strip. Fold the pastry over to enclose the filling and form a triangle. Continue folding the triangle over until you reach the end of the pastry. Put the triangles on the baking trays and brush with the remaining butter mixture. Bake for 20–25 minutes, or until the pastry is golden brown.

NOTE: Feta is a traditional Greek-style salty cheese that should be stored immersed in lightly salted water and kept refrigerated. Rinse and pat dry before using.

RIGHT: Spinach and feta triangles

LAMB AND FILO PIE

Preparation time: 20 minutes
Total cooking time: 55 minutes
Serves 6

2 tablespoons oil

2 onions, chopped

I clove garlic, chopped

I teaspoon ground cumin

I teaspoon ground coriander

½ teaspoon ground cinnamon

I kg (2 lb) lamb mince

3 tablespoons chopped fresh parsley

2 tablespoons chopped fresh mint

I tablespoon tomato paste (tomato purée)

10 sheets filo pastry

250 g (8 oz) butter, melted

I Heat the oil in a large frying pan. Add the onion and garlic and cook for 3 minutes, or until just soft. Add the cumin, coriander and cinnamon to the pan and cook, stirring constantly, for another minute.

2 Add the mince to the pan and cook over medium heat for 10 minutes, or until the meat is brown and all the liquid has evaporated. Use a fork to break up any lumps of mince as it cooks. Add the herbs, tomato paste and ¼ teaspoon salt and mix well. Cool completely.

3 Preheat the oven to moderate 180°C (350°F/ Gas 4). Lightly grease a 33 x 23 cm (13 x 9 inch) ovenproof dish. Remove 3 sheets of filo. Cover the remainder with a damp tea towel to prevent them drying out. Brush the top sheet of filo with melted butter. Cover with another 2 sheets of filo and brush the top one with butter. Line the baking dish with these sheets, leaving the excess overhanging the dish.

4 Spread the lamb mixture over the pastry and fold the overhanging pastry over the filling. Butter 2 sheets of filo, place one on top of the other and fold in half. Place over the top of the filling and tuck in the edges. Butter the remaining sheets of filo, cut roughly into squares and then scrunch these over the top of the pie. Bake for 40 minutes, or until crisp and golden.

FILO PASTRY
This is a pastry commonly used in Middle Eastern, Turkish, Greek, Austrian and Hungarian cuisines. It is a very thin pastry that is layered and used to fill and wrap around both sweet and savoury foods. When baked, the flaky layers are light, crisp and golden. It is readily available in supermarkets. When working with filo, keep the unused sheets covered with a slightly damp tea towel. The pastry is so thin that it dries out very quickly and becomes unworkable. Brush the filo sheets lightly with oil or melted butter using a wide pastry brush so that the pastry is covered as quickly as possible and doesn't have time to dry out. Spray oil can also be used if preferred.

ABOVE: Lamb and filo pie

213

FETA CHEESE

This Greek cheese is popular in Greek salads and savoury pastries. It is a soft, white cheese with a sharp, salty taste. It is made using the milk from sheep or goats and sometimes cows. The salty taste is intense because the cheese is ripened or pickled in a brine solution. It has a short ripening period of about one month. When buying feta, make sure it looks moist and is sitting in a briny solution. To store feta, place it in a container and cover with a salty solution. Change the solution each day and use the feta within four days. Feta cheese is made in many countries where it is quite popular, including Italy, Bulgaria, Denmark, Germany and Australia.

ABOVE: Sweet potato, feta and pine nut strudel

SWEET POTATO, FETA AND PINE NUT STRUDEL

Preparation time: 25 minutes
Total cooking time: 55 minutes
Serves 6

450 g (14 oz) sweet potato, cut into
  2 cm (³/4 inch) cubes
1 tablespoon olive oil
¹/2 cup (80 g/2³/4 oz) pine nuts, toasted
250 g (8 oz) feta, crumbled
2 tablespoons chopped fresh basil
4 spring onions, chopped
40 g (1¹/4 oz) butter, melted
2 tablespoons olive oil, extra, for brushing
7 sheets filo pastry
2– 3 teaspoons sesame seeds

1 Preheat the oven to moderate 180°C (350°F/ Gas 4). Brush the sweet potato with oil and bake for 20 minutes, or until softened and slightly coloured. Transfer to a bowl and cool slightly.
2 Add the pine nuts, feta, basil and spring onion to the bowl, mix gently and season, to taste.
3 Mix the butter and extra oil. Remove one sheet of filo and cover the rest with a damp tea towel. Brush each sheet of filo with the butter mixture and layer them into a pile.
4 Spread the prepared filling in the centre of the filo, covering an area about 10 x 30 cm (4 x 12 inches). Fold the sides of the pastry into the centre, then tuck in the ends. Carefully turn the strudel over and place on a baking tray, seam-side down. Lightly brush the top with butter mix and sprinkle with sesame seeds. Bake for 35 minutes, or until the pastry is crisp and golden. Serve warm.
NOTE: You can use 450 g (14 oz) of pumpkin instead of the sweet potato.

VOL-AU-VENTS

Preparation time: 20 minutes
  + 15 minutes refrigeration
Total cooking time: 30 minutes
Makes 4

250 g (8 oz) home-made or bought puff pastry
  (see page 150)
1 egg, lightly beaten

Sauce and filling

40 g (1¼ oz) butter
2 spring onions, finely chopped
2 tablespoons plain flour
1½ cups (375 ml/12 fl oz) milk
your choice of filling (see Note)

1 Preheat the oven to hot 220°C (425°F/Gas 7). Line a baking tray with baking paper.
2 Roll out the pastry to a 20 cm (8 inch) square. Cut 4 circles of pastry with a 10 cm (4 inch) cutter. Place the rounds onto the tray and cut 6 cm (2½ inch) circles into the centre of the rounds with a cutter, taking care not to cut right through the pastry. Place the baking tray in the refrigerator for 15 minutes.
3 Using a floured knife blade, 'knock up' the sides of each pastry round by making even indentations about 1 cm (½ inch) apart around the circumference. This should allow even rising of the pastry as it cooks. The dough can be made ahead of time up to this stage and frozen until needed. Carefully brush the pastry with the egg, avoiding the 'knocked up' edge as any glaze spilt on the sides will stop the pastry from rising.
4 Bake for 15–20 minutes, or until the pastry has risen and is golden brown and crisp. Cool on a wire rack. Remove the centre from each pastry circle and pull out and discard any partially cooked pastry from the centre. The pastry can be returned to the oven for 2 minutes to dry out if the centre is undercooked. The pastry cases are now ready to be filled with a hot filling before serving.
5 For the sauce, melt the butter in a saucepan, add the spring onion and stir over low heat for 2 minutes, or until soft. Add the flour and stir for 2 minutes, or until lightly golden. Gradually add the milk, stirring until smooth. Stir constantly over medium heat for 4 minutes, or until the mixture boils and thickens. Season well. Remove and stir in your choice of filling (see Note).

NOTE: Add 350 g (12 oz) of any of the following to your white sauce: sliced, cooked mushrooms; peeled, cooked prawns; chopped, cooked chicken breast; poached, flaked salmon; dressed crab meat; oysters; steamed asparagus spears.

VOL-AU-VENTS

Cut out 4 circles from the puff pastry with a 10 cm (4 inch) cutter.

Cut circles part of the way through the pastry using a 6 cm (2½ inch) cutter.

Make indentations around the outside of the pastry with a sharp knife.

LEFT: Vol-au-vents

215

BREAD

We've all been there, innocently walking past a bakery, not feeling particularly hungry, then it suddenly hits you. The smell of freshly baked bread can drive you mad with a craving that must be satisfied immediately. Imagine having a private bakery in your own kitchen, devouring still-warm bread with a slathering of butter or a good drizzle of extra virgin olive oil. Once you've mastered the basics, you'll quickly see how easy it is to add seeds, fruit, nuts, olives or cheese to produce another masterpiece. But remember, as tempting as it may seem, man cannot live by bread alone.

ALL ABOUT BREAD

When you master the techniques described here, in no time you will be delighted

by the wonderful aroma of freshly baked bread all over the house.

PLAIN BREAD

Once you have an understanding of some of the important elements of bread making, such as working with yeast, and kneading techniques, you will find that delicious bread is simple to make. As with all cookery, first read the recipe thoroughly, carefully weigh all the ingredients and assemble the equipment you need.

MYSTERIES OF YEAST SOLVED

Working with yeast, probably the most important ingredient in bread, is not as difficult as you may think. Yeast is available dried or fresh. Dried yeast, available at supermarkets, generally comes in a box containing 7 g (¼ oz) sachets, one of which is enough for a standard loaf. Fresh yeast, sometimes harder to obtain, is available at some health food shops and bakeries. It has quite a short storage life. 15 g (½ oz) of fresh yeast is equivalent to a 7 g (¼ oz) sachet of dried. We used dried yeast in our recipes as it is readily available, can be stored in the pantry and carries a use-by date.

TYPES OF FLOUR

The type and quality of flour you use is vital. The correct flour makes a big

difference to the quality of bread. Many of the recipes call for the use of flour that is labelled as bread flour. This is high in protein and will form gluten, which helps the bread rise well and bake into a light airy loaf with a good crust. For most breads, if you use a regular flour the loaf will not rise well, gluten will not form and the loaf will be heavy and dense.

TO MAKE YOUR LOAF

This basic recipe is an excellent starting point as similar techniques are used in all bread making. Put a 7 g (¼ oz) sachet of dried yeast, ½ cup (125 ml/4 fl oz) warm water and 1 teaspoon caster sugar in a small bowl and stir well to combine. Leave in a warm, draught-free place for 10 minutes, or until bubbles appear on the surface. The mixture should be frothy and slightly increased in volume. If it

isn't, discard it and start again. Sift 4 cups (500 g/1 lb) white bread flour, 1 teaspoon salt, 2 tablespoons dried whole milk powder and 1 tablespoon caster sugar into a large bowl. Make a well in the centre, add the yeast mixture, ¼ cup (60 ml/2 fl oz) vegetable oil and 1 cup (250 ml/8 fl oz) warm water. Mix to a soft dough using a large metal spoon. The moisture content of flour can vary greatly between brands and even between batches so add extra water or flour, 1 tablespoon at a time, if the dough is too dry or sticky. Do not add too much flour because the dough will absorb more flour during kneading.

KNEADING THE DOUGH

The dough is then formed into a ball on a lightly floured surface and kneaded. Don't be tempted to cut short the

kneading time as it affects the texture of the finished bread. Kneading firstly distributes the yeast evenly throughout the dough and, secondly, allows the flour's protein to develop into gluten. Gluten gives the dough elasticity, strength and the ability to expand, as it traps the carbon dioxide gas created by the yeast and this allows the bread to rise.

The kneading action is simple and it is quite easy to get into a rhythm. Hold one end of the dough down with one hand, and stretch it away from you with the other hand. Fold the dough back together, make a quarter turn and repeat the action. Knead for 10 minutes, or until smooth and elastic. When you have finished, gather the dough into a ball, then follow the instructions on the next page to complete the bread-making process.

PREPARE TO BAKE

PROVING THE BREAD

After kneading, put the dough into a lightly greased bowl to prevent it from sticking. Cover loosely with plastic wrap or a clean damp tea towel. This helps retain moisture and stop the formation of a skin. Leave the bowl in a warm place (around 30°C is ideal) to allow the dough to rise—this stage is called proving. Do not put the dough in a very hot environment in an attempt to speed up the rising process as it will give an unpleasant flavour to the bread, and may damage the yeast action. The dough will take longer to rise in a cooler environment, but with no adverse effect. When the dough is ready it should be doubled in volume and not spring back when touched with a

fingertip. This will take about an hour. Lightly grease a bread tin that measures 22 x 9 x 9 cm (9 x 3½ x 3½ inches) with melted butter or oil. Heavy-gauge baking tins and trays are best as they resist buckling at high temperatures and prevent the loaf from burning on the base.

PUNCHING DOWN

After proving, punch down the dough (literally—one punch) to expel the air, and knead again briefly for 1 minute, or until smooth. The dough is now ready for shaping. Handle the dough carefully and gently and avoid excessive reshaping. Shape the loaf to fit into the prepared tin, placing it in with any seam at the base. Cover with plastic wrap or a damp tea

towel and place the tin in a warm, draught-free place until the dough is well risen and doubled in size. This will take about 45–60 minutes. This is the final rise for the dough.

BAKING

Preheat the oven to hot 210°C (415°F/Gas 6–7). To glaze, beat 1 egg with 1 tablespoon milk and brush over the top of the dough with a pastry brush. Place the bread in the middle of the hot oven and bake for 10 minutes. Don't open the oven during the first 10 minutes of baking as intense heat is needed during this time. Reduce the oven temperature to moderate 180°C (350°F/Gas 4) and bake for another 30–40 minutes. At the

end of cooking time, test for doneness by turning the loaf out of the tin and tapping the base with your knuckles. The bread will sound hollow when cooked. If it is not cooked, return it to the tin and bake for another 5– 10 minutes. Remove from the tin and cool on a wire rack.

OTHER SHAPES

Bread dough can be made into many shapes and does not have to be baked in a bread or loaf tin. You will need to grease a baking tray, and, as an option, sprinkle the tray with fine cornmeal or polenta.

BLOOMER: At the shaping stage, roll out the dough on a lightly floured surface to a rectangle about 2.5 cm (1 inch) thick. Starting from the short end, roll up the dough like you would a swiss roll. Roll quite firmly to make a short, rather thick loaf. Place with the seam underneath on the baking tray. Cover the dough with a cloth and leave in a warm, draught-free place for an hour, or until doubled in size. Using a sharp knife, make 6 evenly-spaced slashes across the top of the dough. Spray the loaf with water and place in a hot 220°C (425°F/Gas 7) oven for 10 minutes. Reduce to moderately hot 200°C (400°F/Gas 6) and bake for 30 minutes, or until the loaf is golden brown and sounds hollow when tapped underneath. Cool on a wire rack.

PLAITED LOAF: After knocking back, divide the dough into three. Gently roll each portion into a 30 cm (12 inch) sausage, then transfer to a greased baking tray. Arrange next to one another on the tray, then join the strands at one end and start plaiting them together. Pinch and tuck under at both ends to seal the plait. Cover with a tea towel and set aside in a warm, draught-free place for 1 hour, or until doubled in size. Brush with milk and bake in a hot 220°C (425°F/Gas 7) oven for 10 minutes. Reduce the oven to moderately hot 200°C (400°F/Gas 6) and cook for 30 minutes, or until the loaf is golden brown and sounds hollow when tapped underneath. Cool on a wire rack.

STORAGE

Home-baked bread is best eaten on the day of baking, or otherwise used to make toast. Because it has no preservatives it doesn't keep as long as commercial bread, but it can be tightly wrapped and frozen for up to 3 months. When required, thaw at room temperature, then refresh in a moderate 180°C (350°F/Gas 4) oven for 10 minutes.

VARIATION: A good flavour can be made by substituting 1 cup (125 g/4 oz) of the bread flour with 1 cup (150 g/5 oz) wholemeal or stoneground bread flour. Follow the instructions for the white loaf.

WHAT WENT WRONG?

YEAST

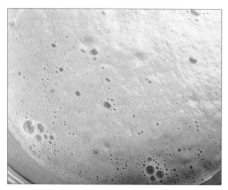

PERFECT The mixture above looks frothy and has doubled in size.

DEAD If your yeast mixture has not risen and is not frothy, the yeast is dead. If this happens, you will have to throw away the mixture and start again. Take care when measuring the yeast. The temperature of the water should be tepid, not too warm, or you may kill the yeast. If using dry yeast, check the expiry date on the back of the packet before you start.

OTHER PROBLEMS

STRONG SMELL AND TASTE OF YEAST
If there is a strong smell and taste of yeast, the bread was undercooked or there was too much yeast used in proportion to the amount of flour.

LOAF DIDN'T RISE OR ROSE POORLY
If the loaf didn't rise or rose poorly, the yeast was old or dead. The liquid may have been too hot and killed the yeast. The yeast may have worked itself out too early by being placed to rise in a spot that was too warm. It may have been left too long to prove.

LOAF OVER-RISEN AND PUFFY
If there are large holes in the loaf and it is risen too much and puffy, the dough may have been insufficiently kneaded during the first kneading stage. The rising time for the dough may have too long, or the dough may not have been correctly knocked backed before shaping the loaf.

LOAF CRUST AND CRUMB SEPARATE
If the crumb and crust separate from one another, the bread dough was not properly knocked back before shaping the loaf.

LOAF ROSE UNEVENLY
If the loaf rises unevenly, or is cracked along one side, the oven temperature was uneven or the bread was not placed in the centre of the oven or was too close to the oven heating elements. The baking tin used may have been too small.

LOAF HAS UNEVEN COLOUR
If the bread is unevenly coloured, the oven temperature was uneven, too high or the bread was placed too low in the oven. A hard crust forms if the dough is not covered during the rising stage, allowing the surface to dry out and thus form a crust.

BREAD

PERFECT The bread has a good even crumb and the loaf has risen evenly and well. It has even spring on the sides and sounds hollow when tapped. The bread is coloured to a golden brown.

OVERCOOKED The crust is too dark and is cracked on top. The crumb is dry. The oven may have been too hot or the cooking time too long or there may have been too much sugar. The bread may have been placed too high in the oven.

UNDERCOOKED The crumb is damp and sticky and the crust soft and pale. If very under-baked, the loaf may not hold its shape and may be wet or have wet holes. If the loaf does not sound hollow when tapped, bake it for another 10 minutes. Check that the oven is the correct temperature before putting the dough in the oven.

FOCACCIA

PERFECT The bread is evenly and well risen and has coloured to a golden brown. The crust is crisp but not hard.

SOGGY, UNDER-BAKED The crust is soft and pale and the crumb is dense and wet. The bread may not have been cooked long enough, or the oven temperature may have been too low. The yeast may have been stale or 'killed' by using hot water when dissolving it. Also, the dough may have been too wet because of the addition of too much water.

UNEVEN RISING, PUFFY The dough was not rolled evenly. Also the dough may not have been sufficiently kneaded during the first stage. The rising time for the dough may have been too long or too much yeast may have been used for the amount of flour.

PIZZA

PERFECT The dough is well risen and lightly browned. It is crisp but not tough. The topping is evenly spread and light golden brown.

RISEN TOO MUCH The dough is unevenly risen and may be dry with a yeasty taste. Too much yeast may have been used or the dough may have been allowed to prove too quickly (too warm) or for too long.

UNEVEN RISING, PUFFY The dough is not evenly rolled and the topping not even. The oven heat may have been uneven or the shelf placed too low or too high.

OTHER PROBLEMS

FOCACCIA
If the focaccia didn't rise or rose poorly, this indicates the yeast was old or expired or the dough was overworked during kneading. The yeast worked itself out too quickly due to being placed in a spot that was too warm for rising.

OTHER PROBLEMS

PIZZA
If the pizza base is soggy, this may be because the base was rolled too thickly or too much topping was used. The topping may have been too wet or not cooked long enough. The oven temperature may have been incorrect.

COTTAGE LOAF

This is a traditional English style of bread with a distinctive look. It has a large round free-form base topped with a smaller top-knot. The smaller loaf is pressed down in the centre with two fingers to attach it firmly to the base loaf. It can be made with both white or wholemeal flours or a combination of the two. The addition of a little oil to bread doughs aids in the keeping quality of the bread after baking. This basic dough can be formed into any shape you like, either free-form or placed in a bread tin. This type of loaf is also delicious cut into thick slices and toasted.

COTTAGE LOAF

Preparation time: 30 minutes
    + I hour 25 minutes rising
Total cooking time: 40 minutes
Makes I large loaf

✷ ✷

7 g (¹/4 oz) sachet dried yeast
I tablespoon soft brown sugar
2 cups (250 g/8 oz) white bread flour
2 cups (300 g/10 oz) wholemeal bread flour
I teaspoon salt
I tablespoon vegetable oil

I Place the yeast, 1 teaspoon of the sugar and ¹/2 cup (125 ml/4 fl oz) warm water in a small bowl and mix well. Leave in a warm, draught-free place for 10 minutes, or until bubbles appear on the surface. The mixture should be frothy and slightly increased in volume. If your yeast mixture doesn't foam it is dead, so you will have to discard it and start again.
2 Place the flours and salt in a large bowl. Make a well in the centre and add the yeast mixture, oil, the remaining sugar and 1 cup (250 ml/ 8 fl oz) warm water. Mix with a wooden spoon, then turn out onto a lightly floured surface. Knead for 10 minutes, or until smooth and elastic. Incorporate a little extra flour into the dough as you knead, to stop the dough from sticking.
3 Place the dough in an oiled bowl and lightly brush oil over the dough. Cover with plastic wrap or a damp tea towel and leave in a warm place for 45 minutes, or until doubled in size.
4 Punch down the dough, then turn out onto a lightly floured surface and knead the dough for 3–4 minutes. Pull away one third of the dough and knead both portions into a smooth ball. Place the large ball on a large floured baking tray and brush the top with water. Sit the smaller ball on top and, using two fingers, press down into the centre of the dough to join the two balls together. Cover with plastic wrap or a damp tea towel and set aside in a warm place for 40 minutes, or until well risen.
5 Preheat the oven to moderately hot 190°C (375°F/Gas 5). Sift some white flour over the top of the loaf and bake for 40 minutes, or until golden brown and cooked. Leave on the tray for 2–3 minutes to cool slightly, then turn out onto a wire rack to cool.

ABOVE: Cottage loaf

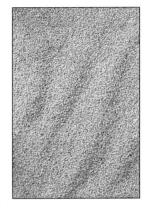

SOY AND LINSEED LOAF

Preparation time: 30 minutes
  + 1 hour 45 minutes rising
Total cooking time: 50 minutes
Makes 1 loaf

✩ ✩

1/2 cup (110 g/3 1/2 oz) pearl barley

7 g (1/4 oz) sachet dried yeast

1 teaspoon caster sugar

1 teaspoon salt

1 tablespoon linseeds

2 tablespoons soy flour

2 tablespoons gluten flour

1 cup (150 g/5 oz) wholemeal bread flour

2 1/2 cups (310 g/10 oz) white bread flour

2 tablespoons olive oil

 Brush a 26 x 10 cm (10 1/2 x 4 inch) bread tin with oil. Put the barley in a saucepan with 2 cups (500 ml/16 fl oz) water, bring to the boil and boil for 20 minutes, or until softened. Drain.
2 Place the yeast, sugar and 155 ml (5 fl oz) warm water in a small bowl and mix well. Leave in a warm, draught-free place for 10 minutes, or until bubbles appear on the surface. The mixture should be frothy and slightly increased in volume. If your yeast doesn't foam it is dead, so you will have to discard it and start again.
3 Place the barley, salt, linseeds, soy and gluten flours, wholemeal flour and 2 cups (250 g/8 oz) of the white flour in a large bowl. Make a well and add the yeast mixture, oil and 155 ml (5 fl oz) warm water. Mix with a wooden spoon to a soft dough. Turn out onto a floured surface and knead for 10 minutes, or until smooth and elastic. Incorporate enough of the remaining flour until the dough is no longer sticky.
4 Place in an oiled bowl and brush the dough with oil. Cover with plastic wrap or a damp tea towel and leave in a warm, draught-free place for 45 minutes, or until doubled in size. Punch down and knead for 2–3 minutes.
5 Pat the dough into a 24 x 20 cm (9 1/2 x 8 inch) rectangle. Roll up firmly from the long side and place, seam-side-down, in the bread tin. Cover with plastic wrap or a damp tea towel and set aside in a warm, draught-free place for 1 hour, or until risen to the top of the tin. Preheat the oven to moderately hot 200°C (400°F/Gas 6).
6 Brush the dough with water and make two slits on top. Bake for 30 minutes, or until golden. Remove from the tin and cool on a wire rack.

SOY BEANS
Soy beans have been cultivated in Asia for centuries and were introduced to Europe in the seventeenth century. America is now the largest producer of soy beans. They are used mostly to make soy bean oil, but the bean is also used whole and manufactured into a wide range of food products. Soy flour is a high-protein food, but lacks gluten, which is essential for the rising of breads. Soy flour is added to bread to give a different flavour and as it is high in fat, it enriches the bread. A high proportion of wheat flour and/or gluten flour is necessary to give a satisfactorily risen loaf.

ABOVE: Soy and linseed loaf

1 Grease four 13 x 6½ x 5 cm (5 x 2¾ x 2 inch) baking tins. Place the yeast, sugar and milk in a small bowl and mix well. Leave in a warm, draught-free place for 10 minutes, or until bubbles appear on the surface. The mixture should be frothy and slightly increased in volume. If your yeast doesn't foam it is dead, so you will have to discard it and start again.

2 Place the flour and salt in a large bowl, make a well in the centre and add the yeast mixture, oil and 1 cup (250 ml/8 fl oz) warm water. Mix to a soft dough and gather into a ball. Turn out onto a floured surface and knead for 10 minutes. Add a little extra flour if the dough is too sticky.

3 Place the dough in a large oiled bowl, cover loosely with plastic wrap or a damp tea towel and leave in a warm place for 1 hour, or until well risen.

4 Punch down the dough, turn out onto a floured surface and knead for 1 minute, or until smooth. Divide into four portions, knead into shape and put in the tins. Cover loosely with plastic wrap or a damp tea towel and leave in a warm place for 45 minutes, or until risen.

5 Preheat the oven to hot 210°C (415°F/ Gas 6–7). Brush the loaf tops with the beaten egg. Bake for 10 minutes, then reduce the oven temperature to moderate 180°C (350°F/Gas 4) and bake for another 30–35 minutes, or until the base sounds hollow when tapped. Cover with foil if the tops become too brown.

MINI BAGUETTES

Preparation time: 25 minutes
  + 2 hours 30 minutes rising
Total cooking time: 30 minutes
Makes 3 loaves

★ ★

7 g (¼ oz) sachet dried yeast
1 teaspoon sugar
¾ cup (90 g/3 oz) plain flour
3 cups (375 g/12 oz) white bread flour
½ teaspoon salt
2 tablespoons polenta, to sprinkle

1 Place the yeast, sugar and 1¼ cups (315 ml/ 10 fl oz) warm water in a small bowl and mix well. Leave in a warm place for 10 minutes, or until bubbles appear on the surface. The mixture should be frothy and slightly increased in volume. If your yeast doesn't foam it is dead and you will have to discard it and start again.

MINI WHOLEMEAL LOAVES

Preparation time: 40 minutes
  + 1 hour 45 minutes rising
Total cooking time: 45 minutes
Makes 4 small loaves

★ ★

7 g (¼ oz) sachet dried yeast
1 tablespoon caster sugar
½ cup (125 ml/4 fl oz) warm milk
4 cups (600 g/1¼ lb) wholemeal
  bread flour
1 teaspoon salt
¼ cup (60 ml/2 fl oz) oil
1 egg, lightly beaten

ABOVE: Mini wholemeal loaves

2 Mix together the flours and salt and transfer half the dry ingredients to a large bowl. Make a well in the centre and add the yeast mixture. Using a large metal spoon fold the flour into the yeast mixture. This should form a soft dough. This forms the 'sponge'. Cover the bowl with a damp tea towel or plastic wrap and set aside for 30–35 minutes, or until frothy and risen by about one third of its original size.

3 Mix in the remaining dry ingredients and add up to ¼ cup (60 ml/2 fl oz) warm water, enough to form a soft, but slightly sticky dough. Knead the dough on a lightly floured surface for about 10 minutes, until smooth and elastic. If the dough sticks to the work surface while kneading, flour the surface sparingly, but try to avoid adding too much flour. Shape the dough into a ball and place in a large lightly greased bowl. Cover with a damp tea towel or plastic wrap and leave in a warm place for about 1 hour, until the dough has doubled in size.

4 Lightly grease two large baking trays and sprinkle with polenta. Punch down the dough and knead for 2–3 minutes. Divide the dough into 3 portions and press or roll each into a rectangle about 20 x 40 cm (8 x 16 inches). Roll each up firmly into a long sausage shape and place seam-side down, well spaced on the prepared trays. Cover loosely with a damp tea towel or plastic wrap and set aside in a warm place for 40 minutes, or until doubled in size.

5 Preheat the oven to hot 220°C (425°F/ Gas 7). Lightly brush the loaves with water and make diagonal slashes across the top at 6 cm (2½ inch) intervals using a safety blade. Place the trays in the oven and spray the oven with water. Bake the bread for 20 minutes, spraying the oven with water twice during this time. Lower the temperature to moderate 180°C (350°F/Gas 4) and bake for another 5–10 minutes, or until the crust is golden and firm and the base sounds hollow when tapped underneath. Cool on a wire rack. Baguettes are best eaten within a few hours of baking.

NOTE: In some countries, special flour is available for making baguettes.

BAGUETTES

A baguette, meaning 'little rod', is the famous long, cylindrical and narrow French bread. It has a very crisp, brown crust and a chewy texture. Baguettes always seem to feature in old French movies sticking out of bicycle baskets. The French say that it is best to buy two baguettes because one always gets half eaten on the way home! Baguettes can be cooked free-form on a baking tray but special purpose half-cylinder containers can be bought from speciality kitchenware shops.

LEFT: Mini baguettes

227

SHERRY

Sherry is a fortified wine made from white grapes. Sherry production takes place the world over but the most famous comes from the region in southwest Spain called Jerez. Sherries have a very concentrated flavour and are usually drunk in small glasses as the alcohol content is about twenty per cent compared with wine at ten to twelve per cent. Sherries are sweet, medium or dry in flavour. In baking, sweet sherry is usually used. It is commonly used in sauces, puddings and fruit cakes. A small glass of sherry with a piece of fruit cake is an English tradition.

OPPOSITE PAGE:
Light fruit bread (top);
Dense fruit bread

LIGHT FRUIT BREAD

Preparation time: 25 minutes
  + 1 hour 30 minutes rising
Total cooking time: 35 minutes
Makes 1 loaf

1 cup (160 g/5 1/2 oz) raisins
1 tablespoon sherry
1 tablespoon grated orange rind
7 g (1/4 oz) sachet dried yeast
1 cup (250 ml/8 fl oz) warm milk
1/4 cup (60 g/2 oz) caster sugar
3 cups (375 g/12 oz) white bread flour
1/2 teaspoon salt
30 g (1 oz) butter, cubed

Glaze

1 egg yolk
2 tablespoons cream

1 Combine the raisins, sherry and rind in a small bowl and set aside.
2 Place the yeast, milk and 1 teaspoon of the sugar in a small bowl and mix well. Leave in a warm, draught-free place for 10 minutes, or until bubbles appear on the surface. The mixture should be frothy and slightly increased in volume. If your yeast doesn't foam it is dead, so you will have to discard it and start again.
3 Place 2 3/4 cups (340 g/11 oz) of the bread flour and the salt in a large bowl. Rub in the butter and remaining sugar with your fingertips. Make a well, add the yeast mixture and mix to a soft dough. Turn out onto a floured surface and knead for 10 minutes, or until smooth and elastic, incorporating the remaining flour as necessary.
4 Place the dough in an oiled bowl and brush with oil. Cover with plastic wrap or a damp tea towel and leave for 1 hour, or until well risen. Punch down, knead for 2 minutes, then roll to a rectangle, 40 x 20 cm (16 x 8 inches). Scatter with raisins and roll up firmly from the long end.
5 Grease a loaf tin with a base measuring 21 x 8 cm (8 1/2 x 3 inches) and line the base with baking paper. Place the dough in the tin, cover with plastic wrap or a damp tea towel and leave for 30 minutes, or until well risen. Preheat the oven to moderate 180°C (350°F/Gas 4).
6 Combine the egg yolk and cream and brush a little over the loaf. Bake for 30 minutes, or until cooked and golden. Glaze again, bake for 5 minutes then glaze again. Cool on a wire rack.

DENSE FRUIT BREAD

Preparation time: 25 minutes
  + 1 hour 40 minutes rising
Total cooking time: 50 minutes
Makes 1 large loaf

★ ★

7 g (1/4 oz) sachet dried yeast
1/4 teaspoon sugar
450 g (14 oz) white bread flour
1/4 teaspoon salt
25 g (3/4 oz) butter
1/2 teaspoon ground ginger
1/4 teaspoon grated nutmeg
1/3 cup (90 g/3 oz) caster sugar
2 cups (320 g/11 oz) sultanas
1 1/4 cups (185 g/6 oz) currants
1/4 cup (45 g/1 1/2 oz) mixed peel

1 Place the yeast, sugar and 1 1/4 cups (315 ml/ 10 fl oz) warm water in a small bowl and mix well. Leave in a warm, draught-free place for 10 minutes, or until bubbles appear on the surface. The mixture should be frothy and slightly increased in volume. If your yeast doesn't foam it is dead, so you will have to discard it and start again.
2 Place the flour and salt in a large bowl and rub in the butter with your fingertips until the mixture resembles coarse breadcrumbs. Stir in the spices and three quarters of the caster sugar. Make a well in the centre and stir in the yeast mixture. Mix well until the dough comes together and leaves the side of the bowl clean. Turn onto a lightly floured surface and knead for 10 minutes, or until elastic and smooth. Place in a clean bowl, cover with plastic wrap or a damp tea towel and leave in a warm, draught-free place for 1 hour, or until doubled in size.
3 Turn the dough onto a lightly floured surface, add the fruit and knead for a couple of minutes, or until the fruit is incorporated. Shape the dough into a large round and place on a greased baking tray. Cover with plastic wrap or a damp tea towel and leave in a warm, draught-free place for 30– 40 minutes, or until doubled in size.
4 Preheat the oven to moderately hot 200°C (400°F/Gas 6). Bake on the middle shelf for 40– 45 minutes, or until the loaf is nicely coloured and sounds hollow when tapped on the base. Transfer to a wire rack to cool slightly.
5 Dissolve the remaining caster sugar in 1 tablespoon hot water and brush over the loaf. Bake for 2– 3 minutes, then cool on a wire rack.

DAMPER

Preparation time: 20 minutes
Total cooking time: 25 minutes
Makes 1 damper

3 cups (375 g/12 oz) self-raising flour
1–2 teaspoons salt
90 g (3 oz) butter, melted
1/2 cup (125 ml/4 fl oz) milk
milk, extra, to glaze
flour, extra, to dust

1 Preheat the oven to hot 210°C (415°F/ Gas 6–7). Grease a baking tray. Sift the flour and salt into a bowl and make a well. Combine the butter, milk and 1/2 cup (125 ml/4 fl oz) water and pour into the well. Stir with a knife until just combined. Turn the dough onto a lightly floured surface and knead for 20 seconds, or until smooth. Place the dough on the baking tray and press out to a 20 cm (8 inch) circle.

2 Using a sharp pointed knife, score the dough into 8 sections about 1 cm (1/2 inch) deep. Brush with milk, then dust with flour. Bake for 10 minutes.

3 Reduce the oven temperature to moderate 180°C (350°F/Gas 4) and bake the damper for another 15 minutes, or until the damper is golden and sounds hollow when the surface is tapped. Serve with butter.

NOTE: Damper is the Australian version of soda bread. It is traditionally served warm with slatherings of golden syrup. If you prefer, you can make four rounds instead of one large damper and slightly reduce the cooking time. Cut two slashes in the form of a cross on the top.

BELOW: Damper

BROWN SODA BREAD

Preparation time: 10 minutes
Total cooking time: 30 minutes
Makes 1 loaf

2 cups (250 g/8 oz) self-raising flour
2 cups (250 g/8 oz) unbleached self-raising flour
1 teaspoon bicarbonate of soda
3 cups (750 ml/24 fl oz) buttermilk

1 Preheat the oven to moderately hot 190°C (375°F/Gas 5). Lightly grease a baking tray. Sift the flours and bicarbonate of soda into a large bowl, add the husks to the bowl and make a well in the centre. Add 2 1/2 cups (625 ml/21 fl oz) of the buttermilk and mix with a knife to form a soft dough, adding some of the remaining buttermilk if required.

2 Turn the dough onto a floured surface and knead gently and briefly—don't knead too much as this will make it tough. Press the dough out to a 20 cm (8 inch) round and place on the baking tray. Score a deep cross with a floured knife one third the depth of the dough. Lightly brush with water and sprinkle with a little flour. Bake for 20–30 minutes, or until the bread sounds hollow when tapped.

NOTE: You can use wholemeal self-raising flour instead of the plain self raising-flour to make a heavier bread. You can substitute natural yoghurt, or milk soured with a little lemon juice, for the buttermilk.

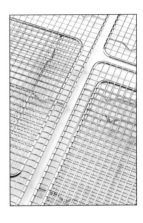

RYE BREAD

Preparation time: 40 minutes
+ 2 hours 30 minutes rising
Total cooking time: 45 minutes
Makes 1 loaf

✩✩

7 g (1/4 oz) sachet dried yeast
1 teaspoon sugar
3/4 cup (185 ml/6 fl oz) warm milk
2 cups (200 g/6 1/2 oz) rye flour
1 1/3 cups (165 g/5 1/2 oz) white bread flour
1 teaspoon salt
rye flour, extra, to dust

1 Place the yeast, sugar and milk in a small bowl and mix well. Leave in a warm place for 10 minutes, or until bubbles appear on the surface. The mixture should be frothy and slightly increased in volume. If your yeast doesn't foam it is dead, so you will have to discard it and start again.

2 Sift the flours and salt into a large bowl and make a well in the centre. Add the yeast mixture and 3/4 cup (185 ml/6 fl oz) warm water and, using your fingers, gradually incorporate the flour to form a dough.

3 Turn the dough onto a lightly floured surface and knead for 10 minutes, or until smooth and elastic. Place the dough in a large lightly oiled bowl and cover with plastic wrap or a damp tea towel. Leave in a warm place for up to 1 1/2 hours, until doubled in size.

4 Lightly grease a baking tray and dust lightly with flour. Punch down the dough and turn onto a lightly floured surface. Knead for 1 minute, or until smooth. Shape into an 18 cm (7 inch) circle and, using a sharp knife, score a shallow criss-cross pattern on top of the loaf. Lightly dust the top with the extra rye flour.

5 Cover the dough with plastic wrap or a damp tea towel and leave in a warm place for 1 hour, or until doubled in size. Preheat the oven to moderate 180°C (350°F/Gas 4) and bake the bread for 40–45 minutes, or until golden brown and the bread sounds hollow when tapped. Transfer to a wire rack to cool completely before cutting.

RYE FLOUR

Rye is cultivated mainly in northern Europe, notably Scandinavia, and Eastern Europe, particularly Russia. Only a small proportion of the cereal is used for human consumption, the majority being produced to feed livestock. It grows well in these regions, as unlike most cereals, it is tolerant to poor soils and cold temperatures. A by-product of the cereal is rye flour which is used to make bread. Because it lacks the protein gluten, which is responsible for the elasticity of bread, rye bread is a much denser and more compact bread. It is also very strong in flavour and makes a distinctive-tasting bread that marries well with cheese, herrings and pickles. It is a moist bread so it keeps well.

ABOVE: Rye bread

231

CHEESE AND HERB PULL-APART

Preparation time: 30 minutes
  + I hour 30 minutes rising
Total cooking time: 30 minutes
Makes I loaf

★★

7 g (¹/4 oz) sachet dried yeast
I teaspoon sugar
4 cups (500 g/I lb) plain flour
I¹/2 teaspoons salt
2 tablespoons chopped fresh parsley
2 tablespoons chopped fresh chives
I tablespoon chopped fresh thyme
60 g (2 oz) Cheddar, grated
milk, to glaze

I Place the yeast, sugar and ¹/2 cup (125 ml/ 4 fl oz) warm water in a small bowl and stir well. Leave in a warm place for 10 minutes, or until bubbles appear on the surface. The mixture should be frothy and slightly increased in volume. If your yeast doesn't foam it is dead,

so you will have to discard it and start again.
2 Sift the flour and salt in a large bowl. Make a well in the centre and add the yeast mixture and 1 cup (250 ml/8 fl oz) warm water. Mix to a soft dough. Turn onto a lightly floured surface and knead for 10 minutes, or until smooth. Place the dough in an oiled bowl, cover with plastic wrap or a damp tea towel and leave for 1 hour, or until doubled in size.
3 Punch down the dough and knead for 1 minute. Divide the dough in half and shape each half into 10 flat discs, 6 cm (2¹/2 inches) in diameter. Mix the fresh herbs with the Cheddar and place 2 teaspoons of the mixture on one of the discs. Press another disc on top, then repeat with the remaining discs and herb mixture.
4 Grease a 21 x 10.5 x 6.5 cm (8¹/2 x 4¹/4 x 2¹/2 inch) loaf tin. Stand the filled discs upright in the prepared tin, squashing them together. Cover the tin with plastic wrap or a damp tea towel and leave in a warm place for 30 minutes, or until the dough is well risen. Preheat the oven to hot 210°C (415°F/Gas 6–7).
5 Lightly brush the loaf with a little milk and bake for 30 minutes, or until the bread is brown and crusty and sounds hollow when tapped on the base.

ABOVE: Cheese and herb pull-apart

ROSETTAS

Preparation time: 40 minutes + 2 hours rising
Total cooking time: 25 minutes
Makes 10

7 g (¹/₄ oz) sachet dried yeast
1 teaspoon sugar
4¹/₂ cups (560 g/1 lb 2 oz) unbleached plain
  flour, sifted
1 teaspoon salt
50 g (1³/₄ oz) butter, softened
¹/₄ cup (60 ml/2 fl oz) olive oil
¹/₄ cup (60 g/2 oz) caster sugar
milk, to glaze
plain flour, extra, to dust

1 Grease two baking trays. Place the yeast, sugar and ¹/₂ cup (125 ml/4 fl oz) warm water in a small bowl and stir well. Leave in a warm, draught-free place for 10 minutes, or until bubbles appear on the surface. The mixture should be frothy and slightly increased in volume. If your yeast doesn't foam it is dead, so you will have to discard it and start again.
2 Set aside ¹/₄ cup (30 g/1 oz) of the flour and put the rest in a large bowl with the salt. Make a well in the centre. Add the yeast mixture, butter, oil, sugar and 1¹/₄ cups (315 ml/10 fl oz) warm water. Stir with a wooden spoon, until the dough leaves the side of the bowl and forms a rough, sticky ball. Turn out onto a floured surface. Knead for 10 minutes, or until the dough is smooth and elastic. Add enough of the reserved flour, if necessary, to make a smooth dough. Place in a large, lightly oiled bowl and brush the surface with melted butter or oil. Cover with plastic wrap and leave in a warm place for 1 hour, or until well risen.
3 Punch down the dough, then knead for 1 minute. Divide into 10 portions and shape each into a smooth ball. Place the balls 5 cm (2 inch) apart on the trays. Using a 3 cm (1¹/₄ inch) round cutter, press a 1 cm (¹/₂ inch) deep indent into the centre of each ball. With a sharp knife, score five evenly-spaced, 1 cm (¹/₂ inch) deep cuts down the side of each roll. Cover with plastic wrap or a damp tea towel and leave in a warm place for 1 hour, or until well risen.
4 Preheat the oven to moderate 180°C (350°F/ Gas 4). Brush the rolls with milk and sift a fine layer of the extra flour over them. Bake for 25 minutes, or until golden. Rotate the trays in the oven if one tray is browning faster than the other. Cool on a rack.
NOTE: These are best eaten on the day of cooking and can be frozen for up to 1 month.

ROSETTAS

Press a deep round indent into the centre of each ball of dough.

Sift a fine layer of plain flour over the tops of the rolls before baking.

BELOW: Rosettas

BEER BREAD

Preparation time: 15 minutes
Total cooking time: 40 minutes
Makes 1 loaf

3¼ cups (405 g/13 oz) white bread flour
3 teaspoons baking powder
1 teaspoon salt
1 tablespoon caster sugar
2 teaspoons dill seeds
50 g (1¾ oz) butter, chilled and cubed
375 ml (12 fl oz) can beer
plain flour, extra
dill seeds, extra
coarse sea salt

1 Preheat the oven to hot 210°C (415°F/ Gas 6–7). Lightly grease a baking tray. Sift the flour, baking powder and salt into a large bowl. Add the sugar and dill seeds and combine. Rub the butter into the dry ingredients using your fingers, until the mixture resembles breadcrumbs. Make a well in the centre and add the beer all at once. Using a wooden spoon, quickly mix to form a soft dough.
2 Turn out onto a floured surface, sprinkling extra flour on your hands and on the surface of the dough. Knead for 1–2 minutes, or until the dough forms a smooth ball. Elongate the ball slightly, flatten a little, and with the blunt end of a large knife press down 2 cm (¾ inch) along the centre. Brush the surface with water, and sprinkle liberally with the extra dill seeds and sea salt.
3 Bake for 20 minutes, then reduce the oven to moderate 180°C (350°F/Gas 4) and bake for another 15–20 minutes, or until the bread sounds hollow when tapped. Remove from the oven, place on a wire rack and leave to cool.
NOTE: This bread is best eaten on the day of baking and it freezes well for up to a week.

CORN BREAD

Preparation time: 20 minutes
Total cooking time: 25 minutes
Makes 1 loaf

1 cup (125 g/4 oz) self-raising flour
1 cup (150 g/5 oz) fine cornmeal
1 teaspoon salt
1 egg
1 cup (250 ml/8 fl oz) buttermilk
¼ cup (60 ml/2 fl oz) oil

1 Preheat the oven to hot 220°C (425°F/Gas 7). Generously grease a 20 cm (8 inch) cast iron frying pan with an ovenproof or screw off handle, or round cake tin, with oil. Place in the oven to heat while making the batter.
2 Sift the flour into a bowl, add the cornmeal and salt and make a well in the centre. Whisk together the egg, buttermilk and oil, add to the dry ingredients and stir until just combined. Do not overbeat.
3 Pour into the hot cast iron pan or cake tin and bake for 25 minutes, or until firm to the touch and golden brown. Serve, cut into wedges, warm or at room temperature.

QUICK MIX ONION AND BUTTERMILK BREAD

Preheat the oven to moderate 180°C (350°F/Gas 4). Sift 3 cups (375 g/12 oz) self-raising flour into a large bowl and stir in a 35 g (1¼ oz) packet of dried French onion soup and 2 tablespoons chopped chives. Mix in 1¾ cups (440 ml/14 fl oz) buttermilk with a knife, using a cutting action, until the mixture forms a soft dough. Add extra buttermilk if the mixture is too dry. Turn out onto a lightly floured surface and quickly knead into a smooth ball. Cut into 4 even-sized pieces and shape each into a ball. Place on a floured tray, allowing room for each to rise. Sift extra flour over the top and make a slash with a sharp knife across the top of each loaf. Bake the loaves for 25–30 minutes, or until cooked and golden. Makes 4 loaves.

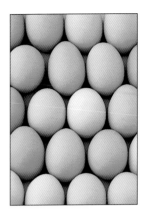

CORNMEAL
Corn is the only native American cereal grain, believed to have originated in Mexico or Central America. Archeologists have discovered evidence of corn as far back as 7000 years ago. The first explorers to the New World found corn growing from Canada to Chile. The native Indians made great use of corn as did the early settlers. Corn has a large variety of culinary uses. It can be cooked fresh or processed into cornstarch, cornflour, hominy, corn germ, corn oil, corn flakes and cornmeal. Cornmeal is obtained by grinding dried corn kernels into a coarse white or yellow meal, and is ground into degrees of coarseness. It is used slightly coarse in the baking of corn bread and muffins. Polenta is more porridge-like. It is also used to make tortillas, corn chips and tamales.

OPPOSITE PAGE: Corn bread (top); Beer bread

BREAD ROLLS

Create your own selection of delicious rolls using plain (page 218) or wholemeal (page 226) bread dough and the following toppings and glazes.

SPIRAL ROLLS

Divide the dough into 16–24 even pieces. Roll each into a 30 cm (12 inch) long rope. Shape into tight spirals, tuck under the ends, then seal. Place 5 cm (2 inches) apart on lightly oiled baking trays. Cover with plastic wrap and leave in a warm place for 20 minutes, or until well risen. Brush with a glaze or topping. Bake in a moderate 180°C (350°F/Gas 4) oven for 15–20 minutes, or until risen and golden.

KNOT ROLLS

Divide the dough into 16–24 even pieces. Roll into 30 cm (12 inch) long ropes. Tie each rope into a loose knot. Place 5 cm (2 inches) apart on lightly oiled baking trays. Proceed as for spiral rolls.

CLOVER LEAF ROLLS

Divide the dough into 16–24 even pieces. Divide each piece into 3 even-sized balls. Place the trio of balls from each piece close together on lightly oiled baking trays and 5 cm (2 inches) apart. Proceed as for spiral rolls.

OVAL ROLLS

Divide the dough into 16–24 even pieces, and then shape into ovals. Leave plain or slash the tops once lengthways, or twice diagonally. Place 5 cm (2 inches) apart on lightly oiled baking trays. Proceed as for spiral rolls.

TOPPINGS AND GLAZES

Glazing dough and adding toppings will change the appearance as well as the taste of the bread. Glazing affects the result of the crust and is done before or after baking, depending on the result you are after. The high oven temperature used for baking bread may cause some toppings to brown too quickly. If you notice this happening, lower the oven temperature slightly or place a sheet of foil or double thickness of baking paper on top of the rolls to prevent them from burning.

TOPPINGS

Lightly sprinkle the dough with a topping such as flour, rolled oats, crushed rock salt, cracked wheat or grated Cheddar. You can also try seeds such as poppy, sesame, caraway, pumpkin, dill, fennel or sunflower. Cereals such as cornmeal (polenta), barley flakes, cracked wheat and rye flakes also make interesting toppings and add a little flavour.

GLAZES

Use a wide pastry brush to brush one of these glazes over the dough, choosing the appropriate glaze for your desired result.

AFTER BAKING

Soft crust: Brush the cooked, hot bread with melted butter and return to the oven for 2 minutes. Remove, brush again with melted butter and leave to cool.
Glossy crust: Whisk 1 egg white with 1 tablespoon water. Brush the cooked, hot bread with the glaze, then return to the oven for 5 minutes. Cool.
Sweet glossy crust: Combine 1 tablespoon sugar with 2 tablespoons milk and brush over the hot bread. Return to the oven for 5 minutes. Cool.

Sugar glaze: Dissolve 1/4 cup (60 g/2 oz) sugar in 2 tablespoons water over low heat. Boil for 2 minutes, or until the mixture is syrupy. Brush on the hot bread.

BEFORE BAKING

Deep colour in the crust: Beat 1 whole egg with 1 teaspoon water. For a very deep colour, beat 1 egg yolk with 1 teaspoon water.
Rich, dark gleam on savoury breads: Beat 1 egg with 1 teaspoon oil and some salt and pepper.
Crisp crust: Whisk together 1 egg white with 1 teaspoon water.
Light sheen: Brush with milk, cream or melted butter.

FROM LEFT: Spiral rolls; Knot rolls; Clover leaf rolls; Oval rolls; Knot rolls. Toppings (rack on right): Sesame seeds; Poppy seeds; Rock salt; Sunflower seeds

SOURDOUGH BREAD

Gradually draw the flour into the yeast mixture and stir to form a thick paste.

For the sponge, stir the flour into the starter mixture and whisk in warm water to form a smooth mixture.

Knead the dough until it is smooth and elastic, incorporating more flour if necessary.

Use a sharp knife to make diagonal cuts along the loaves.

ABOVE: Sourdough bread

SOURDOUGH BREAD

Preparation time: 30 minutes + 2 days standing + 1 hour 45 minutes rising
Total cooking time: 40 minutes
Makes two loaves

Starter

1 cup (125 g/4 oz) white bread flour
2 teaspoons fresh yeast

Sponge

1 cup (125 g/4 oz) white bread flour

Dough

3 cups (375 g/12 oz) white bread flour
1 teaspoon salt
2 teaspoons fresh yeast

1 To make the starter, sift the flour into a bowl and make a well in the centre. Cream the yeast and 1 cup (250 ml/8 fl oz) warm water together, pour into the flour and gradually draw the flour into the centre to form a thick smooth paste. Cover with plastic wrap or a damp tea towel and leave at room temperature for 24 hours. The starter will begin to ferment and bubble.
2 To make the sponge, stir the flour into the starter mixture and gradually whisk in 1/2 cup (125 ml/4 fl oz) warm water to form a smooth mixture. Cover with plastic wrap and leave for 24 hours.
3 To make the dough, sift the flour and salt into a large bowl and make a well in the centre. Cream the yeast and 1/3 cup (80 ml/2¾ fl oz) warm water together and add to the dry ingredients with the starter and sponge mixture. Gradually incorporate the flour into the well. Turn the dough onto a lightly floured surface and knead for 10 minutes, or until smooth and elastic, incorporating extra flour if needed.
4 Place the dough in a lightly oiled bowl, cover with plastic wrap or a damp tea towel and place in a warm place for 1 hour, or until doubled in size. Lightly grease two baking trays and dust lightly with flour. Punch the dough down and turn onto the work surface. Knead for 1 minute, or until smooth. Divide into two equal portions and shape each into a 20 cm (8 inch) round. Using a sharp knife, score diagonal cuts 1 cm (1/2 inch) deep along the loaves.
5 Place the loaves on the trays and cover with plastic wrap or a damp tea towel. Leave in a warm place for 45 minutes, or until doubled. Preheat the oven to moderately hot 190°C (375°F/Gas 5). Bake for 35– 40 minutes, changing the breads around halfway through. Bake until the bread is golden and crusty and sounds hollow when tapped. Cool on a wire rack before cutting.

POTATO BREAD

Preparation time: 45 minutes
   + I hour 45 minutes rising
Total cooking time: 35 minutes
Makes I loaf

☆ ☆

7 g (¹/4 oz) sachet dried yeast

4 cups (500 g/I lb) unbleached plain flour

I teaspoon salt

2 tablespoons full-cream milk powder

I cup (230 g/7¹/2 oz) warm cooked mashed
   potato

¹/2 cup (25 g/³/4 oz) chopped fresh chives

I egg white, to glaze

2 teaspoons cold water

sunflower or pumpkin (pepita) seeds

I Lightly grease a 25 cm (10 inch) round cake tin and line the base with baking paper. Place the yeast and ¹/4 cup (60 ml/2 fl oz) warm water in a small bowl and stir well. Leave in a warm, draught-free place for 10 minutes, or until bubbles appear on the surface. The mixture should be frothy and slightly increased in volume. If your yeast doesn't foam it is dead, so you will have to discard it and start again.
2 Sift 3¹/2 cups (435 g/14 oz) of the flour, the salt and milk powder into a large bowl. Using a fork, mix the potato and chives through the dry ingredients. Add the yeast mixture and 1 cup (250 ml/8 fl oz) warm water and mix until combined. Add enough of the remaining flour to make a soft dough.
3 Turn the dough onto a lightly floured surface. Knead for 10 minutes, or until the dough is smooth and elastic. Place in an oiled bowl, then brush the surface of the dough with oil. Cover with plastic wrap and leave in a warm place for 1 hour, or until well risen.
4 Punch down the dough, then knead for 1 minute. Divide into 12 equal pieces and form each piece into a smooth ball.
5 Place evenly spaced balls in a daisy pattern in the tin, piling 2 balls in the centre. Cover with plastic wrap and leave to rise for 45 minutes, or until the dough has risen to the top of the tin. Preheat the oven to hot 210°C (415°F/Gas 6–7).
6 Brush the top with the combined egg white and water and sprinkle the seeds onto the centre ball. Bake for 15 minutes. Reduce the oven to moderate 180°C (350°F/Gas 4) and bake for another 20 minutes, or until a skewer inserted in the centre comes out clean. Leave for 10 minutes, then turn out onto a wire rack.
NOTE: Depending on the moisture content of the potato, extra flour may have to be added to make a soft, slightly sticky dough. The bread keeps for three days in an airtight container.

POTATO BREAD

The addition of cooked mashed potato to bread results in a moist, springy crumb and a dense bread, due to the moisture in the potatoes. Potato also adds interest, flavour and keeping qualities to the bread. The best potatoes to use for mashing are the floury varieties such as King Edward and pontiac, rather than the waxy potatoes. To prepare the potatoes, cut the peeled potatoes into even-sized pieces and boil or steam until softened. Drain well and mash while hot.

ABOVE: Potato bread

GLUTEN-FREE BREAD

Preparation time: 25 minutes
+ 1 hour rising
Total cooking time: 45 minutes
Makes 1 loaf

☆ ☆

7 g (1/4 oz) sachet dried yeast

2 teaspoons sugar

2 1/4 cups (400 g/13 oz) gluten-free plain
flour (see Note)

1/2 teaspoon salt

1/2 cup (50 g/1 3/4 oz) milk powder

1 tablespoon xanthan gum (see Note)

2 eggs, lightly beaten

1/4 cup (60 ml/2 fl oz) oil

1 tablespoon sesame seeds

1 Lightly grease a loaf tin with a base measuring 22 x 9 x 5.5 cm (9 x 3 1/2 x 2 1/4 inches). Place the yeast, sugar and 1 3/4 cups (440 ml/14 fl oz) warm water in a small bowl and stir well. Leave in a warm, draught-free place for 10 minutes, or until bubbles appear on the surface. The mixture should be frothy and slightly increased in volume. If your yeast doesn't foam it is dead, so you will have to discard it and start again.
2 Sift the flour, salt, milk powder and xanthan gum into a large bowl. Make a well in the centre and add the yeast mixture, egg and oil. Using a wooden spoon, stir together well until it forms a soft moist mixture. Beat with the spoon for 1 minute.
3 Spoon the mixture into the loaf tin and smooth the surface with moist hands. Sprinkle the sesame seeds over the top. Cover with lightly greased plastic wrap and leave in a warm, draught-free place for 1 hour, or until the mixture has nearly risen to the top of the tin. Preheat the oven to moderately hot 190°C (375°F/Gas 5). Bake the bread for 40–45 minutes, or until it is golden and sounds hollow when tapped. Leave in the tin for 5 minutes before transferring to a wire rack to cool. Allow the bread to cool completely before cutting.
NOTE: You can buy gluten-free plain flour in the health food section of the supermarket. Xanthan gum is used as a gluten substitute as it gives structure to the bread. It is available from health food shops.

WALNUT BREAD

Preparation time: 45 minutes
+ 2 hours 30 minutes rising
Total cooking time: 50 minutes
Makes 1 loaf

☆ ☆

2 1/2 teaspoons dried yeast

1/4 cup (90 g/3 oz) liquid malt

2 tablespoons olive oil

3 cups (300 g/10 oz) walnut halves, lightly
toasted

4 1/4 cups (530 g/1 lb 1 oz) white bread flour

1 1/2 teaspoons salt

1 egg, lightly beaten

1 Grease a baking tray. Place the yeast, liquid malt and 1 1/3 cups (350 ml/11 fl oz) warm water in a small bowl and stir well. Leave in a warm, draught-free place for 10 minutes, or until bubbles appear on the surface. The mixture should be frothy and slightly increased in volume. If your yeast doesn't foam it is dead, so you will have to discard it and start again. Stir in the oil.
2 Process 2 cups (200 g/6 1/2 oz) of the walnuts in a food processor to a coarse meal. Combine 4 cups (500 g/1 lb) of the flour and the salt in a large bowl and stir in the walnut meal. Make a well and add the yeast mixture. Mix with a large metal spoon until a loose clump forms. Turn out onto a lightly floured surface and knead for 10 minutes, or until smooth, incorporating enough of the remaining flour to keep the dough from sticking—it should be soft and moist, but it won't become very springy. Shape the dough into a ball. Place in a lightly oiled bowl, cover with plastic wrap or a damp tea towel and leave in a warm place for up to 1 1/2 hours, or until doubled.
3 Punch down the dough and turn out onto a lightly floured surface. With very little kneading, shape the dough into a 25 x 20 cm (10 x 8 inch) rectangle. Spread with the remaining walnuts and roll up firmly from the short end. Place the loaf on the baking tray, cover with plastic wrap or a damp tea towel and leave to rise for 1 hour, or until well risen and doubled in size.
4 Preheat the oven to moderately hot 190°C (375°F/Gas 5). Glaze the loaf with the egg and bake for 45–50 minutes, or until golden and hollow sounding when tapped. Transfer to a wire rack to cool.
NOTE: Use good-quality pale and plump walnuts as cheaper varieties can be bitter.

Firmly roll the loaf from the short end and place on the greased baking tray.

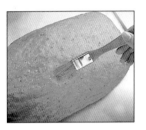

When the dough has doubled in size, brush with the beaten egg.

OPPOSITE PAGE:
Walnut bread (top);
Gluten-free bread

ABOVE: Pumpernickel

PUMPERNICKEL

Preparation time: 1 hour
   + 2 hours 15 minutes rising
Total cooking time: 50 minutes
Makes 2 loaves

★ ★

2 x 7 g (1/4 oz) sachets dried yeast
1 teaspoon caster sugar
1/4 cup (90 g/3 oz) molasses
1/4 cup (60 ml/2 fl oz) cider vinegar
90 g (3 oz) butter
30 g (1 oz) dark chocolate, chopped
1 tablespoon instant coffee powder
4 1/2 cups (560 g/1 lb 2 oz) unbleached
   plain flour

3 cups (300 g/10 oz) rye flour
1 cup (75 g/2 1/2 oz) bran
1 tablespoon caraway seeds
2 teaspoons fennel seeds
1 teaspoon salt
1 egg white
caraway seeds, extra

1 Grease a 20 cm (8 inch) round cake tin and a 28 x 12 cm (11 x 4 1/2 inch) loaf or bread tin, or use any baking tin that has a 1.75 litre capacity. Line the base of each tin with baking paper. Put 1/2 cup (125 ml/4 fl oz) warm water, the yeast and sugar in a small bowl and stir well. Leave in a warm, draught-free place for 10 minutes, or until bubbles appear on the surface. The mixture should be frothy and slightly increased in volume. If your yeast doesn't foam it is dead, so you will have to discard it and start again.
2 Put the molasses, vinegar, butter, dark chocolate, coffee powder and 2 cups (500 ml/ 16 fl oz) cold water into a saucepan and stir over low heat until the butter and chocolate have melted and the mixture is just warmed.
3 Place 3 1/2 cups (435 g/14 oz) of the plain flour, the rye flour, bran, caraway and fennel seeds and salt in a large bowl. Make a well in the centre and add the yeast and chocolate mixtures. Using a wooden spoon, and then your hands, combine the dough until it leaves the side of the bowl and forms a firm, sticky ball.
4 Turn out onto a heavily floured surface and knead for 10 minutes. Incorporate enough of the remaining plain flour to make a dense but smooth and elastic dough. Divide in half and place in separate lightly oiled bowls. Brush the surface of the dough with melted butter or oil. Cover with plastic wrap or a damp tea towel and leave in a warm, draught-free place for 1 1/4 hours, or until well risen. Punch down the dough and knead each for 1 minute. Shape each portion to fit a tin and place one in each tin. Cover with lightly oiled plastic wrap or a damp tea towel and leave in a warm place for 1 hour, or until well risen.
5 Preheat the oven to moderate 180°C (350°F/ Gas 4). Glaze the dough with combined egg white and 1 tablespoon water and sprinkle with caraway seeds. Bake for 50 minutes, or until well browned. During the last 15 minutes, cover with foil to prevent excess browning. Leave in the tins for 15 minutes before turning out onto a wire rack to cool.
NOTE: Pumpernickel is a dense rye bread that originated in Germany. It is delicious with soft cheeses, olives, smoked salmon and dill pickles.

ENGLISH MUFFINS

Preparation time: 20 minutes
  + 1 hour 40 minutes rising
Total cooking time: 15 minutes
Makes 15

7 g (¹/₄ oz) sachet dried yeast
¹/₂ teaspoon sugar
4¹/₄ cups (530 g/1 lb 1 oz) plain flour
1 teaspoon salt
1¹/₃ cups (350 ml/11 fl oz) lukewarm milk
1 egg, lightly beaten
40 g (1¹/₄ oz) butter, melted

1 Lightly dust two 32 x 28 cm (13 x 11 inch) baking trays with flour. Put the yeast, sugar, 1 teaspoon of the flour and ¹/₄ cup (60 ml/ 2 fl oz) warm water in a small bowl and mix well. Leave in a warm place for 10 minutes, or until bubbles appear on the surface. The mixture should be frothy and slightly increased in volume. If your yeast doesn't foam it is dead, so you will have to discard it and start again.

2 Sift the salt and remaining flour into a large bowl. Make a well in the centre and add the milk, egg, butter and yeast mixture all at once. Using a flat-bladed knife, mix to a soft dough.

3 Turn the dough onto a lightly floured surface and knead lightly for 2 minutes, or until smooth. Shape the dough into a ball and place in a large, lightly oiled bowl. Cover with plastic wrap or a damp tea towel and leave in a warm place for 1¹/₂ hours, or until well risen.

4 Preheat the oven to hot 210°C (415°F/ Gas 6–7). Punch the dough down and knead again for 2 minutes, or until smooth. Roll to 1 cm (¹/₂ inch) thick, then cut into rounds with a lightly floured plain 8 cm (3 inch) cutter and place on the trays. Cover with plastic wrap or a damp tea towel and leave in a warm, draught-free place for 10 minutes.

5 Bake for 15 minutes, turning once halfway through cooking. Transfer to a wire rack to cool. Serve warm or cold.

BELOW: English muffins

FOCACCIA

Preparation time: 50 minutes
  + 1 hour 50 minutes rising
Total cooking time: 25 minutes
Makes 1 flat loaf

★★

7 g (¼ oz) sachet dried yeast
1 teaspoon caster sugar
2 tablespoons olive oil
3¼ cups (405 g/13 oz) white bread flour
1 tablespoon full-cream milk powder
½ teaspoon salt

Topping

1 tablespoon olive oil
1–2 cloves garlic, crushed
black olives
fresh rosemary sprigs or leaves
1 teaspoon dried oregano
1–2 teaspoons coarse sea salt

BELOW: Focaccia

1 Lightly grease a 28 x 18 cm (11 x 7 inch) baking tin. Put the yeast, sugar and 1 cup (250 ml/8 fl oz) warm water in a small bowl and stir well. Leave in a warm, draught-free place for 10 minutes, or until bubbles appear on the surface. The mixture should be frothy and slightly increased in volume. If your yeast doesn't foam it is dead, so you will have to discard it and start again. Add the oil.
2 Sift 3 cups (375 g/12 oz) of the flour, the milk powder and salt into a large bowl. Make a well in the centre and add the yeast mixture. Beat with a wooden spoon until the mixture is well combined. Add enough of the remaining flour to form a soft dough, and then turn onto a lightly floured surface.
3 Knead for 10 minutes, or until the dough is smooth and elastic. Place the dough in a large, lightly oiled bowl. Brush the surface of the dough with oil. Cover with plastic wrap or a damp tea towel and leave in a warm place for 1 hour, or until well risen. Punch down the dough and knead for 1 minute. Roll into a rectangle, 28 x 18 cm (11 x 7 inches) and place in the prepared tin. Cover with plastic wrap and leave to rise in a warm place for 20 minutes. Using the handle of a wooden spoon, form indents 1 cm (½ inch) deep all over the dough at regular intervals. Cover with plastic wrap and set aside for 30 minutes, or until the dough is well risen. Preheat the oven to moderate 180°C (350°F/Gas 4).
4 For the topping, brush the combined olive oil and garlic over the surface of the dough. Top with the olives and rosemary sprigs, then sprinkle with the oregano and salt.
5 Bake for 20– 25 minutes, or until golden and crisp. Cut into large squares and serve warm.
NOTES: Focaccia is best eaten on the day of baking. It can be reheated if necessary. Variations to use as toppings are only limited by your imagination. Remember that focaccia was originally a rustic bread that was brushed with olive oil and sprinkled with salt. Make indentations in the top of the dough as described in the above recipe, brush with olive oil, then top with any of the following suggestions. Chop 6 sun-dried tomatoes and spread evenly over the top of the foccacia before baking. Top with green olives and 1 teaspoon chopped fresh sage leaves before baking. Sliced onion that has been softened in a little olive oil over low heat until golden also makes a delicious topping. Spread over the focaccia before baking. Alternatively, you can spread pesto or tapenade over the dough then brush with the oil and add olives as we have done in the recipe.

MALT BREAD

Preparation time: 45 minutes
  + 1 hour 40 minutes rising
Total cooking time: 40 minutes
Makes 1 loaf

 ✱ ✱

7 g (¼ oz) sachet dried yeast

1 teaspoon sugar

2 cups (300 g/10 oz) plain wholemeal flour

1 cup (125 g/4 oz) white bread flour

2 teaspoons ground cinnamon

½ cup (80 g/2¾ oz) raisins

30 g (1 oz) butter, melted

1 tablespoon treacle

1 tablespoon liquid malt extract

1 tablespoon hot milk

½ teaspoon liquid malt, extra

1 Lightly grease a 21 x 14 x 7 cm (8½ x 5½ x 2¾ inch) loaf tin and line the base with baking paper. Put the yeast, sugar and 1 cup (250 ml/8 fl oz) lukewarm water in a small bowl and stir until dissolved. Leave in a warm place for 10 minutes, or until bubbles appear on the surface. The mixture should be frothy and slightly increased in volume. If your yeast doesn't foam it is dead, so you will have to discard it and start again.

2 Sift the flours and cinnamon into a large bowl and add the raisins. Make a well in the centre and add the butter, treacle, malt and yeast mixture. Using a knife, mix to a soft dough. Turn onto a lightly floured surface and knead for 10 minutes, or until smooth. Shape the dough into a ball and place in a lightly oiled bowl. Cover with plastic wrap or a damp tea towel and leave in a warm place for 1 hour, or until well risen.

3 Punch down the dough, then knead for 3 minutes, or until smooth. Roll the dough into a 20 cm (8 inch) square and roll up. Place, seam-side down, in the tin and set aside. Cover with plastic wrap or a damp tea towel and leave in a warm place for 40 minutes, or until well risen.

4 Preheat the oven to moderate 180°C (350°F/Gas 4). Brush the dough with the combined milk and extra malt. Bake for 40 minutes, or until well browned. Cool in the tin for 3 minutes before transferring to a wire rack to cool. Malt bread is delicious sliced and spread with butter and honey.

ABOVE: Malt bread

PUMPKIN BREAD

Preparation time: 35 minutes
+ 2 hours rising
Total cooking time: 50 minutes
Makes 1 round loaf

✷ ✷

300 g (10 oz) pumpkin, chopped
7 g (¼ oz) sachet dried yeast
1 teaspoon salt
4½ cups (560 g/1 lb 2 oz) white bread flour
1 egg, beaten
pumpkin seeds (pepitas), to decorate

1 Steam or boil the pumpkin for 10 minutes, or until tender. Drain thoroughly, then mash. Grease a 20 cm (8 inch) cake tin and line the base with baking paper. Place the yeast and ¼ cup (60 ml/2 fl oz) warm water in a small bowl and stir well. Leave in a warm, draught-free place for 10 minutes, or until bubbles appear on the surface. The mixture should be frothy and slightly increased in volume. If your yeast doesn't foam it is dead, so you will have to discard it and start again.
2 Sift the salt and 4 cups (500 g/1 lb) of the flour into a large bowl. Add the pumpkin, yeast mixture and ¼ cup (60 ml/2 fl oz) warm water. Mix thoroughly using a wooden spoon, and then your hands, until well combined. The dough will form a rough, slightly sticky ball. Add more liquid if the mixture is too dry—the amount of liquid will depend on the moistness of the pumpkin.
3 Turn onto a floured surface. Knead for 10 minutes, or until the dough is smooth and elastic. Incorporate enough of the remaining flour to form a smooth dough. Place the dough in a lightly oiled bowl and brush the dough with oil. Cover with plastic wrap or a damp tea towel and leave in a warm place for 1 hour, or until well risen.
4 Punch down the dough, knead for 1 minute, then pull away a golf ball-sized piece of dough. Shape the remaining dough into a smooth round ball and place in the tin. Roll the smaller ball into a rope 35 cm (14 inches) long. Tie into a loose knot and place across the top of the dough, then seal with a little water to hold in place. Cover with plastic wrap or a damp tea towel and leave in a warm place for 1 hour, or until risen to the top of the tin.
5 Preheat the oven to hot 210°C (415°F/ Gas 6–7). Beat 2 teaspoons water into the egg and brush over the dough. Sprinkle with the pumpkin seeds and bake for 20 minutes. Reduce the oven to moderate 180°C (350°F/Gas 4), then bake for another 20 minutes, or until cooked. Cover with foil during the last 10 minutes of cooking if the bread is browning too much. Transfer to a wire rack to cool.
NOTE: Pumpkin bread is delicious served with butter. It will keep for up to three days in an airtight container, and it also freezes well for up to a month.

FOUGASSE

Preparation time: 30 minutes
+ 1 hour 20 minutes rising
Total cooking time: 35 minutes
Makes 4

✷ ✷

7 g (¼ oz) sachet dried yeast
1 teaspoon sugar
4 cups (500 g/1 lb) white bread flour
2 teaspoons salt
¼ cup (60 ml/2 fl oz) olive oil

1 Place the yeast, sugar and ½ cup (125 ml/ 4 fl oz) warm water in a small bowl and stir until dissolved. Leave in a warm, draught-free place for 10 minutes, or until bubbles appear on the surface. The mixture should be frothy and slightly increased in volume. If your yeast doesn't foam it is dead, so you will have to discard it and start again.
2 Sift the flour and salt into a bowl and make a well in the centre. Add ¾ cup (185 ml/6 fl oz) warm water, the yeast mixture and oil. Mix to a soft dough and gather into a ball with floured hands. Turn out onto a floured surface and knead for 10 minutes, or until smooth.
3 Place in a large, lightly oiled bowl, cover loosely with plastic wrap or a damp tea towel and leave in a warm place for 1 hour, or until doubled in size.
4 Punch down the dough and knead for 1 minute. Divide the mixture into four equal portions. Press each portion into a large, oval shape 1 cm (½ inch) thick and make several cuts on either side of all of them. Lay on large, floured baking trays, cover with plastic wrap and leave to rise for 20 minutes.
5 Preheat the oven to hot 210°C (415°F/ Gas 6–7). Bake the fougasse for 35 minutes, or until crisp. After 15 minutes, spray the oven with water to make the crust crispy.

FOUGASSE
Also called Provençal hearth bread, fougasse is a branch-shaped bread that is the centrepiece surrounded by twelve desserts that are the traditional Christmas Eve celebrations of the Provence region in France. After midnight mass, families return to their homes to partake in warmed wine and eat a selection of twelve fruits, nuts and sweetmeats. These are placed around the bread and symbolize Christ and his twelve apostles. For this occasion the bread is unsweetened and unflavoured. The bread can be enjoyed throughout the year and may be flavoured with anise seeds or fresh chopped herbs.

OPPOSITE PAGE:
Pumpkin bread (top);
Fougasse

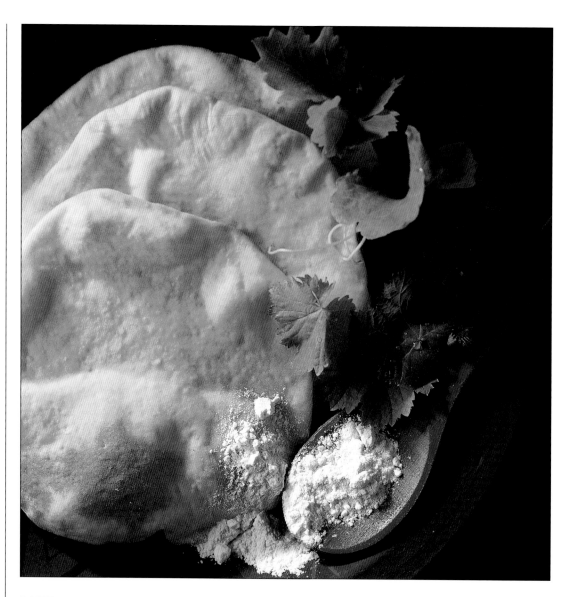

PITTA BREAD

This is the staple bread of the Middle East. It is known as 'khubz' in Arabic but is more commonly known in the west by its Greek name, pitta. It is a flat bread with a chewy crust and a hollow pouch which makes it very versatile. Typically, it is split open and filled with a variety of meats, salads and dips, such as hummus or baba ganouj. It can also be used as a scoop for dips and even to wrap foods such as kebabs with chilli sauce. Keep pitta bread sealed in a plastic bag in the refrigerator. To refresh it, you can sprinkle it lightly with water and reheat it in a warm oven.

ABOVE: Pitta bread

PITTA BREAD

Preparation time: 30 minutes + 40 minutes rising
Total cooking time: 5 minutes
Makes 12

7 g (¼ oz) sachet dried yeast
1 teaspoon caster sugar
3½ cups (435 g/14 oz) plain flour
2 tablespoons olive oil

1 Lightly grease three baking trays. Put the yeast, sugar and 1½ cups (375 ml/12 fl oz) warm water in a small bowl and stir well. Leave in a warm, draught-free place for 10 minutes, or until bubbles appear on the surface. The mixture should be frothy and slightly increased in volume. If your yeast doesn't foam it is dead, so you will have to discard it and start again.

Sift the flour into a bowl and make a well in the centre. Add the yeast mixture and the oil and mix with a wooden spoon until well moistened. Gather the dough together with floured hands.
2 Turn the dough onto a well-floured surface and knead for 10 minutes, or until smooth and elastic. Place the dough in a lightly oiled bowl, cover with plastic wrap or a damp tea towel and leave in a warm place for 20 minutes, or until doubled in size.
3 Punch down the dough and divide into 12 equal portions. Roll each portion into a 5 mm (¼ inch) thick round. Place on the baking trays and brush well with water. Leave to rise for another 20 minutes. Preheat the oven to very hot 250°C (500°F/Gas 10).
4 If the dough rounds have dried, brush them again with water. Bake for 4– 5 minutes. The pitta bread should be soft and pale, slightly swollen and hollow inside. Serve warm with kebabs or felafel, or cool with salad.

PRETZELS

Preparation time: 50 minutes
  + 1 hour 30 minutes rising
Total cooking time: 15 minutes
Makes 12

1 teaspoon dried yeast
1/4 teaspoon sugar
150 ml (5 fl oz) warm milk
1 1/2 cups (185 g/6 oz) white bread flour
1/4 teaspoon salt
30 g (1 oz) butter, melted
1 egg yolk, lightly beaten
coarse sea salt, to sprinkle

1 Place the yeast, sugar and warm milk in a small bowl and stir well. Leave in a warm, draught-free place for 10 minutes, or until bubbles appear on the surface. The mixture should be frothy and slightly increased in volume. If your yeast doesn't foam it is dead, so you will have to discard it and start again.

2 Place the flour and salt in a large bowl and make a well in the centre. Add the yeast mixture and butter and mix to a rough dough with a wooden spoon. Turn out onto a floured surface and knead for 10 minutes until smooth and elastic.

3 Place into an oiled bowl, oil the surface of the dough, cover with plastic wrap or a clean tea towel and set aside in a warm place for 1 hour until doubled in size.

4 Preheat the oven to moderately hot 190°C (375°F/Gas 5). Line a large baking tray with baking paper. Punch down the dough and knead again for 2–3 minutes. Divide into 12 pieces. Cover the dough while working with each piece. Roll each piece into a long rope 40 cm (16 inches) long. Circle and knot into a pretzel shape. Place well spaced on the tray. Cover with a tea towel. Leave to rise in a warm, draught-free place for 20–30 minutes.

5 Lightly brush the pretzels with the beaten egg yolk and sprinkle with sea salt. Place the pretzels in the oven and spray them twice with water before baking for 12–15 minutes, or until crisp and golden brown. Transfer to a wire rack to cool.

BELOW: Pretzels

GRISSINI

Preparation time: 40 minutes
   + 1 hour rising
Total cooking time: 15 minutes
Makes 24

7 g (¼ oz) sachet dried yeast
1 teaspoon sugar
4 cups (500 g/1 lb) white bread flour
1 teaspoon salt
¼ cup (60 ml/2 fl oz) olive oil
¼ cup (15 g/½ oz) chopped fresh basil
4 cloves garlic, crushed
½ cup (50 g/1¾ oz) finely grated Parmesan
2 teaspoons sea salt flakes
2 tablespoons finely grated Parmesan, extra

1 Place the yeast, sugar and 1¼ cups (315 ml/ 10 fl oz) warm water in a small bowl and stir well. Leave in a warm, draught-free place for 10 minutes, or until bubbles appear on the surface. The mixture should be frothy and slightly increased in volume. If your yeast doesn't foam it is dead, so you will have to discard it and start again.

2 Sift the flour and salt into a bowl and make a well in the centre. Add the yeast mixture and oil and mix to combine. Add more water if the dough is dry.

3 Gather the dough into a ball and turn out onto a lightly floured surface. Knead for 10 minutes, or until soft and elastic. Divide the dough into two portions, add the basil and garlic to one portion, and the Parmesan to the other. The best way to do this is to flatten the dough into a rectangle and place the filling on top. Fold the dough to enclose the filling, then knead for a few minutes to incorporate the filling evenly.

4 Place each dough in a lightly oiled bowl and cover with plastic wrap or a damp tea towel. Leave in a warm, draught-free place for 1 hour, or until doubled in volume. Preheat the oven to very hot 230°C (450°F/Gas 8). Lightly grease two baking trays.

5 Punch down the doughs and knead each again for 1 minute. Divide each piece of dough into 12 portions, and roll each portion into a stick about 30 cm (12 inches) long and 5 mm (¼ inch) across. Place on the trays and brush with water. Sprinkle the basil and garlic dough with the sea salt flakes, and the cheese dough with the extra Parmesan. Bake for 15 minutes, or until crisp and golden brown.

GRISSINI

These long thin sticks of crisp bread originated in the city of Turin. They can be pencil thin or as thick as a cigar and are always served at the Italian table as part of an antipasto platter to start a meal. They are a light starter designed so as not to curb one's appetite for the following courses. Toppings vary from coarse salt to seeds, cheese or dried herbs, either on their own or combined for interesting variations.

RIGHT: Grissini

CIABATTA

Preparation time: 30 minutes
  + 5 hours 15 minutes rising
Total cooking time: 30 minutes
Makes 1 freeform loaf

✯ ✯ ✯

7 g (¹/₄ oz) sachet dried yeast

1 teaspoon sugar

2 teaspoons salt

3 cups (750 g/1 ¹/₂ lb) white bread flour

50 ml (1³/₄ fl oz) olive oil

extra flour, to sprinkle

1 Place the yeast, sugar and 75 ml (2¹/₂ oz) warm water in a small bowl and stir well. Leave in a warm, draught-free place for 10 minutes, or until bubbles appear on the surface. The mixture should be frothy and slightly increased in volume. If your yeast doesn't foam it is dead, so you will have to discard it and start again.

2 Place the salt and 2 cups (250 g/8 oz) of the flour in a large bowl and make a well in the centre. Add the yeast mixture, oil and 225 ml (7 fl oz) water to the bowl and stir to combine.

Use a cupped hand to knead the wet dough, lifting and stirring for 5 minutes. The dough will be quite wet at this stage.

3 Shape the dough into a ball and place in a clean bowl. Cover with plastic wrap or a damp tea towel and leave in a warm place for 4 hours, or until doubled in size.

4 Stir in the remaining flour, using a cupped hand, and mix until the flour has been incorporated. Scrape down the side of the bowl. Cover with plastic wrap or a clean tea towel and leave in a warm place for 1– 1¹/₄ hours.

5 Liberally sprinkle a large baking tray with flour. Do not punch down the dough but carefully tip it out onto the tray. Use floured hands to spread the dough into an oval about 30 x 12 cm (12 x 4¹/₂ inches). Use heavily floured hands to spread evenly and tuck under the dough edges to plump up the dough. Sprinkle liberally with flour. Cover with plastic wrap and leave for 30 minutes.

6 Preheat the oven to hot 210°C (415°F/ Gas 6– 7). Place a heatproof container of ice on the base of the oven. Bake the ciabatta for 30 minutes, or until puffed and golden. Remove the melted ice after about 20 minutes. The loaf is cooked when it sounds hollow when tapped.

CIABATTA

Now a popular bread baked all over the world, ciabatta originated in the Emilia Romagna region of Italy. Its name means 'slipper' bread as it is said to resemble a well-worn slipper. Its light airy texture is due to its long rising time and the use of a wet dough. It is an unusual process in that the dough is not punched down to eliminate the air bubbles as with other breads. It needs to be handled with great care so as not to lose the air bubbles that have formed after the long rising.

ABOVE: Ciabatta

BAGELS

Leave the yeast mixture until bubbles appear on the surface.

Knead the dough until smooth and quite stiff.

Roll each ball of dough into a long rope, the same thickness all the way along.

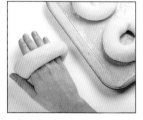

With the circle around the base of your fingers and the overlap under your palm, roll the rope several times. Apply firm pressure to seal the seam.

ABOVE: Bagels

BAGELS

Preparation time: 35 minutes
  + 12 hours refrigeration
Total cooking time: 16 minutes
Makes 8

✷ ✷

7 g (¹/4 oz) sachet dried yeast

1 teaspoon sugar

1 tablespoon barley malt syrup or honey

4 cups (500 g/1 lb) white bread flour

2 teaspoons salt

coarse polenta, for dusting

1 Place the yeast, sugar and 1¹/2 cups (375 ml/ 12 fl oz) warm water in a small bowl and stir until dissolved. Leave in a warm place for 10 minutes, or until bubbles appear on the surface. The mixture should be frothy and slightly increased in volume. If your yeast doesn't foam it is dead, so you will have to discard it and start again. Stir in the malt syrup.
2 Put 2 cups (250 g/8 oz) of the flour in a large bowl, make a well in the centre and add the yeast mixture and salt. Stir with a wooden spoon, adding flour as necessary to make the dough firm. Turn out onto a floured work surface and knead for 10–12 minutes, or until smooth and stiff. Add more flour if necessary to make the dough quite stiff, then divide into 8 portions and roll them into smooth balls. Cover with plastic wrap or a clean tea towel and leave for 5 minutes.
3 Roll each ball under your palms to form a rope 28 cm (11 inches) long. Do not taper the ends of the rope. Dampen the ends slightly, overlap by 4 cm (1¹/2 inches) and pinch firmly together. Place one at a time around the base of your fingers and, with the overlap under your palm, roll the rope several times. Apply firm pressure to seal the seam. It should be the same thickness all the way around. Place them all on polenta-dusted baking trays, cover with plastic wrap and refrigerate for 12 hours.
4 Preheat the oven to very hot 240°C (475°F/ Gas 9). Line two baking trays with baking paper. Remove the bagels from the fridge 20 minutes before baking. Bring a large saucepan of water to the boil and drop the bagels, in batches of 3 or 4, into the water for 30 seconds. Remove and drain, base-down, on a wire rack.
5 Place the bagels on the trays and bake for 15 minutes, or until deep golden brown and crisp. Cool on a wire rack.

SCOTTISH BAPS

Preparation time: 40 minutes
+ 1 hour 15 minutes rising
Total cooking time: 30 minutes
Makes 12

7 g (¹/₄ oz) sachet dried yeast
1 teaspoon caster sugar
3¹/₂ cups (435 g/14 oz) white bread flour
1 cup (250 ml/8 fl oz) lukewarm milk
1¹/₂ teaspoons salt
45 g (1¹/₂ oz) butter, melted
1 tablespoon plain flour, extra

1 Lightly dust two baking trays with flour. Place the yeast, sugar and 2 tablespoons flour in a small bowl. Gradually add the milk, blending until smooth and dissolved. Leave in a warm, draught-free place for 10 minutes, or until bubbles appear on the surface. The mixture should be frothy and slightly increased in volume. If your yeast doesn't foam it is dead, so you will have to discard it and start again.

2 Sift the salt and remaining flour into a large bowl. Make a well in the centre and add the yeast mixture and butter. Using a knife, mix to form a soft dough.

3 Turn the dough onto a lightly floured surface and knead for 3 minutes, or until smooth. Shape into a ball and place in a large oiled bowl. Cover with plastic wrap or a damp tea towel and leave in a warm place for 1 hour, or until well risen.

4 Preheat the oven to hot 210°C (415°F/ Gas 6– 7). Punch down the dough with your fist. Knead the dough again for 2 minutes, or until smooth. Divide into 12 pieces. Knead one portion at a time on a lightly floured surface for 1 minute, roll into a ball and shape into a flat oval. Repeat with the remaining dough.

5 Place the ovals on the trays and dust with the extra flour. Cover with plastic wrap and leave in a warm place for 15 minutes, or until well risen. Make an indent in the centre of each oval with your finger. Bake for 30 minutes until browned and cooked through. Serve warm.

SCOTTISH BAPS

Baps are flattish soft bread rolls that are traditionally from Scotland but are now common all over Britain. Eaten at breakfast time, they are often called 'morning rolls'. They are best eaten warm straight from the oven. Baps are distinguished from other breads in that they are always dusted with white flour and made with milk, which gives the rolls a tender crumb and soft crust. The origins of the bread are not known but the word has been in use since late in the sixteenth century.

LEFT: Scottish baps

TURKISH BREAD

Preparation time: 30 minutes
+ 2 hours rising
Total cooking time: 36 minutes
Makes 3

2 x 7 g (¹/₄ oz) sachets dried yeast
¹/₂ teaspoon sugar
¹/₂ cup (60 g/2 oz) plain flour
3¹/₂ cups (435 g/14 oz) white bread flour
1¹/₂ teaspoons salt
¹/₃ cup (80 ml/2³/₄ fl oz) olive oil
1 egg, lightly beaten with 2 teaspoons water
nigella or sesame seeds, to sprinkle

1 Place the yeast, sugar and ¹/₂ cup (125 ml/
4 fl oz) warm water in a small bowl and stir well.
Add a little of the flour and mix to a paste. Leave
in a warm, draught-free place for 30 minutes, or
until bubbles appear on the surface. The mixture
should be frothy and will more than triple in
size. If your yeast doesn't foam it is dead, so you
will have to discard it and start again.
2 Place the remaining flours and salt in a large
bowl and make a well in the centre. Add the
sponged yeast, olive oil and 1 cup (250 ml/
8 fl oz) warm water. Mix to a rough dough,
then turn out onto a floured surface and knead
for 5 minutes. Add minimal flour as the dough
should remain damp and springy.
3 Shape the dough into a ball and place in a large
oiled bowl. Cover with plastic wrap or a damp
tea towel and leave in a warm place for 1 hour
to triple in size. Punch down and divide into
three. Knead each portion for 2 minutes and
shape each into a ball. Cover with plastic wrap
or a damp tea towel and leave for 10 minutes.
4 Roll each portion of dough into a rectangle
35 x 15 cm (14 x 6 inches). Cover with damp
tea towels and leave in a warm place for
20 minutes. Indent all over the surface with
your fingers, brush with the egg wash and
sprinkle with the seeds. Preheat the oven to
hot 220°C (425°F/Gas 7).
5 For the best results, bake each loaf separately.
Place a baking tray in the oven for a couple of
minutes until hot, remove and sprinkle lightly
with flour. Place one portion of dough on the
hot tray and bake for 10– 12 minutes, or until
puffed and golden brown. Wrap in a clean tea
towel to soften the crust and set aside to cool.
Meanwhile, repeat baking the remaining
portions of dough.

UNLEAVENED LAVASH

Preparation time: 40 minutes
+ 1 hour refrigeration
Total cooking time: 32 minutes
Makes 4

1 cup (125 g/4 oz) plain flour
¹/₂ teaspoon salt
¹/₂ teaspoon sugar
20 g (³/₄ oz) butter, chilled and chopped
¹/₃ cup (80 ml/2³/₄ fl oz) milk
sesame and poppy seeds, to sprinkle

1 Place the flour, salt, sugar and butter in a food
processor. Process in short bursts until the butter
is incorporated. With the machine running,
gradually pour in the milk and process until the
dough comes together—you may need to add an
extra 1 tablespoon milk.
2 Turn out onto a lightly floured surface and
knead briefly until smooth. Wrap in plastic wrap
and refrigerate for 1 hour.
3 Preheat the oven to moderately hot 190°C
(375°F/Gas 5). Lightly grease a large baking tray.
Cut the dough into 4 pieces. Working with one
piece at a time, roll until very thin into a rough
square shape measuring about 20 cm (8 inches)
along the sides.
4 Place the dough shapes on the tray, brush
the tops lightly with water and sprinkle with
the seeds. Roll a rolling pin lightly over the
surface of the dough to press in the seeds.
Bake for 6– 8 minutes, or until golden brown
and dry. Transfer to a wire rack until cool and
crisp. Break into large pieces. Repeat the
process of rolling and baking the remaining
dough. Lavash is delicious served with dips
or soft cheeses.
NOTE: You can use a combination of sesame
and poppy seeds or just one of them.

**LAVASH AND TURKISH
BREAD**
Throughout the Middle
East, bread is revered as a
gift from God, a staple to
life, and is present at every
meal. It is used to scoop
up food as well as being
filled or rolled around a
filling, so it takes the place
of cutlery. It is thought
that lavash originated in
Armenia but it is eaten
throughout Syria, Turkey
and Lebanon. It is rolled
paper-thin and cooked in a
special oven called a
'tannur'. Turkish bread,
or pide, is the Turkish
version of pitta bread.

OPPOSITE PAGE:
Turkish bread (top);
Unleavened lavash

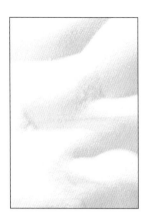

PIZZA DOUGH

Preparation time: 30 minutes
 + 1 hour 30 minutes rising
Total cooking time: 30 minutes
Makes two 30 cm (12 inch) or one 42 cm
 (17 inch) pizza

7 g (¹/₄ oz) sachet dried yeast
3 teaspoons caster sugar
3¹/₂ cups (435 g/14 oz) white bread flour
¹/₂ teaspoon salt
¹/₄ cup (60 ml/2 fl oz) olive oil

1 Place the yeast, sugar and ¹/₃ cup (80 ml/ 2³/₄ oz) warm water in a small bowl and stir well. Leave in a warm, draught-free place for 5 minutes, or until bubbles appear on the surface. The mixture should be frothy and slightly increased in volume. If your yeast doesn't foam it is dead, so you will have to discard it and start again.
2 Sift the flour and salt into a bowl and make a well in the centre. Add the yeast mixture, oil and ¹/₂ cup (125 ml/4 fl oz) warm water and mix together. Add more water if the dough is dry.
3 Gather the dough into a ball and turn out onto a lightly floured surface. Knead for 12 minutes, or until soft and elastic.
4 Place the dough in a lightly oiled bowl and brush over the surface with oil. Cover with plastic wrap or a damp tea towel and leave in a warm place for 1– 1¹/₂ hours, or until doubled in volume.
5 Punch down the dough. Divide the dough and gently knead on a lightly floured surface into the desired size and shape.
NOTE: To make a classic topping, using a half quantity of pizza dough, roll out to a 30 cm (12 inch) circle. Spread ³/₄ cup (185 ml/6 fl oz) bottled tomato pasta sauce over the base. Top with 125 g (4 oz) sliced Italian salami, cut into strips. Follow with 2 tablespoons chopped fresh basil, 125 g (4 oz) sliced small cap mushrooms, 1 onion, cut into thin wedges, ¹/₂ green pepper (capsicum), sliced, and 12 pitted black olives. Place 6 anchovy fillets over the top and sprinkle with 150 g (5 oz) grated mozzarella and 30 g (1 oz) grated Parmesan. Bake in a moderately hot 190°C (375°F/Gas 5) oven for 30 minutes.

PIZZA

The idea of cooking a flat piece of dough with a savoury topping was known to the ancient Greeks and Romans even though the Armenians claim to have invented the pizza. In more modern times, the world was introduced to the pizza via Naples in Italy, although every region in Italy has its own variations. The classic Naples version is basically a very thin dough with a simple tomato and mozzarella cheese sauce, maybe with a few herbs, anchovies and black olives added for extra flavour. It was the Americans, though, who transformed pizza into the ultimate fast food item with its many variations. It is now usually made with a thick bready crust topped with a variety of ingredients.

RIGHT: Pizza dough (with classic topping)

POTATO AND ONION PIZZA

Preparation time: 40 minutes
 + 1 hour 30 minutes rising
Total cooking time: 45 minutes
Serves 4

7 g (¹/4 oz) sachet dry yeast
¹/2 teaspoon sugar
1¹/2 cups (185 g/6 oz) white bread flour
1 cup (150 g/5 oz) wholemeal
   plain flour
1 tablespoon olive oil

Topping

1 large red pepper (capsicum)
1 potato
1 large onion, sliced
125 g (4 oz) soft goat's cheese,
   crumbled into small pieces
3 tablespoons capers
1 tablespoon dried oregano
1 teaspoon cracked pepper
1 teaspoon olive oil

1 Mix the yeast, sugar, a pinch of salt and 1 cup (250 ml/8 fl oz) warm water in a bowl. Leave in a warm, draught-free place for 10 minutes, or until foamy. Sift both flours into a bowl. Make a well, add the yeast mixture and mix to a firm dough. Knead on a lightly floured surface for 5 minutes, or until smooth. Place in a lightly oiled bowl, cover with plastic wrap or a damp tea towel and leave in a warm, draught-free place for 1– 1¹/2 hours, or until doubled in size.
2 Preheat the oven to moderately hot 200°C (400°F/Gas 6). Brush a 30 cm (12 inch) pizza tray with oil. Punch down the dough and knead for 2 minutes. Roll out to a 35 cm (14 inch) round. Put the dough on the tray and tuck the edge over to form a rim.
3 For the topping, cut the red pepper into large flat pieces and remove the membrane and seeds. Place, skin-side-up, under a hot grill until blackened. Cool in a plastic bag, then peel away the skin and cut the flesh into narrow strips.
4 Slice the potato paper-thin and arrange over the base with the red pepper, onion and half the cheese. Sprinkle with capers, oregano and cracked pepper and drizzle with oil. Brush the crust edge with oil and bake for 20 minutes. Add the remaining cheese and bake for 15– 20 minutes, or until the crust has browned. Serve in wedges.

ABOVE: Potato and onion pizza

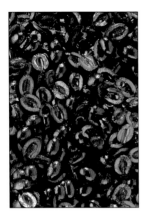

PISSALADIERE

A southern French dish from Provence, pissaladière is their version of the pizza. It gets its name from the Niçoise dialect word 'pissalat' which means a combination of anchovies or sardines, herbs and olive oil. This substantial dish of bread dough with a tomato, onion, anchovy and olive topping is often sold by the slice by bakers and street vendors in cities such as Marseille and Toulon. Although there are many varieties of small silver fish caught worldwide that are sold as anchovies, the only true anchovies come from the Mediterranean. They are filleted, salt-cured and canned in oil for export all over the world.

ABOVE: Pissaladière

PISSALADIERE

Preparation time: 50 minutes + 30 minutes rising
Total cooking time: 2 hours
Serves 8

✫ ✫

7 g (^{1}/4 oz) dried yeast
1 teaspoon caster sugar
2^1/2 cups (310 g/10 oz) white bread flour
^{1}/2 teaspoon salt
2 tablespoons milk powder
1 tablespoon vegetable oil

Tomato and onion topping

^{1}/3 cup (80 ml/2^3/4 fl oz) olive oil
3–4 cloves garlic, finely chopped
6 onions, cut into thin rings
425 g (14 oz) can chopped tomatoes
1 tablespoon tomato paste (tomato purée)
^{1}/4 cup (15 g/^{1}/2 oz) chopped fresh parsley

1 tablespoon chopped fresh thyme
3 x 45 g (1^1/2 oz) cans anchovy fillets,
    drained and halved lengthways
36 small black olives

1 Lightly grease two 30 cm (12 inch) pizza trays. Place the yeast, sugar and 1 cup (250 ml/8 fl oz) warm water in a small bowl and stir well. Leave in a warm, draught-free place for 10 minutes, or until bubbles appear on the surface. The mixture should be frothy and slightly increased in volume. If your yeast doesn't foam it is dead, so you will have to discard it and start again.
2 Sift 2 cups (250 g/8 oz) of the plain flour, the salt and milk powder into a large bowl and make a well in the centre. Add the oil and yeast mixture and mix thoroughly. Turn out onto a lightly floured surface and knead for 10 minutes, gradually adding small amounts of the remaining flour, until the dough is smooth and elastic.
3 Place in an oiled bowl and brush the surface with oil. Cover with plastic wrap and leave in

a warm place for 30 minutes, or until doubled.

4 For the topping, heat the oil in a saucepan. Add the garlic and onion and cook, covered, over low heat for about 40 minutes, stirring frequently. The onion should be softened but not browned. Uncover and cook, stirring frequently, for another 30 minutes, or until lightly golden. Take care not to burn. Allow to cool.

5 Put the tomato in a saucepan and cook over medium heat, stirring frequently, for 20 minutes, or until thick and reduced to about 1 cup (250 ml/8 fl oz). Remove from the heat and stir in the tomato paste and herbs. Season, to taste. Cool, then stir into the onion mixture.

6 Preheat the oven to hot 220°C (425°F/Gas 7). Punch down the dough, then turn out onto a floured surface and knead for 2 minutes. Divide in half. Return one half to the bowl and cover. Roll the other out to a 30 cm (12 inch) circle and press into the tin. Brush with olive oil. Spread half the onion and tomato mixture evenly over the dough, leaving a small border. Arrange half the anchovy fillets over the top in a lattice pattern and place an olive in each square. Repeat with the rest of the dough and topping. Bake for 15–20 minutes, or until the dough is cooked through and lightly browned. If your oven can accommodate both pissaladière at once and you want to cook them together, the cooking time will be longer. Rotate the trays towards the end of cooking time.

YORKSHIRE PUDDINGS

Preparation time: 10 minutes
 + 1 hour refrigeration
Total cooking time: 30 minutes
Makes 6

¾ cup (90 g/3 oz) plain flour

½ teaspoon salt

½ cup (125 ml/4 fl oz) milk

2 eggs

30 g (1 oz) oil, ghee, dripping or lard, melted

1 Sift the flour and salt into a bowl, make a well in the centre and whisk in the milk. In a separate bowl, whisk the eggs until fluffy, then add them to the batter and mix well. Add ½ cup (125 ml/ 4 fl oz) water and whisk until large bubbles form. Cover with plastic wrap and refrigerate for 1 hour.

2 Preheat the oven to hot 220°C (425°F/Gas 7). Put ½ teaspoon oil into 6 of the holes in a twelve hole ⅓ cup (80 ml/2¾ fl oz) muffin tray. Heat the tray in the oven for 3–4 minutes, or until the oil is smoking. Beat the batter again until bubbles form and pour into each hole to three-quarters full. Bake for 20 minutes, then reduce the oven to moderate 180°C (350°F/ Gas 4) and bake for 10 minutes, or until puffed and golden. Serve immediately. Traditionally, these are served with roast beef and gravy.

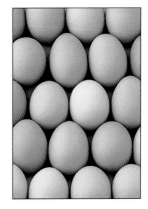

YORKSHIRE PUDDINGS
These first appeared on English tables in the eighteenth century when a batter made with dripping was cooked underneath the roasting joint (usually mutton) so that it would absorb the juices from the meat. This was called 'dripping pudding'. Later, a lighter version based on eggs, milk and flour and prepared in individual muffin tins was developed. Today it is served with a traditional roast. It is a cross between a soufflé and an American popover. Yorkshire puddings puff up when baked but can deflate rapidly and therefore should be served immediately.

LEFT: Yorkshire puddings

SALLY LUNN

Preparation time: 35 minutes
 + 2 hours 30 minutes rising
Total cooking time: 45 minutes
Makes 1 bun

★★☆

7 g (1/4 oz) sachet dried yeast
1 teaspoon caster sugar
3 eggs, at room temperature
3/4 cup (185 ml/6 fl oz) warm milk
1/3 cup (115 g/4 oz) honey
125 g (4 oz) butter, melted
1/2 teaspoon salt
4 cups (500 g/1 lb) plain flour
1 tablespoon sugar, extra
1 tablespoon milk, extra

1 Grease a deep 25 cm (10 inch) round tin and line the base with baking paper. Place the yeast, sugar and 1/4 cup (60 ml/2 fl oz) warm water in a small bowl and stir well. Leave in a warm, draught-free place for 10 minutes, or until bubbles appear on the surface. The mixture should be frothy and slightly increased in volume. If your yeast doesn't foam it is dead, so you will have to discard it and start again.

2 Place the eggs, milk, honey, butter, salt, 2 cups (250 g/8 oz) of the flour and the yeast mixture in a large bowl. Beat with electric beaters at medium speed for 5 minutes, then stir in enough of the remaining flour to make a thick batter. Cover loosely with plastic wrap and leave in a warm place for 1–1 1/2 hours, or until well risen. Stir down the batter.

3 Spoon the batter into the tin with a ladle or spoon, then flatten the surface of the batter with lightly oiled hands. Cover and leave to rise again for 1 hour, or until the batter reaches the top of the tin.

4 Preheat the oven to moderate 180°C (350°F/ Gas 4). Bake for 35– 40 minutes, or until a skewer inserted in the centre comes out clean. Brush with the combined extra sugar and milk, then return to the oven for 5 minutes. Turn out onto a wire cooling rack and leave for 20 minutes. Slice and serve while still warm.

NOTE: Sally Lunn is a cake-like bread that is often served for afternoon tea. It is traditionally served in the following way: leave the bread to cool, then slice it horizontally into three equal layers. Toast and butter each side, then reassemble into the original bun shape. It is then sliced for serving. It can also be simply sliced in the same way you usually slice bread. It keeps for up to five days in an airtight container and can be frozen for up to a month.

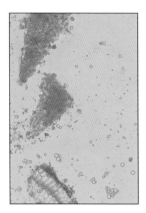

SALLY LUNN

One of the many tales of the origins of Sally Lunn has it that the name comes from a baker in the late eighteenth century called Sally Lunn who had a bakery in Bath. Another more romantic variation of the story is that a well-known baker and musician bought the bakery and wrote a song about Sally Lunn and named the bun after her. It is popular not just in England and France, but the United States, where it is baked, especially in the south. Sally Lunn is a term used for a variety of yeast and soda breads and can be made as sweet large buns or teacakes.

RIGHT: Sally Lunn

BRIOCHE

Preparation time: I hour
+ 3 hours rising
Total cooking time: 50 minutes
Makes 6 small and I medium brioche

★★★

7 g (¹/₄ oz) sachet dried yeast

I teaspoon caster sugar

¹/₂ cup (125 ml/4 fl oz) warm milk

4¹/₄ cups (530 g/I lb I oz) plain flour

I teaspoon salt

2 tablespoons caster sugar, extra

4 eggs, at room temperature, lightly beaten

175 g (6 oz) butter, softened

I egg yolk, to glaze

I tablespoon cream

1 Grease 6 small brioche moulds and a 21 x 11 cm (8¹/₂ x 4¹/₂ inch) bread or loaf tin (see Note). Place the yeast, sugar and warm milk in a small bowl and stir well. Leave in a warm, draught-free place for 10 minutes, or until bubbles appear on the surface. The mixture should be frothy and slightly increased in volume. If your yeast doesn't foam it is dead, so you will have to discard it and start again.

2 Sift 4 cups (500 g/I lb) of the flour, the salt and extra sugar into a large bowl. Make a well in the centre and pour in the yeast mixture and egg. Beat the mixture with a wooden spoon until well combined and the mixture forms a rough ball.

3 Turn out onto a lightly floured surface and knead for 5 minutes, or until the dough is smooth and firm. Gradually incorporate small amounts of the butter into the dough. This will take about 10 minutes and the dough will be very sticky.

4 Sprinkle a clean work surface, your hands and the dough with a small amount of the remaining flour. Knead the dough lightly for 10 minutes, or until smooth and elastic. Place in a large buttered bowl and brush the surface with oil. Cover with plastic wrap and leave in a warm place for 1¹/₂– 2 hours, or until well risen.

5 Punch down the dough and divide in half. Cover one half with plastic wrap and set aside. Divide the other half into 6 even-sized pieces. Remove a quarter of the dough from each piece. Mould the larger pieces into even rounds and place into the brioche moulds. Brush the surface with the combined egg yolk and cream glaze. Shape the small pieces into small even-sized balls and place on top of each roll. Push a floured wooden skewer through the centre of the top ball to the base of the roll, then remove—this will secure the ball to the roll. Brush again with the glaze, cover and leave in a warm place for 45 minutes, or until well risen.

6 Meanwhile, place the remaining dough in the bread tin and brush with glaze. Cover and set aside for 1 hour, or until well risen.

7 Preheat the oven to hot 210°C (415°F/ Gas 6– 7). Bake the small brioche for 10 minutes. Reduce the oven to moderate 180°C (350°F/ Gas 4) and bake for 10 minutes, or until golden and cooked. Turn out immediately onto a wire rack to cool. Increase the oven to hot 210°C (415°F/Gas 6– 7).

8 Bake the medium loaf for 15 minutes. Reduce the oven to moderate 180°C (350°F/Gas 4) and bake for 15 minutes, or until golden and cooked. Turn out onto a wire rack to cool.

NOTE: If the brioche moulds are not available you may prefer to prepare the dough and bake as two loaves.

ABOVE: Brioche

HOT CROSS BUNS

Preparation time: 30 minutes + 1 hour rising
Total cooking time: 25 minutes
Makes 12

2 x 7 g (¼ oz) sachets dried yeast or
   30 g (1 oz) fresh yeast
4 cups (500 g/1 lb) white bread flour
2 tablespoons caster sugar
1 teaspoon mixed spice
1 teaspoon ground cinnamon
40 g (1¼ oz) butter
1¼ cups (200 g/6½ oz) sultanas

Paste for crosses

¼ cup (30 g/1 oz) plain flour
¼ teaspoon caster sugar

Glaze

1½ tablespoons caster sugar
1 teaspoon gelatine

ABOVE: Hot cross buns

1 Lightly grease a baking tray. Place the yeast, 2 teaspoons of the flour, 1 teaspoon of the sugar and ½ cup (125 ml/4 fl oz) warm water in a small bowl and stir well. Leave in a warm, draught-free place for 10 minutes, or until bubbles appear on the surface. The mixture should be frothy and slightly increased in volume. If your yeast doesn't foam it is dead, so you will have to discard it and start again.

2 Sift the remaining flour and spices into a large bowl, stir in the sugar and rub in the butter with your fingertips. Stir in the sultanas. Make a well in the centre, stir in the yeast mixture and up to ¾ cup (185 ml/6 fl oz) water to make a soft dough. Turn the dough out onto a lightly floured surface and knead for 5 minutes, or until smooth, adding more flour if neccessary, to prevent sticking.

3 Place the dough in a large floured bowl, cover with plastic wrap or a damp tea towel and leave in a warm, draught-free place for 30–40 minutes, or until doubled in size.

4 Preheat the oven to moderately hot 200°C (400°F/Gas 6). Turn the dough out onto a lightly floured surface and knead gently to deflate. Divide into 12 portions and roll each into a ball. Place the balls on the tray, just touching each other, in a rectangle 3 rolls wide and 4 rolls long. Cover loosely with plastic wrap or a damp tea towel and leave in a warm place for 20 minutes, or until nearly doubled in size.

5 To make the crosses, mix the flour, sugar and 2½ tablespoons water into a paste. Spoon into a paper piping bag and pipe crosses on top of the buns.

6 Bake for 20 minutes, or until golden brown. Put the sugar, gelatine and 1 tablespoon water in a small pan and stir over the heat until dissolved. Brush over the hot buns and leave to cool.

NOTES: These spiced, sweet yeasted traditional Easter buns are heavily glazed and usually served warm or at room temperature. They are split open and buttered, or sometimes toasted.

The dried fruit in these buns can be varied. Often, currants and chopped candied peel are used. The crosses are sometimes made with pastry instead of flour and water paste, or crosses can be scored into the dough prior to proving.

As a variation, make up the dough as per the recipe but, instead of shaping in the traditional way, make individual buns of varying shapes. For example, try rolling the dough into a sausage shape about 15 cm (6 inches) long, then shaping into a knot, or rolling into a circular snail shape, or folding in half and twisting the dough for a twist roll. Bake as for the hot cross buns, without the crosses, but glaze them if you like.

CHALLAH

Preparation time: I hour + 2 hours rising
Total cooking time: I hour
Makes I loaf

★ ★ ★

275 g (9 oz) floury potatoes, cubed

7 g (¼ oz) sachet dried yeast

⅓ cup (80 ml/2¾ fl oz) oil

2 large eggs

2 large egg yolks

2 tablespoons honey

1½ teaspoons salt

4½ cups (560 g/1 lb 2 oz) white bread flour

1 egg yolk, extra

poppy seeds or sesame seeds

1 Boil the potato in 2½ cups (625 ml/20 fl oz) water for 10 minutes, or until very soft. Drain well, reserving the potato water. Leave to cool for 5 minutes, then mash the potato until very smooth.

2 Grease and lightly flour a baking tray. Place the yeast and ½ cup (125 ml/4 fl oz) warm water in a small bowl and stir well. Leave in a warm, draught-free place for 10 minutes, or until bubbles appear on the surface. The mixture should be frothy and slightly increased in volume. If your yeast doesn't foam it is dead, so you will have to discard it and start again.

3 Place the oil, eggs, egg yolks, honey, salt, ½ cup (125 ml/4 fl oz) reserved potato water and the mashed potato in a large bowl and beat with a wooden spoon until smooth. Leave to cool. Add the yeast mixture and gradually mix in 2 cups (250 g/8 oz) of the flour, beating until smooth. Add another 1½ cups (185 g/6 oz) flour and mix until a rough soft dough is formed. Place the dough on a lightly floured work surface. Knead for 10 minutes, or until the dough is smooth. Incorporate the remaining flour as required to keep the dough from sticking. Place in an oiled bowl and brush the surface with oil. Cover with plastic wrap or a damp tea towel and leave in a warm place for 1½ hours, or until doubled in size.

4 Turn the dough out onto a floured work surface and knead for 4 minutes. Divide the dough into two, a one-third portion and a two-thirds portion, then divide each portion into three equal parts. Leave to rest for 10 minutes. Roll each part into ropes about 35 cm (14 inches) long, with the centre slightly thicker than the ends. Braid the three thicker ropes, pinching the ends together firmly. Place the larger braid on the prepared tray. Whisk the extra egg yolk and 1 tablespoon water and brush some over the surface of the challah. Repeat the process with the remaining three ropes and place on top of the first braid, making sure the ends of the braids overlap. Secure tightly and brush the surface with some of the egg wash. Cover with plastic wrap and leave in a warm, draught-free place for 30 minutes, or until doubled in size. Preheat the oven to moderate 180°C (350°F/Gas 4).

5 Brush the dough with the remaining egg wash and sprinkle with either poppy or sesame seeds. Bake for 50–55 minutes, or until golden brown. Cool on a wire rack.

NOTE: No Shabbat dinner would be complete without a loaf of this rich, braided bread. Challah is made in various sizes and shapes, each with its own meaning. As the strands look like intertwined arms, these breads have come to symbolise love.

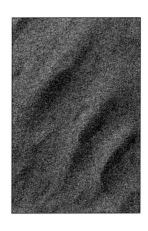

BELOW: Challah

GREEK EASTER BREAD

Put the dough on the tray and sprinkle sesame seeds, almonds and sugar on top.

If you are using dyed eggs, press them into the dough after plaiting.

GREEK EASTER BREAD

Preparation time: 1 hour + 1 hour
  40 minutes standing
Total cooking time: 45 minutes
Makes 1 loaf

★ ★

7 g (¹/4 oz) sachet dried yeast
¹/2 cup (125 ml/4 fl oz) milk
60 g (2 oz) butter
¹/2 teaspoon salt
¹/4 cup (60 g/2 oz) caster sugar
1 teaspoon grated orange rind
3 cups (375 g/12 oz) white bread flour
1 teaspoon ground anise
1 egg, lightly beaten

Topping

1 egg, lightly beaten
1 tablespoon milk
1 tablespoon sesame seeds
1 tablespoon chopped slivered almonds
1 tablespoon caster sugar

1 Place the yeast and 2 tablespoons warm water in a small bowl and stir well. Leave in a warm, draught-free place for 10 minutes, or until bubbles appear on the surface. The mixture should be frothy and slightly increased in volume. If your yeast doesn't foam it is dead, so you will have to discard it and start again.

2 Combine the milk, butter, salt, sugar and orange rind in a small saucepan. Heat until the butter has melted and the milk is just warm. Sift 2¹/2 cups (310 g/10 oz) of the flour and the ground anise into a large bowl. Make a well in the centre, add the yeast and the milk mixtures, then the egg. Gradually beat into the flour for 1 minute, or until a smooth dough forms.

3 Turn out onto a lightly floured surface. Knead for 10 minutes, incorporating the remaining flour, or until the dough is smooth and elastic. Place in an oiled bowl and brush the surface with oil. Cover with plastic wrap and leave in a warm place for 1 hour, or until well risen.

4 Lightly grease a baking tray. Punch down the dough and knead for 1 minute. Divide the dough into three equal pieces. Roll each portion into a sausage 35 cm (14 inches) long. Plait the strands and fold the ends under. Place on the tray, brush with the combined egg and milk, then sprinkle with sesame seeds, almonds and sugar (if using dyed eggs, add them at this stage— see Note). Cover with lightly oiled plastic wrap and leave in a warm place for 40 minutes, or until well risen.

5 Preheat the oven to moderate 180°C (350°F/ Gas 4). Bake for 30– 40 minutes, or until cooked. It should sound hollow when tapped.
NOTE: Decorate with one or two dyed hard-boiled eggs. Push the eggs onto the dough after plaiting. Use Greek red dye which is available in some Greek speciality food stores, and comes with detailed instructions on how to dye eggs.

*RIGHT: Greek
Easter bread*

SAFFRON BUNS

Preparation time: 40 minutes + 2 hours rising
Total cooking time: 10 minutes per tray
Makes 16

★ ★

2 x 7 g (¹/₄ oz) sachets dry yeast
2 cups (500 ml/16 fl oz) warm milk
¹/₂ teaspoon saffron threads
150 g (5 oz) butter, chopped
7 cups (875 g/1 lb 12¹/₂ oz) white bread flour
1 teaspoon salt
²/₃ cup (160 g/5¹/₂ oz) sugar
1 cup (160 g/5¹/₂ oz) raisins
2 eggs

1 Combine the yeast and ¹/₂ cup (125 ml/ 4 fl oz) warm milk and saffron in a small bowl and stir well. Leave in a warm draught-free place for 10 minutes, or until bubbles appear on the surface. The mixture should be frothy and slightly increased in volume. If your yeast doesn't foam, it is dead, so you will have to discard it and start again. Melt the butter in a small saucepan, add the remaining milk and stir over low heat until warm. Remove from the heat and cover.

2 Sift the flour into a large bowl, stir in the frothy yeast, salt, sugar and half the raisins, then make a well in the centre. Add the just warm saffron milk mixture and 1 lightly beaten egg. Mix with a flat-bladed knife, using a cutting action, until the mixture comes together to form a soft dough.

3 Turn the dough onto a lightly floured work surface and knead for 5–7 minutes, or until the dough is smooth. Place the dough in a large, lightly oiled bowl, cover with plastic wrap or a damp tea towel, and leave for 1–1¹/₂ hours in a warm place or until doubled in size.

4 Turn out the dough onto a lightly floured work surface and knead for 5 minutes. Cut into 16 portions. Roll each portion into a sausage shape about 20 cm (8 inches) long and form each into an 'S' shape. Place on greased baking trays. Cover loosely with plastic wrap or a damp tea towel and leave in a warm, draught-free place for 30 minutes, or until doubled in size. Preheat the oven to moderately hot 200°C (400°F/Gas 6).

5 Brush with the remaining beaten egg and decorate with the remaining raisins, placing them gently into the 'S' shape, being careful not to deflate the buns. Bake for 10 minutes, or until the tops are brown and the buns feel hollow when tapped underneath. Transfer to a wire rack to cool. Serve warm or cold, plain or buttered.

SAFFRON
This is the most expensive spice in the world. It comes from the dried stigma of a crocus plant species. The word comes from the Middle East and can be traced as far back as Phoenician times. Saffron has been used for centuries for colouring and flavouring food. It is well known for its use in savoury dishes, especially rice dishes such as paella and risotto, but is also used to add colour and a slightly bitter flavour to yeasted breads and cakes. Saffron can be bought in small containers from speciality food stores. Keep in an airtight container in a cool dark place as saffron strands will lose their colour and flavour if exposed to light.

ABOVE: Saffron buns

INDIVIDUAL PANETTONE

Preparation time: 30 minutes + 1 hour soaking
+ 1 hour 40 minutes rising
Total cooking time: 35 minutes
Makes 8

★★

1/2 cup (95 g/3 oz) chopped dried apricots

1/2 cup (75 g/2 1/2 oz) currants

1/2 cup (80 g/2 3/4 oz) sultanas

1/2 cup (125 ml/4 fl oz) Marsala

2 x 7 g (1/4 oz) sachets dried yeast

3/4 cup (185 ml/6 fl oz) milk, warmed

1/2 cup (125 g/4 oz) caster sugar

180 g (6 oz) butter, softened

2 teaspoons vanilla essence

3 eggs

2 egg yolks

4 cups (500 g/1 lb) white bread flour

1 teaspoon ground aniseed

*ABOVE: Individual
panettone*

1 Combine the fruit and Marsala in a bowl, cover with plastic wrap and stand for 1 hour, or until most of the liquid is absorbed. Put the yeast, milk and 1 teaspoon of the sugar in a bowl, mix well and leave in a warm, draught-free place for about 10 minutes, or until bubbles appear on the surface. The mixture should be frothy and slightly increased in volume. If your yeast doesn't foam it is dead, so you will have to discard it and start again.
2 Place the butter, vanilla and the remaining sugar in a bowl and beat with electric beaters until light and fluffy. Add the eggs and yolks one at a time, beating well after each addition.
3 Sift the flour and aniseed into a bowl, make a well in the centre and add the yeast mixture, butter mixture and fruit mixture. Mix with a flat-bladed knife, until the mixture forms a soft, sticky dough. Cover with plastic wrap or a damp tea towel and leave in a warm place for 40 minutes, or until the dough has doubled in size.
4 Lightly oil the base and sides of eight 1/2 cup (125 ml/4 fl oz) soufflé dishes. Cut a strip of brown paper long enough to fit around the inside of each dish and tall enough to come 10 cm (4 inches) above the edge. Fold down a cuff about 2 cm (3/4 inch) deep along the length of each strip. Make diagonal cuts up to the fold line on each strip, about 1 cm (1/2 inch) apart. Fit the strips around the inside of the dishes, pressing the cuts so they sit flat around the bottom edge of the dish. Cut circles of brown paper using the dish as a guide, place in the base of each dish, and grease the paper.
5 Turn the dough out onto a floured surface and knead for 3 minutes, or until smooth. You will need more flour, up to 1/2 cup (60 g/2 oz), and the dough should be soft but not sticky. Divide into eight equal portions and press into the dishes. Cover with plastic wrap or a damp tea towel and leave in a warm, draught-free place for 1 hour, or until doubled in size.
6 Preheat the oven to moderately hot 200°C (400°F/Gas 6). Bake for 30– 35 minutes, or until golden brown and cooked through when tested with a skewer. Remove from the soufflé dishes, leaving the paper attached. Dust with icing sugar, if desired. Serve warm or cold.
NOTE: If your panettone has gone stale and dried too much, you can still eat it. It is good for toasting or can be used to make bread and butter pudding.

STOLLEN

Preparation time: 30 minutes
+ 2 hours 45 minutes rising
Total cooking time: 40 minutes
Makes 1

★★

1/3 cup (80 ml/2¾ fl oz) lukewarm milk

2 teaspoons sugar

7 g (¼ oz) sachet dried yeast

125 g (4 oz) butter, softened

1/3 cup (90 g/3 oz) caster sugar

1 egg

2 teaspoons vanilla essence

1/2 teaspoon ground cinnamon

3 cups (375 g/12 oz) white bread flour

1/2 cup (80 g/2¾ oz) raisins

1/2 cup (75 g/2½ oz) currants

1/2 cup (95 g/3 oz) mixed peel

1/2 cup (60 g/2 oz) slivered almonds

30 g (1 oz) butter, melted

icing sugar, for dusting

1 Put the milk, sugar and yeast with 1/3 cup (80 ml/2¾ fl oz) warm water in a small bowl and mix well. Leave in a warm, draught-free place for 10 minutes, or until bubbles appear on the surface. The mixture should be frothy and slightly increased in volume. If your yeast doesn't foam it is dead, so you will have to discard it and start again.

2 Beat the butter and sugar with electric beaters until light and creamy, then beat in the egg and vanilla. Add the yeast mixture, cinnamon and almost all the flour and mix to a soft dough, adding more flour if necessary. Turn out onto a lightly floured surface and knead for 10 minutes, or until the dough is smooth and elastic. Place in a lightly oiled bowl, cover with plastic wrap or a damp tea towel and leave in a warm, draught-free place for 1 hour 45 minutes or until doubled in volume.

3 Knock back the dough by punching it to expel the air. Press it out to a thickness of about 1.5 cm (5/8 inch). Sprinkle the fruit and nuts over the dough, then gather up and knead for a few minutes to mix the fruit and nuts evenly through the dough.

4 Shape the dough into an oval about 18 cm (7 inches) wide and 30 cm (12 inches) long. Fold in half lengthways, then press down to flatten slightly, with the fold slightly off centre on top of the loaf. Place on the tray, cover with plastic wrap and leave in a warm place for 1 hour, or until doubled in size. Preheat the oven to moderate 180°C (350°F/Gas 4). Lightly grease a baking tray.

5 Bake the dough for 40 minutes, or until golden. As soon as it comes out of the oven, brush with the melted butter, allowing each brushing to be absorbed until you have used all the butter. Cool on a wire rack. Dust with icing sugar.

BELOW: Stollen

CELEBRATION CAKES

Cakes tenaciously make an appearance at most significant occasions in our lives. You're sure to find them prominently on display at christenings, engagement parties, weddings, birthdays and Christmas celebrations. These beautifully adorned cakes bring with them a lovely sense of festive gaiety and make us feel we are indulging ourselves in something rather extravagant. Definitely not a time for 'less is more'. The tempting array of recipes on the following pages show you how with a little time and care you can create a perfectly over-the-top cake to star at your next special event.

TRIPLE TRUFFLE CAKE

Total preparation time: 1 hour
  + 45 minutes refrigeration
Total cooking time: 1 hour 10 minutes
Makes 1

✷ ✷ ✷

Chocolate cake

185 g (6 oz) unsalted butter, softened

330 g (11 oz) caster sugar

2½ teaspoons vanilla essence

3 eggs

75 g (2½ oz) self-raising flour

225 g (7 oz) plain flour

1½ teaspoons bicarbonate of soda

90 g (3 oz) cocoa powder

280 ml (9 fl oz) buttermilk

Chocolate glaze

250 g (8 oz) dark chocolate, chopped

½ cup (125 ml/4 fl oz) cream

⅔ cup (160 g/5½ oz) sugar

Truffles

300 g (10 oz) Madeira cake crumbs

2 tablespoons jam of your choice

3 tablespoons cream

60 g (2 oz) unsalted butter, melted

300 g (10 oz) milk or dark chocolate, melted

2 tablespoons rum

150 g (5 oz) each of white, milk and dark
  compound chocolate

1 egg white, lightly beaten

24 carat edible gold leaf

1 Preheat the oven to moderate 180°C (350°F/
Gas 4). Lightly grease a deep 22 cm (9 inch)
round cake tin and line the base with baking
paper.

2 Cream the butter and sugar with electric
beaters until light and fluffy, then beat in the
vanilla essence. Add the eggs, one at a time,
beating well after each addition.

3 Using a metal spoon, fold in the combined
sifted flours, bicarbonate of soda and cocoa
powder alternately with the buttermilk.
Stir until just smooth.

4 Spoon the mixture into the tin and smooth
the surface. Bake for 1 hour, or until a skewer
comes out clean when inserted into the centre.
Leave the cake to cool in the tin for at least
5 minutes before turning out onto a wire rack
to cool completely.

5 For the glaze, put the chocolate, cream and
sugar in a saucepan and stir over low heat until
smooth. Bring to the boil, then reduce the heat
and simmer for 4–5 minutes, stirring occasionally
to prevent the mixture catching. Remove from
the heat and stir gently, to cool a little.

6 Cut the dome off the cake to give a flat
surface. Turn the cake upside-down on a rack
over a tray, to catch the glaze that runs over.

7 Pour the cooled glaze over the cake, letting
it run evenly down the side. Tap the tray on
the bench to level the surface. Leave to set
completely.

8 Line a tray with baking paper or foil. To make
truffles, mix together the cake crumbs, jam,
cream, butter, chocolate and rum, stirring until
moistened. Refrigerate for 20–30 minutes, or
until firm. Roll teaspoons of the mixture into
balls and place on the tray. Refrigerate for
10–15 minutes, or until firm.

9 Line three baking trays with baking paper or
foil. Melt the white, milk and dark compound
chocolate separately: put the chocolate in a
heatproof bowl, bring a saucepan of water to
a simmer, remove from the heat and place the
bowl over the saucepan (don't let the bowl
touch the water). Stir the chocolate occasionally
until melted.

10 Using a fork, dip the truffles in the different
chocolates, tapping gently on the edge of the
bowl to drain away the excess. Dip a third of the
truffles in the white chocolate, a third in the
milk and the rest in the dark. Leave on the trays
to set. Don't have the chocolate too hot, or the
truffles may melt and the chocolate discolour.
If you find the chocolate too thick, add 15 g
(½ oz) Copha (white vegetable shortening).

11 Dab a spot of egg white onto the dark
chocolate truffles, then remove the gold leaf
from the sheet with tweezers and press onto
the egg white. Put the cake on a serving plate
and pile the truffles on top.

NOTE: The chocolate cake can be refrigerated
in an airtight container for up to a week, or for
three days in a cool dry place. It can also be
frozen for up to two months. It can be glazed
up to a day in advance. Pile with the truffles just
prior to serving (use a little melted chocolate to
stick them to the cake). The truffles can be kept
for three days in an airtight container in a cool,
dry place. Refrigerate in warm weather. You
can substitute the butter cake recipe from the
Valentine cake (see page 276), but it will take
about 15 minutes longer to cook because of
the different tin size.

Put the glaze ingredients in
a saucepan and stir until
smooth before bringing to
the boil.

Pour the glaze over the
cake, letting it run down to
completely cover the side
of the cake.

Use a fork, or a special
chocolate dipper, to cover
the truffles with chocolate.

Remove the gold leaf from
the sheet with tweezers
and press onto the truffles.

OPPOSITE PAGE:
Triple truffle cake

ROSE PETAL CAKE

Paint egg white over the petals, so they are covered, but not too heavily.

Sprinkle caster sugar over the petals, then shake off any excess.

Press a layer of petals around the base of the cake, then overlap the petal layers upwards.

OPPOSITE PAGE:
Rose petal cake

ROSE PETAL CAKE

Preparation time: 2 hours + 2 hours drying of flowers
Total cooking time: 1 hour 15 minutes
Makes 1

✶ ✶ ✶

Rose decorations

1 bunch pale pink roses
3 white roses
1 egg white
caster sugar

Coconut cake

2 cups (250 g/8 oz) self-raising flour
1/2 cup (45 g/1 1/2 oz) desiccated coconut
220 g (7 oz) caster sugar
2/3 cup (60 g/2 oz) ground almonds
1 cup (250 ml/8 fl oz) buttermilk
2 eggs
1 teaspoon vanilla essence
150 g (5 oz) butter, melted

Meringue frosting

3 egg whites
2/3 cup (160 g/5 1/2 oz) caster sugar
250 g (8 oz) unsalted butter

1 Line two or three large trays with paper towels. Carefully separate the rose petals, discarding any that are very small or blemished. Whisk the egg white lightly until just foamy. Spread the caster sugar on a large plate. Use a small brush to paint the egg white lightly over each petal—make sure the entire petal is coated, but not too heavily. Sprinkle the petals with caster sugar, gently shake off any excess and place the petals on the tray to dry. Leave them for at least 1 or 2 hours. The drying time will vary according to the weather and the humidity.
2 Preheat the oven to moderate 180°C (350°F/ Gas 4). Lightly grease a 2-litre charlotte tin and line the base with baking paper.
3 Mix the sifted flour, coconut, sugar and almonds in a large bowl and make a well in the centre. Pour the combined buttermilk, eggs, vanilla and butter into the well and stir with a metal spoon until smooth.
4 Pour the mixture into the tin and smooth the surface. Bake for 1 1/4 hours. Cover the cake for the last 15 minutes if necessary. The cake is ready when a skewer comes out clean when inserted into the centre of the cake. Leave in the tin for 10 minutes before turning out onto a wire rack to cool.
5 For the meringue frosting, put the egg whites and sugar in a heatproof bowl. Bring a small pan of water to simmering point and place the bowl over the pan, making sure the base of the bowl doesn't touch the water. Stir continuously to dissolve the sugar, but be careful not to cook the egg whites.
6 When the sugar has dissolved, remove the bowl from the pan and beat the mixture with electric beaters for 3–5 minutes, or until stiff peaks form. Cut the butter into about 8 pieces and add, piece by piece, beating after each addition. The mixture should thicken when you have about 2 pieces of butter left, but continue until you have added all of it.
7 Place the cake on a serving plate and spread the frosting evenly over the cake, as smoothly as possible. Starting from the base, press a layer of pink rose petals around the cake. Start the next layer slightly overlapping the first and continue working up towards the top of the cake. In the final few layers, alternate white petals with the pink. The cake should look like an open flower from the top.
NOTE: The coconut cake can be kept in an airtight container in the refrigerator for up to a week, or for three days in an airtight container in a cool dry place. It can also be frozen for up to two months. You can decorate it up to a day in advance as long as the rose petals are dry. Store in an airtight container in a cool dark place.

STRAWBERRIES AND CREAM SPONGE WITH SPUN TOFFEE

Preparation time: 40 minutes
Total cooking time: 25 minutes
Makes 1

✿ ✿ ✿

75 g (2¹/₂ oz) plain flour
150 g (5 oz) self-raising flour
6 eggs
220 g (7 oz) caster sugar
2 tablespoons boiling water
3 cups (750 ml/24 fl oz) cream
2 tablespoons icing sugar
500 g (1 lb) strawberries
Kirsch or Cointreau
1 cup (250 g/8 oz) caster sugar

1 Preheat the oven to moderate 180°C (350°F/ Gas 4). Grease two deep 22 cm (9 inch) round cake tins and line the bases with baking paper. Lightly dust the tins with flour, shaking off the excess.
2 Sift the flours three times onto greaseproof paper. Beat the eggs in a large bowl with electric beaters for 7 minutes, or until thick and pale.
3 Gradually add the sugar to the eggs, beating well after each addition. Using a metal spoon, fold in the sifted flour and boiling water. Spread the mixture evenly into the tins and bake for 25 minutes, or until the sponges are lightly golden and shrink slightly from the sides of the tins. Leave the sponges in their tins for 5 minutes before turning out onto a wire rack to cool.
4 Using a serrated knife, slice each cake horizontally in half (you will only need three layers of cake, so freeze the remaining portion for trifles or cake crumbs).
5 Whip the cream and icing sugar into stiff peaks. Hull half the strawberries and slice thinly.
6 Place one layer of cake on a serving plate or board and brush lightly with a little liqueur. Spread with a quarter of the cream and scatter with half the sliced strawberries. Repeat with another layer of cake, liqueur, cream and strawberries. Place the last cake layer on top and spread the remaining cream roughly over the top. Arrange the remaining whole strawberries on top. Refrigerate until the toffee is ready.
7 To make the toffee, put a heavy-based frying pan over medium heat, gradually sprinkle with some of the sugar and, as it melts, sprinkle with the remaining sugar. Stir to melt any lumps and prevent the sugar burning. When the toffee is golden brown, remove the pan immediately from the heat.
8 Dip two forks in the toffee, then rub the backs of the forks together until the toffee begins to stick. Gently pull the forks apart to check whether the toffee is cool enough to spin. If it drips or dips, it probably needs a little longer to cool. If not, continue pulling the toffee apart over the cake, pressing the forks together to spin a second time when they meet. Re-dip and continue spinning backwards and forwards and over the cake. Serve as soon as you've spun the toffee.
NOTE: The layered cake can be kept in the refrigerator for up to two hours before serving. Once you have spun the toffee over the top, serve immediately—the spun toffee will start to soften if left.

STRAWBERRIES AND CREAM SPONGE WITH SPUN TOFFEE

Once the toffee has turned golden brown, remove from the heat. Use two forks to make the toffee strands.

Gently pull the forks apart. If the toffee dips or drips it needs to cool a little longer.

Spin the toffee strands over the cake, pressing the forks together when they meet.

OPPOSITE PAGE:
Strawberries and cream sponge with spun toffee

VALENTINE CAKE

Fold the paper circle in half, draw half a heart on one side and cut out.

Put the paper template over the cake and cut with a serrated knife.

Ease the icing into the corners and around the edges until it fits snugly.

Roll out the balls of coloured icing and cut heart shapes of various sizes.

OPPOSITE PAGE:
Valentine cake

VALENTINE CAKE

Preparation time: 50 minutes
Total cooking time: 1 hour 15 minutes
Makes 1

★★★

Butter cake

280 g (9 oz) butter
225 g (7 oz) caster sugar
1½ teaspoons vanilla essence
4 eggs
225 g (7 oz) self-raising flour
150 g (5 oz) plain flour
185 ml (6 fl oz) milk

Pink buttercream

50 g (1¾ oz) unsalted butter
120 g (4 oz) icing sugar, sifted
3 teaspoons liqueur (e.g. Cointreau,
    Grand Marnier)
few drops of red food colouring

500 g (1 lb) ready-made soft icing
icing sugar
few drops of red food colouring

1 Preheat the oven to moderate 180°C (350°F/ Gas 4). Lightly grease a deep 20 cm (8 inch) round cake tin with melted butter or oil and line the base with baking paper.
2 Cream the butter and sugar with electric beaters until light and fluffy. Beat in the vanilla essence. Add the eggs one at a time, beating well after each addition.
3 Using a large metal spoon, fold in the combined sifted flours alternately with the milk, until smooth. Spoon the mixture into the tin and smooth the surface. Bake for 1¼ hours, or until a skewer comes out clean when inserted into the centre of the cake.
4 Leave the cake in the tin for 5 minutes before turning out onto a wire rack to cool completely.
5 Draw around the base of the cake tin and cut out a 20 cm (8 inch) circle from a piece of paper. Fold the circle in half and draw on half a heart shape using the fold as the middle of the heart and the outside edge as the edge of the heart. Cut along this line and unfold the paper to make a heart-shaped template.
6 Cut the domed top off the cake to give a flat surface. Turn the cake upside-down and use the template to cut into a heart with a serrated knife. The cake should cut easily and leave a clean edge.

7 For the pink buttercream, beat the butter until soft, add the sifted sugar and continue beating until light and fluffy. Add the liqueur and colouring and beat well.
8 Cut the cake in half horizontally. Spread the bottom layer with a third of the buttercream and sandwich the halves together. Spread the remaining buttercream over the cake in a thin layer, to help the next layer of icing stick. Place the cake on a serving plate or board.
9 Knead the soft icing until smooth on a surface dusted with icing sugar. Add a couple of drops of food colouring and knead into the icing until it is pale pink (you may need to add more icing sugar as you go along). Pull off a piece the size of a golf ball and add another few drops of food colouring to make it darker. Wrap it in plastic wrap and set aside. Continue doing this until you have three or four different shades of pink icing set aside. Roll out the remaining icing into a circle large enough to cover the top and side of the cake. Carefully drape this over the cake, easing it into the corners and around the edges until it fits snugly all over. As long as you don't over-roll your icing you should not have any folds or pleats—if you do, just smooth them in. Trim away any excess and set it aside.
10 Roll out the balls of coloured icing and stamp out heart shapes using varying sized cutters. If you want any of the hearts to be red, paint them with the food colouring and leave to dry. Mix 1 tablespoon of icing sugar with a little water to make a runny paste and use a tiny dab of this to stick each heart onto the cake.
NOTE: Butter cake can be kept in an airtight container in the refrigerator for up to a week. It can be frozen for up to two months. The iced cake can be kept for up to three days in an airtight container.

LEMON CURD MERINGUE CAKE

Preparation time: 1 hour 30 minutes
+ several hours refrigeration
Total cooking time: 2 hours 25 minutes
Makes 1

 ✫ ✫ ✫

Sponge cakes

300 g (10 oz) plain flour
8 eggs
220 g (7 oz) caster sugar
100 g (3 1/2 oz) unsalted butter, melted
1 cup (250 ml/8 fl oz) thick (double) cream
icing sugar, to dust

Meringue

4 egg whites
220 g (7 oz) caster sugar
few drops of pink food colouring
40 g (1 1/4 oz) flaked almonds

Lemon syrup

110 g (3 1/2 oz) caster sugar
3 tablespoons lemon juice

Lemon curd

5 egg yolks
150 g (5 oz) caster sugar
1 tablespoon grated lemon rind
2/3 cup (170 ml/5 1/2 fl oz) lemon juice
180 g (6 oz) unsalted butter, chopped

1 Preheat the oven to moderate 180°C (350°F/ Gas 4). Brush two deep 22 cm (9 inch) round cake tins with melted butter. Line the bases with baking paper and then grease the paper. Dust the tins lightly with flour, shaking off any excess. Sift the flour three times onto greaseproof paper.
2 Mix the eggs and sugar in a large heatproof bowl. Place the bowl over a pan of simmering water and beat with electric beaters for 8 minutes, or until the mixture is thick and fluffy and a ribbon of mixture drawn in a figure of eight doesn't sink immediately. Remove from the heat and beat for 3 minutes, or until slightly cooled.
3 Add the cooled butter and sifted flour to the bowl. Using a large metal spoon, fold in quickly and lightly until the mixture is just combined.
4 Spread the mixture evenly into the tins. Bake

for 25 minutes, or until the sponge is lightly golden and shrinks slightly from the side of the tin. Leave the cakes in their tins for 5 minutes before turning out onto a wire rack to cool.
5 Reduce the oven to very slow 120°C (250°F/ Gas 1/2). Cover four baking trays with baking paper. Mark a 21 cm (8 1/2 inch) circle on the baking paper on three of the trays and turn the marked paper over. To make the meringue, beat the egg whites into soft peaks. Gradually add the sugar, beating well after each addition, until smooth and glossy. Tint the meringue pale pink with a little colouring. Spoon a quarter of the meringue into a piping bag fitted with a 1 cm (1/2 inch) plain nozzle. Pipe strips 1.5 cm (5/8 inch) apart along the length of the unmarked tray and sprinkle with the almonds. Divide the remaining meringue into three and spread over the circles marked on the trays (they will spread slightly). Bake in two batches for 1 hour each. After cooking, turn off the oven and leave to cool in the oven with the door ajar. Break each of the strips into 3 pieces and store in an airtight container for up to two days, until required.
6 Meanwhile, for the lemon syrup, put the sugar and lemon juice in a small saucepan with 3 tablespoons water and stir over medium heat until the sugar has dissolved. Leave to cool.
7 To make the lemon curd, beat the egg yolks and sugar in a jug and strain into a heatproof bowl. Add the lemon rind, juice and butter and place the bowl over a pan of barely simmering water (don't let the bowl sit in the water). Stir over the heat for 20 minutes, or until the mixture thickens enough to coat the back of a wooden spoon. Cool slightly, then cover the surface with plastic wrap and leave until completely cold.
8 Cut the cakes in half horizontally with a long serrated knife. Place one layer on a plate, brush with the syrup and spread with a thin layer of lemon curd. Top with a round of meringue, trimming the edge to fit. Spread with lemon curd and top with another layer of cake. Repeat the layers, finishing with the last round of cake and syrup. Chill for several hours, at least, to soften the meringue.
9 Beat the cream into stiff peaks and spread over the cake. Pile the meringue fingers on the top and dust liberally with icing sugar.
NOTE: Ideally, this should be made a day in advance to let the meringue soften. However, the decorated cake will not keep for longer than two days.

LEMON CURD MERINGUE CAKE

Pipe strips of pink meringue along the length of the baking tray.

Spread the remaining mixture over the marked circles on the baking paper.

Stir the lemon curd over the heat until it coats the back of a wooden spoon.

Spread a layer of lemon curd over the cake, then top with a meringue circle.

OPPOSITE PAGE: Lemon curd meringue cake

MERINGUE AND BERRY CAKE

Stir the egg whites and sugar to dissolve the sugar without cooking the egg whites.

Brush the cake with the syrup, spread with a layer of frosting, then repeat the layers.

Use a palette knife to spread the frosting up the side of the cake, making furrows.

OPPOSITE PAGE:
Meringue and berry cake

MERINGUE AND BERRY CAKE

Preparation time: 1 hour
Total cooking time: 1 hour 30 minutes
Makes 1 cake

☆ ☆ ☆

Coconut cake

4 cups (500 g/1 lb) self-raising flour

1 cup (90 g/3 oz) desiccated coconut

440 g (14 oz) caster sugar

1⅓ cup (120 g/4 oz) ground almonds

2 cups (500 ml/1 lb) buttermilk

4 eggs

2 teaspoons vanilla essence

300 g (10 oz) butter, melted

110 g (3½ oz) caster sugar

3 tablespoons Cointreau or orange juice

750 g (1½ lb) assorted fresh berries
(blueberries, raspberries, blackberries
or loganberries)

Meringue frosting

3 egg whites

165 g (5½ oz) caster sugar

250 g (8 oz) unsalted butter, softened

1 Preheat the oven to moderate 180°C (350°F/ Gas 4). Lightly grease two deep 20 cm (8 inch) round cake tins and line the bases with baking paper.

2 Sift the flour into a large bowl and add the coconut, sugar and almonds. Mix well, then make a well in the centre. Pour the combined buttermilk, eggs, vanilla and butter into the well and stir with a metal spoon until smooth. If you don't have a bowl big enough, then make the mixture in two batches.

3 Pour the mixture into the tins and smooth the surface. Bake for 1¼ hours. If your oven is large enough, it is best to cook both cakes on the middle shelf, but make sure that the tins are not touching each other and that they are not touching the sides of the oven. Alternatively, the cakes can be baked on different shelves but they will need to be rotated after 50 minutes cooking time because the cake on the higher shelf may colour a little more than the other cake. Cover the cakes lightly with foil for the last 15 minutes, if necessary, so they don't burn. The cakes are ready when a skewer comes out clean when inserted into the centre of the cake. Leave in the tin for 10 minutes before turning out onto a wire rack to cool.

4 For the meringue frosting, put the egg whites and sugar in a heatproof bowl. Bring a small pan of water to a simmer and place the bowl over the pan (don't let the base of the bowl sit in the water). Stir to dissolve the sugar, but be careful not to cook the egg whites.

5 When the sugar has dissolved, remove from the heat and beat with electric beaters for 5 minutes, or until stiff peaks form. Cut the butter into about 10 pieces and add, piece by piece, beating after each addition. The mixture should thicken when you have a couple of pieces of butter left, but continue until you have added it all.

6 Put the sugar in a small pan with ¾ cup (185 ml/6 fl oz) water and stir over the heat until the sugar has dissolved. Stir in the Cointreau.

7 Trim the domed top off each cake to give a flat surface. Slice each cake in half horizontally and place one layer on a serving plate or board. Brush well with the Cointreau syrup and spread with a thin layer of frosting. Repeat this to build up the layers, finishing with a layer of cake.

8 Spread the remaining frosting evenly over the top and side of the cake with a palette or flat-bladed knife. Spread the frosting up the side of the cake to make furrows. Pile the berries on top of the cake. Dust with a little icing sugar if you prefer your berries sweetened.

NOTES: If you prefer, you can use two butter cakes (see page 276) for this recipe.

The cake can be iced up to a day in advance, but don't add the berries until you are ready to serve.

If you prefer, use a white chocolate ganache instead of the frosting: put 150 g (5 oz) white chocolate melts, 130 g (4½ oz) chopped white chocolate, ½ cup (125 ml/4 fl oz) cream and 250 g (8 oz) butter in a pan and stir over low heat until melted and smooth. Transfer to a small bowl, cover the surface with plastic wrap and leave overnight to cool. Beat with electric beaters for 3–5 minutes, or until thick, pale and creamy.

HAZELNUT TORTE

Preparation time: 1 hour + setting
 of the chocolate leaves
Total cooking time: 20 minutes
Makes 1

6 egg whites
1¼ cups (310 g/10 oz) caster sugar
180 g (6 oz) ground hazelnuts
2 tablespoons plain flour, sifted
100 ml (3½ fl oz) white rum
chopped roasted hazelnuts, to decorate

Chocolate leaves

150 g (5 oz) white chocolate
non-toxic leaves (choose leaves with
 prominent veins)

White chocolate cream

125 g (4 oz) white chocolate
1¾ cups (435 ml/14 fl oz) cream

Dark chocolate cream

40 g (1¼ oz) dark chocolate
½ cup (125 ml/4 fl oz) cream

1 Lightly grease two 20 cm (8 inch) sandwich tins. Line the bases with baking paper and then grease the paper. Dust the tins lightly with flour, shaking off any excess. Preheat the oven to moderate 180°C (350°F/Gas 4).

2 Beat the egg whites in a clean, dry bowl, with electric beaters, until stiff peaks form. Gradually add the sugar to the bowl, beating until thick and glossy. Lightly fold in the ground hazelnuts and flour. Divide evenly between the prepared tins and smooth the tops with wet fingers. Bake for 15–20 minutes, or until the cakes feel spongy to touch. Leave in the tins to cool a little before turning out onto wire racks to cool completely. Cut each cake in half horizontally with a long serrated knife.

3 To make the chocolate leaves, chop the white chocolate into small even-sized pieces and place in a heatproof bowl. Bring a saucepan of water to the boil, then remove the saucepan from the heat. Sit the bowl over the pan, making sure the base of the bowl doesn't sit in the water. Stir occasionally until the chocolate has melted. Use a fine brush to paint the chocolate over the underside of the leaves. Leave to set, then peel away the leaf. If the coating of chocolate is too thin, it will break when the leaf is removed.

4 For the white chocolate cream, bring a saucepan of water to the boil and remove the pan from the heat. Place the white chocolate in a heatproof bowl and sit the bowl over the water, making sure the bowl does not touch the water. Stir occasionally until the chocolate melts, then allow to cool. Whip the cream in a bowl, with beaters, until it begins to hold its shape. Add the chocolate and beat it in, then allow to cool. Make the dark chocolate cream in the same way.

5 Put a layer of cake on a serving plate, brush the cut surface with rum and spread with a quarter of the white chocolate cream.

6 Top with a second cake layer. Brush with rum and spread with all the dark chocolate cream. Add another layer of cake and spread with rum and a quarter of the white chocolate cream. Top with the final cake layer and spread the remaining white chocolate cream over the top and side of the cake.

7 Decorate the torte with the chopped hazelnuts and chocolate leaves.

HAZELNUT TORTE

Bake for up to 20 minutes, until the cake feels spongy.

Spread the layers of cake with chocolate cream.

OPPOSITE PAGE:
Hazelnut torte

CROQUEMBOUCHE

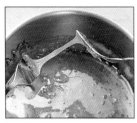

Rub the backs of the forks together until the toffee is tacky, then gently pull apart.

Spin fine lengths of toffee around, pressing the forks together when they meet.

OPPOSITE PAGE:
Croquembouche

CROQUEMBOUCHE

Preparation time: 1 hour 30 minutes
Total cooking time: 1 hour 30 minutes
Makes 1 croquembouche

★ ★ ★

1¹⁄₂ cups (185 g/6 oz) plain flour
100 g (3¹⁄₂ oz) unsalted butter
6 eggs, beaten
4 cups (1 kg/2 lb) sugar

Filling

1¹⁄₂ cups (375 ml/12 fl oz) milk
1 vanilla bean
3 egg yolks
¹⁄₄ cup (60 g/2 oz) caster sugar
2 tablespoons plain flour
¹⁄₄ cup (60 ml/2 fl oz) Grand Marnier
1¹⁄₂ cups (375 ml/12 fl oz) cream

1 Preheat the oven to hot 210°C (415°F/ Gas 6–7). Sift the flour three times onto a piece of baking paper. Put the butter in a large heavy-based saucepan with 1¹⁄₂ cups (375 ml/12 fl oz) water and stir over medium heat until the mixture comes to the boil. Remove from the heat and quickly beat in the flour with a wooden spoon. Return to the heat and continue beating until the mixture forms a ball and leaves the side of the pan. Transfer to a large clean bowl and cool slightly.

2 Beat the mixture to release any heat. Gradually add the beaten egg about 3 teaspoons at a time. Beat well after each addition until all the egg has been added and the mixture is thick and glossy—a wooden spoon should stand upright in it. (If it is too runny, the egg has been added too quickly. Beat for several minutes more, or until thickened.) Sprinkle three baking trays with water. Spoon the mixture onto the trays, leaving plenty of room for spreading. You will need about eight large puffs, using about 2 tablespoons of the mixture for these—vary the remainder, gradually reducing the size. One small puff is equal to about 1 heaped teaspoon of mixture. Sprinkle the puffs lightly with a little water— this creates steam, helping the puffs to rise and the outer surface become crisp. Bake for 20–30 minutes, or until browned. Remove the profiteroles from the oven and make a small hole in the base of each one, then reduce the heat to moderate 180°C (350°F/Gas 4) and bake for another 5 minutes so they dry out. You may

need to prepare and cook them in two batches.

3 For the filling, put the milk and vanilla bean in a saucepan. Heat gently until the milk almost boils. Remove from the heat and cool slightly. Beat the yolks, sugar and flour in a bowl until thick and pale. Gradually whisk in the warm milk. Return to a clean saucepan and stir over medium heat until the custard boils and thickens. Remove from the heat and stir in the liqueur. Discard the vanilla bean. Cover the surface of the custard with plastic wrap to prevent a skin forming and leave to cool completely.

4 Whip the cream into stiff peaks and fold into the cold custard, then put into a piping bag with a nozzle less than 1 cm (¹⁄₂ inch) in diameter. Poke a small hole in the base of each puff and fill with the custard cream.

5 Put 2 cups (500 g/1 lb) of the sugar in a pan with 1 cup (250 ml/8 fl oz) water. Stir over low heat without boiling until dissolved. Simmer over low heat without stirring until the toffee is light gold (watch it carefully as it can burn quickly).

6 To assemble, begin with the large puffs. Dip the base of each in enough toffee to coat it and arrange in a large circle, with the sides touching. It is not necessary to have any in the centre. Build up into a cone shape, using smaller puffs nearer the top.

7 Use the remaining sugar to make another batch of toffee as in step 5 and then dip two forks in it. Rub the backs of the forks together until the toffee begins to stick. Gently pull the forks apart to check whether the toffee is cool enough to spin. If it drips or dips, it probably needs a little longer to cool. Spin toffee around the Croquembouche. Re-dip and continue spinning to make a decorative pattern as shown in the picture.

NOTE: You can make the puffs a couple of days ahead and store them in an airtight container. The custard can be made a day or two in advance and stored, covered, in the refrigerator. The toffee decoration can be added a couple of hours ahead of serving time.

Croquembouche, literally, *crunch in the mouth*, is a traditional French dessert usually served at celebrations such as weddings and first communions.

MODERN WEDDING CAKE

Preparation time: 1 hour + 30 minutes
refrigeration
Total cooking time: 40 minutes
Makes 1

✩ ✩ ✩

Genoise sponge

2¹/3 cups (290 g/10 oz) plain flour

8 eggs

220 g (7 oz) caster sugar

100 g (3¹/2 oz) unsalted butter, melted
and cooled

White chocolate ganache

150 g (5 oz) white chocolate melts

135 g (4¹/2 oz) white chocolate

¹/2 cup (125 ml/4 fl oz) cream

250 g (8 oz) unsalted butter

Custard filling

75 g (2¹/2 oz) cornflour

¹/2 cup (60 g/2 oz) custard powder

²/3 cup (160 g/5¹/2 oz) caster sugar

2 teaspoons vanilla essence

1¹/2 cups (375 ml/12 fl oz) cream

2 cups (500 ml/16 fl oz) milk

2 egg yolks

³/4 cup (185 ml/6 fl oz) Cointreau

300 g (10 oz) white chocolate melts, melted

²/3 cup (160 g/5¹/2 oz) sugar

coloured ribbon

1 To make the genoise sponges, lightly grease an 18 cm (7 inch) and a 25 cm (10 inch) deep cake tin with melted butter. Preheat the oven to moderate 180°C (350°F/Gas 4). Line the base with baking paper, then grease the paper. Dust the tin with a little flour, shaking off any excess.

2 Sift the flour three times onto baking paper. Mix the eggs and sugar in a large heatproof bowl. Sit the bowl over a saucepan of simmering water, making sure the base doesn't touch the water, and beat with electric beaters for 8 minutes, or until the mixture is thick and fluffy and a ribbon of mixture drawn in a figure of eight doesn't sink immediately. Remove from the heat and beat for 3 minutes, or until the mixture is slightly cooled.

3 Add the cooled butter and sifted flour. Using a large metal spoon, fold in quickly and lightly until the mixture is just combined.

4 Spread the mixture evenly into the tins. Bake for 25 minutes, or until the sponges are lightly golden and have shrunk slightly from the side of the tins. Leave the cakes in the tins for 5 minutes before turning out onto a wire rack to cool.

5 To make the ganache, put all the ingredients in a saucepan and stir over low heat until smooth. Transfer to a bowl, cover with plastic wrap and leave until cold (don't refrigerate). Beat for 3–5 minutes, or until light and fluffy.

6 For the custard filling, put the cornflour, custard, sugar and vanilla in a pan. Gradually add the cream and milk, whisking until free of lumps. Stir over low heat until the mixture just comes to the boil. Reduce the heat and simmer for 3 minutes. Remove from the heat and quickly stir in the egg yolks. Transfer to a bowl, cover with plastic wrap and refrigerate for 30 minutes, stirring occasionally.

7 Slice each cake horizontally into three layers with a long serrated knife. Put the bottom layer of the large cake on a plate. Brush with Cointreau and spread with a third of the custard filling. Top with another layer of cake, Cointreau and custard. Brush the underside of the top layer of cake with Cointreau and place on top. Cover with two thirds of the ganache.

8 Place the bottom layer of the small cake on top of the larger cake. Brush with Cointreau and spread with half the remaining custard. Top with the next layer, brush with Cointreau and spread with the rest of the custard. Brush the underside of the top layer with Cointreau and place on top. Cover with the remaining ganache. Chill.

9 Lay out 2 sheets of plastic wrap. Wrinkle the surface and spread with 2 rows of melted white chocolate about 10 cm (4 inches) long. Leave to set. Break into pieces. Arrange around the cakes, overlapping the pieces slightly.

10 Cover three baking trays with foil. Put a heavy-based saucepan over medium heat and sprinkle with a little sugar. As the sugar melts, add the rest gradually. Stir to melt any lumps and prevent burning. When the sugar is golden brown, remove from the heat. Drizzle on the trays, cool, then peel away the foil. Tie ribbon around the cake and top with toffee.

NOTE: This cake can be kept for two days once assembled but don't add the toffee until closer to the time you are ready to serve or it will soften.

MODERN WEDDING CAKE

Brush the cake liberally with Cointreau, then spread with custard filling.

Spread two rows of the melted chocolate over the wrinkled plastic wrap.

Break the chocolate into pieces, then arrange around the cake, overlapping.

Once the toffee is a dark caramel colour, drizzle over the foil-covered trays.

OPPOSITE PAGE:
Modern wedding cake

TRADITIONAL
WEDDING CAKE

Gently press your finger
into the rounded end of
the petal to make a hollow.

When all five petals are
ready, gently roll them
together, pinching the ends.

Place the flowers into a
padded egg carton, then
ease open the petals.

TRADITIONAL WEDDING CAKE

Preparation time: 2 hours + overnight soaking
    of fruit + overnight drying of icing
Total cooking time: 3 hours 15 minutes
Makes 1 cake

★ ★ ★

double quantity of Rich fruit cake (see page 90)
brandy, for brushing

1 quantity ready-made modelling paste
cornflour and icing sugar, to dust
medium frangipani petal cutter
edible yellow chalks and green, brown and
    yellow food colourings
medium-long leaf cutter
15 cm (6 inch) and 40 cm (16 inch) round
    cake boards
2 tablespoons apricot jam
3 x 500 g (1 lb) packets soft icing
4 wooden skewers
1 teaspoon egg white
1–2 tablespoons pure icing sugar
ribbon

1 Preheat the oven to slow 150°C (300°F/
Gas 2). Grease a 30 cm (12 inch) and a 15 cm
(6 inch) round cake tin and line with a double
thickness of baking paper. Fit a paper collar on
the outside of the tin (see page 49).
2 Spoon the mixture into the tins and smooth
the surface. Tap the tins on the bench to remove
any air bubbles. Dip your hand in water and
level the surface. Sit the cake tins on several
layers of newspaper in the oven and bake the
small cake for 2 hours 40 minutes and the large
one for 3 hours 10 minutes, or until a skewer
comes out clean when inserted into the centre.
Brush the cakes with brandy. Cover the top of
the cakes with baking paper and wrap in a tea
towel. Cool completely in the tin.
3 To decorate, roll a small amount of modelling
paste to 2 mm (1/8 inch) thick on a bench lightly
dusted with cornflour and, working quickly, cut
out petals with a cutter. Only cut 10 petals at a
time (enough for 2 frangipanis) and cover with
plastic wrap. Dust your fingers lightly with
cornflour and smooth the cut edges of the petal.
Gently press your finger into the rounded end
of the petal and make a slight hollow by easing
your finger towards you. Place a dab of water at
the point of each petal and press the next petal,

slightly overlapping, onto this. When all five
petals are ready, gently roll together, pinching
the ends to join. Put in a padded egg carton and
ease the petals open to form a full flower. Make
at least 20 flowers, all at varying degrees of
opening. Make buds by rolling cigar shapes and
pressing lines down outside, then give a gentle
twist. When dry, dust the centre of the flower
with a little yellow chalk.
4 Knead green food colouring into a little
modelling paste. Roll out thinly on a bench
lightly dusted with cornflour and, with an
elongated leaf cutter or sharp knife, cut out
leaves about 5 cm (2 inches) long. Gently press
in half, then open out and mark veins on either
side with the back of the knife. Twist at angles
and leave to dry before placing in airtight
containers. Paint with green and brown
colouring and a little water. Leave to dry.
5 Trim the domes from the cakes so they are
the same height. Invert onto the boards. Heat
the jam, strain and brush all over the cakes.
6 Knead the icing on a work surface dusted
with icing sugar. Add enough yellow colouring
to tint cream. Roll two thirds of the icing out
to 5 mm (1/4 inch) thick and large enough to
cover the large cake. Roll the icing over the
rolling pin and re-roll over the top of the cake.
Press and smooth over the cake, using the palms
of your hands dusted with icing sugar. Trim off
any excess. Repeat with the remaining icing and
small cake. Leave the icing to dry for a day
before decorating.
7 Insert skewers into the bottom cake, equal
distances apart, so they will be covered by the
top cake. Cut off level with the icing. Place the
small cake on top.
8 Mix the egg white into a soft paste with a little
icing sugar. Wrap ribbon around the base of each
cake and secure with paste; hold with pins while
the paste dries (don't forget to remove them
before serving the cake). Arrange the flowers
and leaves on the cakes, securing with paste.
NOTES: The un-iced cake can be kept, tightly
wrapped in plastic wrap, in a cool dry place for
up to eight months or frozen for at least twelve
months.

Dry the flowers for at least a day. Then they
can be kept for a month in an airtight container
with a stick of chalk or a little raw rice to absorb
any moisture. The decorated fruit cake can be
kept for up to a year.

OPPOSITE PAGE:
Traditional wedding cake

CHRISTENING CAKE

Preparation time: 2 hours + 1 day resting
 the icing before decorating
Total cooking time: 1 hour 10 minutes
Makes 1 cake

★ ★ ★

Butter cake

280 g (9 oz) unsalted butter, softened

1 cup (250 g/8 oz) caster sugar

1½ teaspoons vanilla essence

4 eggs

1¾ cups (215 g/7 oz) self-raising flour

1¼ cups (155 g/5 oz) plain flour

¾ cup (185 ml/6 fl oz) milk

21 x 28 cm (8 x 11 inch) oval board

2 tablespoons apricot jam

2 x 500 g (1 lb) packets soft icing

assorted food colourings

pure icing sugar

thin ribbon

wide ribbon

1 tablespoon egg white

sugar flowers

1 Preheat the oven to moderate 180°C (350°F/ Gas 4). Brush an 18 x 25 cm (7 x 10 inch) oval cake tin with melted butter or oil and line the base with baking paper.

2 Cream the butter and sugar with electric beaters until light and fluffy. Beat in the vanilla essence. Add the eggs one at a time, beating well after each addition.

3 Using a large metal spoon, fold in the combined sifted flours alternately with the milk, until smooth. Spoon the mixture into the tin and smooth the surface. Bake for 1 hour 10 minutes, or until a skewer comes out clean when inserted into the centre of the cake.

4 Leave the cake in the tin for at least 5 minutes before turning out onto a wire rack to cool completely.

5 Trim the dome from the cake to give a flat surface. Turn upside down onto the board. Heat the jam in a pan and sieve through a fine strainer. Brush all over the cake.

6 Remove two golf-ball sized pieces of soft icing and one walnut-sized ball and wrap in plastic (for the bootees and leaves). Knead a little colouring into the remaining icing. Roll out large enough to cover the cake, dusting the bench and rolling pin with icing sugar

to prevent sticking. Roll the icing over the rolling pin and re-roll over the cake. Gently press over the cake with the palms of your hands dusted with icing sugar. Smooth and trim the excess. Leave for a day before decorating.

7 Knead a little green colouring into the walnut-sized ball of icing. Roll out thinly on a bench lightly dusted with icing sugar and cut out leaves with a knife or cutter. Gently press in half, then open out and mark the veins by gently pressing with the back of the knife. Twist at different angles and leave to dry.

8 Knead a little colouring into the golf balls of icing to make it a darker colour than the cake. Roll into two short sausages. Make a bootee by bending the sausage in half and moulding the icing (see photograph to the right). Hollow out the top of the bootee with your finger and thin the edges to make a frill. Leave for 2 hours, then tie a thin ribbon bow around each bootee. Tie the wide ribbon around the bottom of the cake.

9 Trace the baby's name onto paper in simple letters. Place on a board and cover with non-stick baking paper. Blend the egg white and enough icing sugar to make a smooth icing that holds its shape when drawn across the surface. Tint with colouring if you want. Spoon into a paper piping bag and pipe over the letters. (Pipe a few extra letters in case of breakages.) If the icing is too stiff and doesn't sit flat, while it is still wet, brush gently with a small clean paintbrush dipped in egg white. Leave to dry overnight. Put the remaining icing in a small bowl and cover with plastic. Lift the letters from the paper with a palette knife. Spoon the reserved icing into a small paper piping bag and use a little on the back of each letter, to stick them to the cake. Stick the bootees, leaves and sugar flowers to the cake with icing.

NOTES: Butter cake can be kept in an airtight container in the fridge for up to a week, or for up to four days in an airtight container in a cool dry place. It can be frozen for up to two months. The cake can be decorated up to three days ahead. If using a fruit cake, it will keep for a month after decorating.

 You can also make this cake in a 20 cm (8 inch) round cake tin. You may need to bake it for about 5 minutes longer.

CHRISTENING CAKE

Use leaf cutters or a sharp knife to cut out the leaves, then mark veins on them.

To make a bootee, bend each sausage of icing in half and mould into shape.

Hollow out the top of the bootee with your fingertip, then frill the edge.

Fill a paper piping bag with the coloured icing and pipe over the letters.

OPPOSITE PAGE:
Christening cake

SIMNEL CAKE

Spoon the rest of the mixture over the marzipan.

Brush apricot jam over the surface of the cooled cake.

SIMNEL CAKE

Preparation time: 40 minutes
Total cooking time: 2 hours
Makes 1

★ ★ ★

500 g (1 lb) commercial marzipan
185 g (6 oz) unsalted butter, softened
1 cup (185 g/6 oz) soft brown sugar
1 teaspoon grated lemon rind
4 eggs, lightly beaten
1¼ cups (155 g/5 oz) self-raising flour
¾ cup (110 g/3½ oz) wholemeal self-raising
    flour
1 cup (160 g/5½ oz) sultanas
½ cup (105 g/3½ oz) glacé cherries,
    cut in halves
1¼ cups (185 g/6 oz) currants
2 tablespoons apricot jam

1 Preheat the oven to warm 160°C (315°F/ Gas 2– 3). Lightly grease a deep 17 cm (7 inch) cake tin and line the base and sides with baking paper, preferably using two layers.
2 Roll out 300 g (10 oz) of the marzipan between two sheets of baking paper. Using a plate as a guide, cut out a 20 cm (8 inch) round, then cover with plastic wrap and set aside. Repeat the rolling and cutting process with the remaining 200 g (6 oz) of marzipan to make a 17 cm (7 inch) thinner round.
3 Cream the butter, sugar and lemon rind in a small bowl with electric beaters until light and fluffy. Gradually add the eggs, beating thoroughly after each addition. Add 2 tablespoons of the sifted flours, to stop the mixture curdling, and continue beating until well combined. Transfer the mixture to a large bowl. Using a metal spoon, fold in the combined sifted flours including the husks. Add the fruit and stir until well combined and the mixture is smooth.
4 Spoon half the mixture into the prepared tin. Carefully place the thinner circle of marzipan over the mixture and gently press down. Spoon the remaining mixture over the marzipan and smooth the surface. Bake for 1 hour, then reduce the oven temperature to slow 150°C (300°F/Gas 2) and bake for another 45– 60 minutes, or until a skewer comes out clean when inserted into the centre of the cake. Remove from the oven and set aside to cool.

5 Put the apricot jam in a small saucepan and stir over low heat until warm. Brush the jam over the surface of the cake. Place the remaining circle of marzipan on top of the cake and pinch the edges to decorate. Heat a grill to medium and briefly place the cake under the grill until the marzipan is light golden. Allow to cool completely, then dust with icing sugar and decorate with coloured marzipan eggs, if desired. Tie a wide colourful ribbon around the side of the cake.
NOTES: Because this cake does not contain alcohol and is iced with marzipan, it should be eaten within four weeks of baking. During humid weather, store it in an airtight container in the refrigerator.

This English fruit cake is traditional Easter fare and was also served on Mothering Sunday, which fell during Lent. The top was sometimes decorated with twelve small balls, moulded from leftover marzipan, representing the twelve apostles. A small Easter chick often tops the marzipan eggs.

OPPOSITE PAGE:
Simnel cake

INDEX

Page numbers in *italics* refer to photographs. Page numbers in **bold** type refer to margin notes.

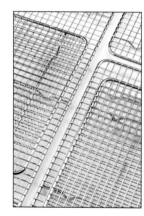

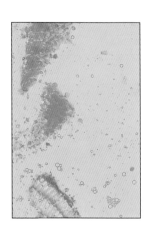

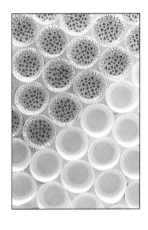

ACKNOWLEDGEMENTS

HOME ECONOMISTS: Alison Adams, Laura Ammons, Anna Beaumont, Kate Brodhurst, Wendy Brodhurst, Rebecca Clancy, Michelle Earl, Jo Forrest, Maria Gargas, Joanne Glynn, Wendy Goggin, Kathy Knudsen, Michelle Lawton, Beth Mitchell, Kerrie Mullins, Kate Murdoch, Justine Poole, Kerrie Ray, Tracy Rutherford, Maria Sampsonis, Margot Smithyman, Maria Villegas

RECIPE DEVELOPMENT: Roslyn Anderson, Anna Beaumont, Wendy Berecry, Wendy Brodhurst, Janelle Bloom, Janene Brooks, Amanda Cooper, Alex Diblasi, Michelle Earl, Stephanie Elias, Joanne Glynn, Wendy Goggin, Lulu Grimes, David Herbert, Eva Katz, Coral Kingston, Kathy Knudsen, Jane Lawson, Barbara Lowery, Voula Mantzouridis, Jean Miles, Kerrie Mullins, Denise Munro, Sally Parker, Tracey Port, Jennene Plummer, Justine Poole, Wendy Quisumbing, Kerrie Ray, Jo Richardson, Tracy Rutherford, Maria Sampsonis, Christine Sheppard, Sylvia Sieff, Dimitra Stais, Beverly Sutherland Smith, Angela Tregonning, Alison Turner, Jody Vassallo, Maria Villegas, Lovoni Welch

PHOTOGRAPHY: Jon Bader, Craig Cranko; Joe Filshie, Phil Haley, Chris Jones, André Martin, Luis Martin, Reg Morrison, Peter Scott, Tony Lyon

STYLISTS: Marie-Hélène Clauzon, Rosemary De Santis, Carolyn Fienberg, Kay Francis, Mary Harris, Vicki Liley, Michelle Noerianto, Sylvia Seiff, Maria Villegas, Sophie Ward

The publisher wishes to thank the following, all in NSW, for their assistance in the photography for this book:
The Bay Tree Kitchen Shop; Bertoli Olive Oil, Breville Holdings Pty Ltd; Chief Australia; Limoges Australia; Peter McInnis Pty Ltd/Kitchenaid; MEC-Kambrook Pty Ltd; Orson & Blake Collectables; Pavillion Christofle; Sheldon & Hammond; Sunbeam Corporation Ltd; Waterford Wedgwood Australia Ltd.